THEOLOGICAL-
POLITICAL TREATISE

BARUCH SPINOZA

THEOLOGICAL-POLITICAL TREATISE

(Gebhardt Edition)

Second Edition

Translated by

SAMUEL SHIRLEY

Introduction and Annotation by

Seymour Feldman

Hackett Publishing Company, Inc.

Indianapolis/Cambridge

22 21 20 19 18   3 4 5 6 7

For further information, please address:
 Hackett Publishing Company, Inc.
 P.O. Box 44937
 Indianapolis, IN 46244–0937

 www.hackettpublishing.com

Thanks to Steven Barbone, Rondo Keele, Michael Morgan, and Daniel Werner for their
editorial contributions.

Cover design by Listenberger & Associates.

Library of Congress Cataloging-in-Publication Data

Spinoza, Benedictus de, 1632–1677.
  [Tractatus theologico-politicus. English]
  Theological-political treatise / Baruch Spinoza ; (Gebhardt edition)
translated by Samuel Shirley ; introduction and annotation by
Seymour Feldman.— 2nd ed.
     p. cm.
  Includes bibliographical references (p.) and index.
  ISBN 0-87220-607-6 (paper)
     1. Philosophy and religion—Early works to 1800. 2. Free
thought—Early works to 1800. I. Shirley, Samuel, 1912– II. Feldman,
Seymour. III. Title.
B3985.E5 S4513 2001
199'.492—dc21   2001039608

ISBN-13: 978-0-87220-607-6 (pbk.)

CONTENTS

INTRODUCTION

Among the various epithets that greeted the publication of Spinoza's *Theological-Political Treatise* (henceforth the *TTP*) in 1670 were "harmful and vile," "most pernicious," "intolerably unrestrained," "subversive," "blasphemous," "diabolical," and "atheistic." In our day it has been described as "unscrupulous," "Machiavellian," even "anti-Semitic," and "anti-Jewish." Yet this work has had its defenders and praisers. It has been characterized as "pioneering," indeed "revolutionary," "liberal," "democratic," "bold," and "a neglected masterpiece." In the face of these diverse and incompatible assessments, how are we to understand this book and its author? Was he really the Devil in disguise, the Antichrist, whose aim was to destroy all religion, especially those religions based upon the Hebrew Bible? Was he the originator of what was to become known to some in modern times as biblical criticism and to others as Higher anti-Semitism? Or was he the philosophical advocate of the liberal values of religious tolerance, free speech, and democratic politics? Indeed, some have even regarded him as the first political Zionist and solver of the "Jewish Question."

The Preface to the treatise makes it quite clear that the *TTP* is a polemical, political, indeed personal book, despite the paucity of references to either contemporary events or his own life. Spinoza is quite explicit that this is no abstract ivory-tower treatise in philosophy, as his more famous work the *Ethics*[1] has seemed to its superficial readers. The *TTP* is openly a political and theological tract aimed at solving several specific practical issues facing contemporary Dutch society, in whose midst Spinoza had been born and in which he lived all his life, never leaving its borders, even for a vacation or visit. It also contains a response to an important event, indeed a turning point, in Spinoza's own life, his excommunication from the Jewish community of Amsterdam in 1656. Some scholars have maintained that the *TTP* is a later version of a reply that Spinoza had written to the Jewish community, defending his actions and opinions.[2] It is therefore important to understand what led to Spinoza's severance from Judaism and how he responded to it.

---

1. Baruch Spinoza, *Ethics, Treatise on the Emendation of the Intellect, and Selected Letters,* translated by Samuel Shirley (Indianapolis: Hackett Publishing Company, 1992).

2. L. Strauss, *Spinoza's Critique of Religion,* translated by E. M. Sinclair (New York: Schocken Books, 1982). W. Klever, "Spinoza's Life and Works," in *The*

I

Although he was born (1632) and raised a Jew, Spinoza's parents had been
born and raised as Catholics, as were most of the original Jewish community of Amsterdam. They were *Conversos*, Jews who had converted to
Christianity, either under compulsion or willingly, yet retained their Jewish identity in secret.[3] Modern scholars have uncovered many of the
important facts of Spinoza's early years and the events surrounding his
excommunication.[4] After receiving the traditional Jewish elementary education, consisting primarily of the study of Hebrew and of the Bible and
rabbinic literature, Spinoza entered his father's dried-fruit-importing
business, most likely at the age of fourteen or fifteen. Nevertheless, he
continued to study on his own, but what he studied at this time is still not
altogether certain. Since even his early writings show that he had mastered
Cartesian philosophy and science, it is obvious that, at some time previous
to these writings, Spinoza had begun to study Latin, then still the language of philosophy and other scholarly literature. However, we do not
know exactly when and where he began to study Latin, nor are we certain
when and how he encountered the philosophy and science of Descartes.
However the chronology of Spinoza's acquisition of Latin and of Cartesian philosophy is settled, it is most probable that he became somewhat
proficient in Latin and that he knew something of Cartesianism before his
excommunication.[5] What is also highly likely is that, on the basis of his
own readings, he was already quite familiar with the classics of medieval
Jewish biblical exegesis and philosophy, especially the biblical commentaries of Abraham ibn Ezra and the philosophical writings of Moses
Maimonides and Hasdai Crescas.[6] At some point before 1656 these stud-

---

Cambridge Companion to Spinoza, ed. D. Garrett (Cambridge: Cambridge University Press, 1996), 18.

3. Among the more recent studies of the *Converso* experience are B. Netanyahu,
The Origins of the Spanish Inquisition in 15th Century Spain (New York: Random
House, 1995); D. Gitlitz, *Secrecy and Deceit: The Religion of the Crypto-Jews*
(Philadelphia: Jewish Publication Society, 1996).

4. J. Freudenthal, ed., *Die Lebensgeschichte Spinozas: Quellenschriften, Urkunden
und nichtnamlichen Nachrichten* (Leipzig, 1899). The works of I. Revah are fundamental, especially his *Spinoza et le Dr Juan de Prado* (The Hague: Mouton, 1959).
More recently the studies of Richard Popkin have been most illuminating, if
controversial. (See Select Bibliography.)

5. Klever, 17–21.

6. Abraham ibn Ezra (c.1090–1164), Moses Maimonides (1135–1204), and
Hasdai Crescas (1340–1410) were all Spanish Jews. Ibn Ezra's biblical commen-

ies had led him to entertain serious doubts about Judaism and biblical religion in general. What was needed now was some catalytic agent or stimulant to bring about the break.

This was provided, some scholars have argued, by the recently arrived *Converso* physician, Juan de Prado, who had already become skeptical of Judaism, even though he professed it.[7] Evidence indicates that Spinoza and Prado were friends, and that Prado himself was excommunicated a few years after Spinoza for entertaining unorthodox beliefs, such as a naturalistic, philosophical conception of the deity and the denial of personal immortality. Doubts about biblical revelation were also attributed to him. It is not unlikely that Spinoza, too, had shared these views even before his meeting with Prado, but they were probably confirmed and fortified by their discussions. Whatever the influence of Prado upon Spinoza, it is clear that beliefs such as these would surely have raised concern among the Jewish community, whose admittance to and permission to stay within Amsterdam depended upon the suppression of any heterodoxy that would disturb the general community, non-Jewish as well as Jewish.

Some scholars have argued that an important influence on Spinoza's turn from Judaism was that of liberal or even heterodox Christianity. Claims have been made that Spinoza had contacts with English Quakers engaged in missionary activities in the Netherlands[8] or that he had been exposed to the views of the Socinians, the precursors of modern Unitarianism.[9] It has also been maintained that Spinoza was influenced by Isaac La Peyrère, a heterodox Protestant, perhaps of Jewish background, who came to Amsterdam in 1655 and whose book *Prae Adamitae* was published in 1655 by Spinoza's former teacher, Menasseh ben Israel, and was in Spinoza's own library. La Peyrère had argued that Adam was not the first human and that the Bible cannot be taken to be "the Gospel truth." Indeed, the biblical text that we now possess, he maintained, is an "edited" version of several sources. La Peyrère also denied the existence of miracles.[10]

---

tary became one of the more widely studied commentaries by Jews, even to this day. Maimonides and Crescas wrote classic philosophical-theological treatises: Maimonides, *The Guide of the Perplexed;* Crescas, *The Light of the Lord.*

7. Revah, *passim.*

8. R. Popkin, "Spinoza, the Quakers and the Millenarians," *Manuscrito* 6 (1982), 113–133.

9. H. Mechoulan, "Morteira et Spinoza au Carrefour du Socianisme," *Revue des Etudes Juives,* 135 (1976), 51–65.

10. Strauss, 64–85. Popkin, *Isaac La Peyrère (1596–1676): His Life, Work and Influence* (Leiden: Brill, 1987).

The actual writ of excommunication that expelled Spinoza is relatively silent on the specifics of Spinoza's own "heterodoxies": all it says is that he behaved monstrously, and that he believed and taught "abominable things."[11] If the *TTP* is indeed some indication of what he had believed in 1656, the elders of the Jewish community were certainly justified in getting rid of this upstart and "troubler of Israel." As we shall see, the main theses of this treatise are indeed subversive of traditional biblical religion. But however Spinoza arrived at these ideas, it is important to recognize two facts about him: 1) he was a genius, as his subsequent career proves; 2) he was well read in medieval Jewish philosophical and exegetical literature. These considerations can easily explain how a young intellectual could have religious doubts about his tradition, some of which at least were even raised and discussed in the books of his Jewish teachers. Maimonides did not solve all the "perplexities" that he attempted to, and Jewish biblical exegetes, such as Abraham ibn Ezra, Levi ben Gershom (Gersonides), and Isaac Abravanel, were not uncritical readers of the Bible.[12] It is not difficult to picture the young Spinoza mulling over these authors, thinking through the doubts and problems that they raised, finding their solutions to be inadequate, and then reaching the conclusion that traditional Judaism, indeed the Bible itself, could no longer be regarded as the "Word of God." Thousands of Jews and Christians since Spinoza have reached similar conclusions by an analogous route.

Spinoza remained in Amsterdam for a couple of years after his severance from the Jewish community, continuing his study of Latin, philosophy, and science under the tutelage of an ex-Jesuit schoolmaster, Franciscus van den Enden, who ran a school that was already known for its "free-thinking" tendencies and curriculum. It is probable that it was in this environment that Spinoza began to study Cartesian philosophy and science, since van den Enden himself was a professed Cartesian.[13] However, it is not clear whether Spinoza began his studies with van den Enden before or after his excommunication. In any case, Spinoza eventually left Amsterdam, and during the next few years resided in several villages nearby, ultimately taking up permanent residence in The Hague, where he died in 1677, most likely from tuberculosis or some other lung disease, which had caused the death of his mother as well. Tradition relates that he earned his living as a lens-grinder. But it is not certain whether his exper-

11. Klever, 16.

12. Levi ben Gershom (Gersonides, 1288–1344) was a Provençal Jewish philosopher, mathematician, scientist, and biblical exegete. Isaac Abravanel (1437–1509) was a Spanish Jewish theologian and biblical exegete.

13. Klever, 17, 21, 26.

tise in optics was merely economically motivated or scientifically driven. His correspondence clearly shows that he was highly regarded as an expert in optics, but it also suggests that this proficiency was theoretical as well as practical. His correspondents seem to have been quite interested in Spinoza's solutions to certain physical and mathematical problems involved in optical research.[14] It is not unlikely that he was supported by "research grants" given to him by several friends and patrons.[15] At any rate, Spinoza lived the rest of his life deeply engaged in scientific and philosophical pursuits and, as we shall see, occasionally addressing political issues that were vexing the Netherlands. He was by no means isolated from his world: his friends and correspondents kept him well informed of what was taking place not only in the Netherlands but also in England and in France. Spinoza was not, as he has often been depicted, divorced from the practical problems of his day or the passions that often are associated with these concerns. There are indications that several times he acted "politically," protesting the murder of the de Witt brothers, who were the leaders of the republican government, and attempting to visit the French general who led an army into the Netherlands.[16] Indeed, as the *TTP* will prove, he was altogether a "political" person.

II

Spinoza's literary activity was produced during a relatively short intellectual career that lasted only about seventeen years. It should be kept in mind that he was a "late starter": whereas Descartes began to learn and speak Latin when he was about six, Spinoza did not begin his Latin studies until his late teens or early twenties; whereas Descartes studied mathematics, physics, and philosophy in one of the most famous Jesuit colleges in Europe, Spinoza was primarily an autodidact. But as his writings show, he was a quick learner.

His early letters, from 1661 to 1663,[17] indicate that he had already begun to formulate some of the fundamental ideas in metaphysics and epistemology that were to appear in full form in his *Ethics*, which, although completed and ready for publication during his lifetime, appeared in print only posthumously, in 1677. In these early letters Spinoza refers to his two short treatises, most likely the *Treatise on the Emendation of the*

---

14. See Spinoza's *Letters,* translated by S. Shirley (Indianapolis: Hackett Publishing Company, 1995), especially Letters 32, 36, 39–40, 45–46. Klever, 33–34.
15. Freudenthal, 17–18.
16. Klever, 40.
17. Spinoza, *Letters,* 2, 4, 9, and 12.

Intellect (henceforth the *TIE*) and the *Short Treatise,* which was apparently lost for more than a hundred years and discovered and published only in the nineteenth century. In 1663 Spinoza published the only work to appear under his own name during his lifetime: *Principles of Cartesian Philosophy Geometrically Demonstrated,* along with an appendix entitled *Metaphysical Thoughts.* The book was intended as a kind of introduction to Cartesian philosophy and physics, written for a friend or student of Spinoza. The prefatory letter to the treatise, written by Spinoza's close friend and physician, Ludwig Meyer, tells the reader that this work is not to be taken as a specimen of Spinoza's own philosophy; it is just a more rigorous exposition of Descartes's system. In several places Spinoza distances himself from Descartes's views, especially those in metaphysics; indeed, already in his first letter he criticizes Descartes along with Francis Bacon for having made some basic errors in philosophy. (See Letter 2.)

As Spinoza's correspondence from 1665 indicates, it appears that he had already completed a first draft of *Ethics,* which he was reluctant to publish at this time. (See Letters 23, 27, and 28.) By 1675 a final version of *Ethics* had been completed and was ready to be published.[18] Although initially Spinoza wanted to see it in print, he decided to withdraw it from publication. It was now too dangerous for him to have it out in the world for everyone to read and discuss. What had brought about this situation?

In September of 1665 Henry Oldenburg, Spinoza's first and most important correspondent, wrote to Spinoza, asking him whether it was true that he was then occupied with theological matters (Letter 29). Soon thereafter Spinoza responded that he was indeed writing a treatise on his interpretation of Scripture. He had undertaken this task for three reasons: 1) he wanted to expose and remove the "prejudices of the theologians"; 2) he wanted to counter the accusation of the masses that he was an atheist; and finally, 3) he wished to defend the right to philosophize freely and to express one's thoughts without fear of punishment or harassment. (Letter 30.) As the second reason clearly shows, Spinoza had acquired a reputation as a free-thinker, as an excommunicated Jew whose "atheistical" views were already part of the public domain and beginning to provoke the political and theological authorities as well as the masses. Accordingly, he believed, perhaps naively, that he should disabuse these authorities of their prejudices and persuade them that the dispassionate study of philosophy is not dangerous or subversive and hence ought to be allowed and practiced without political or religious restraints. Consequently Spinoza turned his attention to these matters and put the *Ethics* back into his desk drawer, for its publication could only make things worse, and began to

18. Spinoza, *Letters,* 62 and 68.

work on the *TTP.* This work was the second and only other work to be published during his life, but anonymously and under the name of a fictitious publisher, in 1670. It was an immediate best-seller, although it didn't make Spinoza rich, only more notorious than he had been before. People saw through its disguises and recognized the author as that "atheistical Jew," who was "rightly" expelled from the synagogue. Spinoza was utterly mistaken in believing that his treatise would accomplish the goals for which he had written it. Both in the Netherlands and in France, where it was immediately translated into French, the *TTP* occasioned considerable uproar and opposition.[19] When the great German mathematician and philosopher Leibniz learned of its contents secondhand, he begged a learned theologian friend to write a counter-treatise refuting Spinoza's "monstrous" heresies.[20]

Nevertheless, three years after the publication of the *TTP,* Spinoza received an invitation from the University of Heidelberg in Germany to become a professor of philosophy (Letter 47). The letter of invitation clearly stipulated that Spinoza would "have the most extensive freedom in philosophizing." Thus, in spite of the outrage that the *TTP* had raised, there were some who appreciated its author. Yet, the very same letter concluded with the words, "you will not misuse [this freedom] to disturb the publicly established religion." Evidently the author of the letter did not read the *TTP* or did not read it carefully, for, as we shall see, it is precisely one of Spinoza's main theses in the *TTP* that intellectual freedom should not be bound by religious authority and that no particular religion ought to be established. It should be no surprise, then, that a month later Spinoza courteously declined the offer (Letter 68). Had he accepted the invitation, he would have become the first Jewish professor of philosophy appointed to an academic post without having to convert to Christianity.

During the remaining four years of his life, Spinoza continued to work on his *Ethics,* which was now expanded into a five-part book. He continued to occupy himself in scientific research, not only in optics but in anatomy as well. He also composed a treatise on Hebrew grammar, apparently at the request of a friend or student. Just before his death he began another political work, the *Political Treatise,* which unfortunately was not completed. Two short essays, apparently written originally in Dutch, have also been attributed to Spinoza: one on the rainbow, the other on proba-

19. *The Spinozistic Heresy: The Debate on the* Tractatus Theologico-Politicus, *1670–1677,* ed. P. Cristofolini (Amsterdam: APA Holland Press, 1995).

20. E. Curley, "Homo Audax: Leibniz, Oldenburg and the *TTP,*" *Studia Leibnitiana,* Supplement 27 (1990), 277–312.

bility. However, scholars have expressed doubt about the authenticity of these works.[21]

III

Despite the expressed impartiality and philosophical neutrality that Spinoza espouses, the *TTP* is permeated with Spinoza's own philosophical biases or assumptions. As we indicated above, Spinoza had pretty much worked out the main ideas of his *Ethics* before embarking upon the *TTP,* and some of these ideas are found in and indeed underlie several of the more important discussions in the latter work. In the first few chapters of the *TTP* Spinoza offers a detailed analysis of biblical prophecy. Although much of his discussion here presupposes and eventually undermines Maimonides' theory of prophecy, Spinoza had already reached the conclusion in his earlier works that prophecy is not the highest form of cognition, contrary to what Maimonides and almost all the medieval Jewish and Christian philosophers and theologians had maintained.[22] Insofar as prophecy involves the use of the imagination, as Maimonides had emphasized, it is an inferior mode of cognition, since the imagination, Spinoza insists, is the source of error and illusion. Moreover, since prophecy is a form of communication, both to the prophet and to his or her audience, it uses language. But language too is for Spinoza a source of confusion and falsity. These ideas are developed both in the *TIE* and the *Ethics,* and they are used by Spinoza in the *TTP* to show that prophecy need not be taken seriously as a source of truth.[23]

Another place where Spinoza's philosophical theories are used as a critical tool against traditional biblical religion is his treatment of miracles. In the *Ethics* Spinoza reached the conclusion that God and Nature are not two completely different things, that, as he put it in his letter (via Oldenburg) to the famous English chemist Robert Boyle: "I do not differentiate between God and Nature in the way all those known to me have done" (Letter 6, end). One of the consequences of this virtual identification of God with Nature[24] is that the laws of nature, i.e., the laws discovered by

21. J. J. de Vet, "Spinoza's Authorship of *Stelkonstige Reeckening van den Regenboog* (*Algebraic Calculation of the Rainbow*) and of *Reeckening van Kanssen* (*Calculation of Chances*), Once More Doubtful," *Studia Spinozana* 2 (1986), 267–307.

22. Maimonides, *Guide of the Perplexed,* 2.32–45.

23. Spinoza, *TIE,* paragraphs 52–64; *Ethics,* 1.15, Scholium, Appendix, 2.40, Scholia 1 and 2, 2.41.

24. The famous formula "God, or Nature" first appears in the *Ethics* in Part 4, Preface. This equation is more explicit in the *TTP,* especially chapters 1 and 6.

natural science, are the divine laws and conversely. Hence, if a miracle is supposed to be a break in or violation of a law of nature, it would be tantamount to a change of a divine law, which is impossible, since God is, not only for Spinoza but for many of the medievals as well, immutable. Throughout his discussion of miracles, as we shall see, Spinoza assumes his theory of natural determinism, the thesis that all events in nature follow strict determinate laws, that there is no real contingency and teleology in nature. Given this metaphysical infrastructure, the biblical doctrine of miracles, as traditionally understood, turns out to be an illusion.[25]

In reading the *TTP* it will be helpful to consult not only the *Ethics* but also Spinoza's *Letters*. The latter not only contain useful information concerning the chronology and motivation for his writing the *TTP* but offer important commentary on and expansion of points discussed in the treatise. This is especially true in his exchange with the merchant and amateur theologian Blyenburgh (Letters 18–24, 28) as well as in his correspondence with the more sophisticated Oldenburg (Letters 29–30, 61, 68, 71, 73, 74–75, 77–79). Examples of a more emotional Spinoza, especially in these matters, can be found in his exchange with a former friend or student, Albert Burgh, who had converted to Roman Catholicism and tried to convince Spinoza of the truth and advantages of his newly adopted religion (Letters 67 and 76). Spinoza's reply to Burgh is especially interesting not only for its sarcastic and trenchant refutation of Burgh's arguments but for its somewhat more sympathetic statements about the Jewish religion and his former coreligionists, one of whom, a recent victim of the Inquisition, was just as much a martyr to religious and political persecution as was Jesus, who after all was also a Jew. This letter makes it quite clear that although he rejected Judaism, Spinoza was not a Christian either. He was a philosopher and a scientist, to whom traditional religion, insofar as it is based upon the Bible, was no longer a viable option for those who had achieved philosophical enlightenment and emancipation.

IV

In the Preface to the *TTP* Spinoza makes it clear why he is writing this book and to whom it is primarily addressed. In this sense there is no "hidden agenda" in the treatise. Although the work consists of twenty chapters and over three hundred pages, it is in an important sense an "occasional" pamphlet, written to remedy a serious "disease" infecting the lives of the citizens of the Netherlands—political and religious intol-

25. Spinoza, *Ethics*, 1.16–end, Appendix.

erance and fanaticism. To be sure, these plagues have been endemic throughout human history. Nevertheless, Spinoza—whose parents had been victims of these diseases, indeed he himself believed that he too was the innocent victim of religious persecution—saw that his native country was now the locus of political and religious bigotry and fanaticism, and that the latter were serious threats to the peace and security of the state. Something had to be done, and soon.

The particular situation in which Spinoza found himself was brought about by a mixture of political and religious factions and alliances that were ripping apart the Dutch republic, which had only recently won its independence from Spanish domination. The republican government, ruled by a merchant class favoring decentralization and moderate liberal policies in religion, was opposed by a royalist faction headed by the House of Orange, which wanted to transform the republic into a monarchy. To complicate matters, each political party was allied with religious groups that had their own agenda: the Remonstrants and the Counter-Remonstrants. The republicans sided with the more "liberal" Remonstrants, whereas the monarchists favored the more orthodox Counter-Remonstrants. The particular religious bones of contention need not detain us here, since Spinoza had no interest in them. What bothered him was the interference of religious parties in political affairs and the willingness of political leaders to make alliances with religious factions. As he perceived the political situation, this unholy alliance was the main cause of all the political unrest and discord that was destroying his country. Moreover, and now Spinoza becomes more personal, this political strife made the pursuit of philosophy and science difficult, even impossible. To defend both political and intellectual freedom Spinoza argued for the secularization of politics and the emancipation of philosophy from both political and religious supervision and influence.

But to whom is this book addressed? That Spinoza wrote it in Latin immediately rules out two groups: 1) the masses, or *"vulgus,"* who, not knowing this language, would not be able to read the *TTP;* and 2) the Jews, most of whom did not know Latin. The former are, according to Spinoza, incapable of either understanding or appreciating the ideas in the *TTP;* moreover, if they did understand some of its contents, they would be utterly unreceptive to it and vigorously oppose it. Throughout the *TTP* Spinoza exhibits a not too well disguised disdain for the masses. Assuming his theory of human nature, worked out in detail in Parts 3–5 of the *Ethics,* Spinoza claims that most people are ruled by passion and hence are in "bondage." One specific consequence of this "imprisonment" is their addiction to superstition, false beliefs based on the unrestrained exercise of the imagination, and fanaticism. Since the road to liberation is long and difficult (*Ethics* 5.42, Scholium), Spinoza had no illusion that most people would either undertake or complete this journey.

The Jews, even the ones who did know Latin, would not read the *TTP,* since it was written by an outcast. The writ of excommunication expressly prohibited not only any personal contact with Spinoza but also reading anything he had written or would write. This prohibition seems to have been quite successful since, with one known exception,[26] there are no surviving published responses to Spinoza from the Jewish community until the late eighteenth century.[27]

For those who have, either through their own efforts or from study of Spinoza's philosophy emancipated themselves from prejudice and super- stition, the *TTP* is superfluous. Having attained philosophical maturity, they no longer need the lessons of the *TTP.* They have already been convinced that philosophy, which is concerned only with truth, is not harmful either to the state or to true religion. It leads to freedom and tranquillity. If the masses, the Jews, and the philosophers are not, for diverse reasons, the audience for the *TTP,* who, then, are its intended readers?

Not all educated people are philosophers. Even some theologians and theologically literate readers have made some progress toward true free- dom. The Netherlands seemed to have had a goodly number of such people, many of whom had been exposed to Cartesian philosophy and science as well as to more liberal conceptions of Christianity. Besides the established Protestant Church, there was a variety of smaller groups of "heterodox," or nonconformist, Christians, such as the Socinians, Col-

---

26. The earliest known extant Jewish response to Spinoza's philosophy is from the former *Converso* physician Isaac Orobio de Castro, who arrived in Amsterdam in 1662. A friend and former classmate of Juan de Prado, Orobio engaged in a series of polemical debates with Prado. He also wrote an essay attacking the efforts of a Dutch amateur theologian to incorporate Spinoza's philosophy into Christianity. In this work Orobio criticizes some of the fundamental ideas of Spinoza. For an excellent discussion of Orobio see Joseph Kaplan, *From Christianity to Judaism: The Life and Works of Isaac Orobio de Castro* (Oxford: Oxford University Press, 1989). On Orobio's critique of Spinoza see S. Feldman, "The First Jewish Cri- tique of Spinoza" (Hebrew), *Iyyun,* 37 (1988), 222–237.

27. The history of Spinoza's impact upon modern Jewish thought has received considerable recent attention. See Z. Levy, "On some early responses to Spinoza's philosophy in Jewish thought," *Studia Spinozana,* 6 (1990), 251–278, and S. Feld- man, "Spinoza," in *History of Jewish Philosophy, Routledge History of World Philoso- phies,* vol. 2, ed. D. Frank and O. Leaman (London: Routledge, 1997), 612–635.

legiants, and others. Many of Spinoza's friends after his excommunication were of this sort of "enlightened" Christianity.[28] Spinoza wanted to convince them that their authentic and legitimate political and religious goals were being subverted by certain views about religion and politics that they still held. They needed to be shown that the troubles facing their country were brought about by superstitions and prejudices, many of which were rooted in an erroneous conception of biblical reading and interpretation. If Spinoza can demonstrate that this misconception is based on certain assumptions that are arbitrary, perhaps even false, then he will have succeeded in removing these superstitions and prejudices. The Bible is the focus of his attention, since it is the authoritative book for Christians; moreover, for many of the Protestants of the Netherlands it is the source of their political theory that makes the state and religion partners in governing the lives of the citizens. To many Dutch Protestants, especially those following John Calvin, the ancient Israelite polity led by Moses is the model for the Christian political regime. Spinoza wants to demonstrate that this view of politics and religion is harmful and dangerous. The philosophers have already been convinced; the masses will never be convinced. Yet there is hope that an open-minded, educated person will be persuaded by arguments based upon logic and facts.[29]

Already in the Preface to the *TTP* Spinoza introduces two methodological principles that will govern his discussions throughout the treatise. First, he makes it quite clear that one of the basic errors of previous exegetes of the Bible had been their tendency to read into the text ideas that they derived from some nonbiblical source, especially but not exclusively from philosophy. These ideas then became authoritative, and the interpreters attained the status of an exegetical elite who believed that they alone had the right to interpret the Bible. Spinoza rejects this approach as arbitrary and arrogant: arbitrary, since it assumes that the Bible is a philosophical book from which all kinds of philosophical and scientific truths can be learned, at least by those competent to recognize these truths behind or beneath the literal text; arrogant, since it makes a pretense to a level of intellectual insight that is unwarranted and self-serving. Spinoza proposes that we read the Bible as it is, literally, that we try our best to

---

28. L. Kolakowski, *Chrétiens sans Eglise,* translated by A. Posner (Paris: Gallimard, 1969). R. Popkin; "Spinoza, the Quakers and the Millenarians," *Manuscrito* 6 (1982), 113–133.

29. L. Strauss, *Spinoza's Critique of Religion,* 28, 111–123; idem, "How to Study Spinoza's *Theological-Political Treatise,*" in his *Persecution and the Art of Writing* (Glencoe: Free Press, 1952), 162–163, 190. Steven Smith, *Spinoza, Liberalism and the Question of Jewish Identity* (New Haven: Yale University Press, 1997), chapter 2.

understand what it really says, not attempt to make it say what we want it to say. Secondly, in reading the Bible as it is written, we must rely upon our best tool, reason. This means that we must not, especially at the outset of our reading, subordinate reason to any theological dogmas or principles. The medieval doctrine that philosophy is the "handmaiden" of theology[30] Spinoza explicitly and scornfully rejects. But lest one think that Scripture will be made a handmaiden to philosophy, as some of the medieval philosophers attempted,[31] Spinoza will argue that philosophy and theology are separate and independent disciplines, a theme that will be developed in detail in a later chapter of the *TTP*. Having openly stated his motives, goals, and method, Spinoza opens up the Bible to see what is really there.

V

The first six chapters of the *TTP* are devoted to an analysis of some of the root beliefs of biblical religion. Once Spinoza has made clear what these beliefs mean and entail, he proceeds to a close examination of the biblical text itself, reaching some radical conclusions about the authorship of the Bible and its transmission and interpretation throughout the ages. Since the Bible is a book that purports to be revealed to man by God, it is necessary to consider first what revelation means; in particular, we must investigate the vehicle of biblical revelation, prophecy. What is the nature of prophecy? What kind of person is a prophet? What is the content of a prophetic message? Are prophets privileged persons? Is one nation in particular the unique recipient of prophetic revelation? The framework of Spinoza's discussion of these topics was provided by Moses Maimonides, especially in his influential treatise *Guide of the Perplexed*, a work that in many respects is devoted to biblical exegesis.[32] One of the central themes in the *Guide* is the nature of prophecy and the special cognitive status of

---

30. Thomas Aquinas, *Summa Theologica*, I, q. 1, a. 5.

31. Two medieval Muslim philosophers, Al-Farabi (d. 950) and Averroës (1126–1198), could be read as suggesting this conception of religion. See Al-Farabi's *The Attainment of Happiness*, translated by M. Mahdi, included in *Medieval Political Philosophy*, ed. R. Lerner and M. Mahdi (Ithaca: Cornell University Press, 1963), 74–81; Averroës, *The Decisive Treatise Determining What the Connection Is between Religion and Philosophy*, translated by G. Hourani, included in *Medieval Political Philosophy*, ed. R. Lerner and M. Mahdi, 163–187.

32. Maimonides, *Guide of the Perplexed*. A complete modern English translation was provided by S. Pines (Chicago: University of Chicago Press, 1963). A good English translation is given by C. Rabin in the abridged version edited by Julius Guttman (Indianapolis: Hackett Publishing Company, 1995).

the prophet. Spinoza uses Maimonides' theory, but to undermine the special claims Maimonides and others made for prophecy.

According to Maimonides, a prophet is a person who has attained a level of moral, religious, and philosophical perfection such that he or she is eligible to receive the prophetic illumination. Indeed, the only thing that prevents such a person from receiving prophecy is divine intervention; otherwise, the person will necessarily be enlightened by this extraordinary mode of cognition. The perfection required involves the maximal development not only of one's intellect but also of the imagination, the capacity to form mental images and to express these images in language accessible to the masses. Prophecy is then a mode of cognition that employs both intellect, or reason, and imagination. There is one exception to this principle: according to Maimonides, Moses was a prophet who did not make use of or need the imagination. His prophecies were purely intellectual, devoid of imagery; his speeches to the Israelites were for the most part nonparabolic and prosaic (as opposed to poetical). When the Bible says of Moses that he spoke to God "face to face," "mouth to mouth," this means that he received his prophetic messages without the mediation of the imagination. His prophetic information was "pure," not covered up or obscured by metaphor or parables. As a consequence, Moses as prophet barely differs from a philosopher, who strictly speaking, does not or should not use the imagination in his speculation and communication.[33]

Spinoza takes this theory and turns it against Maimonides and all those who want to make prophecy a mode of cognition superior to philosophy. For if it is the case that prophets, excluding Moses, necessarily employ the imagination, then precisely for that reason their messages are infected with an epistemic disease. For the imagination is an impediment to knowledge; as we have mentioned earlier, it is for Spinoza the lowest level of cognitive development. Indeed, Maimonides admits as much when he excluded the imagination from the prophecies of Moses.[34] The "pure" perception and communication of the truth does not need, indeed cannot use, the imagination. Truth is a matter of intellect, not fantasy. To the extent that prophets receive their messages through visions and dreams and then communicate these messages by means of stories and poetry, it is no wonder that we find their language, such as that employed by Ezekiel and Zechariah, obscure and difficult. Moreover, it is not only a question of language: since the prophets use the imagination in their reception of prophecy, it is also not surprising that their insights are themselves not

33. Maimonides, *Guide,* 2.32–45.
34. Ibid., 2.34–35, 45–end.

clear. This accounts for the fact, Spinoza claims, that we find different conceptions about God and other matters in the prophetic books. Consider, for example, those passages wherein God is portrayed as not omniscient: God asks Adam, "Where are you?" or God goes to Sodom and Gomorrah to find out whether or not their citizens were as evil as he thought (Genesis 3:9 and 18:20–21). Yet in other passages God is said to be all-knowing: "All is on record before me" (Isaiah 65:6). Accordingly, on a very important issue no consistent doctrine can be found in the Scriptures.

Sometimes the prophets, although in agreement among themselves, proclaim false doctrines. This is especially the case with their common depiction of God as having corporeal characteristics and human emotions. Now, traditional exegetes were aware of this problem and attempted to solve it. Maimonides, for example, used the rabbinic rule "The Torah [i.e., the Bible] speaks the language of men." Accordingly, these anthropomorphic expressions were to be construed metaphorically. Indeed, Maimonides went so far in this direction as to declare someone a heretic if that person believed that God had any of these objectionable features.[35] Spinoza will have none of this Scriptural "sanitizing." The Bible means what it says, even when what it says is false. The Bible is not a philosophical or scientific text, so we should not expect it to contain correct propositions about these matters. In the language of Maimonides, Spinoza maintains that the Bible is a book of imagination, speaking to our emotions and moral intuitions. It is not surprising, then, to find in it a great deal of poetry, parables, and stories, many quite beautiful and edifying. But where are its arguments and proofs?[36]

Didn't Maimonides say, on the basis of what Scripture itself says, that Moses did not use the imagination in his prophecies? Since, for the believing Jew and Christian, Moses is the greatest of the prophets in the Hebrew Bible, it would be sufficient to claim that he alone attained the level of intellectual prophecy, whereby he reached cognitive insights not reached by any other human, including the other prophets. Spinoza uses this thesis but modifies it to deprive Moses of this special status: Jesus, not Moses, is the man of pure intellect. According to Spinoza, Jesus, not Moses, had a direct insight into the truth, or he communicated with God mentally, without the mediation of language or visions. For if Moses spoke to God "mouth to mouth," he was still using words, and this for Spinoza is a limitation. Jesus, he claims, is never described as speaking with God, or God as speaking with him. (Of course, this can be construed in a very

35. Maimonides, *Guide*, 1.26 and 1.35.

36. Spinoza, *TTP*, chapters 1–2.

different manner, implying some quite radical conclusions.) If Jesus was a prophet, then his prophecies, and his alone, are purely intellectual. On the other hand, if he was not a prophet, since prophets are bound by their imagination, then he was a man who had attained the highest level of intellectual insight. In other words, he was a philosopher.[37]

However, lest one get the wrong impression, it should be clearly recognized that Spinoza had no patience with the traditional Christian conceptions of Jesus. Although he was almost always respectful, indeed reverential, in his references to Jesus in the *Ethics* and the *TTP,* in his letters Spinoza exhibits a different attitude and tone. In these more personal and private testimonies he definitely denies the divinity of Jesus and indicates the incomprehensibility of such doctrines as the incarnation and resurrection of Jesus (Letters 73 and 78). In Letter 76 he mocks the doctrines of the Eucharist and the Devil. In fact, if Jesus is to be regarded as having great intellectual insight, and in this sense he can be considered the human embodiment of divine wisdom (*TTP,* chapters 1 and 4), this achievement is in principle attainable by others. Indeed, Spinoza is quite generous in his praise of King Solomon, who in his opinion is the most philosophical of all the biblical authors (*TTP,* chapters 4 and 6). It is not surprising then that Spinoza often uses the Solomonic books—Proverbs and Ecclesiastes—as biblical confirmations of his own philosophical views.

The upshot of the first two chapters of the *TTP* is that prophecy is not the source of truth, that its function is not to teach us principles of philosophy or science, as Maimonides had maintained, but to inculcate certain moral and religious values and practices that are politically and socially useful. In other words, the Bible is a practical, not a theoretical, book. A prophet is someone who teaches us to be just, charitable, and obedient. This is true piety. Although prophets may and do differ among themselves as to whether or not God repents or whether man differs from the beasts, they do agree on the correct way to live. And that is what's important to most people, and why the Bible is a popular book.

But before Spinoza leaves the topic of prophecy, he addresses an issue that in some respects seems to be out of place, indeed irrelevant to his purposes—the election of the Israelites.

More than ten years had passed since his excommunication, so why was it so important to Spinoza to discuss his former people, especially since very few of them would read this book? Keep in mind, however, that even though his Christian audience believed that they were now the "true Israel," they also admitted that the ancient Israelites did receive authentic

---

37. Ibid., chapters 1–2, 4.

divine prophecy and that the Old Testament was still a valid source of inspiration and model for living. In this respect, Christians also believed that the Jews *were*, at least, a "chosen people." But what does this exactly mean, Spinoza now asked?

At the outset Spinoza declares that the ancient Israelites did not excel other nations in their intellectual or moral virtues. The Bible itself makes this quite explicit. Their chosenness was actually something quite ordinary, an achievement that other nations too have achieved at various times—political success. In chapter 3 Spinoza offers us a completely secularized version of biblical Jewish history. Moses, Joshua, and their successors prior to the kings, created an effective government which was able to settle the land and preserve its autonomy despite the number and strength of the surrounding peoples. Even under the first kings, Saul, David, and Solomon, the Israelites had created a kingdom that was militarily, politically, and economically successful, something Spinoza was not too happy to admit, since monarchy was a form of government he did not like, as we shall see. In enjoying these material benefits, the Israelites were "chosen" by God. But all this means is that God, or Nature, had favored them with political success for a certain period of time. This election is perfectly consistent with other nations having been equally blessed and with the Israelites eventually losing these benefits, or as the Bible puts it, being "cursed." And that is exactly what happened. After a while, the Israelites were conquered and lost their sovereignty. They were and are no longer chosen. Indeed, for Spinoza this has the radical corollary that Mosaic law is no longer valid for the Jews. Since there is no Jewish state, this legal system has become obsolete. In the ancient Jewish regime, there was no distinction between religious and civil law: the Law of Moses was the Law. But when the Jews lost their political independence after the Roman conquest, Mosaic law ceased to have any legal validity. Political defeat resulted in the obsolescence of Jewish law.[38]

Spinoza's conclusions here have both backward and forward implications. Looking back at his former coreligionists who had rejected him, Spinoza tells them that their excommunication of him has no legal force, since Jewish law itself has lost its validity. Not only was Spinoza not bound by it, but the Jews as a group were living under a legal yoke as obsolete as it was burdensome. Indeed, it is a cause of anti-Semitism insofar as it segregates the Jews from the rest of their social environment; Jewish law is the cause of the alienation of the Jews. The forward-looking aspect of Spinoza's argument is evident: the solution to anti-Semitism, Spinoza suggests, is total assimilation. And a prerequisite for this is the elimination of

38. Ibid., chapter 3.

Jewish law or all those features of it that isolate the Jews from their surroundings. If Judaism is to be retained, it should literally be "domesticated," restricted to the private realm and decentralized, with the individual as the focal point, not some group vested with authority or power.[39]

Nevertheless, for Spinoza there is nothing in the nature of things, i.e., in the divine order, that would prevent the Jews from reconstituting themselves as an independent nation, except their present condition as a people untutored in political and military skills, partly the result of their stubborn adherence to Jewish law and partly the effect of the exile. If they were to throw off many of their dysfunctional habits and succeed in reestablishing a sovereign state, they would again be "chosen by God."[40] So there is nothing mysterious or supernatural in the doctrine of the election of Israel. Like everything else, it is a purely natural phenomenon, explicable within the framework of political science and history. Spinoza has utterly stripped the traditional notions of divine providence and election of their supernatural meaning and has reduced them to the raw facts of political power and success.

VI

Both Jews and Christians understood Mosaic prophecy to be primarily the revelation of a legal system that was divinely mandated. The Torah, the "Five Books of Moses," or Pentateuch, is a code of law consisting of commandments given by God, who is pictured as a king, with Israel his subjects and Moses as his prime minister. This is the traditional concept of the divine law. For the Jews this law is perfect and absolutely binding. Although Christians are not obliged to follow all the prescriptions of this law, especially its ceremonial commandments, its moral precepts are considered valid.

Several medieval philosophers incorporated this notion of divine law into a general theory of law according to which there is a law of nature, natural law, on the one hand, and the laws of particular societies, human, or civil, law. The divine law is a supernatural supplement to the natural and civil law, providing information on what to do in cases where the latter do not inform and telling us what we need to do in order to gain divine salvation, on which subject both natural and civil law are silent.[41] Like human law, divine law is prescriptive, the commandments of a recognized sovereign; like natural law, it has a validity that is almost absolute. Indeed,

---

39. S. Smith, chapter 8.
40. Spinoza, *TTP*, chapter 3–end.
41. Thomas Aquinas, *Summa Theologica*, I–II, questions 90–95.

according to some its validity is eternal, just as the laws of nature are.[42] Spinoza rejects this theory and replaces it with a theory of divine law consistent with his general philosophy of nature.

For Spinoza there is no fundamental distinction between God and Nature. Spinoza's God is, as he often insists, not transcendent, but immanent in the world. The world of natural processes is not something God created to keep him company but necessarily follows from his nature as an eternal and infinite being.[43] Now, if the equation God = Nature is true, then, Spinoza argues, this equation is also true: the divine law = the laws of nature, or natural law. The medieval doctrine of the divine law as a supranatural code coming down to us from a God who sits on his throne issuing decrees from time to time to a specific people or to particular individuals is for Spinoza an infantile fable. It depicts God as an arbitrary sovereign who can decree anything he wishes; his mere decree makes the law binding. Spinoza's God is very different; there is nothing capricious or arbitrary about it: everything this God does is a necessary feature or consequence of its nature. Thus the laws of God are necessarily true, eternal, and universally valid. One important implication of this new theory is that, if you want to study God's laws, you should take courses in physics and biology, not the Bible, Talmud, or Canon Law. We know the "ways of the Lord" by studying nature, not some book.[44]

Another significant consequence of Spinoza's identification of divine law with the laws of nature is that the ceremonial, or ritual, law is of no intrinsic value. Since such laws by definition teach no moral principles, they are not essential to our daily lives or to our attainment of salvation. What does it matter if we eat pork or a wafer with wine? Neither act is going to make us morally better or lead to our ultimate happiness. This does not mean that ritual has no meaning or utility at all. Some ceremonies may be of value in habituating us to cultivate morality and piety, which for Spinoza means obedience. Others may function as a kind of "social glue," preserving and uniting the community. Thus, Spinoza comments, circumcision has maintained Jewish identity throughout ages of persecution and exile.[45] But religious ceremonies are not divine laws in the strict sense; if they are to be legislated and followed, this is because of their status as civil law or by virtue of their social utility. They are customs, not divine decrees.

42. Joseph Albo, *The Book of Principles*, translated by I. Husik (Philadelphia: Jewish Publication Society, 1946), vol. 1, chapters 5–10.

43. Spinoza, *Ethics*, 1.16–18.

44. Spinoza, *TTP*, chapter 4.

45. Ibid., chapters 3 (end), 5.

Another interesting and radical consequence of Spinoza's rejection of the traditional notion of divine law is that the equally traditional doctrine of miracles is no longer tenable. If a miracle is understood as some supranaturally caused event that violates or contravenes some law of nature, then there cannot be such events. A law of nature is, as we have just seen, a divine law. If a miracle occurs, some law of nature has been broken or annulled. But this would mean that God has changed, for a change in his laws is a change in his nature. This is absurd. So if God is eternal and immutable, as most of the medieval philosophers and theologians had maintained, then the laws of nature, i.e., the decrees of God, cannot change or be suspended, even momentarily. In short, miracles are an impossibility. If they could occur, there would be no God. But for Spinoza the existence of God is the most certain truth we know.[46] So to believe in miracles is to deny the existence of God. Not Spinoza, but the traditional believer is the atheist![47]

Spinoza's critique of the doctrine of miracles goes further than this logical argument based upon his own metaphysics. He opens up the Bible and shows that the text itself supports his view. At first this seems to be a joke. The Bible is full of stories of miraculous events. How can Spinoza be serious? But we have to consider who wrote the Bible and for whom it was written. Spinoza claims that neither the prophets, including Moses, nor the Israelites knew much natural science. Moreover, as Maimonides himself admitted, it is a feature of biblical narrative style to attribute all natural events to the will of God, even when there are perfectly good and sometimes obvious natural explanations for them.[48] So there was a well-ingrained habit among the Israelites to account for surprising and unusual natural phenomena by appealing to divine intervention. But had the prophets been physicists and the ancient Israelites students of natural science, they either would have known the true natural causes of these phenomena or would have undertaken to find out these causes. Miracles are then just a sign of our ignorance and laziness.[49]

Actually, the belief in miracles is motivated by a deep-seated "prejudice": the assumption that natural phenomena are somehow human-oriented. This is the fallacy of anthropocentrism. We tend to think that whatever happens occurs for us. If what happens turns out to be beneficial, people attribute their good fortune to their merit or to divine grace; if what occurs is not favorable, we say that it is our fault, or we complain. In

46. Spinoza, *TIE*, paragraphs 38–39.
47. Spinoza, *TTP*, chapter 6.
48. Maimonides, *Guide*, 2.48.
49. Spinoza, *TTP*, chapter 6.

either case, we believe that we are the focal point of the universe. This is an utter illusion, manifesting an absolutely erroneous conception of nature and, in particular, of our place within nature. Whatever happens must happen, since all of nature is governed by laws that are necessarily true. Natural phenomena take place not for man but because they follow necessarily from the divine nature. If anything, nature is "theocentric." Once we realize this fact, we shall abandon the bad habit of thanking God for miraculous interventions when we like what happens and blaming God or ourselves when things don't turn out as we want.[50]

In fact, Spinoza maintains, a close reading of the Bible reveals that it often describes these so-called "miracles" in naturalistic terms or that these events can be given naturalistic explanations that are consistent with the biblical text. Consider, for example, the plagues that afflicted the Egyptians. The locusts arrived by a blast of the east wind.[51] The parting of the Sea of Reeds, too, came about as the result of the blowing of the east wind.[52] From these and other examples Spinoza infers that the Bible situates the occurrence of these unusual events *within* nature, not outside it.[53]

Spinoza's attitude toward the miraculous is nicely illustrated in his analysis of perhaps the most extraordinary "miracle" reported in the Bible: the cessation of the motion of the sun at the behest of Joshua while he was engaged in battle.[54] Obviously the narrator of and the actors in this story believed that normally the sun moves; the miracle consisted in the sun's stopping, resulting in a longer day than usual. Now, whereas medieval philosophers and exegetes struggled to make sense of this event within the context of what they took to be the correct astronomical theory, i.e., the geocentric cosmos of Aristotle and Ptolemy,[55] Spinoza laughs at this attempt as another vain effort of trying to read into the Bible something that is not there. The text clearly indicates that the Israelites, including the prophet Joshua, believed in the false theory of solar motion around a stationary earth. As we have already seen, the prophets were not physicists. They and their followers had no idea of the true state of affairs in the celestial realm, nor were they interested in finding out the truth in these

---

50. Spinoza, *Ethics*, 1, Appendix.

51. Exodus 10:13.

52. Exodus 14:21.

53. Spinoza, *TTP*, chapter 6.

54. Joshua 10:12–14.

55. Spinoza, *TTP*, chapter 2. S. Feldman, "'Sun Stand Still': A Philosophical-Astronomical Midrash," *Proceedings of the Ninth World Congress of Jewish Studies*, Division C, Jerusalem 1986, 77–84.

matters. They saw or thought they saw something unusual, and, as they were used to doing, they attributed this event to God's intervention. But this was simply an appeal to ignorance. Although Spinoza is not too interested in providing a detailed explanation of this alleged event, he does suggest that perhaps because of the excessive hailstones in the air at that time, a fact reported in Joshua 10:11, there was a greater refraction of light, and thus the appearance of a longer day. Not knowing any science, the Israelites believed that God had done something extraordinary for them; in fact, if anything strange did happen, it came about through natural causes.

VII

As we have already seen, Spinoza has not only announced his intention to read the biblical text as it was written but has used this principle in his interpretation of miracles. At this juncture in the *TTP* Spinoza takes off his philosophical hat and replaces it with his philological-historical cap. He now offers us a general theory of biblical exegesis, a set of principles on how to read the Bible, indeed for that matter any literary text, and then uses these principles to examine several biblical books and narratives.[56] Many scholars have claimed that in chapters 7–13 Spinoza has made very important contributions to biblical studies; indeed, some have maintained that Spinoza is the founder of modern "Biblical Criticism." However these claims are to be evaluated, it is clear that in this section of the *TTP* Spinoza shows that he learned his early lessons in Hebrew and Bible well. Using the highly sophisticated tradition of medieval Jewish biblical exegesis, Spinoza applies these lessons to the biblical text, but with greater consistency and daring. It is no surprise that he reaches conclusions far more radical and significant than those of his predecessors.[57]

Spinoza himself claims that he is doing something new. Like the new physicists of his own day—Galileo, Descartes, Boyle, and Huyghens, who attempted and in some cases succeeded in inferring true laws of nature from the critical observation and analysis of nature—Spinoza announces his intention to do the same with the Bible. He will look at the data, i.e., the stories, language, and literary composition and structure of the text, and see what facts about the Bible can be safely asserted. To do this the "biblical scientist" will need to have mastery of the relevant languages and

56. For a recent discussion of the relevance of the *TTP* for literary theory, see C. Norris' *Spinoza and the Origins of Modern Critical Theory* (Oxford: Blackwell, 1991).

57. R. Popkin, "Spinoza and Bible Scholarship," in *The Cambridge Companion to Spinoza*, 383–407.

historical background. These are our tools, just as mathematics and empirical observation are the tools of the natural scientist. Once the particular facts about the Bible have been ascertained, one can then proceed to formulate and derive general laws about biblical religion and society. After these principles have been determined, they can be ordered into some kind of logical system analogous to Euclidean geometry or Spinoza's own *Ethics*. No matter how this will be done or turn out, the important thing is to use a method based upon sound philological and historical facts and principles.

Above all, we must not distort the text to read into it our philosophical, religious, or political "prejudices." Just as nature is "out there" waiting to be studied objectively, so the biblical text is lying on our desk, ready to be read scientifically. In doing so we must always remember that our main and first task is to determine the exact meaning of the text. Questions about the truth of the Bible must be postponed until we have succeeded in arriving at an accurate text and an understanding of what this text says. If we allow questions about truth to enter too early in our inquiries, our conception of the truth of Scripture will determine what Scripture means. Let us use the example discussed above of the "miracle" of the cessation of the sun's motion. If we antecedently assume the principle of biblical infallibility, that the Bible is true in every one of its details, then either we shall say that what the Bible describes as having occurred did occur exactly as it is described, or we shall interpret the verse to make it fit some independently adopted philosophical or scientific theory that we believe to be true, which the Bible either esoterically teaches or is consistent with. The first option is that taken by Fundamentalists who believe without question that the Bible is true and that if anything is inconsistent with the biblical text, it is to be rejected. The second approach is the route adopted by several medieval Jewish exegetes, such as Maimonides, who reads a biblical passage in such a way that it accords with some philosophical theory, which he takes to be true independently of his reading of Scripture. Indeed, Spinoza states, Maimonides goes so far as to claim that, if a biblical verse contradicts some demonstrated philosophical or scientific proposition, this verse must be interpreted in such a manner as to make it consistent with the philosophical and scientific facts.[58] Spinoza scornfully labels this latter approach "dogmatism," since it assumes a priori a set of philosophical theories and twists the biblical text to fit these principles; moreover, it sets up the philosophers as the infallible and authoritative interpreters of the text. The Fundamentalists, however, are derided as "Skeptics," since they deny the authority and applicability of reason to

58. Maimonides, *Guide*, 2.25.

religion and to the biblical text: *Whatever* the Bible says is true. If this means that we have to reject Darwin or Einstein, so be it. What is truly divine in man, reason, they reject or demean. Spinoza's new "biblical science" avoids both these approaches and forges an alternative method to the study of the Bible, one that is free from philosophical dogmatism or skepticism.

Having formulated the guiding methodological principles of his new biblical science, Spinoza then turns to the texts, both of the Hebrew Bible and of the New Testament. His main attention is given to the former, for he says that his knowledge of Hebrew is superior to his knowledge of Greek. But it is also likely that Spinoza focusses upon the Hebrew Bible because it served as the model for the Calvinists' political theory of a state in which religion is the law of the land. Some scholars have claimed that Spinoza concentrates upon the Hebrew Bible because it was safer to do so. A detailed critical analysis of the New Testament would have been more dangerous.[59] Some of the conclusions Spinoza reaches are quite striking and, in some cases, radical. With respect to the question of authorship Spinoza announces that the traditional ascription of the Pentateuch to Moses is false. Obviously, he says, Moses could not have written the chapter describing his death and burial. More important, there are passages elsewhere in the Pentateuch that indicate that they were written after Moses, indeed in some cases much later than Moses. For example, Genesis 36:31 provides a list of the Edomite kings who ruled *before* there were any kings in Israel. Now, the Israelite kings were instituted several centuries *after* Moses had died. In reaching this conclusion Spinoza acknowledges his debt to the medieval Jewish exegete Abraham ibn Ezra (d. 1167), who in his commentary on the Pentateuch noted twelve passages that seemed to have been written after Moses' death. But whereas ibn Ezra couched this conclusion in obscure and elusive language, Spinoza is out in the open. Moreover, he makes the same claim with respect to several other books in the Hebrew Bible: their authors are not the ones traditionally assigned to them. In short, the books of the Bible represent a library of documents dating from different times, written by various authors, many anonymous, and finally compiled and put together by an editor, considerably after their original composition, most likely Ezra the Scribe in the fifth century B.C.[60]

Spinoza devotes only one chapter to a detailed discussion of the New Testament, but his conclusions are equally "subversive," even though

---

59. Strauss, *Spinoza's Critique of Religion*, 20, 192; idem, "How to Read Spinoza's *Theological-Political Treatise*," 162–169.

60. Spinoza, *TTP*, chapter 8.

more muted. First, he curtly dismisses the contention, favored by many modern Christian theologians and biblical scholars, that Jesus' message represents a radical innovation, that it is a major improvement upon the Judaism of his day. Spinoza claims that Jesus' teachings did not depart from the conventional ideas and values of his Jewish contemporaries. The only novelty in his mission was that it was addressed to a wider audience, to all the nations, not just to the Jews.[61]

Second, in chapter 11, which is specifically concerned with the New Testament, Spinoza considers the question whether the Apostles wrote as prophets. He begins by conceding that the Apostles were prophets. But of course this doesn't mean very much, since prophets aren't the most knowledgeable people. His main point, however, is that although the Apostles were prophets, they wrote not as prophets but as individuals who spoke to their audience in an argumentative manner, rather than in the imperative and authoritative style of the biblical prophets. They told their auditors that they had come to them not by the command of God but as private men who had been granted the privilege of hearing what Jesus had said and had undertaken to spread his teachings. When they committed their messages to writing, they wrote as preachers, not prophets. Indeed, their writings, especially those of Paul, often exhibited a philosophical tone. On the other hand, since the Apostles spoke and wrote as ordinary men, what they said often contained manifest contradictions. Paul, for example, taught predestination and the primacy of faith and grace, whereas James asserted the centrality of deeds and human merit. Thus, Paul made Jewish law unnecessary for the Christian, whereas James insisted upon its validity.[62]

This "deconstruction" of the New Testament is taken a step further when Spinoza remarks in a later chapter that the four-fold repetition of Jesus' biography is strange. After all, the Israelite exodus from Egypt isn't repeated even once. Moreover, each Gospel gives a different account; sometimes they contradict each other. So why should we take these narratives to be authoritative? Like the stories in the Hebrew Bible, the New Testament writings are human documents, to be read and studied as we do all human histories.[63]

One doesn't have to think too deeply to see that what Spinoza is telling us here is that the Bible as we have it is a human book, written and edited

---

61. Ibid., chapter 4. This is, however, not true. Several passages in the New Testament indicate that Jesus had no such intention, that he saw his mission as directed toward the Jews only (Matthew 6:7–8, 10:5–6, 15:24–27).

62. Spinoza, *TTP,* chapter 11.

63. Ibid., chapter 12.

by humans for humans. It is, as we have already seen, not free from scientific doctrines that are false, philosophical ideas that are not true, and laws that are not necessary for our moral and spiritual betterment. Its transmission to us from earliest times has not been flawless; the text manifests scribal errors and lacunae. It is not clear why certain books were included and others excluded. These decisions were made much later than the actual composition of most of the biblical books and were made by men, whose reliability and authority may be questioned. For all we know, tomorrow a book will be found in the Judean desert that looks like it should be in the Bible but currently isn't. What should we do then?

Fully aware of the radical and potentially provocative character of these conclusions, Spinoza immediately tries to dissipate their apparent heterodoxy by informing his readers that he is faithful only to what Scripture really says and in particular to what Scripture says about itself as the "Word of God." For what does this phrase really mean? To be sure, many believe that the word of God is literally some spoken or written linguistic formulation. For the Jew and the Christian, the word of God is found in the Bible; for the Muslim in the Quran. But for Spinoza this is a mistake, if only because the texts that allegedly contain the words of God have been shown to be faulty. But perhaps more important, the fact that Scripture itself says that the word of God is really in our hearts, i.e., in our minds, shows that the text, at best, can only be a record of what the prophet believed to be given in revelation. Deuteronomy 30:11–14 clearly says that the divine commandments are not "in heaven . . ." such that someone has to go up to heaven and bring these words to us; rather, the divine words are "very near . . . in our hearts. . . ." To Spinoza this means that the true divine message is revealed not in any written text or by some prophet speaking to us but in and through our own mind, or reason. After all, if a person comes to us and performs all kinds of wonders but tells us not to worship the one eternal God but Stalin or Hitler, the Bible explicitly tells us to kill him; for what this person teaches, regardless of the wondrous signs, is false and clearly prohibited by the Bible. So what really counts is the truth of the message, and the truth can only be recognized and discovered through the use of reason. In sum, the word of God is for Spinoza "inscribed in our intellect."[64] Indeed, those who believe that an engraved stone tablet or parchment filled with scriblings written in ink is divine are guilty of idolatry and victims of superstition. What is true is divine. After all, when Moses broke the tablets because of the Israelites' lapse into idolatry, he didn't destroy the Word of God. The latter was and

---

64. Ibid., chapter 12.

is totally independent of any material embodiment: it can no more be destroyed than a mathematical equation is annulled when the mathematics teacher erases the blackboard.

Does this mean that the Bible does not contain any divine words or commandments? By no means. There are true principles and laws in the Bible, and for that matter in books written by us, such as the *Ethics*. In particular, many of the moral commandments can be considered true insofar as they inculcate in us virtue and obedience, e.g., to love God and our neighbor. Similarly, there are certain philosophical beliefs in the Bible, albeit expressed in somewhat less than philosophically acceptable language, that if properly understood do convey truths about God, e.g., the unity of God. In this sense we can say that the Bible is divine or that God is its author: to the extent that there are truths in this text, especially those relevant to human perfection. So the novel or radical conclusions reached by biblical science really do not affect negatively the importance and value of Scripture. The Bible can still serve as a useful guide in our everyday lives, especially if it influences us to live morally and peacefully.[65]

VIII

Indeed, when we have followed the methods of this new way of reading and studying the Bible, we shall see that there is in it a conception of faith and piety that all reasonable people can and should assent to. Genuine faith and piety consist in those principles of religion and morality the adherence to which induces the practice of obedience. This is for Spinoza the "aim and object of Scripture." These principles are relatively few in number and simple in meaning; they are therefore not difficult to follow or understand. Moreover, they constitute a common set of beliefs, shared by all the various sects of Christians, as well as by Jews and Muslims. So there would be no questions of heresies and religious conflict. Spinoza calls this ecumenical religion "the true universal religion."[66] It is governed by two basic principles: 1) the love of God; and 2) the love of our neighbor. In chapter 14 of the *TTP* Spinoza lists the seven specific beliefs that comprise its dogmatic content:

1. A divine being exists who is just and merciful and whom we are obliged to obey.
2. This deity is one.

65. Ibid., chapters 13–14.
66. Ibid., chapter 14.

3. God is omnipresent and omniscient.
4. God is omnipotent and a free agent.
5. The worship of God consists only in justice and charity, or love of our neighbor.
6. Only those who obey God are saved.
7. God forgives those who repent.

One of the advantages of this universal religion is that it constitutes a sufficiently broad conception of religious faith: it is virtually neutral and thus not harmful, either to the state or to the various religious groups within a state. In addition, its principles are general in meaning, such that they can be interpreted in various ways, allowing for a certain latitude in religious belief. This exegetical liberalism is necessary for the preservation of society. In this respect it functions as a kind of civic religion, or secularized theology, to which all can pledge allegiance. Without such a religion people would be dogmatically divided from each other by their parochial beliefs and practices, and this can result and often has resulted in civil war and religious imperialism. As a child of *Conversos* Spinoza knew what religious dogmatism could lead to; and as a resident of the Netherlands he was an eyewitness to the religious-political conflicts that were splitting Dutch society. The "true universal religion" is not infected with the diseases of fanaticism and intolerance. It preaches fair-mindedness and tolerance, virtues that are necessary for the health of any society.

Now, it is important to recognize that this universal religion is not philosophical in origin or content. Indeed, from a purely philosophical point of view some of its principles, especially the ways in which they are formulated, may not be strictly true. But no matter. What is needed here is that they are believed to be salutary and useful. For example, the last principle of this religion is that God forgives the sins of those who repent. This is surely a teaching that is found in the Bible and the Quran. But, according to the philosophy of the *Ethics*, this principle is false. For according to Spinoza repentance is idle; it presupposes the false belief that one could have done otherwise than what in fact one did do (*Ethics*, Part 3, Proposition 51, Scholium, Appendix, Definition 27; Part 4, Proposition 54). Nevertheless, the belief in repentance does foster the idea that one should do better in the future and that if one does better, this will be acceptable to God. Society needs this belief; so we or, better, the non-philosophers, should believe it.

By divorcing philosophy from the universal religion, Spinoza believes that he is ready to enunciate one of the more significant theses of the *TTP:* philosophy and theology are or should be independent of each other. The province of philosophy is truth; the domain of religion is obedience. No longer is one the servant of the other. Each has its own function and purpose; each is legitimate in its own sphere. So long as one does not go beyond its proper range, nothing that endangers public peace and security will result. Threats to the peace occur when religion transgresses its legitimate boundary and attempts to philosophize and in particular when it tries to enlist the government to its illegitimate cause. There is no fear that genuine philosophy will commit this sin, since philosophy clearly recognizes its scope and has no interest in political domination. This divorce has a happy consequence: philosophy emancipates itself from the illicit and injurious intrusion of theology into its domain; religion rids itself of the excess baggage of inappropriate and irrelevant ideas from philosophy. And neither needs to appeal to the state to enforce its views and doctrines.

This "divorce" needs to be properly understood, especially in the context of the revival of an ancient doctrine with which it may be confused—fideism. The fideist defends faith (the Latin term '*fides*' means "faith") by means of philosophical skepticism: he denies the applicability of human reason to the domain of religion, since human reason is weak and unreliable. The classic formula of the second-century Christian theologian Tertullian nicely expresses this idea: "I believe because it is absurd."[67] In our day a less extreme version of fideism has been espoused by the followers of Ludwig Wittgenstein, such as Norman Malcolm and D. Z. Phillips. This recent form of fideism is more interested in showing that religious belief has its own "grammar" or logic, which is essentially different from that employed in the sciences. Rather than defending religion by denying the power of human reason, the modern fideist makes a more modest claim: religious beliefs are not hypotheses that need to be supported and confirmed. They constitute instead a "form of life" to which their adherents conform. The religious framework is not a scientific theory that requires testing before it can be accepted; one just lives by it.[68]

Spinoza's notion of faith in the *TTP* is not fideistic, although he clearly

---

67. Tertullian, *On the Flesh of Christ,* chapter 5. See Harry Wolfson, *The Philosophy of the Church Fathers* (Cambridge, Mass.: Harvard University Press, 1956, first edition), 102–106.

68. Ludwig Wittgenstein, "A Lecture on Religious Belief," in his *Lectures and Conversations,* edited by C. Barrett (Berkeley: University of California Press, 1966), 53–59. Norman Malcolm, "The Groundlessness of Belief," in *Religion and Reason,* edited by Stuart Brown (Ithaca: Cornell University Press, 1977), 143–157. D. Z. Phillips, *Religion without Explanation* (Oxford: Oxford University Press, 1976).

separates faith from philosophy. The fideist, ancient and modern, defends religious belief by "building a rampart" around it.[69] Questions of truth are not asked because they are for the fideist irrelevant and inappropriate. In this sense, the fideist is "beyond truth or falsity." Not so Spinoza. His separation of faith from philosophy is not so peaceful as it looks. He believes, indeed, he believes he knows, that many traditional religious beliefs are false, including some in his universal religion. The philosopher is no longer committed to these doctrines; indeed, he is "beyond" them. Some of them are politically useful, and so the philosopher will give them their due. His concerns are elsewhere.

Moreover, in chapter 15 of the *TTP* Spinoza expresses disdain for the fideistic strain in Judaism. This attitude is also evident in his contemptuous and sarcastic responses to the orthodox Christians who tried to convert him or defend their traditional views against Spinoza's explicit or implicit criticisms.[70] Unlike Tertullian, Spinoza believed in the reliability of human reason; unlike Wittgenstein and his fideistic disciples, he did not immunize religious beliefs from rational inquiry and testing. Truth mattered to him; indeed, it mattered more than anything else.

IX

The main goals of the *TTP* as announced in its Preface have been achieved. Spinoza has specified the necessary conditions for establishing and preserving a society free from internal conflict. A society that has achieved and preserves these conditions will be tolerant and peaceful, and that is what Spinoza ardently desired and argued for in the *TTP.* Nevertheless, Spinoza writes five more chapters, in which he develops the main outlines of his political theory and uses the ancient Israelite state as a case study for empirical confirmation of his theoretical conclusions and as a "moral-political" lesson for the present and future.

Like his older contemporary, Hobbes, Spinoza employs the vocabulary of the social-contract theory of the state, according to which man's original, or natural, condition is apolitical; it is transformed into the condition of civility by the realization that life in the state of nature is intolerable. This change is effected by a contract, or covenant, that establishes a government, or sovereign, whose sovereignty guarantees or is supposed to guarantee the peace and security for which the state is originally in-

69. The metaphor is from Maimonides, although he was not a fideist (Maimonides, *Guide,* 2.17).

70. In addition to his response to Albert Burgh (Letter 76), the letters to William Blyenburgh (Letters 19, 21, 23, 27) and to Hugo Boxel (Letters 53, 54, 56) are pertinent to this issue.

stituted. Yet, as we shall see, Spinoza differs from Hobbes on several important issues.[71]

The Hobbesian derivation of the state seems to be a rejection of the view of Plato and Aristotle that the state is a natural development growing out of human need and character. For these ancient philosophers, man is a "political animal."[72] This conception of human nature and society was rejected by some of the Sophists, who argued that political organization is "artificial," a contrived convention manufactured by the weak multitude to overcome the minority of the naturally superior.[73] A later version of the artificial theory of the state is found in some medieval Christian thinkers, especially in Augustine, who saw the state as little better than a "pack of thieves" or as punishment for original sin.[74]

Hobbes constructed a model of political development according to which human nature is in essence nonpolitical or even antipolitical. We are naturally antisocial and selfish, even to the point of being hostile to fellow members of the human species. In this "natural state," however, life is "brutish and short," since no one is strong enough to succeed always in getting what he or she wants. So, to avoid harmful and unpleasant outcomes we make a deal: we give up our natural right to everything for an arrangement wherein security and peace are obtained by obedience to a sovereign, who is now invested with the authority and power to issue decrees, thus creating a system of laws and morality. Without this "contract" there is no such thing as justice; with this contract a person can be confident that his life and goods will be respected by others. We now have a commonwealth, or government, all of whose subjects are united in their agreement to obey the sovereign in all that the sovereign commands. Although for Hobbes the sovereign is defined in general terms, such that no particular form of sovereignty is presupposed or implied, Hobbes explicitly argues for the superiority of monarchy, indeed absolute monarchy, as the most efficient type of government.[75]

71. The relationship between Hobbes and Spinoza has been discussed by many scholars. Several issues of the *Studia Spinozana* are devoted to some of these topics: volumes 3 (1987) and 7 (1991). See also S. Zac's insightful essay "Etat et Nature chez Spinoza" in his collection of essays *Philosophie, théologie, politique dans l'oeuvre de Spinoza* (Paris: Vrin, 1979), 117–143. More recently Douglas Den Uyl discusses the differences between Hobbes and Spinoza in his *Power, State and Freedom* (Van Gorcum: Assen, The Netherlands, 1983), especially in Appendix A.

72. Aristotle, *Politics*, 1.2, 1253a2–3.

73. Plato, *Gorgias*, 483a ff.

74. Augustine, *City of God*, Book 14, chapter 1; Book 4, chapter 4.

75. Hobbes, *Leviathan*, Part 2, chapter 19.

Spinoza too sees the state originating in a contract. Like Hobbes, Spinoza insists that in the state of nature there is no morality or legality: everyone enjoys a natural right to anything as far and as long as he has the power to acquire and hold on to it. But of course this power is limited, and sooner or later someone more powerful will come along and take from us what we have. So the state of nature is not a happy state, as Hobbes saw. But unlike Hobbes, Spinoza underplays the artificial, unnatural motivation behind the state's establishment. Although he uses the language of the social contract, Spinoza sees the state as more of a natural outgrowth of our humanity and needs. In this respect he is closer to Plato and Aristotle. Although he is perfectly aware of man's selfishness, he is also cognizant of his need for other human beings, not only to satisfy our material and economic needs but also for the fulfillment of our emotional and intellectual capacities. The reasonable man is one who seeks out other like-minded people to enjoy together the life of the intellect, or freedom.[76] True, most people are not creatures of reason; yet, even the most dull among us recognize that it is better to be part of a society than to live like an ape in a jungle. So self-interest dictates that we make this pact with others and create a social order that insures our safety and at least the minimum satisfaction of our needs. After all, none of us is a farmer, carpenter, plumber, physician, and stockbroker altogether. Yes, the state is "manufactured"; but it is made because we need it, and we need it because we are human, not tigers. So there are in Spinoza's contract theory of the state features of Plato's theory of the reciprocal satisfaction of natural needs. In his *Political Treatise* Spinoza admits that in this sense his theory is more classical than Hobbesian: ". . . if this is why the schoolmen want to call man a sociable animal—I mean because men in the state of nature can hardly be independent—I have nothing to say against them" (*Political Treatise*, 2.15).

Another significant difference between Hobbes and Spinoza lies in their conceptions of the contract that establishes the state. The Hobbesian contract is instituted by a group of individuals among themselves to establish a sovereign, in whom is vested ultimate legal and political authority. The sovereign, however, stands outside this contract; hence, it is not bound by the contract or any particular law it decrees. This agreement is almost absolutely binding upon the subjects, who are obliged to obey the sovereign completely.[77] The one exception admitted by Hobbes is when the sovereign decrees that a subject is to be executed. Although the decree is legally valid and just, since the laws of the sovereign are just by defini-

76. Spinoza, *Ethics*, 4.35–37, 40.
77. Hobbes, *Leviathan*, 2.18.

tion, the subject still has the natural right to defend himself. The right to self-preservation is in this sense inalienable, or nontransferable.[78] The subject may attempt to flee the state, but the sovereign is justified in pursuing the subject, and in capturing and killing him. At this point the state of nature has resurfaced, at least between the former subject and the sovereign. What transpires in this situation is just a matter of raw might.

On this issue Spinoza explicitly distinguishes his theory from that of Hobbes in one of his letters to his friend Jarig Jelles:

> With regard to political theory, the difference between Hobbes and myself, which is the subject of your inquiry, consists in this, that *I always preserve the natural right in its entirety,* and I hold that the *sovereign* power in a State has right over a subject only in proportion to the excess of its power over that of a subject. This is always the case in a state of nature (Letter 50, emphasis added).

In this passage the italicized phrase is crucial. Whereas Hobbes speaks of transferring our original right to everything to a sovereign who thereby acquires this right, Spinoza prefers to speak of a transfer of power and the retention of our natural right.[79] Hobbes' focus upon the transference of a right leads him to stress the formal-legalistic dimensions of the initial contract and the obedience to it. If I have a car and sell it, I have transferred my right to the car to another person who now has the right to it. I no longer have any legal claim to that car. Spinoza's account of the contract, however, stresses the aspect of power: the contractees agree to establish a more powerful means in order obtain security. This results in a reduction of their already limited power, but not of their right to anything that they have the power to acquire. The transfer of power involved here is beneficial, and so less is really more. Thus, even in the state, or society, our original natural right is preserved "in its entirety," although we have transferred our power to implement this right absolutely to someone else.

This distinction allows Spinoza a more flexible attitude toward the contract and promises in general. In the *TTP,* chapter 16, he claims that a contract is binding so long as it is useful to its participants. He expresses this "realistic" view in very blunt terms: "Everyone has the natural right to act deceitfully and is not bound to keep his engagements except through hope of greater good or fear of greater evil."[80] This is as true in the public domain as it is in the private realm. What makes the contract binding is its

---

78. Ibid., 1.14.

79. Edwin Curley, "Kissinger, Spinoza, and Genghis Khan," in *The Cambridge Companion to Spinoza,* 322–327.

80. Spinoza, *TTP,* chapter 16.

utility, not the mere act of saying "I promise X," as it is for Hobbes. Accordingly, if the sovereign is unable to provide for and preserve the security for which the state was contracted, then the deal is off. The sovereign's failure is comparable to the bouncing of the car purchaser's check. When this occurs, the car returns to the original owner. If the sovereign doesn't do its job, it ceases to be a sovereign; it loses its sovereignty over the subjects. Sovereignty is legitimate as long as it is effective, that is, useful.[81]

Indeed, on this very question of sovereignty, there is another significant difference between Hobbes and Spinoza. As mentioned before, Hobbes shows a clear sympathy for absolute monarchy. Spinoza, like the biblical prophet Samuel, abhors it. For Spinoza, the best form of sovereignty is democracy; indeed, this is the most natural form of the state, since democracy is the rule of all the subjects by and over itself. A democratic polity is one where all those who constitute the state by their contract become equally, by this pact, sovereigns, either directly, as in ancient Athens, or indirectly, as in a representative democracy, or republic. In this sense, as Kant was to maintain, the laws issued by the sovereign are literally the laws of each subject. To obey the laws of a democracy is really to obey ourselves. In a democracy the citizen is truly free, or independent, since no one subject has more legal right than another, and the sovereign is just the collectivity of the subjects. Thus, the original condition of equality in the state of nature is preserved.[82]

We shouldn't rush to the conclusion, however, that Spinoza's utilitarian conception of the contract and his preference for democracy countenance civil disobedience and rebellion. A state without obedience and order is no state. There are limits to what the citizen may do; liberty is not the license to do anything one wants. Spinoza makes it quite clear that he has no use for revolutions, which generally turn out worse than the original situation, or even civil disobedience. At this point Spinoza's strong advocacy of the liberty of speech and thought undergoes an interesting and significant modification. If the sovereign passes a law that we find to be impractical or unnatural, we do have the right to argue against it, either through our representatives or through our own efforts. But we must obey the law while we fight against it and after we fail to have it changed. We don't have the option to disobey the law. All cases of civil disobedience ought to be punished, even though the right to argue against a law is allowed. Speech is permitted, although action is proscribed.[83]

81. Ibid.
82. Ibid., chapters 19–20.
83. Ibid., chapter 20.

This seeming ambiguity is evident even in Spinoza's argument for freedom of religion and philosophy. Although he has defended the right to worship God in a variety of ways and the liberty to philosophize as one wishes, Spinoza bestows upon the sovereign the right to curtail such activities if it believes that they are dangerous to the public welfare.[84] To use our previous example: we have the right to speak our minds; but we don't have the right to disobey the law. We have the right to establish or practice a religion in accordance with our conception of what religion is about, but if this religion advocates or results in social disruption and anarchy, then the sovereign has the right, indeed the duty, to forbid this religious practice. Spinoza is then not so much a defender of liberty of speech, if this is interpreted in an absolute sense, as an advocate of liberty of conscience and thought. Our thoughts are our own: no one can stop us from thinking what we think, although we can be influenced to a considerable extent to think what others want us to think. Yet, for Spinoza there is always a "private domain" in our minds that cannot be invaded or controlled. The sovereign has no right over our minds since it has no power to control them. In language similar to that used by John Stuart Mill two centuries later, Spinoza lists the advantages resulting from a generous right to free speech and the disadvantages that accrue to society when it is abrogated or significantly curtailed.[85] But, as Mill too noted,[86] this right or liberty cannot be absolute. We don't allow someone to yell "Fire!" in a crowded theater or stadium. Nor, Spinoza maintains, should we permit people to advocate the dissolution of the state or the assassination of the sovereign.[87]

In this context Spinoza makes an interesting comment that again reveals his greater affinity with ancient Greek political thought than with Hobbes. Right after he states that freedom of speech cannot be absolutely unrestricted, he claims that the goal of government is to free us from fear, and this freedom from fear includes the removal of anxiety that is often present in absolute monarchy or in other forms of nondemocratic polities.

> It is not . . . the purpose of the state to transform men from rational beings into beasts or puppets, but rather to enable them to develop their mental and physical faculties in safety, to use their reason without restraint. . . . Thus, the purpose of the state is, in reality, freedom.[88]

84. Ibid.
85. Ibid.
86. J. S. Mill.
87. Spinoza, *TTP,* chapters 18, 20.
88. Ibid., chapter 20.

Aristotle would have agreed. Peace and security for both Aristotle and Spinoza have "positive consequences," i.e., the promotion and preservation of human culture; for Hobbes, they are primarily "negative," i.e., the removal of threats to one's physical existence. Spinoza's claim—"For peace is not the mere absence of war, but a virtue based upon strength of mind" (*Political Treatise*, 5.4)—echoes the Platonic-Aristotelian notion that the political domain is conducive to and necessary for human development and progress.

Several commentators have considered Spinoza to be the first founder and defender of democracy and liberalism.[89] But we need to be more reserved in our praise, especially if we conceive of democracy and liberalism in contemporary terms. As we have mentioned earlier, Spinoza clearly indicated his "low regard" for the masses. When the republican leaders of the Netherlands were assassinated, Spinoza called their murderers "the ultimate barbarians."[90] Nor was he generous in granting the right to vote: women and men engaged in "lowly" occupations would be disenfranchised.[91] Some scholars have noted, however, that Spinoza's principle of exclusion is based upon his notion of the citizen as autonomous, as not being subject to or dependent upon any other person. In his day women were for the most part economically dependent and undereducated, as were many men.[92] And, after all, in the United States of America women didn't get the vote until the twentieth century. So we have to be a bit patient with Spinoza's "biases."

X

In the concluding chapters of the *TTP* Spinoza returns to ancient Israelite history to find confirming evidence to support his theory. Politics, he insists, is a practical science and must fit the facts.[93] One could ask, however, why use ancient Israel as an example? Indeed, earlier in the treatise, Spinoza explicitly stated that, not only has the Israelite state ceased to exist, but that it suffered from some serious internal defects.[94] So why does Spinoza select this obsolete and unsuccessful state for extensive analysis in these closing chapters?

89. Smith, 121–122. Den Uyl, 157.
90. Klever, 40.
91. Spinoza, *Political Treatise*, 11.3.
92. Den Uyl, 162–167.
93. Spinoza, *Political Treatise*, chapter 1.
94. Spinoza, *TTP*, chapter 3.

Two reasons seem to be pertinent. First, many of the theologians and politicians of Spinoza's own day regarded the ancient Israelite society as a model, perhaps *the* model, for the kind of state they wanted to establish in the Netherlands. To persuade them that this is not a good idea, Spinoza has to examine this particular society in detail to show his ideological opponents its shortcomings and irrelevance to the present. A "New Jerusalem" cannot, indeed, ought not to be, created in Amsterdam. Second, Spinoza believes and will argue that some of the more serious problems facing Dutch society and politics were present in the ancient Hebrew state. By pinpointing these problems and seeing what resulted from them in Israelite history, we can perhaps avoid their recurrence in our own times.

Curiously, though, Spinoza's second visit to ancient Israel results in a somewhat more favorable impression. The earlier hostility to Judaism and Jewry is absent; the strengths and positive features of ancient Israel are given their due. Moses is depicted in a more positive fashion: he is a strong and effective leader who refuses to create a hereditary monarchy after him, although he is in a good position to do so. He knows his limits, shows his modesty in wanting all the Israelites to become worthy of the prophetic gift,[95] and obeys God, even when God forbids him to enter the Promised Land. Wisely he creates a citizen army, as against hiring mercenaries; he establishes "welfare" laws that attempt to eliminate or at least minimize poverty; and he preserves the autonomy of the judiciary system, as against the encroachments of the priesthood, by instituting independent courts and judges. Indeed, the original priesthood was completely subordinate to Moses, who appointed the high priest, and was not permitted to issue laws on its own, even laws pertaining to its own proper activities. The Israelite polity was indeed a theocracy, in the sense that its ultimate authority was God, but in practice it was a kind of limited monarchy, since it was really governed on a practical level by Moses, whose authority was always subject to divine limitation and intervention.

Israelite history also furnishes Spinoza with a real example of his theory of the formation of the state. After the exodus from Egypt, the Israelites, according to Spinoza, were in the state of nature, a condition that they found to be intolerable. They thus entered into a covenant, or contract, with God, who henceforth became their sovereign. This covenant was entered into by the whole people, and thus there were elements of democracy in this contract: 1) all the people were equal; 2) they were dependent only upon God, not any other human; 3) even after they ceded their rights to Moses, God's representative, or vicar, on earth, they re-

95. Numbers 11:26–30.

verted to a kind of federated democracy after Joshua's death, during the period of the Judges. The real effective ruler of the people at this period was the Torah, or Law, which applied to all the people and which was supposed to be studied by all.

At this juncture two significant changes come about that led to the irreparable decline of the Israelite polity. The people asked for a king, and the priests became more powerful, especially after the return to Judea from the Babylonian exile. Under the kings, even the successful ones such as David and Solomon, there was continual conflict between political authority and religious institutions, both priests and prophets. Many of the kings acted arbitrarily and tyrannically. The situation became worse during the reign of the Maccabean princes in the second and first centuries and the Herodian puppet-rulers after the Roman conquest of Judea. The Maccabees were originally priests and had no right to assume political rule, which was supposed to reside only in the House of David. Moreover, in their attempt to exercise political power the priests became corrupt and later seditious, as in the rebellion against Rome. Eventually religious sects arose, something that did not exist formerly. These diverse groups differed primarily in dogma, in some cases using philosophy to bolster or formulate their views. Worse still, they intervened in politics, and the political authorities used or abused these religious parties to further their own interests. This is the infamous history of the conflicts between the Sadducees and the Pharisees, a story, Spinoza insists, full of fanaticism, mutual hostility, and persecution.[96]

From this sad story Spinoza learns several lessons with which he closes his treatise. First and foremost, the clergy cannot be given power or authority, either political or religious. They are not to be permitted to interfere in the political affairs of the state. They are not to be given the authority to legislate religious practice, even to their own followers, if this practice is deemed dangerous to the state. They certainly do not have the right to persecute those who disagree with them. Second, the political authorities should stay out of religious matters as much as is practical. They should certainly refrain from dictating religious or philosophical ideas, in particular declaring one particular religious sect as the established church. On the other hand, it may be necessary for the political authority to legislate in religious affairs, if the circumstances warrant such activity. In doing so the sovereign is within its right. But such legislation should concern only practice, not thought. Third, changes in government usually have deleterious consequences, as the Israelite request for a mon-

---

96. Spinoza, *TTP,* chapter 18. Spinoza's account of postbiblical Jewish history owes much to the writings of Josephus, the Jewish historian (A.D. 37–c.100).

archy demonstrated. The state was originally instituted to secure peace and stability. Sudden and violent eruptions can only cause disorder and terror.

The experience of the ancient Israelite state is then instructive. We cannot, indeed, ought not go back and revive an exact replica of it. It was established by God through his prophets, and there are no universally accepted prophets today. Its legal system was historically conditioned insofar as it was given to a people at a certain stage of spiritual develop-ment that no longer applies to many people today. We no longer need to or should picture God as an arbitrary lawgiver issuing decrees, many of which have nothing to do with our moral and intellectual perfection and happiness. Whatever advantages the ancient Israelite state possessed were rooted in the particular historical circumstances of those times. Not only is it no longer the obligatory system for the Israelites of modern times, but it is also not the model for anyone else. True, we have learned many positive lessons from its history. And we can thank the Israelites for having taught us these lessons. But we have gone beyond them, precisely by reading their history.

Seymour Feldman

SELECT BIBLIOGRAPHY

Original Latin Editions of the *TTP*

Opera, ed. Carl Gebhardt. Heidelberg: C. Winter, 1972 (reprint of 1925 edition). 4 vols. The *TTP* is included in volume 3.

Spinoza, Political Works, ed. and trans. A. G. Wernham. Oxford: Clarendon Press, 1958. Contains only parts of the *TTP* with an English translation, but all of the *Political Treatise.*

Translations

English

Elwes, R. H. M. *The Chief Works of Benedict de Spinoza*. New York: Dover Books, 1951. Vol. 1.

French

Lagrée, J., and P.-F. Moreau, in *Oeuvres* III (*Traité théologico-politique*), with Latin text by F. Akkerman. Paris: Presses Universitaires de France, 1999.

German

Theologisch-politischer Traktat, trans. C. Gebhardt and G. Gawlik. Hamburg: F. Meiner Verlag, 1976.

Hebrew

Wirszubski, C. Jerusalem: Magnus Press, Hebrew University, 1961.

Italian

Trattato teologico-politico, trans. A. Droetto and E. Giancotti Boscherini. Turin: Einaudi, 1972.

Spanish

Tratado teológico-político, trans. A. Domínguez. Madrid: Alianza Editorial, 1986.

Studies

Albiac, G. *La sinagoga vacía. Un estudio de las fuentes marranas del espinosismo.* Madrid: Ediciones Hiperion, 1987.

Bagley, P. (Ed.) *Piety, Peace, and the Freedom to Philosophize: Studies in Baruch Spinoza's* Theological-Political Treatise. Dordrecht: Kluwer Acadamic Publishers, 1999.

Curley, E. "Notes on a Neglected Masterpiece (I): Spinoza and the Science of Hermeneutics," in G. Hunter (Ed.), *Spinoza: The Enduring Questions* (pp. 64–99). Toronto: University of Toronto Press, 1994.

———. "Notes on a Neglected Masterpiece (II): The TTP as a Prolegomenon to the Ethics." In A. Cover and M. Kulstad (Eds.), *Central Themes in Early Modern Philosophy* (pp. 109–159). Indianapolis: Hackett Publishing Company, 1990.

———. "Homo Audax: Leibniz, Oldenburg, and the TTP." *Studia Leibnitiana*, Supplement 27 (1990), 277–312.

Den Uyl, D., and S. Warner. "Liberalism and Hobbes and Spinoza." *Studia Spinozana* 3 (1987), 261–318.

Donagan, A. "Spinoza's Theology." In D. Garrett (Ed.), *Cambridge Companion to Spinoza* (pp. 343–382). Cambridge: Cambridge University Press, 1996.

Feldman, S. "Spinoza: A Marrano of Reason?" *Inquiry* 35 (1992), 37–53.

Feuer, L. *Spinoza and the Rise of Liberalism*. Boston: Beacon Press, 1958.

Franck, I. "Spinoza's Onslaught on Judaism." *Judaism* 28 (1979), 177–193.

Joël, M. *Spinozas Theologisch-Politischer Traktat, auf seine Quellen geprüft*. Breslau: Schletter, 1870.

Klever, W. "Spinoza's Life and Works." In D. Garrett (Ed.), *Cambridge Companion to Spinoza* (pp. 13–60). Cambridge: Cambridge University Press, 1996.

Matheron, A. *Individu et communauté chez Spinoza*. Paris: Editions de Minuit, 1969.

———. *Le Christ et le salut des ignorants chez Spinoza*. Paris: Aubier, 1971.

Popkin, R. "Spinoza and La Peyrère." In J. Biro and R. Shahan (Eds.), *Spinoza: New Perspectives* (pp. 177–195). Norman: University of Oklahoma Press, 1978.

———. "Spinoza, the Quakers and the Millenarians." *Manuscrito* 6 (1982), 113–133.

———. "Spinoza and Bible Scholarship." In D. Garrett, *Cambridge Companion to Spinoza* (pp. 383–407). Cambridge: Cambridge University Press, 1996.

Revah, I. *Spinoza et le Dr Juan de Prado*. Paris: Mouton, 1959.

Smith, Steven. *Spinoza, Liberalism and the Question of Jewish Identity*. New Haven: Yale University Press, 1997.

Strauss, Leo. "How to Study Spinoza's *Theological-Political Treatise*. In his collected essays, *Persecution and the Art of Writing* (pp. 142–201). Glencoe: Free Press, 1952.

———. *Spinoza's Critique of Religion*. Trans. E. Sinclair. New York: Schocken Books, 1965.

Yovel, Y. *Spinoza and Other Heretics*. Vol. 1: The Marrano of Reason. Princeton: Princeton University Press, 1989.

Zac, S. *Spinoza et l'interprétation de l'écriture*. Paris: Presses Universitaires de France, 1965.

———. *Philosophie, théologie, politique dans l'oeuvre de Spinoza*. Paris: Vrin, 1979.

TRANSLATOR'S FOREWORD

The text followed in this translation is that of Gebhardt's Heidelberg edition of 1925, with a few exceptions that are noted.

Hebrew texts and letters have been omitted except where necessary to the sense.

The lengthy paragraphs of the original text would create unnecessary difficulty for the modern reader. I have therefore adopted a system of shorter paragraphs, at my discretion.

In rendering quotations from the Bible I have in general followed the Authorised Version. Where Spinoza is not in full accord with the Authorised Version, I have adhered to Spinoza.

Although an excellent translation of part of this work is included in Wernham's *Spinoza, Political Works,* the only complete English translation is that of R. H. M. Elwes, 1883, and reprinted many times. This was made from the Bruder text, since superseded; and although admirable in many respects, it contains a number of inaccuracies. The Gebhardt text, besides being more authoritative, includes many Adnotationes not available to Elwes. With regard to these Adnotationes, I have used my discretion in omitting some of Gebhardt's bracketed insertions when these do not appear to cast further light on the point at issue.

Samuel Shirley

Editorial note: Notes in the text are of two distinct kinds, those of Spinoza and those of the translator or editor. Spinoza's notes themselves take two forms, those that occur throughout the text and those that appear as Supplementary Notes at the end of the treatise. Spinoza's footnotes are signaled by asterisks. The translator's and editor's footnotes are indicated by numerals. The editor's notes and bibliography were inadvertently omitted from the first edition.

Throughout the *TTP* Spinoza quotes Scriptural passages and occasionally interjects his own explanatory comments. He marks off these comments with parentheses, which are retained in the present translation.

THE THEOLOGICAL-POLITICAL TRACTATE

Containing

Various Disquisitions,

By means of which it is shown not only that Freedom of Philosophising
can be allowed in Preserving Piety and the Peace of the Republic:
but also that it is not possible for such Freedom to be upheld
except when accompanied
by the Peace of the Republic and Piety Themselves.

The First Epistle of John, Chapter 4, Verse 13.
*Through this means we recognise that we remain in God, and God remains
in us—that He gave to us from His own Spirit.*

Hamburg,
from Heinrich Künraht.
1670

PREFACE

If men were able to exercise complete control over all their circumstances, or if continuous good fortune were always their lot, they would never be prey to superstition. But since they are often reduced to such straits as to be without any resource, and their immoderate greed for fortune's fickle favours often makes them the wretched victims of alternating hopes and fears, the result is that, for the most part, their credulity knows no bounds. In critical times they are swayed this way or that by the slightest impulse, especially so when they are wavering between the emotions of hope and fear; yet at other times they are overconfident, boastful and arrogant.

No one can be unaware of these truths, even though I believe that men generally know not their own selves. For no one can have lived in this world without realising that, when fortune smiles at them, the majority of men, even if quite unversed in affairs, are so abounding in wisdom that any advice offered to them is regarded as an affront, whereas in adversity they know not where to turn, begging for advice from any quarter; and then there is no counsel so foolish, absurd or vain which they will not follow. Again, even the most trivial of causes are enough to raise their hopes or dash them to the ground. For if, while possessed by fear, they see something happen that calls to mind something good or bad in the past, they believe that this portends a happy or unhappy issue, and this they therefore call a lucky or unlucky omen, even though it may fail them a hundred times. Then again, if they are struck with wonder at some unusual phenomenon, they believe this to be a portent signifying the anger of the gods or of a supreme deity, and they therefore regard it as a pious duty to avert the evil by sacrifice and vows, susceptible as they are to superstition and opposed to religion. Thus there is no end to the kind of omens that they imagine, and they read extraordinary things into Nature as if the whole of Nature were a partner in their madness.

This being the case, we see that it is particularly those who greedily covet fortune's favours who are the readiest victims of superstition of every kind, and it is especially when they are helpless in danger that they all implore God's help with prayers and womanish tears. Reason they call blind, because it cannot reveal a sure way to the vanities that they covet, and human wisdom they call vain, while the delusions of the imagination, dreams and other childish absurdities are taken to be the oracles of God. Indeed, they think that God, spurning the wise, has written his decrees not in man's mind but in the entrails of beasts, or that by divine inspiration and instigation these decrees are foretold by fools, madmen or birds. To

1

such madness are men driven by their fears.

It is fear, then, that engenders, preserves and fosters superstition. If anyone seeks particular examples to confirm what I have said, let him consider Alexander. It was only when he first learnt to fear fortune at Pylae Susidis (Curtius, Book 5, ch. 4) that superstition drove him to employ seers.[1] After his victory over Darius he ceased to consult prophets and seers until he was once more dismayed by his plight. With the Bacrians having deserted and Scyths taking the offensive while he himself lay wounded on his sickbed, he again (Curtius, Book 7, ch. 7) "having recourse once more to superstition, that mockery of human wisdom, bade Aristander, in whom he had instilled his own credulity, enquire the issue by sacrifices." Numerous examples of this kind can be cited, illustrating quite clearly the fact that only while fear persists do men fall prey to superstition, that all the objects of spurious religious reverence have been no more than phantoms, the delusions springing from despondency and timidity, and that, finally, it is in the times of the state's gravest perils that seers have held the strongest sway over the people and have been most formidable to their own rulers. But since I consider that this is quite common knowledge, I will say no more.

This being the origin of superstition—in spite of the view of some who assign it to a confused idea of deity possessed by all mortals—it clearly follows that all men are by nature liable to superstition. It follows that superstition, like all other instances of hallucination and frenzy, is bound to assume very varied and unstable forms, and that, finally, it is sustained only by hope, hatred, anger and deceit. For it arises not from reason but from emotion, and emotion of the most powerful kind. So men's readiness to fall victim to any kind of superstition makes it correspondingly difficult to persuade them to adhere to one and the same kind. Indeed, as the multitude remains ever at the same level of wretchedness, so it is never long contented, and is best pleased only with what is new and has not yet proved delusory. This inconstancy has been the cause of many terrible uprisings and wars, for—as is clear from the above, and as Curtius, too, says so well in Book 4, ch. 10—"the multitude has no ruler more potent than superstition." So it is readily induced, under the guise of religion, now to worship its rulers as gods, and then again to curse and condemn them as mankind's common bane. To counteract this unfortunate tendency, immense efforts have been made to invest religion, true or false,

---

1. Spinoza makes ample use here and in chapter 17 of the first-century (A.D.) Roman historian Quintus Curtius Rufus, the author of a biography of Alexander the Great, *Historiae Alexandri Magni*.

with such pomp and ceremony that it can sustain any shock and constantly evoke the deepest reverence in all its worshippers. In this the Turks have achieved the greatest measure of success. They hold even discussion of religion to be sinful, and with their mass of dogma they gain such a thorough hold on the individual's judgment that they leave no room in the mind for the exercise of reason, or even the capacity to doubt.

Granted, then, that the supreme mystery of despotism, its prop and stay, is to keep men in a state of deception, and with the specious title of religion to cloak the fear by which they must be held in check, so that they will fight for their servitude as if for salvation, and count it no shame, but the highest honour, to spend their blood and their lives for the glorification of one man. Yet no more disastrous policy can be devised or attempted in a free commonwealth. To invest with prejudice or in any way coerce the citizen's free judgment is altogether incompatible with the freedom of the people. As for those persecutions that are incited under the cloak of religion, they surely have their only source in this, that law intrudes into the realm of speculative thought, and that beliefs are put on trial and condemned as crimes. The adherents and followers of these beliefs are sacrificed, not to the public weal, but to the hatred and savagery of their opponents. If under civil law 'only deeds were arraigned, and words were not punished',[2] persecutions of this kind would be divested of any appearance of legality, and disagreement would not turn into persecution.

Now since we have the rare good fortune to live in a commonwealth where freedom of judgment is fully granted to the individual citizen and he may worship God as he pleases, and where nothing is esteemed dearer and more precious than freedom, I think I am undertaking no ungrateful or unprofitable task in demonstrating that not only can this freedom be granted without endangering piety and the peace of the commonwealth, but also the peace of the commonwealth and piety depend on this freedom.

This, then, is the main point which I have sought to establish in this treatise. For this purpose my most urgent task has been to indicate the main false assumptions that prevail regarding religion—that is, the relics of man's ancient bondage—and then again the false assumptions regarding the right of civil authorities. There are many who, with an impudence quite shameless, seek to usurp much of this right and, under the guise of religion, to alienate from the government the loyalty of the masses, still prone to heathenish superstition, so that slavery may return once more.

2. Tacitus, *Annals*, I, 12.

But before going on to discuss briefly my arrangement of this exposition, I shall first set forth the causes that have induced me to write.

I have often wondered that men who make a boast of professing the Christian religion, which is a religion of love, joy, peace, temperance and honest dealing with all men, should quarrel so fiercely and display the bitterest hatred towards one another day by day, so that these latter characteristics make known a man's creed more readily than the former. Matters have long reached such a pass that a Christian, Turk, Jew or heathen can generally be recognised as such only by his physical appearance or dress, or by his attendance at a particular place of worship, or by his profession of a particular belief and his allegiance to some leader. But as for their way of life, it is the same for all. In seeking the causes of this unhappy state of affairs, I am quite certain that it stems from a wide-spread popular attitude of mind which looks on the ministries of the Church as dignities, its offices as posts of emolument and its pastors as eminent personages. For as soon as the Church's true function began to be thus distorted, every worthless fellow felt an intense desire to enter holy orders, and eagerness to spread abroad God's religion degenerated into base avarice and ambition. The very temple became a theatre where, instead of Church teachers, orators held forth, none of them actuated by desire to instruct the people, but keen to attract admiration, to criticise their adversaries before the public, and to preach only such novel and striking doctrine as might gain the applause of the crowd. This inevitably gave rise to great quarrels, envy and hatred, which no passage of time could assuage. Little wonder, then, that of the old religion nothing is left but the outward form—wherein the common people seem to engage in base flattery of God rather than his worship—and that faith has become identical with credulity and biased dogma. But what dogma!—degrading rational man to beast, completely inhibiting man's free judgment and his capacity to distinguish true from false, and apparently devised with the set purpose of utterly extinguishing the light of reason. Piety and religion—O everlasting God—take the form of ridiculous mysteries, and men who utterly despise reason, who reject and turn away from the intellect as naturally corrupt—these are the men (and this is of all things the most iniquitous) who are believed to possess the divine light! Surely, if they possessed but a spark of the divine light, they would not indulge in such arrogant ravings, but would study to worship God more wisely and to surpass their fellows in love, as they now do in hate. They would not persecute so bitterly those who do not share their views: rather would they show compassion, if their concern was for men's salvation, and not for their own standing.

Furthermore, if they did indeed possess some divine light, this would surely be manifested in their teaching. I grant that they have expressed boundless wonder at Scripture's profound mysteries, yet I do not see that they have taught anything more than the speculations of Aristotelians or Platonists, and they have made Scripture conform to these so as to avoid appearing to be the followers of heathens. It was not enough for them to share in the delusions of the Greeks: they have sought to represent the prophets as sharing in these same delusions. This surely shows quite clearly that they do not even glimpse the divine nature of Scripture, and the more enthusiastic their admiration of these mysteries, the more clearly they reveal that their attitude to Scripture is one of abject servility rather than belief. And this is further evident from the fact that most of them assume as a basic principle for the understanding of Scripture and for extracting its true meaning that it is throughout truthful and divine—a conclusion which ought to be the end result of study and strict examination; and they lay down at the outset as a principle of interpretation that which would be far more properly derived from Scripture itself, which stands in no need of human fabrications.

When I pondered over these facts, that the light of reason is not only despised but is condemned by many as a source of impiety, that merely human suppositions are regarded as divine doctrine and that credulity is looked upon as faith; and when I saw that the disputes of philosophers are raging with violent passion in Church and Court and are breeding bitter hatred and faction which readily turn men to sedition, together with other ills too numerous to recount here, I deliberately resolved to examine Scripture afresh, conscientiously and freely, and to admit nothing as its teaching which I did not most clearly derive from it. With this precaution I formulated a method of interpreting the Bible, and thus equipped I began first of all to seek answers to these questions: What is prophecy? In what way did God reveal himself to the prophets? Why were these men acceptable to God? Was it because they attained rare heights in their understanding of God and Nature? Or was it only because of their piety? With the answers to these questions I had no difficulty in deciding that the authority of the prophets carries weight only in matters concerning morality and true virtue, and that in other matters their beliefs are irrelevant to us.

I then went on to enquire why the Hebrews were called God's chosen people. When I realised that this was for no other reason than that God chose for them a certain territory where they might live in security and wellbeing, I was led to understand that the Law revealed by God to Moses was simply the laws of the Hebrew state alone, and was therefore binding on none but the Hebrews, and not even on them except while their state still stood. Furthermore, to ascertain whether Scripture taught that the human intellect is naturally corrupt, I resolved to enquire whether universal religion—i.e. the divine law revealed to all mankind through the Prophets and the Apostles—differed from the teachings of the natural light of reason; and, again, whether miracles contravene the order of Nature, and whether they demonstrate God's existence and providence with greater clarity and certainty than events which we understand clearly and distinctly through their prime causes.

Now I found nothing expressly taught in Scripture that was not in agreement with the intellect or that contradicted it, and I also came to see that the prophets taught only very simple doctrines easily comprehensible by all, setting them forth in such a style and confirming them by such reasoning as would most likely induce the people's devotion to God. So I was completely convinced that Scripture does not in any way inhibit reason and has nothing to do with philosophy, each standing on its own footing. To demonstrate this in logical order and to settle the whole question conclusively, I show in what way Scripture must be interpreted, and how all our understanding of Scripture and of matters spiritual must be sought from Scripture alone, and not from the sort of knowledge that derives from the natural light of reason. I then pass on to indicate the prejudiced beliefs that originate from the fact that the common people, prone to superstition and prizing the legacy of time above eternity itself, worship the books of Scripture rather than the Word of God. Thereafter I show that the revealed Word of God is not to be identified with a certain number of books, but is a simple conception of the divine mind as revealed to the prophets; and that is—to obey God with all one's heart by practising justice and charity. I point out how this teaching in Scripture is adapted to the understanding and beliefs of those to whom the Prophets and Apostles were wont to proclaim the Word of God, with the purpose that men might embrace it willingly and with all their heart. Then, the fundamental principles of faith being now made clear, I reach the conclusion that the object of knowledge by revelation is nothing other than obedience, and so it is completely distinct from natural knowledge in its purpose, its basis and its method, that these two have nothing in common, that they each have a separate province that does not intrude on the other, and that neither should be regarded as ancillary to the other.

Furthermore, as men's ways of thinking vary considerably and different beliefs are better suited to different men, and what moves one to reverence provokes ridicule in another, I repeat the conclusion already stated, that everyone should be allowed freedom of judgment and the right to interpret the basic tenets of his faith as he thinks fit, and that the moral value of a man's creed should be judged only from his works. In this way all men would be able to obey God whole-heartedly and freely, and only justice and charity would be held in universal esteem.

After thus making clear the freedom granted to every man by the revelation of the Divine Law, I pass on to the second part of our subject, namely, the claim that this freedom can be granted without detriment to public peace or to the right of civil authorities, and should be so granted, and cannot be withheld without great danger to peace and grave harm to the entire commonwealth. To establish these points, I begin with the natural right of the individual; this is co-extensive with the individual's desire and power. Nobody is bound by natural right to live as another pleases, each man being the guardian of his own freedom. I go on to prove that nobody can really part with this right except by transferring his power of self-defence to another, and he to whom each man has transferred his right to live as he pleases together with his power of self-defence must necessarily retain absolute control over this natural right. Hence I show that those who hold the sovereignty possess the right over everything that is within their power and are the sole guardians of law and freedom, and that subjects should act in all matters solely in accordance with the sovereign's decree. However, since nobody can so deprive himself of the power of self-defence as to cease to be a human being, I conclude that nobody can be absolutely deprived of his natural rights, and that by a quasi-natural right subjects do retain some rights which cannot be taken from them without imperilling the state, and which therefore are either tacitly conceded or explicitly agreed by the rulers.

From these considerations I pass on to the Hebrew commonwealth, which I describe at some length so as to show in what way and by whose decision religion began to acquire the force of law, together with numerous other incidental matters of interest. Thereafter I prove that governments are the guardians and interpreters of religious law as well as civil law, and they alone have the right to decide what is just and unjust, what is pious and impious. I finally conclude that they can best retain this right and preserve the state in safety only by granting to the individual citizen the right to have his own opinions and to say what he thinks.

Such, learned reader, are the topics which I here submit for your consideration, topics which I am sure you will find interesting by reason of the great importance of the issues discussed in the entire work and in each separate chapter. I would say more, but I do not want my Preface to expand to a volume, especially since I believe its main points are quite familiar to philosophers. To others I seek not to commend this treatise, for I have no reason to expect them to approve it in any way. I know how deeply rooted in the mind are the prejudices embraced under the guise of piety. I know, too, that the masses can no more be freed from their superstition than from their fears. Finally, I know that they are unchanging in their obstinacy, that they are not guided by reason, and that their praise and blame is at the mercy of impulse. Therefore I do not invite the common people to read this work, nor all those who are victims of the same emotional attitudes. Indeed, I would prefer that they disregard this book completely rather than make themselves a nuisance by misinterpreting it after their wont. For without any advantage to themselves they would stand in the way of others for whom a more liberal approach to philosophical questions is prevented by this one obstacle, that they believe that reason must be the handmaiden of theology. These latter, I am confident, will derive great profit from this work.

However, as there are many who will not have the leisure, or perhaps the inclination, to peruse the whole of this work, I feel obliged to state at this point, as also at the conclusion of the treatise, that I have written nothing that I would not willingly submit to the scrutiny and judgment of my country's government. If anything of what I say is deemed by them to contravene the laws of our country or to be injurious to the common good, I am ready to withdraw it. I realise that I am human and may have erred. But I have taken great pains to avoid error and to ensure that my writing should be in complete agreement with our country's laws, with piety, and with morality.

CHAPTER 1

Of Prophecy [1]

Prophecy, or revelation, is the sure knowledge of some matter revealed by
God to man. A prophet is one who interprets God's revelations to those
who cannot attain to certain knowledge of the matters revealed, and can
therefore be convinced of them only by simple faith. For the Hebrew word
for prophet is '*nabi*',* that is, speaker and interpreter; but it is always used
in Scripture in the sense of interpreter of God, as we gather from Exodus
chapter 7 v. 1, where God says to Moses, "See, I have made thee a God to
Pharaoh, and Aaron thy brother shall be thy prophet." This implies that
because Aaron was acting the part of prophet in interpreting Moses'
words to Pharaoh, Moses would be to Pharaoh as God, or one acting in
God's place.

Prophets will be the subject of my next chapter; here I shall treat of
prophecy. From the definition given above, it follows that natural knowledge can be called prophecy, for the knowledge that we acquire by the
natural light of reason depends solely on knowledge of God and of his
eternal decrees. However, since this natural knowledge is common to all
men—for it rests on foundations common to all men—it is not so highly
prized by the multitude who are ever eager for what is strange and foreign
to their own nature, despising their natural gifts. Therefore prophetic
knowledge is usually taken to exclude natural knowledge. Nevertheless,
the latter has as much right as any other kind of knowledge to be called
divine, since it is dictated to us, as it were, by God's nature insofar as we
participate therein, and by God's decrees. It is no different from what is
generally termed divine knowledge except that the latter transcends the
bounds of the former and cannot be accounted for by the laws of human
nature considered in themselves. Yet in respect of the certainty involved in
natural knowledge and the source from which it derives, i.e. God, it is in
no way inferior to prophetic knowledge. I discount the fantastic view that
the prophets had human bodies but nonhuman minds, so that their sensa-
tions and consciousness were of an entirely different order from our own.

But although natural knowledge is divine, its professors cannot be

---

1. Throughout chapters 1 and 2 Spinoza has Maimonides' *Guide of the Perplexed*
before him. The reader should consult Part 2, chapters 32–45 of the *Guide*.

* See Supplementary Note 1.

called prophets;* for the rest of mankind can apprehend and be convinced of what they teach with an assurance in no way inferior to theirs, and it is not through mere faith that they do so.

Since, then, the human mind contains the nature of God within itself in concept, and partakes thereof, and is thereby enabled to form certain basic ideas that explain natural phenomena and inculcate morality, we are justified in asserting that the nature of mind, insofar as it is thus conceived, is the primary cause of divine revelation. For, as I have just pointed out, all that we clearly and distinctly understand is dictated to us by the idea and nature of God—not indeed in words, but in a far superior way and one that agrees excellently with the nature of mind, as everyone who has tasted intellectual certainty has doubtless experienced in his own case.[2] However, my main purpose being to treat only of what concerns Scripture alone, these few words on the natural light will suffice. So I pass on to treat more fully of other sources of knowledge, and other means by which God reveals to man that which transcends the bounds of natural knowledge— and also that which is within its scope, for there is nothing to prevent God from communicating by other means to man that which we can know by the natural light.

However, our discussion must be confined to what is drawn only from Scripture. For what can we say of things transcending the bounds of our intellect except what is transmitted to us by the prophets by word or writing? And since there are no prophets among us today, as far as I know, our only recourse is to peruse the sacred books left to us by the prophets of old, taking care, however, not to make metaphorical interpretations or to attribute anything to the prophets which they themselves did not clearly declare. Now it is important to note here that the Jews never make mention of intermediate or particular causes nor pay any heed to them, but to serve religion and piety or, as it is commonly called, devoutness, they refer everything to God. For example, if they make money by some transaction, they say it has come to them from God; if it happens that they desire something, they say that God has so disposed their hearts; and if some thought enters their heads, they say that God has told them this. Hence we must not accept as prophecy and supernatural knowledge whatever Scripture says God told someone, but only what Scripture expressly declares, or can be deduced from the particular context, to have been prophecy or revelation.

An examination of the Bible will show us that everything that God

---

* See Supplementary Note 2.
2. Spinoza, *Ethics*, 2.34, 49 Scholium, 4.30; Letter 32.

revealed to the prophets was revealed either by words, or by appearances, or by a combination of both. The words and appearances were either real and independent of the imagination of the prophet who heard or saw, or they were imaginary, the prophet's imagination being so disposed, even in waking hours, as to convince him that he heard something or saw something.

With a real voice God revealed to Moses the laws which he willed to be enjoined on the Hebrews, as is clear from Exodus ch. 25 v. 22 where God says, "And there I will meet with thee and commune with thee from that part of the cover which is between the two Cherubim." This clearly shows that God employed a real voice, since Moses found God there ready to speak with him whenever he wished. This voice, whereby the Law was proclaimed, was the only instance of a real voice, as I shall presently show.

There may be a case for believing that the voice with which God called Samuel was real, for in 1 Sam. ch. 3 v. 21 we read, "And the Lord appeared to Samuel again in Shiloh, for the Lord revealed himself to Samuel in Shiloh by the word of the Lord," implying that the appearing of the Lord to Samuel consisted in God's manifesting himself to him by word; that is to say, Samuel heard God speaking. However, since we are required to make a distinction between the prophesying of Moses and that of other prophets, we are bound to take the view that this voice heard by Samuel was imaginary. This view is supported by the fact that the voice resembled the voice of Eli, which was quite familiar to Samuel, and so might be the more readily imagined. When thrice called by God, he thought it was Eli calling.

The voice heard by Abimelech was imaginary, for in Gen. ch. 20 v. 6 we read, "And God said unto him in a dream. . . ." So the will of God was conveyed to him not in waking hours but in sleep, a time when the imagination is not naturally apt to depict what is most existent.

Some Jews take the view that the words of the Decalogue were not pronounced by God, but that the Israelites heard only a noise without distinct words, and during its continuance they apprehended the Ten Commandments by direct intuition. I was at one time inclined to this view, seeing that the words of the Decalogue in Exodus differ from the words of the Decalogue in Deuteronomy. Since God spoke only once, it would seem to follow that the Decalogue is intended to convey the meaning, and not the actual words, of God. However, unless we would do violence to Scripture, it must undoubtedly be conceded that what the Israelites heard was a real voice; for in Deut. ch. 5 v. 4 it expressly says, "The Lord talked with you face to face," that is, just as two men ordinarily exchange thoughts through the medium of their two bodies. So it would be more in conformity with Scripture that God did really create a voice by which he revealed the Decalogue. As for the reason for the discrepancy in the wording and reasoning of the two versions, I refer you to chapter 8.

Yet even so, the difficulty is not entirely removed. It seems quite alien to reason to assert that a created thing, dependent on God in the same way as other created things, should be able to express or display, factually or verbally, through its own individuality, God's essence or existence, declaring in the first person, "I am the Lord your God, etc." Granted, when someone utters the words "I understand," we all realise that it is the speaker's mind, not his mouth, that understands. But it is because the mouth is identified with the person of the speaker, and also because the hearer knows what it is to understand, that he readily grasps the speaker's meaning through comparison with himself. Now in the case of people who previously knew nothing of God but his name, and desired to speak with him so as to be assured of his existence, I fail to see how their need was met through a created thing (which is no more related to God than are other created things, and does not pertain to God's nature) which declared, "I am the Lord." What if God had manipulated the lips of Moses—but why Moses? the lips of some beast—so as to pronounce the words "I am the Lord"? Would the people thereby have understood God's existence?

Again, it is the indisputable meaning of Scripture that God himself spoke (for which purpose he descended from Heaven to Mount Sinai) and that not only did the Jews hear him speaking but their chief men even beheld him (Exodus ch. 24). Nor did the Law revealed to Moses—to which nothing might be added and from which nothing might be taken away, and which was established as the nation's statutes—ever require us to believe that God is incorporeal or that he has no form or figure, but only that he is God, in whom the Jews must believe and whom alone they must worship. And to dissuade them from forsaking his worship, it forbade them to assign any image to him or to make any; for, as they had not seen God's image, any image they could make would not resemble God but must necessarily resemble some created thing which they had seen. So when they worshipped God through that image, their thoughts would not be of God but of that which the image resembled, and so in the end they would attach to that thing the glory and worship of God. But indeed, Scripture does clearly indicate that God has a form, and that when Moses heard God speaking, it befell him to see God, but to behold only his back parts. So I have no doubt that here lies some mystery, which I shall discuss more fully later on. For the present I shall go on to point out those passages in Scripture which indicate the means whereby God has revealed his decrees to man.

That revelation has occurred through images alone is clear from 1 Chron. ch. 21, where God displays his anger to David through an angel grasping a sword. So, too, in the case of Balaam. Maimonides and some others take the view that this and all other instances of an apparition of an angel—as to Manoah and to Abraham when he was about to sacrifice his son—occurred in dreams, on the grounds that nobody could have seen an angel with his eyes open. But this is mere rubbish. They are concerned only to extort from Scripture some Aristotelian nonsense and some fabrications of their own; and this I regard as the height of absurdity.

It was by images, unreal and dependent only on the prophet's imagination, that God revealed to Joseph his future dominion.

It was through images and words that God revealed to Joshua that he himself would fight on their behalf. He caused to appear to him an angel with a sword as if to lead his army, and he had also revealed this in words, which Joshua had heard from an angel. In the case of Isaiah, too (ch. 6), it was conveyed to him through a vision that God's providence was forsaking the people: he saw God, the thrice Holy, sitting on his throne on high, and the Israelites stained with the filth of their sins, sunk in foulness, and thus far removed from God. Thereby he understood the present miserable plight of the people, while its future calamities were revealed to him by words that seemed to issue from God. I could quote many similar examples from the Bible, but I think they are sufficiently familiar to all.

But the position here outlined receives even clearer confirmations in Numbers ch. 12 v. 6, 7, "If there be a prophet among you, I the Lord will make myself known unto him in a vision (that is, through figures and symbols, for in the case of Moses' prophecy God declared that there was vision without symbols) and I will speak unto him in a dream (that is, not in actual words and a real voice). But not thus (will I reveal myself) to Moses. With him will I speak mouth to mouth, by seeing and not by dark speeches, and the similitude of the Lord shall he behold"; that is to say, beholding me as a friend might do, and not in terror, shall he speak with me—Exodus ch. 33 v. 11. Therefore there can be no doubt that other prophets did not hear a real voice, and this is further confirmed by Deut. ch. 34 v. 10, "And there stood (meaning 'arose') not a prophet since in Israel like unto Moses, whom the Lord knew face to face," which must be taken to mean 'through voice alone', for not even Moses ever saw the Lord's face (Exodus ch. 33).

These are the only means of communication between God and man that I find in the Bible, and so, as I have previously shown, no other means should be alleged or admitted. We may quite clearly understand that God can communicate with man without mediation, for he communicates his essence to our minds without employing corporeal means. Nevertheless, a man who can perceive by pure intuition that which is not contained in the basic principles of our cognition and cannot be deduced therefrom must needs possess a mind whose excellence far surpasses the human mind. Therefore I do not believe that anyone has attained such a degree of perfection surpassing all others, except Christ. To him God's ordinances leading men to salvation were revealed not by words or by visions, but directly, so that God manifested himself to the Apostles through the mind of Christ as he once did to Moses through an audible voice. The Voice of Christ can thus be called the Voice of God in the same way as that which Moses heard. In that sense it can also be said that the Wisdom of God— that is, wisdom that is more than human—took on human nature in Christ, and that Christ was the way of salvation.

But I must here ask it to be noted that I am certainly not alluding to the doctrines held by some Churches about Christ, nor am I denying them; for I freely confess that I do not understand them. What I have just stated I gather from Scripture itself. Nowhere have I read that God appeared to Christ or spoke with him, but that God was revealed to the Apostles through Christ, that Christ is the way of salvation, that the ancient Law was transmitted through an angel, not directly by God and so on. Therefore, if Moses spoke with God face to face as a man may do with his fellow (that is, through the medium of their two bodies), then Christ communed with God mind to mind.

Therefore we may conclude that, with the exception of Christ, God's revelations were received only with the aid of the imaginative faculty, to wit, with the aid of words or images. Hence it was not a more perfect mind that was needed for the gift of prophecy, but a more lively imaginative faculty, as I shall demonstrate more clearly in the next chapter. At this point we must ask what is meant in the Bible by the prophets' being filled with the Spirit of God, or the prophets speaking with the Spirit of God. To this end we must first ask the meaning of the Hebrew word '*ru'aḥ*', which is commonly translated as Spirit.[3]

The basic meaning of the word '*ru'aḥ*' is wind, as is well known, but it is often used in many other senses, which nevertheless derive from this source. It is used to mean:

1. Breath. Psalm 135 v. 17, "Neither is there any Spirit in their mouths."

2. Life, or breathing. 1 Samuel ch. 30 v. 12, "His Spirit came again to him," that is, he started breathing.

3. Hence, courage and strength, as in Joshua ch. 2 v. 11, "Neither did

3. Maimonides, *Guide of the Perplexed*, 1.40.

there remain any more spirit in any man." Likewise Ezekiel ch. 2 v. 2, "And the Spirit (i.e. strength) entered into me and set me on my feet."

4. Hence—virtue or capacity, as in Job ch. 32 v. 8, "But there is a Spirit in man," that is, wisdom is not to be sought exclusively among the old, for I now see that it depends on the virtue and capacity of the individual person. So also Numbers ch. 27 v. 18, ". . . a man in whom there is the Spirit."

5. Disposition of mind. Numbers ch. 14 v. 24, ". . . because he had another Spirit in him," that is, a different disposition or attitude of mind. Likewise Proverbs ch. 1 v. 23, "I will pour out my Spirit unto you," that is, my mind. In this sense, too, it is used to mean will, or decision, desire, and urge, as in Ezekiel ch. 1 v. 12, "Whither the Spirit was to go, they went." Likewise Isaiah ch. 30 v. 1, ". . . for weaving schemes, but not of my Spirit." Also ch. 29 v. 10, ". . . for the Lord hath poured out on you the Spirit (i.e. the desire) of deep sleep." Also Judges ch. 8 v. 3, ". . . then their Spirit (i.e. urge) was abated." Likewise Proverbs ch. 16 v. 32, "He that ruleth his Spirit (i.e. desire) is better than he who taketh a city." Again, ch. 25 v. 28, "He that hath no rule over his own Spirit." Also Isaiah ch. 33 v. 11, "Your Spirit as fire shall devour you." Moreover, the word "ruagh," insofar as it means the mind, serves to express all the passions, and also the gifts, of the mind. Lofty spirit means pride, lowly spirit humility, evil spirit hatred and melancholy, good spirit kindliness. There is the spirit of jealousy, the spirit (i.e. desire) of fornication, the spirit of wisdom, of counsel, of bravery, that is to say (Hebrew tends to use nouns rather than adjectives), a wise, prudent, courageous mind, or the virtue of wisdom, prudence, courage. Then there is the spirit of kindness, and so on.

6. Mind itself, or Soul, as in Eccles. ch. 3 v. 19, "They all have the one Spirit (or Soul)"; ". . . and the Spirit shall return to God."[4]

7. Finally, it can mean the quarters of the world (because of the winds that blow thence), and also the sides of any thing facing towards those quarters. See Ezekiel ch. 37 v. 9, and ch. 42 v. 16, 17, 18, 19 etc.

We should now note that a thing is referred to God and said to be of God in the following ways:

1. As belonging to God's nature, being, so to speak, a part of God, in such phrases as 'the power of God,' 'the eyes of God.'

2. Because it is in God's power and acts at God's behest, as in the Bible the heavens are called 'the heavens of God,' as being God's chariot and habitation, Assyria is called 'the scourge of God,' Nebuchadnezzar, 'the servant of God' and so on.

---

4. Eccles. ch. 12 v. 7. The reference is omitted in the text.

3. As being dedicated to God; e.g. 'the temple of God,' 'a Nazarene of God,' 'the bread of God' and so on.

4. As being told us by the prophets, not revealed through the natural light of reason. Thus the Law of Moses is called the Law of God.

5. As an expression of the superlative degree, as 'the mountains of God,' that is, very high mountains; 'the sleep of God,' that is, very deep sleep. In this sense we should explain Amos ch. 4 v. 11, where God himself says, "I have overthrown you as the overthrow of the Lord came upon Sodom and Gomorrah," meaning that memorable overthrow; for since God is speaking in the first person, the passage cannot properly be explained in any other way. The natural wisdom of Solomon, too, is called 'the wisdom of God'; that is, divine, or above normal. In the Psalms, too, cedars are called 'the cedars of God' to express their extraordinary size. And in 1 Samuel ch. 11 v. 7, ". . . and the fear of God fell upon the people," very great fear is meant.

In this same sense, whatever the Jews did not understand, being at that time ignorant of its natural causes, was referred to God.[5] Thus a storm was called the chiding of God, thunder and lightning were called the arrows of God; for they thought that God kept the winds shut up in caves, which they called the treasuries of God. In this belief they differed from the Gentiles, in that they believed the ruler of the winds to be God, not Aeolus. For the same reason miracles are called the works of God, that is, wonderful works. For surely all natural phenomena are the works of God, existing and acting through the divine power alone. So in this sense the Psalmist calls the Egyptian miracles 'the powers of God,' because, to the surprise of the Hebrews, they opened the way to salvation in the midst of perils, thus evoking their extreme wonder.

Since unusual works of Nature are called works of God, and trees of unusual size are called trees of God, it should occasion us no surprise that in Genesis men of extraordinary strength and great stature are called sons of God, although impious robbers and whoremongers. So any quality whatsoever whereby one surpassed all others used to be referred to God in olden days, and not only by Jews but by Gentiles too. When Pharaoh heard the interpretation of his dream, he said that Joseph possessed the mind of the gods; and Nebuchadnezzar, too, told Daniel that he possessed the mind of the holy gods. Indeed, this is quite common in Latin literature. Works of art are said to have been 'wrought by a divine hand,' which, translated into Hebrew, would be 'wrought by the hand of God,' as any Hebrew scholar would know.

So those passages of Scripture that make mention of the Spirit of God

---

5. Maimonides, *Guide of the Perplexed,* 2.48.

can now be readily understood and explained. In certain passages 'the
Spirit of God' and 'the Spirit of Jehovah' mean simply a very fierce, dry,
deadly wind, as in Isaiah ch. 40 v. 7, "the wind of Jehovah blew upon it,"
that is, a very dry, deadly wind. Also Genesis ch. 1 v. 2, ". . . and the wind
of God moved upon the water," i.e. a very strong wind. Then again, it is
used to mean high courage. The courage of Gideon and of Samson is
called in the Bible 'the Spirit of God,' that is, a bold disposition, ready for
anything. So, too, any virtue or power above the normal is called the Spirit
(i.e. Virtue) of God, as in Exodus ch. 31 v. 3, ". . . and I will fill him
(Bezaleel) with the Spirit of God," that is, as Scripture explains, with
talent and skill above the common lot of mankind. Similarly, Isaiah ch. 11
v. 2, "and the Spirit of the Lord shall rest upon him," that is, as the
prophet goes on to explain in more detail in the manner customary to
biblical writing, the virtue of wisdom, of counsel, of might and so on. So,
too, the melancholy of Saul is called 'the evil Spirit of God,' that is, a very
profound melancholy; for Saul's servants who called his melancholy 'the
melancholy of God' suggested to him that he should send for a musician to
divert him by playing the harp, which indicates that by the melancholy of
God they understood a natural melancholy.

Again, the Spirit of God can mean man's mind, as in Job ch. 27 v. 3,
". . . and the Spirit of God in my nostrils," the allusion being to Genesis
"And God breathed into man's nostrils the breath of life." So, too, Ezekiel,
prophesying to the dead (ch. 37 v. 14), ". . . and I shall put my Spirit into
you and ye shall live," that is, I shall restore you to life. The same meaning
occurs in Job ch. 34 v. 14, "if he will (meaning God), he will gather unto
himself his Spirit (that is, the mind he has given us) and his breath." In the
same way we should understand Genesis ch. 6 v. 3, "my Spirit shall not
always reason (or strive) in man, for that he is flesh"; that is, man hereafter
will act from the dictates of his flesh, and not of the mind which I gave him
so that he might discern the good. So, too, Psalm 51 v. 10, 11, "Create in
me a clean heart, O God, and renew a seemly (or orderly) Spirit (that is,
desire) in me. Cast me not away from Thy presence, and take not the Spirit
of Thy holiness from me." Since sin was believed to arise from the flesh
alone and the mind was the cause of only good impulses, he invokes God's
help against fleshly desire, but he prays that the mind which God, the
Holy One, gave him, should be preserved merely.

Again, since Scripture, in concession to the frailty of the multitude, is
wont to depict God in the likeness of man and to attribute to him mind,
heart, emotions, and even body and breath, the Spirit of God is often used
in the Bible to mean the mind, disposition, emotion, strength and breath
of God. Thus Isaiah ch. 40 v. 13, "Who hath directed the Spirit (i.e. mind)
of God?" that is, who but God himself has determined God's mind to will

anything; and ch. 63 v. 10, ". . . and with bitterness and pain they vexed his Holy Spirit." Hence it comes to be used for the Law of Moses, which displays God's mind, as it were; as in Isaiah ch. 63 v. 11, "Where is he that put his Holy Spirit within him?"—to wit, the Law of Moses, as can be gathered from the context. Also Nehemiah ch. 9 v. 20, "Thou gavest also Thy good Spirit (i.e. mind) to instruct them," for he is speaking of the occasion of the giving of the Law. And the same allusion is made in Deut. ch. 4 v. 6 where Moses says, "for this (namely, the Law) is your wisdom and your understanding." So, too, Psalm 143 v. 10 "Thy good Spirit will lead me unto the level land," that is, your mind revealed to me will lead me to the right way.

The Spirit of God may also mean, as we have seen, the breath of God; for breath, too, just like mind, heart and body, is incorrectly attributed to God in Scripture, as in Psalm 33 v. 6. Again, it can mean the power, force, or virtue of God, as in Job ch. 33 v. 4, "The Spirit of God hath made me," that is, the virtue or power, or, if you prefer, the decree of God. For the Psalmist, in the language of poetry, also says, "By the command of God were the heavens made, and all the host of them by the spirit (or breath) of his mouth," that is, by his decree, uttered, as it were, in one breath. Likewise, in Psalm 139 v. 7, "Whither shall I go from thy Spirit, or whither shall I flee from thy sight?" That is, as the Psalmist goes on to amplify his words, Whither can I go as to beyond thy power and thy presence?

Finally, the Spirit of God is used in the Bible to express the emotions of God, namely, his kindness and his mercy, as in Micah ch. 2 v. 7, "Is the Spirit of the Lord (that is, his mercy) straitened? Are these (cruelties) his works?" Likewise Zechariah ch. 4 v. 6, "Not by my might, nor by power, but by my Spirit alone," that is, by my mercy. It is also in this sense, I think, that we should understand ch. 7. v. 12 of the same prophet, "They made their hearts of adamant stone, lest they should obey the Law and the commands that God hath sent from his Spirit (that is, his mercy) by the prophets of old." In the same sense, again, Haggai says, "My Spirit (i.e. my grace) remains among you. Fear ye not" (ch. 2 v. 5).

As for Isaiah ch. 48 v. 16, "And now the Lord God, and his Spirit, hath sent me," this can be taken as referring either to God's merciful heart or to his mind as revealed in the Law. For he says, "From the beginning (that is, from the time when I first came to you to preach God's anger and his sentence pronounced against you) I spoke not in secret. From the time when sentence was pronounced, there was I (as he himself has testified in chapter 7); but now I am a messenger of joy, sent by God's mercy to prophesy your restoration." But he can also, as I said, be understood as referring to God's mind as revealed in the Law, meaning that he had come to warn them again by command of the Law, namely, Leviticus ch. 19 v.

17; and therefore he warns them in the same circumstances and the same manner as Moses was wont to warn them, and like Moses, he ends by preaching the restoration. However, the first explanation seems to me more likely.

To return now to the main purpose of this chapter, the following Scriptural expressions are now quite clear: the Spirit of the Lord was upon a prophet, the Lord poured his Spirit into men, men were filled with the Spirit of God and with the Holy Spirit and so on. They mean merely this, that the prophets were endowed with an extraordinary virtue exceeding the normal,* and that they devoted themselves to piety with especial constancy. Furthermore, they perceived the mind and thought of God; for we have seen that in Hebrew 'Spirit' means both the mind and the mind's thoughts, and it was for this reason that the Law, since it displays the mind of God, is called the Spirit or the mind of God. Therefore the imaginative faculty of the prophets, insofar as it was the instrument for the revelation of God's decrees, could equally well be called the mind of God, and the prophets could be said to have possessed the mind of God. Now the mind of God and his eternal thoughts are inscribed in our minds, too, and therefore we also, in Scriptural language, perceive the mind of God. But since natural knowledge is common to all men, it is not so highly prized, as I have already said, and particularly in the case of the Hebrews, who vaunted themselves above all men—indeed, despising all men, and consequently the sort of knowledge that is common to all men.

Finally, the prophets were said to possess the Spirit of God because men did not know the causes of prophetic knowledge, which evoked their wonder. They therefore referred it like all other portents to God, and were wont to call it divine knowledge.

We can now have no hesitation in affirming that the prophets perceived God's revelations with the aid of the imaginative faculty alone, that is, through the medium of words or images, either real or imaginary. Since we find no mention in Scripture of any other means than these, it is not permissible for us to invent any, as I have already made clear. As to the particular laws of Nature involved in revelation, I confess my ignorance. I might, indeed, have followed others in saying that it happened through the power of God, but this would be mere quibbling: it would be the same as trying to explain the specific reality of a particular thing by means of some transcendental term. For everything takes place through the power of God. Indeed, since Nature's power is nothing but the power of God, it is beyond doubt that ignorance of natural causes is the measure of our ignorance of the power of God. So it is folly to have recourse to the power

* See Supplementary Note 3.

of God when we do not know the natural cause of some phenomenon—
that is, when we do not know the power of God.[6] However, there is no
need anyway for us now to have an understanding of the cause of prophetic
knowledge. As I have already indicated, our enquiry is here confined to the
teachings of Scripture, with view to drawing our own conclusions from
these, as from data presented by Nature. The causes of these Scriptural
teachings are not our concern.

Since, then, the prophets perceived the revelations of God with the aid
of the imaginative faculty, they may doubtless have perceived much that is
beyond the limits of intellect. For many more ideas can be constructed
from words and images than merely from the principles and axioms on
which our entire natural knowledge is based.

Now we see why the perceptions and the teachings of the prophets were
nearly all in the form of parables and allegories, and why all spiritual
matters were expressed in corporeal form; for this is more appropriate to
the imaginative faculty. We shall no longer wonder why Scripture, or the
prophets, speak so strangely or obscurely of the Spirit, or mind, of God, as
in Numbers ch. 11 v. 17 and in 1 Kings ch. 22 v. 2 etc., and again why God
was seen by Micaiah as seated, by Daniel as an old man clothed in white
garments, by Ezekiel as fire; why the Holy Spirit was seen by those with
Christ as a dove descending, by the Apostles as tongues of flame, and by
Paul at his conversion as a great light. All this is in full agreement with the
common imagination of Gods and Spirits.

Finally, the imaginative faculty being fleeting and inconstant, the gift of
prophecy did not remain with the prophets for long, nor did it often
occur; it was very rare, manifesting itself in very few men, and infre-
quently even in them. This being so, we must now enquire whence the
prophets derived their certainty of what they perceived merely through
their imagination rather than through assured rational principles. However, on this point it is to Scripture that we must once again have recourse,
since on this subject, as I have said, we possess no scientific knowledge,
which is to say that we cannot explain it through its first causes. What
Scripture has to say on the certainty of the prophets will be the subject of
the next chapter, which will be about the prophets.

6. Spinoza, *Ethics*, 1.25, 34–35.

CHAPTER 2

Of the Prophets

It follows from the last chapter, as I have already stated, that the prophets were not endowed with a more perfect mind, but with a more vivid power of imagination. Scripture, too, provides ample material to confirm this. In the case of Solomon, it is clear that he surpassed others in wisdom, but not in the gift of prophecy. Heman, Darda and Kalkol were also men of outstanding wisdom, but not prophets; on the other hand, countrymen who had no learning whatsoever—indeed, even women of humble station, like Hagar, the handmaiden of Abraham—were endowed with the gift of prophecy. This fact is in no way at variance with experience and reason. Those with a more powerful imagination are less fitted for purely intellectual activity, while those who devote themselves to the cultivation of their more powerful intellect, keep their imagination under greater control and restraint, and they hold it in rein, as it were, so that it should not invade the province of intellect.

Therefore those who look to find understanding and knowledge of things natural and spiritual in the books of the Prophets go far astray. In response to the demands of our age, of philosophy, and of truth itself, I have resolved to demonstrate this point at some length, disregarding the rantings of superstition, the bitter enemy of those who are devoted to true knowledge and true morality. Alas, things have now come to such a pass that those who openly declare that they do not possess the idea of God and that they know God only through created things (of whose causes they are ignorant) do not blush to accuse philosophers of atheism.

To treat the subject methodically, I shall show that prophecy varied not only with the imagination and the temperament of each prophet but also with the beliefs in which they had been brought up, and that their prophesying never made the prophets more learned, as I shall go on to explain in more detail. But I must first discuss the question of the certainty of the prophets, for two reasons: because it is relevant to the subject of this chapter, and also because it has some bearing on the general thesis I am seeking to prove.

Imagination by itself, unlike every clear and distinct idea, does not of its own nature carry certainty with it.[1] In order that we may attain certainty of what we imagine, there has to be something in addition to imagination,

---

1. Spinoza, *Ethics*, 2.40, Scholium 2.

namely, reasoning. Hence it follows that prophecy cannot of itself carry certainty, because, as I have shown, it depended solely on the imagination. So the prophets were not assured of God's revelation through the revelation itself, but through a sign. This is clear in the case of Abraham (Gen. ch. 15 v. 8) who, when he heard God's promise, asked for a sign. He did indeed believe in God, and he did not seek a sign so as to have faith in God, but to know that this was God's promise to him. This is even clearer in the case of Gideon, who says to God, "Show me a sign (that I may know) that it is Thou who talkest to me." See Judges ch. 6 v. 17. To Moses, too, God says, "And let this be a sign that I have sent thee." Hezekiah, who had long known Isaiah to be a prophet, asked for a sign of the prophecy predicting his recovery from sickness. This makes it clear that the prophets always received some sign to assure them of the certainty of their prophetic imaginings. It is for this reason that Moses warns the Jews (Deut. ch. 18, last verse) to seek a sign from the prophet, namely, the issue of some future event. In this respect, then, prophecy is inferior to natural knowledge, which needs no sign, but of its own nature carries certainty.

Moreover, the certainty afforded by prophecy was not a mathematical certainty, but only a moral certainty. This, again, is made clear in Scripture, for in Deut. ch. 13 Moses gives warning that if any prophet should seek to introduce new gods, even if he should confirm his teaching by signs and wonders, he must nevertheless be condemned to death. For, as Moses goes on to say, "The Lord also worketh signs and miracles to try his people." Christ, too, gives his disciples a similar warning in Matthew ch. 24 v. 24. Indeed, Ezekiel clearly tells us (ch. 14 v. 9) that God sometimes deceives men by false revelations, "And when a prophet (that is, a false prophet) is deceived and hath spoken a thing, I, the Lord, have deceived that prophet." Micaiah (1 Kings ch. 22 v. 23) bears a similar witness in the case of Ahab's prophets.

Although this seems to prove that prophetic revelation is a matter open to much doubt, it nevertheless did possess a considerable degree of certainty, as I have said. For God never deceives the good and his chosen ones: in accordance with the ancient proverb (1 Samuel ch. 24 v. 13), and as is clearly shown by the story of Abigail and her speech, God uses the good as the instruments of his goodness and the wicked as the executors and tools of his wrath. This is also quite clear from the case of Micaiah quoted above: although God had resolved to deceive Ahab through prophets, he employed only false prophets, whereas to the good prophet he revealed what was true and did not forbid him to proclaim the truth. Still, the prophet's certainty was only of a moral kind, as I have said; for nobody can justify himself before God, or boast that he is the instrument of God's goodness. This is what Scripture tells us, and shows in actuality;

for God's anger misled David to number the people, although Scripture bears ample witness to David's piety.

Therefore the certainty of the prophets was based entirely on these three considerations:

1. That the things revealed were most vividly imagined, just as we are wont to be affected by objects in our waking hours.

2. The occurrence of a sign.

3. Lastly and most important, that the minds of the prophets were directed exclusively towards what was right and good.

Although Scripture does not invariably make mention of a sign, it should nevertheless be assumed that the prophets always received a sign. Scripture does not always relate in full every detail and circumstance, as many scholars have remarked, but tends rather to take such things for granted. Furthermore, we can allow that, when their prophecy revealed nothing beyond what was contained in the Law of Moses, the prophets stood in no need of a sign, for the Law was their assurance. For example, Jeremiah's prophecy concerning the destruction of Jerusalem was supported by the prophecies of other prophets and by the threats of retribution contained in the Law, and so needed no sign; but Hananiah, who in the face of all the prophets prophesied the speedy restoration of the state, necessarily needed a sign, in the absence of which he ought to have doubted his prophecy until it might be confirmed by the event he had prophesied. See Jeremiah ch. 28 v. 9.

Therefore the certainty acquired by the prophets from signs was not a mathematical certainty—that is, the certainty that necessarily derives from the apprehension of what is apprehended or seen—but only of a moral kind, and the signs were vouchsafed only to convince the prophet. It therefore follows that the signs vouchsafed were suited to the beliefs and capacity of the prophet. A sign that would validate his prophecy for one prophet might fail to convince another who held different beliefs, and so the signs varied in the case of each prophet. Similarly, revelation also varied, as we have said, in the case of each prophet according to his temperament, the nature of his imagination, and the beliefs he had previously held. It varied with temperament in this way, that if the prophet was of a cheerful disposition, then victories, peace and other joyful events were revealed to him; for it is on things of this kind that the imagination of such people dwells. If he was of a gloomy disposition, then wars, massacres, and all kinds of calamities were revealed to him. And just as a prophet might be merciful, gentle, wrathful, stern and so forth, so he was more fitted for a particular kind of revelation. In the same way, too, revelation varied with the type of imagination. If the prophet was a man of culture, it was also in a cultivated way that he perceived God's mind; if he lacked an orderly mind, in a disorderly way. The same applies to revelations that took the form of images; the visions were of oxen and cows and the like if the prophet was a countryman, of captains and armies in the case of a soldier, of a royal throne and suchlike if he was a courtier. Finally, prophecy varied with the different beliefs of the prophets. To the Magi (see Matth. ch. 2) who believed in the follies of astrology, Christ's birth was revealed through imagining a star rising in the East. To the augurs of Nebuchadnezzar (see Ezekiel ch. 21 v. 26) the destruction of Jerusalem was revealed in entrails, whereas the king himself understood it from oracles and from the flight of arrows which he shot into the air. To those prophets who believed that men act from free choice and from their own power, God was revealed as one who is aloof and unaware of future human actions. All this we shall illustrate by individual cases taken from Scripture.

The first point is evident from the case of Elisha (2 Kings ch. 3 v. 15) who, in order to prophesy to Jehoram, called for a harp, and could apprehend the mind of God only when he had been beguiled by its music. Only then did he prophesy glad tidings to Jehoram and his company; until then this could not come about because of his anger against the king, and those who are angered against a man are apt to imagine evil, not good, concerning him. As to the view advanced by some[2] that God does not reveal himself to the angry and the gloomy, this has no substance whatsoever. When Moses was angered against Pharaoh, God revealed to him the terrible slaughter of the firstborn (see Exodus ch. 11 v. 8), and this without the assistance of a harp. To Cain, too, in his rage, God was revealed. To Ezekiel, impatient with anger, was revealed the wretched plight and obstinacy of the Jews (see Ezekiel ch. 3 v. 14). Jeremiah, when deeply saddened and utterly weary of life, prophesied the calamities of the Jews, with the result that Josiah refused to consult him, but instead consulted a woman of his time, she being more fitted from her feminine character to receive a revelation of God's mercy (2 Chron. ch. 34). Micaiah, too, never prophesied any good to Ahab, though other true prophets did so (as is clear from 1 Kings ch. 20); throughout his life he prophesied evil (see 1 Kings ch. 22 v. 8), and, more clearly, 2 Chron. ch. 18 v. 7). So the prophets were temperamentally more fitted for one kind of revelation rather than another.

Again, the style of prophecy varied according to the manner of speaking of each prophet. The prophecies of Ezekiel and Amos were lacking in refinement, unlike those of Isaiah and Nahum, which were composed in a

2. Here Spinoza alludes to a rabbinic notion quoted by Maimonides in *Guide* 2.36.

cultured style. Any Hebrew scholar who cares to look into this matter more closely, if he compares certain chapters in the different prophets dealing with the same subject-matter, will find a considerable stylistic difference. Let him compare the courtly Isaiah's chapter 1 v. 11–20 with the rustic Amos' chapter 5 v. 21–24. Then let him compare the arrangement and logical argument of Jeremiah's prophecy concerning Edom (ch. 49) with the arrangement and logical argument of Obadiah. Let him again compare Isaiah chapter 40 v. 19, 20 and chapter 44 from v. 8 with Hosea chapter 8 v. 6 and chapter 13 v. 2. These and other passages, when rightly examined, will readily show that God has no particular style of speech, but in accordance with the learning and capacity of the prophet the style was cultured, compressed, stern, unrefined, prolix or obscure.

Prophetic visions and symbolism, even when conveying the same meaning, varied considerably. For Isaiah and Ezekiel, the glory of the Lord leaving the temple was represented in different ways. Now the Rabbis maintain that both visions were exactly the same, but that Ezekiel, being a countryman, was struck with a boundless wonder, and so he related the vision in every detail.[3] However, unless they have received a trustworthy tradition—which I do not believe—this is plainly an invention. Isaiah saw seraphim with six wings, Ezekiel beasts with four wings; Isaiah saw God clothed and sitting on a royal throne, Ezekiel saw him in the likeness of fire. Doubtless they both saw God as they were wont to imagine him.

Furthermore, there were differences not only in the form taken by revelations but in their clarity. The revelations of Zechariah were too obscure to be understood by him without explanation, as is clear from the narrative. The revelations of Daniel could not be understood by the prophet even when they were explained. This obscurity did not arise from any difficulty in the matter to be revealed (for this was concerned with only human affairs, and these do not exceed human capacity except as relating to the future) but solely from the nature of Daniel's imagination, which was not equally capable of prophecy in waking hours as in sleep. This is evident from the fact that at the very beginning of the revelation he was so terrified that he almost despaired of his strength. So the obscurity of things revealed to him and his failure to understand them even when explained was caused by the inadequacy of his imagination and his strength. And here it should be noted that the words heard by Daniel, as we have pointed out, were only imaginary; so it is not surprising that in his state of terror he imagined these words so confusedly and obscurely that afterwards he could understand nothing of them. Those who say that God did not wish to make a clear revelation to Daniel appear not to have read

3. This is another rabbinic doctrine quoted by Maimonides, in *Guide* 3.6.

the words of the angel, who expressly said (ch. 10 v. 14), "Now I am come to make thee understand what shall befall thy people in the latter days." So those matters remained obscure because no one was found at that time with sufficient power of imagination to receive a clearer revelation. Lastly, the prophets to whom it was revealed that God would take away Elijah tried to convince Elisha that he had been taken to another place where they might still find him; which clearly proves that they had not understood God's revelation.

There is no need to deal with this subject in greater detail. Scripture makes it absolutely clear that God bestowed a far greater gift of prophecy on one prophet than on another. But I shall show in more detail and at greater length that prophecies or revelations also varied in accordance with the ingrained beliefs of the prophets, and that the prophets held various, even contrary beliefs, and various prejudices. (The matters I refer to concern purely philosophic speculation, for with regard to uprightness and morality the case is quite different.) This I consider to be a point of some importance, for I shall eventually conclude from it that the gift of prophecy did not render the prophets more learned, but left them with the beliefs they had previously held, and therefore we are in no way bound to believe them in matters of purely philosophic speculation.

All commentators have displayed an extraordinary eagerness to convince themselves that the prophets knew everything attainable by human intellect; and although certain passages in Scripture make it absolutely clear that there were some things the prophets did not know, rather than admit that there was anything the prophets did not know, they prefer to declare that they do not understand those passages, or alternatively they strive to twist the words of Scripture to mean what they plainly do not mean. If either of these options is permissible, we can bid Scripture farewell. If that which is absolutely clear can be accounted obscure and incomprehensible or else interpreted at will, it will be vain for us to try to prove anything from Scripture. For example, nothing in Scripture could be clearer than that Joshua, and perhaps the writer who composed his history, thought that the sun goes round the earth and the earth does not move, and that the sun stood still for a time. Yet there are many who, refusing to admit that there can be any mutability in the heavens, explain this passage so that it means something quite different. Others, who have adopted a more scientific attitude and understand that the earth moves and the sun is motionless or does not revolve around the earth, make every effort to extort this meaning in the teeth of the Scriptural text. Indeed, I wonder at them. Do we have to believe that the soldier Joshua was a skilled astronomer, that a miracle could not be revealed to him, or that the sun's light could not remain above the horizon for longer than usual without

Joshua's understanding the cause? Both alternatives seem to me ridiculous. I prefer the simple view that Joshua did not know the cause of that extension of daylight, and that he and all the host along with him believed that the sun revolves around the earth with a diurnal motion and on that day it stood still for a while, this being the cause of the prolonged daylight. They did not take account of the fact that, as a result of the excessive coldness of the atmosphere at that time (see Joshua ch. 10 v. 11), there may have been an unusually great refraction of light, or something of the sort, which is not our present concern.[4]

Similarly, the sign of the shadow going back was revealed to Isaiah according to his understanding, namely, through the retrogression of the sun. For he, too, thought that the sun moves and the earth is still. He probably had not the faintest notion of parhelia. We need have no hesitation in maintaining this view, for the sign could really have occurred and Isaiah could have predicted it to the king without knowing its true cause.

As to the building of the Temple by Solomon, if indeed that was revealed to him by God, we must take the same view, namely, that all its measurements were revealed to Solomon in accordance with his understanding and beliefs. As we are not required to believe that Solomon was a mathematician, we may assume that Solomon did not know the ratio between the circumference and diameter of a circle, and that, in common with ordinary workmen, he thought it was three to one. If it is permissible to declare that we do not understand the text of 1 Kings ch. 7 v. 23 I do not know what in Scripture we can understand. The narrative of the building of the Temple is there straightforwardly set forth, and as a mere matter of history. Indeed, if it is permissible to pretend that the writer meant something different, but for reasons unknown to us decided to write in that way, this is nothing else but the utter ruination of the whole of Scripture. Everyone will have equal right to adopt the same attitude to every Scriptural passage, and thus whatever human malice can devise in the way of absurdity and iniquity can be both defended and perpetrated without impairing the authority of Scripture. But the view we are maintaining implies no impiety. Solomon, Isaiah, Joshua and the others were indeed prophets: but they were also men, subject to human limitations.

The revelation to Noah that God was destroying the human race was also made in accordance with his understanding, for he thought that the world beyond Palestine was uninhabited. And not only matters of this kind but other more important matters could have been, and in fact were,

4. S. Feldman, "'Sun Stand Still': A Philosophical-Astronomical Midrash," *Proceedings of the Ninth World Congress of Jewish Studies*, Division C, Jerusalem 1986, 77–84.

beyond the knowledge of the prophets without prejudice to their piety. Their teaching concerning the attributes of God was in no way singular. Their beliefs about God were shared by the vast majority of their time, and their revelations were accommodated to these beliefs, as I shall show by ample Scriptural testimony. Thus one may easily see that they won such praise and repute not so much for sublimity and pre-eminence of intellect as for piety and faithfulness.

Adam, to whom God was first revealed, did not know that God is omnipresent and omniscient, for he hid from God and attempted to excuse his sin before God as if he had to do with a man. So in his case, too, God was revealed in accordance with his understanding, that is, as one who is not everywhere, and as not knowing where Adam was, or Adam's sin. For Adam heard, or thought he heard, God walking in the garden, calling him and seeking him out, and then, seeing his guilty bearing, asking him whether he had eaten of the forbidden tree. Therefore Adam knew none of God's attributes except that God was the maker of all things. To Cain, too, God was revealed in accordance with his understanding, that is, as having no knowledge of human affairs; nor did Cain need to have any higher conception of God before he could repent of his sin.

To Laban God revealed himself as the God of Abraham, because Laban believed that every nation had its own special God. See Gen. ch. 31 v. 29. Abraham, too, did not know that God is everywhere and has foreknowledge of all things; for when he heard the sentence against the people of Sodom, he prayed God not to execute the sentence until he knew whether they all deserved that punishment, saying, "Peradventure there be fifty righteous within the city" (Gen. ch. 18 v. 24). Nor did God appear to him differently in revelation, for in Abraham's imagination God speaks thus, "I will go down now, and see whether they have done altogether according to the cry of it which is come unto me, and if not, I will know." Again, God's testimony concerning Abraham implies only that he was obedient and commanded his household to ways of justice and goodness (see Gen. ch. 18 v. 19); it does not imply that Abraham's conception of God was more sublime than others.

Moses, too, did not completely comprehend that God is omniscient, and that all human actions are governed solely by God's decree. Although God had told him (Exodus ch. 3 v. 18) that the Israelites would hearken to him, he still doubted, and answered (Exodus ch. 4 v. 1), "But if they will not believe me and hearken unto my voice. . . ." So for Moses, too, God was revealed as not determining future human actions and unaware of them; for God gave him two signs, and said (Exodus ch. 4 v. 8), "And it shall come to pass that if they will not believe the first sign, they will believe the latter sign; and if they believe not the latter sign, take some

waters of the river. . . ." Indeed, if anyone will examine without prejudice
what Moses says, he will clearly find that Moses' belief about God was
this, that he is a Being who has always existed, exists, and will always exist.
That is why he gives God the name Jehovah, which in Hebrew expresses
these three tenses of the verb 'to be'. As for God's nature, Moses taught no
more than that God is merciful, gracious etc. and extremely jealous, as is
evident from many passages in the Pentateuch. Further, he believed and
taught that this Being was so different from all other beings that he could
not be expressed by any image of a visible thing, nor even beheld, not so
much because this was intrinsically impossible as because of human inadequacy; and furthermore he was one alone, or unique, in respect of his
power. Moses did indeed concede that there were beings who (doubtless in
accordance with God's arrangement and behest) acted in God's place; that
is, beings to whom God gave the authority, right and power to guide
nations, to look after them and care for them. But he taught that this Being
whom it was their duty to worship was the highest and supreme God or,
(to use the Hebrew phrase), the God of Gods. Thus, in the canticle of
Exodus (ch. 15 v. 11) he said, "Who is like unto thee, O Lord, among the
Gods?" And Jethro says (ch. 18 v. 11), "Now I know that the Lord is
greater than all the Gods," as much as to say, "At last I am forced to admit
to Moses that Jehovah is greater than all the gods and his power is without
equal." There is some doubt as to whether Moses believed those beings
who acted in God's place were created by God; for he said nothing, as far
as we know, about their creation and origin.

He furthermore taught that this Being had reduced our visible world
from chaos to order (Gen. ch. 1 v. 2) and had given Nature its seeds. He
therefore possesses supreme right and power over things, and (Deut. ch.
10 v. 14, 15) in virtue of this supreme right and power he had chosen the
Hebrew nation for himself alone, together with a certain territory (Deut.
ch. 4 v. 19 and ch. 32 v. 8, 9), leaving other nations and lands to the care of
other Gods standing in his place. For this reason he was called the God of
Israel and the God of Jerusalem (2 Chron. ch. 32 v. 19), while other Gods
were called the Gods of other nations. For this same reason the Jews
believed that the land which God had chosen for himself demanded a
special form of worship, quite different from that of other lands; indeed, it
could not suffer the worship of other Gods, a worship belonging to other
lands. It was believed that those peoples whom the king of Assyria brought
into the land of the Jews were torn to pieces by lions because they knew
not the form of worship for the Deity of that land (2 Kings ch. 17 v. 25,
26). And according to ibn Ezra,[5] when Jacob resolved to seek his native

5. Abraham ibn Ezra (1092–1167) was one of the leading figures in the Spanish-

land, it was for this reason that he told his sons to prepare themselves for a new form of worship and to put away strange Gods, that is, the worship of the Gods of the land where they were then dwelling (Gen. ch. 35 v. 2, 3). And David, too, complaining to Saul that because of his persecution he was forced to live away from his native land, said that he was driven out of the heritage of the Lord and sent to worship other Gods (1 Sam. ch. 26 v. 19). And finally, Moses believed that this Being, or God, had his dwelling in the heavens (see Deut. ch. 33 v. 27), a belief wide-spread among the Gentiles.

If we now examine Moses' revelations, we shall find that they were adapted to these beliefs. Since he believed that it was in God's nature to experience those feelings that I have mentioned—mercy, graciousness and so on—God was revealed to him in conformity with this belief and under these attributes (see Exodus ch. 34 v. 6, 7, where we are told in what manner God appeared to Moses; also the Decalogue v. 4, 5). Again, it is related (Exodus ch. 33 v. 18) that Moses asked of God that he might behold him; but since Moses, as we have said, had formed no image of God in his brain, and (as I have already shown) God is revealed to the prophets only in accordance with the nature of their imagination, God did not appear to Moses in the form of an image. This came about, I repeat, because Moses' imagination was not receptive to such an image; for other prophets—Isaiah, Ezekiel, Daniel and the rest—testify that they saw God. For this reason God answered Moses, "Thou canst not see my face"; and since Moses believed that God was visible, that is, visibility was not in contradiction with the divine nature (for otherwise he would not have made such a request), God added, "For no one shall look on me and live." So God gives a reason in conformity with Moses' beliefs; God does not say that to see him is in contradiction with the divine nature—as in fact it is— but that it is impossible because of human inadequacy.

Again, in order to reveal to Moses that through worshipping the calf the Israelites had now become no different from other nations, God said (Exodus ch. 33 v. 2, 3), that he would send an angel, that is, a being, to take care of the Israelites in place of the Supreme Being, but that he himself would withdraw from them. In this way Moses was left with no grounds for supposing that the Israelites were more beloved of God than the rest of

Jewish "Golden Age." He was an outstanding biblical exegete, noted for his rigorous philological approach to the text. He was also a good astronomer and mathematician and wrote several philosophical treatises. Despite Spinoza's praise and use of ibn Ezra, he expresses a surprisingly negative evaluation of him in his own notes to the *TTP* (Supplementary Note 1).

the nations whom God had also entrusted to the care of other beings or angels, as is clear from verse 16, same chapter. Finally, since it was thought that God dwelt in the heavens, he was revealed as descending from heaven onto a mountain, and Moses even climbed the mountain to speak with God, which he certainly need not have done if he could just as well have imagined God as being everywhere.

The Israelites knew scarcely anything of God, although he was revealed to them. This they made abundantly clear when a few days later they transferred to a calf the honour and worship due to him, believing the calf to be the Deity who had led them out of Egypt. Indeed, it would be hardly likely that men addicted to Egyptian superstition, uncultured and sunk in degrading slavery, should have had any sound understanding of God, or that Moses could have taught them anything more than a moral code— not, indeed, as a philosopher might inculcate the morality that is engendered by freedom of spirit, but as a lawgiver, compelling people to live good lives by command of law. Therefore the right way of life, or true living, and the worship and love of God was for them bondage rather than true freedom, the grace and gift of God. For Moses commanded them to love God and keep his Law, to regard their past blessings—such as the escape from Egyptian bondage—as bestowed by God; and he further made terrifying threats if they should transgress these commandments, while promising many blessings if they observed them. So he taught them in the same way as parents teach children who have not reached the age of reason. It is therefore certain that they had no understanding of the excellence of virtue and true blessedness.

Jonah thought to flee from the sight of God, which goes to show that he, too, believed that God had entrusted the care of lands outside Judea to other powers, who were nevertheless installed by him. There is no one in the Old Testament who speaks more rationally of God than Solomon, who possessed the natural light of reason beyond all men of his time. And so he also considered himself above the Law (for that was given only for men not well endowed with reason and the instruction of the natural intellect) and paid little heed to all the laws regarding the king, consisting of three main articles (see Deut. ch. 17 v. 16, 17). Indeed, he plainly violated these laws (in which, however, he did wrong, and by indulgence in pleasures behaved in a way unworthy of a philosopher), and taught that all fortune's gifts to mankind are vanity (see Eccl.), that men possess nothing more excellent than understanding, and can suffer no greater punishment than their folly (see Proverbs ch. 16 v. 22).

But let us return to the prophets, whose different beliefs we have also undertaken to note. The Rabbis who have bequeathed to us the only extant books of the prophets regarding the sayings of Ezekiel as so irreconcilable with those of Moses (as is narrated in the Treatise of Sabbatus[6] ch. 1 fol. 13 p. 2) that they had some thoughts of rejecting his book from the canon, and would doubtless have put it aside if a certain Hananiah had not undertaken to explain it. This he is said to have accomplished with much labour and zeal (as is there narrated), though it is by no means clear how he did so, whether by writing a commentary which has perchance perished, or by having the audacity to alter Ezekiel's words and expressions, embellishing them as he pleased. However that may be, chapter 18 certainly seems to be at variance with Exodus ch. 34 v. 7, with Jeremiah ch. 32 v. 18, and other texts.

Samuel believed that God never repents of any decision he has made (see 1 Sam. ch. 15 v. 29); for when Saul repented of his sin and wished to worship God and seek forgiveness, Samuel said that God would not alter his decree against him. But to Jeremiah, on the other hand, it was revealed (see ch. 18 v. 8, 10) that, whether God has decreed good or whether he has decreed evil for any nation, he turns back the decree provided that men also change for the better or worse from the time of his sentence. Now Joel taught that God repents only of having decreed evil (see Joel ch. 2 v. 13). Finally, it is quite clear from Gen. ch. 4 v. 7 that men can overcome the temptations of sin and act righteously; for this is what was told to Cain— who nevertheless did not overcome those temptations, as is clear from Scripture and from Josephus.[7] This is obviously in agreement with the chapter of Jeremiah just quoted, for it is there said that God repents of his decree pronounced for the good or hurt of men in accordance with their willingness to change their ways and manner of life. But Paul, on the other hand, is quite clear that men have no dominion over the temptations of the flesh save by the special vocation and grace of God. See Epistle to the Romans chapter 9 from verse 10 on. As for his attributing righteousness to God (ch. 3 v. 5 and ch. 6 v. 19), he corrects himself for thus speaking in a merely human fashion and through the frailty of the flesh.

So now the point we set out to prove has been made abundantly clear, namely, that God adapted his revelations to the understanding and beliefs of the prophets, who may well have been ignorant of matters that have no bearing on charity and moral conduct but concern philosophic speculation, and were in fact ignorant of them, holding conflicting beliefs. There-

---

6. The Treatise of Sabbatus—a reference to the Tractate Shabbat of the Babylonian Talmud, mentioned again in chapter 10.

7. Josephus A.D. 37–100. Took part in the revolt of A.D. 66, but surrendered, came over to the Roman side, and took up residence at Rome. His main historical works are the *History of the Jewish War* and *Antiquities of the Jews*.

fore knowledge of science and of matters spiritual should by no means be expected of them. So we conclude that we must believe the prophets only with regard to the purpose and substance of the revelation; in all else one is free to believe as one will. For example, the revelation of Cain teaches us only that God admonished him to live the true life, for that alone is the object and substance of the revelation, which does not teach free will or philosophic doctrines.[8] Therefore, although the wording and the reasoning of admonition seem clearly to imply freedom of the will, we are entitled to hold a contrary opinion, since the wording and reasoning were adapted to Cain's understanding alone. Similarly, the meaning of the revelation to Micaiah is no more than this, that God revealed to Micaiah the true issue of the battle between Ahab and Aram, and so this alone we are bound to believe. Whatever else is contained in that revelation, concerning the true and false Spirit of God, the heavenly host standing on either side of God, and all the other details of that revelation—all this has no relevance for us, and everyone may believe of them as much as is in consonance with his reason.

With regard to the reasonings whereby God showed to Job his power over all things—if indeed it is true that this was revealed to Job and that the author's purpose was to compose a historical narrative and not, as some believe, to display his own ideas—the same point must be made, namely, that these arguments were accommodated to Job's understanding and propounded to convince him alone. They are not arguments of universal validity to convince all men. The same conclusions must be reached regarding the reasonings of Christ whereby he convicts the Pharisees' obstinacy and ignorance and exhorts his disciples to the true life; that is, he adapted his reasonings to the beliefs and principles of each individual. For example, when he said to the Pharisees (see Matth. ch. 12 v. 26), "And if Satan cast out Satan, he is divided against himself; how shall then his kingdom stand?," his only purpose was to refute the Pharisees according to their own principles, not to teach that there are devils, or any kingdom of devils. Similarly, when he said to his disciples (Matth. ch. 18 v. 10), "Take heed that ye despise not one of these little ones; for I say unto you that in heaven their angels. . . ." and so on, the point of his teaching is merely a warning against pride and contempt, and not those other details which he brings into his argument only for the better persuasion of his disciples.

Finally, the same point must be made to cover all the sayings and signs of the Apostles, and there is no need for me to deal with these matters at greater length. If I had to enumerate all the passages of Scripture com-

8. Spinoza, *Ethics*, 2.48–49; Letters 2 and 21.

posed 'ad hominem'—i.e. according to the individual's understanding—and which cannot be upheld as divine doctrine without great prejudice to philosophy, I should depart far from the brevity which is my aim. Let it suffice, then, to have touched on a few instances of general application, and let the zealous reader examine the rest for himself. However, although it is only those points we have made concerning prophets and prophecy that are especially relevant to my main purpose—namely, the differentiation of philosophy from theology—still, as I have touched on this question in a general way, we may well go on to enquire whether the gift of prophecy was peculiar to the Hebrews or whether it was shared by other nations; and then what conclusion should be reached regarding the vocation of the Hebrews. This will be the subject of our next chapter.

CHAPTER 3

Of the vocation of the Hebrews,
and whether the gift of prophecy was peculiar to them

Everyone's true happiness and blessedness consists solely in the enjoyment of good, not in priding himself that he alone is enjoying that good to the exclusion of others. He who counts himself more blessed because he alone enjoys wellbeing not shared by others, or because he is more blessed and fortunate than others, knows not what is true happiness and blessedness, and the joy he derives therefrom, if it be not mere childishness, has its only source in spite and malice. For example, a man's true happiness and blessedness consists solely in wisdom and knowledge of truth, and not in that he is wiser than others, or that others are without true knowledge. This adds nothing at all to his wisdom, that is, his true happiness. So he who rejoices for this reason rejoices at another's misfortune, and is therefore spiteful and malicious, knowing neither true wisdom nor the peace of the true life.[1]

So when Scripture, in exhorting the Hebrews to obey the Law, says that God has chosen them for himself above all other nations (Deut. ch. 10 v. 15), "that he is nigh unto them as he is not unto others" (Deut. ch. 4 v. 4, 7), that for them alone he has ordained just laws (same ch. v. 8), that he has made himself known only to them before all others (same ch. v. 32) and so forth, it is speaking merely according to the understanding of those who, as was shown in the previous chapter and as Moses also testifies (Deut. ch. 9 v. 6, 7), knew not true blessedness. For surely they would have been no less blessed if God had called all men equally to salvation, nor would God have been less close to them for being equally close to others, nor would their laws have been less just or they themselves less wise if those laws had been ordained for all men. Miracles would have displayed God's power no less if they had been wrought for other nations as well, and the Hebrews would have been no less in duty bound to worship God if God had bestowed all these gifts equally upon all men. When God tells Solomon (1 Kings ch. 3 v. 12) that no one shall be as wise as he in time to come, this seems to be just a figure of speech, intending to signify exceptional wisdom. Be that as it may, it is quite incredible that God should have promised Solomon, for his greater happiness, that he would never bestow such wisdom on anyone thereafter. This would in no way have increased Sol-

1. Spinoza, *Ethics*, 4.36–37, 5.42.

omon's understanding, nor would the wise king have been any the less grateful for such a gift even if God had said that he would bestow the same wisdom on all men.

However, although we assert that Moses was speaking to the understanding of the Hebrews in the passages of the Pentateuch just quoted, we do not mean to deny that God ordained those laws in the Pentateuch for them alone, nor that he spoke only to them, nor that the Hebrews witnessed marvels such have never befallen any other nation. Our point is merely this, that Moses wished to admonish the Hebrews in a particular way, using such reasoning as would bind them more firmly to the worship of God, having regard to the immaturity of their understanding. Further, we wished to show that the Hebrews surpassed other nations not in knowledge nor in piety, but in quite a different respect; or (to adopt the language of Scripture directed to their understanding) that the Hebrews were chosen by God above all others not for the true life nor for any higher understanding—though often admonished thereto—but for a quite different purpose. What that purpose was, I shall now proceed to demonstrate.

But before I begin, I wish to explain briefly what I shall hereafter mean by God's direction, by God's help, external and internal, by God's calling, and, finally, by fortune. By God's direction I mean the fixed and immutable order of Nature, or chain of natural events; for I have said above, and have already shown elsewhere, that the universal laws of Nature according to which all things happen and are determined are nothing but God's eternal decrees, which always involve eternal truth and necessity. So it is the same thing whether we say that all things happen according to Nature's laws or that they are regulated by God's decree and direction.[2] Again, since the power of Nature in its entirety is nothing other than the power of God through which alone all things happen and are determined, it follows that whatever man—who is also a part of Nature—acquires for himself to help to preserve his own being, or whatever Nature provides for him without any effort on his part, all this is provided for him solely by the divine power, acting either through human nature or externally to human nature. Therefore whatever human nature can effect solely by its own power to preserve its own being can rightly be called God's internal help, and whatever falls to a man's advantage from the power of external causes can rightly be called God's external help. And from this, too, can readily be deduced what must be meant by God's choosing, for since no one acts except by the predetermined order of Nature—that is, from God's eternal

2. Spinoza, *Ethics*, 1.16, 29, 33, especially Scholium 2.

direction and decree—it follows that no one chooses a way of life for himself or accomplishes anything except by the special vocation of God, who has chosen one man before others for a particular work or a particular way of life. Finally, by fortune I mean simply God's direction insofar as he directs human affairs through causes that are external and unforeseen.

With these preliminary remarks, let us return to our purpose, which is to see why it was that the Hebrew nation was said to have been chosen by God before all others. To demonstrate this, I proceed as follows.

All worthy objects of desire can be classified under one of these three general headings:

1. To know things through their primary causes.
2. To subjugate the passions; i.e. to acquire the habit of virtue.
3. To live in security and good health.

The means that directly serve for the attainment of the first and second objectives, and can be considered as the proximate and efficient causes, lie within the bounds of human nature itself, so that their acquisition chiefly depends on human power alone; i.e. solely on the laws of human nature. For this reason it is obvious that these gifts are not peculiar to any nation but have always been common to all mankind—unless we entertain the delusion that Nature at some time created different species of men. But the means that serve for the attainment of security and physical wellbeing lie principally in external circumstances, and are called the gifts of fortune because they mainly depend on the operation of external causes of which we are in ignorance. So in this matter the fool and the wise man have about an equal chance of happiness or unhappiness. Nevertheless, much can be effected by human contrivance and vigilance to achieve security and to avoid injuries from other men and from beasts. To this end, reason and experience have taught us no surer means than to organise a society under fixed laws, to occupy a fixed territory, and to concentrate the strength of all its members into one body, as it were, a social body.[3] However, a quite considerable degree of ability and vigilance is needed to organise and preserve a society, and therefore that society will be more secure, more stable and less exposed to fortune, which is founded and governed mainly by men of wisdom and vigilance, while a society composed of men who lack these qualities is largely dependent on fortune and is less stable. If the latter nevertheless endures for some considerable time, this is to be attributed to some other guidance, not its own. Indeed, if it overcomes great perils and enjoys prosperity, it cannot fail to marvel at and worship God's guidance (that is to say, insofar as God acts through hidden external

3. Spinoza, *Ethics*, 4.37, especially Scholium 2.

causes, and not through the nature and mind of man); for what it has experienced is far beyond its expectation and belief, and can truly be regarded even as a miracle.

Through this alone, then, do nations differ from one another, namely, in respect of the kind of society and laws under which they live and are governed. Thus the Hebrew nation was chosen by God before all others not by reason of its understanding nor of its spiritual qualities, but by reason of its social organisation and the good fortune whereby it achieved supremacy and retained it for so many years. This is quite evident from Scripture itself. A merely casual perusal clearly reveals that the Hebrews surpassed other nations in this alone, that they were successful in achieving security for themselves and overcame great dangers, and this chiefly by God's external help alone. In other respects they were no different from other nations, and God was equally gracious to all. For in respect of their understanding (as we have shown in the preceding chapter) it is clear that the Hebrews' ideas of God and Nature were quite commonplace, and so it was not in respect of their understanding that they were chosen by God before others. Nor yet in respect of virtue and the true life, for in this matter again they were on the same footing as other nations, very few of them being chosen. Therefore their election and vocation consisted only in the material success and prosperity of their state; nor do we see that God promised anything other than this to the Patriarchs* or their successors. Indeed, in return for their obedience the Law promises them nothing other than the continuing prosperity of their state and material advantages, whereas disobedience and the breaking of the Covenant would bring about the downfall of their state and the severest hardships. This is not surprising, for the purpose of an organised society and state (as is clear from what has just been said, and as I shall show at greater length hereafter) is to achieve security and ease. Now a state can subsist only if the laws are binding on all individuals. If all the members of one society choose to disregard the laws, by that very fact they will dissolve that society and destroy the state. Therefore, in return for their consistent observance of the laws, the only promise that could be made to the society of the Hebrews was their security** with its attendant advantages; whereas for disobedience no surer punishment could be foretold than the downfall of their state, accompanied not only by the usual unhappy consequences but by additional troubles, peculiar to them, entailed by the special constitution of their state. This latter point I need not labour at present, but this I will add, that the laws contained in the Old Testament were revealed and

* See Supplementary Note 4.
** See Supplementary Note 5.

ordained for the Jews alone; for as God chose them only for the establishing of a special kind of society and state, they must also have had laws of a special kind. As to whether God ordained special laws for other nations as well and revealed himself through prophecy for their lawgivers—that is, under those attributes by which they were accustomed to imagine God—I cannot be sure. But this at least is evident from Scripture, that other nations also had their own state and their special laws by God's external guidance. To prove this I shall cite two Scriptural passages only.

In Genesis ch. 14 v. 18, 19, 20 it is related that Melchizedek was king of Jerusalem and priest of the Most High God, and in his capacity of priest (Num. ch. 6 v. 23) he blessed Abraham, and Abraham, the beloved of God, gave a tenth part of all his spoils to this priest of God. All this shows well enough that before God founded the nation of Israel he had established kings and priests in Jerusalem and had appointed rites and laws for them. Whether he did so through prophecy is, as I have said, unclear. But of this, at least, I am sure, that while Abraham lived there he lived religiously according to those laws. For Abraham had not received from God any special rites, and yet it states in Gen. ch. 26 v. 5 that he observed the worship, precepts, statutes and laws of God. This must undoubtedly refer to the worship, precepts, statutes and laws of king Melchizedek. Malachi, in ch. 1 v. 10, 11 rebukes the Jews with these words: "Who is there among you that would shut the doors (of the temple) lest fire be kindled on mine altars for nought? I have no pleasure in you . . . etc. From the rising of the sun even unto the going down of the same my name is great among the nations, and everywhere incense is offered unto me, and a pure offering. For my name is great among nations, saith the Lord of hosts." Surely by these words, which can be interpreted as referring only to his present time unless we do violence to the text, he abundantly testifies that the Jews at that time were no more beloved of God than were other nations. Indeed, he indicates that by his miracles God made himself known to other nations more so than to the Jews of that time—who had then partly regained their independence without miraculous intervention—and that the Gentiles possessed rites and ceremonies by which they were acceptable to God.

But I leave these considerations, for it is sufficient for my purpose to have demonstrated that the choosing of the Jews referred only to the following facts: their temporal material prosperity and freedom—i.e. their political independence—and to the manner and means whereby they achieved it, and consequently to their laws as well, insofar as these were necessary for the preservation of their special kind of state, and, finally, to the way in which these laws were revealed. But in other matters, wherein consists the true happiness of man, they were on the same footing as other nations. So when Scripture says (Deut. ch. 4 v. 7) that no other nation has

its Gods so nigh unto them as the Jews have their God, this must be
understood in respect of independence of their state, and as referring only
to the time when so many miracles befell them, and so forth. For in respect
of understanding and virtue, that is, in respect of blessedness, God is
equally gracious to all, as we have already stated and proved by reason.
This is also well established from Scripture, for the Psalmist says (Psalm
145 v. 18), "The Lord is nigh to all them that call upon him, to all that call
upon him in truth." Likewise in the same Psalm, v. 9, "The Lord is good
to all, and his tender mercies are over all his works." In Psalm 33 v. 15 it is
clearly stated that God has given the same understanding to all, in these
words, "He fashioneth our hearts alike." The Hebrews considered the
heart to be the seat of the soul and the understanding, as I think everybody
knows. Again, from Job ch. 28 v. 28 it is clear that God ordained this law
for the whole human race: to revere God and to abstain from evildoing, i.e.
to act righteously; and so Job, although a Gentile, was to God the most
acceptable of all men, for he surpassed all men in piety and religion.
Finally, it is quite evident from Jonah ch. 4 v. 2 that not only to the Jews
but to all mankind God is gracious, merciful, long-suffering and abundant
in kindness, and loath to punish. For Jonah says, "Therefore I resolved to
flee before to Tarshish, for I knew (namely, from the words of Moses,
Exodus ch. 34 v. 6) that Thou art a gracious God, merciful . . . etc." and
therefore likely to pardon the Ninevites.[4]

  We therefore conclude (since God is equally gracious to all and the
Hebrews were chosen only with respect to their social organisation and
their government) that the individual Jew, considered alone apart from his
social organisation and his government, possesses no gift of God above
other men, and there is no difference between him and a Gentile. Since,
then, it is true that God is equally gracious, merciful etc. to all men, and
since the function of the prophet was to teach not the special laws of his
country but true virtue, and to admonish men thereto, there is no doubt
that all nations possessed prophets and that the gift of prophecy was not
peculiar to the Jews. In actual fact, this is borne out by history, both
secular and sacred; and although the sacred history of the Old Testament
does not specify that other nations had as many prophets as the Hebrews,
or indeed that any Gentile prophet was expressly sent by God to the
nations, this has no significance; for the Hebrews were concerned to
record their own history, not that of other nations. It is therefore sufficient
that in the Old Testament we find that Gentiles and the uncircumcised,
such as Noah, Enoch, Abimelech, Balaam etc., did in fact prophesy, and

---

4. Here, in contrast to his earlier remarks, Spinoza highlights the universal message and content of biblical Judaism.

furthermore that Hebrew prophets were sent by God not only to their own nation but to many others. Ezekiel prophesied for all nations that were then known. Indeed, as far as we know, Obadiah prophesied only to the Idumaeans, and Jonah was chiefly a prophet to the Ninevites. Isaiah bewails and foretells the calamities, and prophesies the restoration, not only of the Jews but of other nations. In chapter 16 v. 9 he says, "Therefore will I bewail Jazer with weeping," and in chapter 19 he foretells first the calamities of the Egyptians and then their restoration (see same chapter v. 19, 20, 21, 25), saying that God will send a saviour to free them, that God will make himself known to them, and that the Egyptians will worship God with sacrifices and gifts; and finally he calls that nation the blessed Egyptians, the people of God. All this is certainly worthy of special note. Lastly, Jeremiah is called the prophet not only of the Hebrew nation but of all nations absolutely (Jer. ch. 1 v. 5). He, too, bemoans the coming calamities of nations and foretells their restoration, for in chapter 48 v. 31 he says of the Moabites, "Therefore will I howl for Moab, I will cry out for all Moab," and in verse 36, "Therefore mine heart will sound for Moab like timbrels"; and he prophesies their eventual restoration, as also the restoration of the Egyptians, the Ammonites and the Elamites.

Therefore there is no doubt that other nations, like the Jews, also had their prophets, who prophesied to them and to the Jews. Although Scripture makes mention of only one man, Balaam, to whom was revealed the future of the Jews and of other nations, we should not suppose that Balaam's prophesying was confined to that one occasion; the narrative makes it quite clear that he had long been renowned for his prophecy and other divine gifts. Balak, ordering him to be summoned, said (Num. ch. 22 v. 6), "For I know that he whom thou blessest is blessed, and he whom thou cursest is cursed." So we see that he possessed the same power that God bestowed on Abraham (Gen. ch. 12 v. 3). Then Balaam, as was his custom in prophesying, told the messengers to await him until God's will should be revealed to him. When he was prophesying, that is, when he was interpreting the true mind of God, he was wont to say of himself, "The word of him who hears the words of God, who knows the knowledge (or mind, or foreknowledge) of the Most High, who sees the vision of the Almighty, falling into a trance, but having his eyes open." Finally, after blessing the Hebrews by God's command, he began, as was his custom, to prophesy to other nations and to foretell their future.[5]

All this abundantly shows that he had always been a prophet, or that he

---

5. The issue of Balaam, especially the question of his prophetic status, was debated in rabbinic literature. Maimonides believed that Balaam was a legitimate prophet (*Guide,* 2.42, 45).

had frequently prophesied, and (another point to be here noted) that he possessed that which especially afforded prophets certainty of truth of their prophecy, namely, a mind bent only on that which is good and right. For he neither blessed nor cursed whomsoever he pleased, as Balak thought, but only those whom God willed to be blessed or cursed. That is why he answered Balak, "If Balak should give me his house full of silver and gold, I cannot go beyond the commandment of the Lord to do good or ill as I will. What the Lord saith, that shall I speak." As for the Lord being angry with him while he was on the way, the same thing befell Moses when he was setting out for Egypt at God's command (Exodus ch. 4 v. 24); as to his receiving money for prophesying, Samuel did the same (1 Sam. ch. 9 v. 7, 8); and if he sinned in any way (see 2 Ep. Peter ch. 2 v. 15, 16 and Jude v. 11), "there is not a just man on earth who always doeth good and sinneth not" (Eccl. ch. 7 v. 20). Indeed, his prayers must have always had much influence with God and his power of cursing must have been very considerable, since it is often found in Scripture, as testimony of God's great mercy towards the Israelites, that God would not hearken to Balaam and changed his cursing to blessing (Deut. ch. 23 v. 6, Josh. ch. 24 v. 10, Nehem. ch. 13 v. 2). He must therefore have been most acceptable to God, for the prayers and cursings of the wicked move God not at all. So since he was a true prophet, and yet Joshua (ch. 13 v. 22) referred to him as a soothsayer or augur, it is clear that this title, too, was an honourable one, and that those whom the Gentiles called augurs and soothsayers were true prophets, while those whom Scripture often accuses and condemns were false soothsayers, deceiving the Gentiles as false prophets deceived the Jews. And this is also quite clearly established from other passages of Scripture. Therefore we conclude that the gift of prophecy was not peculiar to the Jews, but was common to all nations.

The Pharisees,[6] however, vigorously contend that this divine gift was peculiar to their nation, whereas other nations (such is the ingenuity of superstition!) foretold the future with the aid of some diabolical power. The chief evidence they adduce to give authoritative support to this belief is Exodus ch. 33 v. 16, where Moses says to God, "For wherein shall it be known here that I and thy people have found grace in thy sight? Is it not

6. Spinoza's use of the term 'Pharisee' here is contentious and prejudicial. Although in chapter 18 Spinoza correctly applies this term to a particular sect, or party, within the Judaism of the Roman period, here he uses it as a general term for all Jews who follow the Oral Law, codified in the Mishnah and commented upon in the Talmud. To Christians this word connoted a variety of negative attitudes deriving from the New Testament, especially the Gospel of Matthew (see especially chapter 23).

when thou goest with us? So shall we be separated, I and thy people, from all the people that are on the face of the earth." From this, I repeat, they would infer that Moses besought God that he should be present to the Jews and reveal himself to them by prophecy, and, further, that he should grant this grace to no other nation. Surely, it is absurd that Moses should grudge God's presence to the Gentiles, or that he should have ventured to make such a petition to God. The fact is that when Moses realised the character and the obstinate spirit of his nation, he saw clearly that they could not accomplish their undertaking without mighty miracles and the special external help of God, and must assuredly perish without such help; and so he besought this special external help of God so that it should be evident that God willed them to be saved. For he speaks as follows (ch. 34 v. 9), "If now I have found favour in thy sight, O Lord, let my Lord, I pray thee, go among us, for it is a stiff-necked people . . ." and so on. Thus the reason why he sought God's special external help was the obstinacy of the people, and the fact that Moses sought nothing beyond this special external help is made even clearer by God's answer. For God answered at once (same chapter v. 10), "Behold, I make a covenant; before all thy people I will do marvels such as have not been done in all the earth, nor in any nation. . . ." Therefore Moses is here concerned with the choosing of the Hebrews only in the way I have explained, and sought nothing else from God.

However, in Paul's Epistle to the Romans I find another text which carries more weight with me, namely, chapter 3 v. 1, 2, where Paul's teaching appears to differ from that which we have here presented. He says, "What advantage, then, hath the Jew? Or what profit is there of circumcision? Much every way: chiefly because unto them were committed the oracles of God." But if we have regard to the main doctrine that Paul is concerned to teach, we shall find nothing at variance with the view we are here presenting; on the contrary, his doctrine is the same as ours. For in verse 29 of the same chapter he says that God is the God of both Jews and Gentiles, and in chapter 2 v. 25, 26, "If thou be a breaker of the law, thy circumcision is made uncircumcision; on the other hand, if uncircumcision keep the righteousness of the law, his uncircumcision shall be counted for circumcision." Again, in chapter 3 v. 9 and chapter 4 v. 15 he says that all alike, Jews and Gentiles, were under sin, but that there can be no sin without the commandment and the Law. This makes it quite clear (as we have also shown above from Job ch. 28 v. 28) that to all men without exception was revealed the law under which all men lived—namely, the law which has regard only to the true virtue, not that law which is established to suit the requirements of a particular state and is adapted to the character of one nation.

Finally, Paul concludes that, since God is the God of all nations—that is, he is equally gracious to all—and since all mankind were equally under the law and under sin, it was for all nations that God sent his Christ to free all men alike from the bondage of the law, so that no longer would they act righteously from the law's command but from the unwavering resolution of the heart. Thus Paul's teaching coincides exactly with ours. So when he says, "To the Jews alone were entrusted the oracles of God," we should either take it as meaning that only to the Jews were the laws entrusted in writing while to other nations they were communicated by revelation and conception alone, or we must say (since Paul's aim is to refute objections that could be raised only by the Jews) that Paul is answering in accordance with the understanding and beliefs of the Jews of that time. For in order to preach that which he had partly seen and partly heard, he was a Greek with the Greeks and a Jew with the Jews.

It now only remains for us to answer the arguments of those who would convince themselves that the election of the Jews was not a temporal matter, concerned only with their commonwealth, but was eternal; for, they say, we see that the Jews still survive in spite of having lost their commonwealth and being scattered all over the world for so many years, separated from all nations; and that this has befallen no other nation. And again, they say, there are many passages of Holy Scripture that appear to tell us that God has chosen the Jews for himself unto eternity; and so, although they have lost their commonwealth, they nevertheless remain God's chosen ones. The passages which they think most convincing in teaching this eternal election are chiefly the following:

1. Jeremiah chapter 31 v. 36, where the prophet testifies that the seed of Israel shall remain God's people unto eternity, comparing them with the fixed order of the heavens and of Nature.

2. Ezekiel chapter 20 v. 32 and following, where the prophet apparently means that, although the Jews may deliberately turn away from the worship of God, God will nevertheless gather them together again from all the lands where they are scattered and lead them to the wilderness of peoples, as he led their fathers to the wilderness of Egypt; and from there eventually, after separating them from the rebellious and the transgressors, he will bring them to his Holy Mountain, where the whole house of Israel shall worship him.

Other passages are also cited, especially by the Pharisees, but I think I shall satisfy everybody if I reply to these two. This will occasion me no difficulty when I show from Scripture itself that God did not choose the Hebrews unto eternity, but only on the same terms as he had earlier chosen the Canaanites. These also had priests (as I have shown above) who devoutly worshipped God, and yet God rejected them because of their dissolute living, their folly, and their corrupt worship. For Moses (Lev. ch. 18 v. 27, 28) warns the Israelites not to defile themselves with abominations like the Canaanites, lest the land spew them out as it had spewed out those peoples that used to dwell there. And in Deuteronomy ch. 8 v. 19, 20 he threatens them with utter destruction in the plainest possible terms, speaking as follows, "I testify against you this day that ye shall surely perish; as the nations which the Lord destroyed before your face, so shall ye perish." And many other passages to this effect are to be found in the Law, expressly indicating that God did not choose the Hebrew nation absolutely, nor unto eternity. So if the prophets foretold for them a new, eternal covenant involving the knowledge, love and grace of God, it can be easily proved that this promise was made for the godly alone. For in that same chapter of Ezekiel which we have just quoted it is explicitly stated that God will cut off from them the rebellious and the transgressors; and in Zephaniah chapter 3 v. 11, 12 that God will take from their midst the proud, leaving behind the poor. And since this election has regard to true virtue, it is not to be imagined that it was promised only to the godly among the Jews to the exclusion of all others. We must evidently believe that the true Gentile prophets, whom we have shown to be found among all nations, made the same promise to the faithful of their own nations and comforted them thereby. Therefore this eternal covenant involving the knowledge and love of God is universal, as is clearly shown from Zephaniah chapter 3 v. 10, 11, so that in this respect no difference can be granted between Jews and Gentiles, nor therefore any special election of the Jews beyond that which we have already indicated.

As to the fact that the prophets, in speaking of this election which refers only to true virtue, intermingled many sayings regarding sacrifices and other ceremonies and the rebuilding of the Temple and the city, such figurative expressions, after the manner and nature of prophecy, were intended to convey a spiritual message, so that they might also indicate to the Jews, whose prophets they were, the impending restoration of their commonwealth and temple, to be expected at the time of Cyrus. Therefore at the present time there is nothing whatsoever that the Jews can arrogate to themselves above other nations.

As to their continued existence for so many years when scattered and stateless, this is in no way surprising, since they have separated themselves from other nations to such a degree as to incur the hatred of all, and this not only through external rites alien to the rites of other nations but also through the mark of circumcision, which they most religiously observe. That they are preserved largely through the hatred of other nations is demonstrated by historical fact. When the King of Spain formerly compelled the Jews to embrace the religion of his kingdom or else to go into exile, a considerable number of Jews accepted Catholicism. Now since all the privileges of native Spaniards were granted to those who embraced their religion, and they were then considered worthy of full civic rights, they were so speedily assimilated to the Spaniards that after a short while no trace of them was left, nor any remembrance. But just the opposite fate befell those whom the King of Portugal compelled to embrace his country's religion. Although converted to this religion, they lived on their own, because the king declared them unworthy of civic rights.[7]

The mark of circumcision, too, I consider to be such an important factor in this matter that I am convinced that this by itself will preserve their nation forever. Indeed, were it not that the fundamental principles of their religion discourage manliness, I would not hesitate to believe that they will one day, given the opportunity—such is the mutability of human affairs—establish once more their independent state, and that God will again choose them.[8] The Chinese afford us an outstanding example of such a possibility. They, too, religiously observe the custom of the pigtail which sets them apart from all other people, and they have preserved themselves as a separate people for so many thousands of years that they far surpass all other nations in antiquity. They have not always maintained their independence, but they did regain it after losing it, and will no doubt recover it again when the spirit of the Tartars becomes enfeebled by reason of luxurious living and sloth.

In conclusion, should anyone be disposed to argue that the Jews, for this reason or any other, have been chosen by God unto eternity, I shall not oppose him, provided that he holds that this election, be it temporal or eternal, insofar as it is peculiar to the Jews, is concerned only with the

---

7. Spinoza tries to make a distinction between the Inquisition in Spain and the one in Portugal. But he overestimates the openness of Spanish society and government to converted Jews. Not too long after the establishment of the Inquisition in Spain, "laws of blood purity" were passed to prevent converted Jews from obtaining important positions in Spanish government and in the church. Many Spanish Jewish converts attempted to preserve secretly some aspects of Jewish belief and practice while they led Christian lives in public (D. Gitlitz, *Secrecy and Deceit: The Religion of the Crypto-Jews.* Philadelphia: The Jewish Publication Society, 1996; B. Netanyahu, *The Origins of the Inquisition in 15th Century Spain.* New York: Random House, 1995).

8. This passage has had an interesting "history." Some of the early Zionist theoreticians and leaders (e.g., David ben Gurion) saw in this passage hints of the revival of an independent Jewish state grounded in a secular ideology. It is highly unlikely, however, that Spinoza himself had any such thoughts. (See Steven Smith's recent study *Spinoza, Liberalism and the Question of Jewish Identity.* New Haven: Yale University Press, 1997).

nature of their commonwealth and their material welfare (since this is the only distinguishing mark between one nation and another); whereas in respect of understanding and true virtue there is no distinction between one nation and another, and in regard to these matters God has not chosen one nation before another.

CHAPTER 4

Of the Divine Law

The word law, taken in its absolute sense, means that according to which each individual thing—either all in general or those of the same kind—act in one and the same fixed and determinate manner, this manner depending either on Nature's necessity or on human will. A law which depends on Nature's necessity is one which necessarily follows from the very nature of the thing, that is, its definition; a law which depends on human will, and which could more properly be termed a statute [*ius*], is one which men ordain for themselves and for others with view to making life more secure and more convenient, or for other reasons.

For example, the fact that all bodies colliding with smaller bodies lose as much of their own motion as they impart to other bodies is a universal law governing all bodies, and follows from Nature's necessity. Similarly, the fact that a man, in remembering one thing, forthwith calls to mind another like it, or which he has seen along with it, is a law that necessarily follows from the nature of man. But the fact that men give up, or are compelled to give up, their natural right and bind themselves to live under fixed rules, depends on human will. And although I grant that, in an absolute sense, all things are determined by the universal laws of Nature to exist and to act in a definite and determinate way,[1] I still say that these latter laws depend on human will. My reasons are as follows:

1. Man, insofar as he is part of Nature, constitutes a part of the power of Nature. Thus whatever follows from the necessity of man's nature—that is, from Nature as we conceive her to be determinately expressed in man's nature—follows from human power, even though it does so necessarily. Therefore the enacting of these man-made laws may quite legitimately be said to depend on human will, for it depends especially on the power of the human mind in the following respect, that the human mind, insofar as it is concerned with the perception of truth and falsity, can be quite clearly conceived without these man-made laws, whereas it cannot be conceived without Nature's necessary law, as defined above.

2. We ought to define and explain things through their proximate causes. Generalisations about fate and the interconnection of causes can be of no service to us in forming and ordering our thoughts concerning particular things. Furthermore, we plainly have no knowledge as to the

1. Spinoza, *Ethics*, 1.29, 33.

actual co-ordination and interconnection of things—that is, the way in which things are in actual fact ordered and connected—so that for practical purposes it is better, indeed, it is essential, to consider things as contingent. So much for law taken in the absolute sense.

Still, it seems to be by analogy that the word law is applied to natural phenomena, and ordinarily 'law' is used to mean simply a command which men can either obey or disobey, inasmuch as it restricts the total range of human power within set limits and demands nothing that is beyond the capacity of that power. So it seems more fitting that law should be defined in its narrower sense, that is, as a rule of life which man prescribes for himself or for others for some purpose. However, since the true purpose of law is usually apparent only to the few and is generally incomprehensible by the great majority in whose lives reason plays little part, in order to constrain all men alike legislators have wisely devised another motive for obedience, far different from that which is necessarily entailed by the nature of law. For those who uphold the law they promised what most appeals to the masses, while threatening transgressors with dire retribution, thus endeavouring to keep the multitude on a curb, as far as is practicable. Thus it came about that law was mainly regarded as rules of conduct imposed on men through the supremacy of others, and consequently those who obey the law are said to live under the law and appear to be in bondage. And in truth he who renders to each his own through fear of the gallows is constrained in his action by another's command and threat of punishment, and cannot be called a just man. But he who renders to each his own through awareness of the true principle of law and its necessity, is acting steadfastly and at his own will, not another's, and so he is rightly termed a just man. This I take to be Paul's intended meaning when he said that those who lived under the law could not be justified through the law; for justice, as commonly defined, is the steadfast and constant will to render to each his own. It is for this reason, too, that Solomon said in Proverbs ch. 21 v. 15, "It is a joy to the just when judgment is done; but the workers of iniquity are in fear."

So since law is simply a rule of conduct which men lay down for themselves or for others to some end, it can be divided into human and divine law. By human law I mean a prescribed rule of conduct whose sole aim is to safeguard life and the commonwealth; by divine law I mean that which is concerned only with the supreme good, that is, the true knowledge and love of God. This law I call divine because of the nature of the supreme good, which I shall now briefly explain as clearly as I can.

Since our intellect forms the better part of us, it is evident that, if we wish to seek what is definitely to our advantage, we should endeavour above all to perfect it as far as we can, for in its perfection must consist our supreme good. Now since all our knowledge, and the certainty that banishes every possible doubt, depend solely on the knowledge of God—because, firstly, without God nothing can be or be conceived, and secondly, everything can be called into doubt as long as we have no clear and distinct idea of God[2]—it follows that our supreme good and perfection depends solely on the knowledge of God. Again, since nothing can be or be conceived without God, it is clear that everything in Nature involves and expresses the conception of God in proportion to its essence and perfection; and therefore we acquire a greater and more perfect knowledge of God as we gain more knowledge of natural phenomena. To put it another way, since the knowledge of an effect through its cause is nothing other than the knowledge of a property of that cause, the greater our knowledge of natural phenomena, the more perfect is our knowledge of God's essence, which is the cause of all things. So the whole of our knowledge, that is, our supreme good, not merely depends on the knowledge of God but consists entirely therein. This also follows from the principle that man's perfection is the greater, or the reverse, according to the nature and perfection of the thing that he loves above all others. So he who loves above all the intellectual cognition of God, the most perfect Being, and takes especial delight therein, is necessarily most perfect, and partakes most in the highest blessedness.

This, then, is the sum of our supreme good and blessedness,[3] to wit, the knowledge and love of God. So the means required to achieve this end of all human action—that is, God insofar as his idea exists in us—may be termed God's commands, for they are ordained for us by God himself, as it were, insofar as he exists in our minds. So the rules for living a life that has regard to this end can fitly be called the Divine Law. An enquiry as to what these means are, and what are the rules of conduct required for this end, and how there follow therefrom the fundamental principles of the good commonwealth and social organisation, belongs to a general treatise on Ethics. Here my discussion will be confined to a general consideration of the Divine Law.

Since the love of God is man's highest happiness and blessedness, and the final end and aim of all human action, it follows that only he observes the Divine Law who makes it his object to love God not through fear of punishment nor through love of some other thing such as sensual pleasure, fame and so forth, but from the mere fact that he knows God, or knows that the knowledge and love of God is the supreme good. So the sum of the Divine Law and its chief command is to love God as the supreme

2. Spinoza, *Ethics*, 1.15; *TIE*, 39, 49, 79.
3. *Ethics*, 5.24–27, 30–33.

good; that is, as we have said, not from fear of some punishment or penalty nor from love of some other thing from which we desire to derive pleasure. For this truth is told us by the idea of God, that God is our supreme good, i.e. that the knowledge and love of God is the final end to which all our actions should be directed. But carnal man cannot understand these things; he thinks them foolish because he has too stunted a knowledge of God, and in this supreme good, it does only in philosophic thinking and pure activity of mind, he finds nothing to touch, to eat, or to feed the fleshly appetites which are his chief delight. But those who recognise that they have no more precious gift than intellect and a sound mind are sure to regard these as very substantial blessings.

We have now explained the essential nature of the Divine Law, and have defined human laws as all those which have a different aim. But from the latter category we must except laws that have been sanctioned by revelation, for in this case, too, things are referred to God, as we have already shown. And in this sense the Law of Moses, although it was not of universal application but specially adapted to the character and preservation of one particular people, can nevertheless be termed the Law of God, or Divine Law, since we believe it to have been sanctioned by prophetic insight.

If we now consider the nature of the natural Divine Law as we have just explained it, we shall see:

1. That it is of universal application, or common to all mankind. For we have deduced it from human nature as such.

2. That it does not demand belief in historical narratives of any kind whatsoever. For since it is merely a consideration of human nature that leads us to this natural Divine Law, evidently it applies equally to Adam as to any other man, and equally to a man living in a community as to a hermit. Nor can the belief in historical narratives, however certain, give us knowledge of God, nor, consequently, of the love of God. For the love of God arises from the knowledge of God, a knowledge deriving from general axioms that are certain and self-evident, and so belief in historical narratives is by no means essential to the attainment of our supreme good. However, although belief in historical narratives cannot afford us the knowledge and love of God, I do not deny that their study can be very profitable in the matter of social relations. For the more we observe and the better we are acquainted with the ways and manners of men—and it is their actions that best provide this knowledge—the more prudently we can live among them, and the more effectively we can adapt our actions and conduct to their character, as far as reason allows.

3. We see that the natural Divine Law does not enjoin ceremonial rites, that is, actions which in themselves are of no significance and are termed

good merely by tradition, or which symbolise some good necessary for salvation, or, if you prefer, actions whose explanation surpasses human understanding. For the natural light of reason enjoins nothing that is not within the compass of reason, but only what it can show us quite clearly to be a good, or a means to our blessedness. The things whose goodness derives only from authority and tradition, or from their symbolic representation of some good, cannot perfect our intellect; they are mere shadows, and cannot be counted as actions that are, as it were, the offspring and fruit of intellect and sound mind. There is no need for me to go further into this matter.

4. Finally, we see that the supreme reward of the Divine Law is the law itself, namely, to know God and to love him in true freedom with all our heart and mind. The penalty it imposes is the deprivation of these things and bondage to the flesh, that is, an inconstant and irresolute spirit.

Having made these points, we must now enquire:

1. Whether by the natural light of reason we can conceive God as a lawgiver or ruler, ordaining laws for men.

2. What is the teaching of Holy Scripture concerning this natural light and law.

3. For what purpose were ceremonial rites originally instituted.

4. What good is served by knowing the sacred historical narratives, and by believing them.

The first two questions I shall discuss in this chapter, reserving the last two for the next chapter.

Our conclusion as to the first question is easily deduced from the nature of God's will, which is not distinct from his intellect except from the perspective of human reason. That is to say, God's will and God's intellect[4] in themselves are in reality one and the same thing; they are distinct only in relation to the thoughts we form when we think of God's intellect. For example, when we have regard only to the fact that the nature of a triangle is eternally contained in the divine nature as an eternal truth, then we say that God has the idea of a triangle, or that he understands the nature of a triangle. But when thereafter we consider the fact that it is solely from the necessity of the divine nature, and not from the necessity of the essence and nature of a triangle, that the nature of a triangle is thus contained in the divine nature—or rather, the necessity of the essence and properties of a triangle, insofar as they are also conceived as eternal truths, depends not on the nature of a triangle but solely on the necessity of the divine nature and intellect—then that which we termed God's intellect we call God's will or decree. Therefore in respect of God our affirmation is

4. *Ethics*, 1.32.

one and the same, whether we say that God has eternally willed and decreed that the three angles of a triangle should be equal to two right angles, or that God has understood this fact.

Hence it follows that God's affirmations and negations always involve eternal necessity or truth. So if, for example, God said to Adam that he willed that Adam should not eat of the tree of knowledge of good and evil, it would have been a contradiction in terms for Adam to be able to eat of that tree. And so it would have been impossible for Adam to eat of it, because that divine decree must have involved eternal necessity and truth. However, since Scripture tells us that God did so command Adam, and that Adam did nevertheless eat of the tree, it must be accepted that God revealed to Adam only the punishment he must incur if he should eat of that tree; the necessary entailment of that punishment was not revealed. Consequently, Adam perceived this revelation not as an eternal and necessary truth but as a law, that is to say, an enactment from which good or ill consequence would ensue not from the intrinsic nature of deed performed but only from the will and absolute power of some ruler. Therefore that revelation, solely in relation to Adam and solely because of the limitations of his knowledge, was a law, and God was a kind of lawgiver or ruler. For this same reason, namely, their lack of knowledge, in relation to the Hebrews alone the Decalogue was a law; for, not knowing God's existence as an eternal truth, it was inevitable that they should have perceived as a law what was revealed to them in the Decalogue, namely, that God existed, and that God alone must be worshipped. But if God had spoken to them directly, employing no physical means, they would have perceived this not as a law, but as an eternal truth.

What we are here saying about the Israelites and Adam also applies to all the prophets who laid down laws in God's name; they did not perceive God's decrees adequately, as eternal truths. For example, in the case of Moses, too, we have to say that, as a result of revelation or basic principles revealed to him, he perceived a way by which the people of Israel could well be united in a particular territory to form a political union or state, and also a way by which that people could well be constrained to obedience. But he did not perceive, nor was it revealed to him, that this way was the best of all ways, nor that the end for which they were striving would be a consequence necessarily entailed by the general obedience of the people in such a territory. Therefore he perceived all these things not as eternal truths, but as instructions and precepts, and he ordained them as laws of God. Hence it came about that he imagined God as a ruler, lawgiver, king, merciful, just and so forth; whereas these are all merely attributes of human nature, and not at all applicable to the divine nature.

Now what I have said applies only to the prophets who laid down laws in

God's name, but not to Christ. With regard to Christ, although he also appears to have laid down laws in God's name, we must maintain that he perceived things truly and adequately; for Christ was not so much a prophet as the mouthpiece of God. It was through the mind of Christ (as we showed in chapter 1) that God made revelations to mankind just as he once did through angels, i.e. through a created voice, visions etc. Therefore to maintain that God adapted his revelation to Christ's beliefs would be equally irrational as to maintain that God formerly adapted his revelations to the beliefs of angels in communication, that is, to the beliefs of a created voice and visions, so as to communicate to the prophets what was to be revealed. This would be the height of absurdity, especially so since Christ was sent to teach not only the Jews but the entire human race. Thus it was not enough for him to have a mind adapted to the beliefs of the Jews alone; his mind had to be adapted to the beliefs and doctrines held in common by all mankind, that is, to those axioms that are universally true. And surely this fact, that God revealed himself to Christ, or to Christ's mind, directly, and not through words and images as in the case of the prophets, can have only this meaning, that Christ perceived truly, or understood, what was revealed. For it is when a thing is perceived by pure thought, without words or images, that it is understood.[5]

Christ, then, perceived truly and adequately the things revealed to him; so if ever he proclaimed these things as law, he did so because of the people's ignorance and obstinacy. Therefore in this matter he acted in God's place, adapting himself to the character of the people. So although his sayings were somewhat clearer than those of other prophets, his teach-

---

5. *Ethics,* 2.40, Scholium 2. Spinoza's remarks here on Jesus are somewhat curious. In chapter 1 he made it quite clear that he does not subscribe to any of the standard theological beliefs about the divinity of Jesus (see also Letter 76), though he elevates Jesus over Moses by attributing to Jesus a purely intellectual apprehension of God. In this chapter, too, he stresses the uniqueness of Jesus' understanding of God, but he gives no argument for this thesis, except the fact that the New Testament does not describe Jesus as having received any verbal messages or visions from God, and thus communicated with God "mind to mind." Does this mean that Jesus was just a philosopher? Moreover, Spinoza mistakenly universalizes Jesus' message: contrary to his assertion, Jesus wanted his disciples to preach only to the Jews (Matthew 10:5–7). This is a passage, and there are others, where Spinoza is not faithful to his principle of reading the biblical text "as is." To advance his own ideological and political agenda he reads into a text what he wants it to say. (On this issue, see Leo Strauss, *Spinoza's Critique of Religion.* New York: Schocken Books, 1965 and S. Zac, *Spinoza et l'interprétation de l'écriture.* Paris: PUF, 1965.)

ing of things revealed was still obscure and quite often took the form of parables, especially when he was addressing those to whom it had not yet been granted to understand the kingdom of Heaven (see Matth. ch. 13 v. 10, and ff.). But doubtless, to those to whom it was granted to know the mysteries of Heaven, his teaching took the form of eternal truths, not of prescribed laws. In this way he freed them from bondage to the law, while nevertheless giving further strength and stability to the law, inscribing it deep in their hearts.

Paul, too, appears to be making the same point in certain passages, namely, in his Epistle to the Romans, chapter 7 v. 6 and chapter 3 v. 28. Yet he, too, is unwilling to speak openly, but, as he says in the same Epistle chapter 3 v. 5 and in chapter 6 v. 19 he speaks only after the manner of men. This he expressly states when he calls God just, and it was undoubtedly in concession to the frailty of the flesh that he also ascribes to God mercy, grace, anger, and so forth, adapting his words to the character of the common people, or (as he also says in the First Epistle to the Corinthians, chapter 3 v. 1, 2) to the character of carnal man. For in the Epistle to the Romans chapter 9 v. 18 he tells us outright that God's anger and mercy depend not on man's works but on God's vocation, that is, his will; and further, that no one is justified from the works of the law, but only from faith (see Epistle to the Romans chapter 3 v. 28), by which he surely means nothing other than the full consent of the mind. Lastly, he says that no one becomes blessed unless he has in himself the mind of Christ (Rom. ch. 8 v. 9), meaning that he would thereby perceive the laws of God as eternal truths.

We therefore conclude that it is only in concession to the understanding of the multitude and the defectiveness of their thought that God is described as a lawgiver or ruler, and is called just, merciful and so on, and that in reality God acts and governs all things solely from the necessity of his own nature and perfection, and his decrees and volitions are eternal truths, always involving necessity.[6] So much for the first point I had proposed to explain and demonstrate.

Let us, then, pass on to the second point, and perusing the Holy Writ, let us see what it tells us concerning the natural light of reason and this Divine Law. The first thing we encounter is the narrative of the first man, where we are told that God forbade Adam to eat of the tree of knowledge of good and evil. This seems to mean that God commanded Adam to do good and to seek it for its goodness, not insofar as it is contrary to evil; that is, to seek good from love of good, and not from fear of evil. For, as we have

6. *Ethics*, 1.16.

shown, he who does good from true knowledge and love of good acts freely and with a steadfast mind, whereas he who does good from fear of evil acts under constraint of evil, in bondage, and lives under another's sway. This single command given by God to Adam comprehends the natural Divine Law in its entirety, and is in absolute agreement with the dictates of the natural light of reason. It would not be difficult to explain on this basis the whole narrative or parable of the first man, but I refrain from so doing for two reasons. First, I cannot be absolutely sure that my explanation would be in agreement with the author's intention; secondly, there are many who do not grant that this narrative is a parable, firmly maintaining that it is a straightforward account of fact.

It will therefore be better to adduce other passages of Scripture, especially the words of one who speaks from the power of the natural light wherein he surpassed all the sages of his time, one whose sayings have been accepted by the people as having the same sanctity as those of the prophets. I refer to Solomon, who is commended in the Scriptures not so much for prophecy and piety as for prudence and wisdom. In his Proverbs he calls man's intellect the fount of true life, and regards misfortune as consisting only in folly. Thus, he says in chapter 16 v. 22, "Understanding (is) a wellspring of life to him that hath it,* and the punishment of fools is their folly." Here it should be noted that in Hebrew the word 'life' without qualification signifies 'true life', as is clear from Deuteronomy chapter 30 v. 19. He thus identifies the fruit of intellect with true life alone, its privation being itself a punishment, in complete agreement with our remarks on the fourth point concerning the Divine Law. That this fountain of life, i.e. the intellect alone, prescribes laws for the wise—as we have also shown—is plainly taught by this same sage. For he says in chapter 13 v. 14, "The law of the wise is a fountain of life," that is, as is clear from the text just quoted, the intellect. Again, in chapter 3 v. 13 he tells us most explicitly that the intellect makes a man blessed and happy and affords true peace of mind. For he says, "Happy is the man that findeth wisdom, and the son of man that getteth understanding." This is because, as he goes on to say in v. 16, 17, "Length of days** is in her right hand, and in her left hand riches and honour. Her ways" (that is, the ways pointed out by knowledge) "are ways of pleasantness, and all her paths are peace." So Solomon, too, holds the opinion that only the wise live with tranquil and

---

* Latin—*domini*. A Hebrew idiom. That which possesses something, or contains it in its nature, is called lord of that thing. Thus a bird is called lord of wings in Hebrew, because it possesses wings; an intelligent being is called lord of intellect, because it possesses intellect.

** A Hebrew idiom, meaning simply 'life.'

steadfast mind, unlike the wicked, whose minds are agitated by conflicting emotions; and so (as Isaiah, too, says in chapter 57 v. 20) they have neither peace nor rest.

Finally, we should particularly note the passages in the second chapter of the Proverbs of Solomon, which most clearly confirm our view. For in verse 3 of that chapter he begins thus, "If thou criest after knowledge and liftest up thy voice for understanding . . . then shalt thou understand the fear of the Lord and find knowledge of the Lord." ('Knowledge' may perhaps be 'love', for the Hebrew word 'Jadah' can have both meanings.) "For the Lord" (note well) "giveth wisdom. Out of his mouth cometh knowledge and understanding." By these words he is surely indicating as clearly as can be, first, that only wisdom or intellect teaches us to fear God wisely, that is, to worship him with true devotion; and secondly, that wisdom and knowledge flow from the mouth of God and God bestows this upon us. This is the point we have also demonstrated above, namely, that our intellect and knowledge depend solely on the idea or our understanding of God, and spring from it and are perfected by it. Then Solomon goes on to say most explicitly, in verse 9, that this knowledge includes the true principles of Ethics and Politics, which can be deduced therefrom. "Then shalt thou understand righteousness and judgment and equity, yea, every good path." Not content with this, he continues, "When wisdom entereth into thy heart and knowledge is pleasant unto thy soul, discretion* shall preserve thee, and understanding shall keep thee." All this is plainly in accord with natural knowledge, for it is natural knowledge that teaches us ethics and true virtue, once we have arrived at the knowledge of things and have tasted the excellence of understanding.

Thus Solomon, too, takes the view that the happiness and peace of the man who cultivates his natural understanding depends mainly not on the sway of fortune (that is, on God's external help) but on his own internal virtue (or God's internal help), because he owes his self-preservation mainly to his own vigilance, conduct and wise counsel.

Finally, we must here by no means omit the passage in Paul's Epistle to the Romans chapter 1 v. 20, where he speaks thus (as Tremellius translates from the Syriac text), "For the invisible things of God from the creation of the world are clearly seen through the intellect in the things that are made, even his power and his Godhead which is unto eternity, so that they are without excuse." Here he quite clearly indicates that, by the natural light of reason, all can clearly understand the power and eternal divinity of God, from which they can know and infer what they should seek and what they should avoid. So he concludes that all are without excuse and cannot

---

* The Hebrew word '*mezima*' properly means thought, deliberation and vigilance.

plead ignorance, which they could assuredly do if he were speaking of a supernatural light, and of the passion and resurrection of Christ in the flesh, and so forth. And he therefore continues a little later at verse 24 as follows, "Therefore God gave them up to the unclean lusts of their hearts . . ." through the rest of the chapter, describing the vices of ignorance and setting them forth as the punishment of ignorance. This is plainly in accord with the Proverbs of Solomon, chapter 16 v. 22, which we have already quoted, "The punishment of fools is their folly." It is not surprising, then, that Paul says that the wicked are without excuse. For as each sows, so shall he reap; out of evil, unless it be wisely corrected, evil inevitably follows, and out of good, good, if hearts be steadfast.

Therefore Scripture unreservedly commends the natural light and the natural Divine Law. And with this I have completed the task undertaken in this chapter.

CHAPTER 5

Of the reason for the institution of ceremonial observances. Belief in
the Biblical narratives: in what way and for whom it is necessary

In the previous chapter we showed that the Divine Law, which makes men
truly blessed and teaches the true life, is of universal application to all
men. Indeed, our method of deducing it from human nature shows that it
must be considered as innate in the human mind and inscribed therein, as
it were. Now ceremonial observances—those, at least, that are laid down
in the Old Testament—were instituted for the Hebrews alone, and were
so adapted to the nature of their government that they could not be
practised by the individual but involved the community as a whole. So it is
evident that they do not pertain to the Divine Law, and therefore do not
contribute to blessedness and virtue. They have regard only to the election
of the Hebrews, that is (as we demonstrated in chapter 3), to their temporal and material prosperity and peaceful government, and therefore
could have been of practical value only while their state existed. If in the
Old Testament we find them included in God's law, this can only be
because they owed their institution to revelation, or to principles revealed
therein. However, since reason, be it of the soundest, carries little weight
with the common run of theologians, I now intend to confirm by Scriptural authority what we have just demonstrated; and then, for greater
clarity, I shall go on to show how and why ceremonial observances served
to strengthen and preserve the Jewish state.

Of all Isaiah's teachings nothing is clearer than this, that the Divine
Law, taken in a strict sense, signifies not ceremonial observance, but the
universal law that consists in the true way of life. In chapter 1 v. 10, where
the prophet calls upon his countrymen to hear from him the Divine Law,
he first excludes from it sacrifices of every kind and all festivals, and then
goes on to teach the law itself (see verses 16, 17) which he summarises
under these few headings: cleanliness of heart, the habit or practice of
virtue, or good actions, and succouring the helpless. Testimony no less
striking is given by the passage in Psalm 40 v. 6, 8, where the Psalmist
addresses God, "Sacrifice and offering thou didst not desire, mine ears
hast thou opened;* burnt offering and sin-offering hast thou not required;
I delight to do thy will, O my God; yea, thy law is within my heart." So it is
only what is inscribed in the heart, or mind, that the Psalmist calls God's

---

* A Hebrew expression signifying understanding.

law, and he excludes from it ceremonial observances; for the latter are good
not by nature but by convention, and so are not inscribed in the heart.
Besides these passages, Scripture contains others giving the same testimony, but it is enough to have cited these two.

The fact that the observance of ceremonies has regard only to the
temporal prosperity of the state and in no way contributes to blessedness is
also evident from Scripture, which for ceremonial observance promises
nothing but material advantages and pleasures, while blessedness is promised only for observance of the universal Divine Law. In the five books
commonly attributed to Moses the only promise made, as I have already
said, is worldly success—honours or fame, victory, riches, life's pleasures
and health. And although these five books contain much about moral
teaching as well as ceremonial observance, these passages are not set forth
as moral teachings of universal application to all men, but as commands
particularly adapted to the understanding and character of only their state.
For example, it is not as a teacher or prophet that Moses forbids the Jews
to kill or to steal; it is as a lawgiver or ruler that he issues these commands.
He does not justify his precepts by reasoning, but attaches to his commands a penalty, a penalty which can vary, and must vary, to suit the
character of each single nation, as we well know from experience. So, too,
his command not to commit adultery has regard only to the good of the
commonwealth and state. If he had intended this to be a moral precept
that had regard not merely to the good of the commonwealth but to the
peace of mind and the true blessedness of the individual, he would have
condemned not merely the external act but the very wish, as did Christ,
who taught only universal moral precepts (see Matth. ch. 5 v. 28). It is for
this reason that Christ promises a spiritual reward, not, like Moses, a
material reward. For Christ, as I have said, was sent not to preserve the
state and to institute laws, but only to teach the universal law. Hence, we
can readily understand that Christ by no means abrogated the law of
Moses, for it was not Christ's purpose to introduce new laws into the
commonwealth. His chief concern was to teach moral doctrines, keeping
them distinct from the laws of the commonwealth. This was mainly on
account of the ignorance of the Pharisees, who thought that the blessed life
was his who observed the laws of the commonwealth, i.e. the law of Moses;
whereas, in fact, this law concerned only public good, and its aim was to
coerce the Hebrews rather than instruct them.

But let us return to our theme, and cite other passages of Scripture
which promise for ceremonial observance nothing but material benefits,
reserving blessedness solely for the universal Divine Law. None of the
prophets spoke more clearly on this subject than Isaiah. In chapter 58,
after his condemnation of hypocrisy he commends the freeing of the

oppressed and charity towards oneself and one's neighbour, promising in return, "Then shall thy light break forth as the morning, and thine health shall spring forth speedily, and thy righteousness shall go before thee; the glory of the Lord shall gather thee in."* Then he goes on to commend the Sabbath, too, and for its diligent observance he promises, "Then shalt thou delight thyself in the Lord,** and I shall cause thee to ride upon the high places of the earth,*** and feed thee with the heritage of Jacob, thy father; for the mouth of the Lord hath spoken it." So we see that, in return for the freeing of the oppressed and for charity, the prophet promises a healthy mind in a healthy body, and the glory of the Lord even after death; but in return for the observance of ceremonies he promises only the security of the state, prosperity, and material success.

In Psalms 15 and 24 no mention is made of ceremonies but only of moral doctrine, obviously because their only theme is blessedness, and this alone is set before us, although by way of parable. For it is evident that by 'the hill of God' and 'his tabernacle' and the abiding therein is meant blessedness and peace of mind, not the mount of Jerusalem nor the tent of Moses; for nobody dwelt in these places, and they were looked after by those of the tribe of Levi. Then again, all those sayings of Solomon which I quoted in the previous chapter also promise true blessedness simply in return for the cultivation of intellect and wisdom, for from wisdom will the fear of God come to be understood, and the knowledge of God be found.

That the Hebrews are not bound to practise their ceremonial rites since the destruction of their state is clear from Jeremiah, who, when he saw and proclaimed the imminent ruin of the city, said that God delights only in those who know and understand that he exercises lovingkindness, judgment and righteousness in the earth, and so thereafter only those who know these things are to be deemed worthy of praise (see chapter 9 v. 23). This is as much as to say that after the destruction of the city God demanded no special service of the Jews and sought nothing of them thereafter except the natural law by which all men are bound.[1]

---

* A Hebrew expression referring to death. 'To be gathered unto one's people' means to die. See Genesis chapter 49 v. 29, 33.

** Means 'to take honourable pleasure,' as in the Dutch saying, '*Met Godt en met eere.*'

*** Means 'to hold sway,' like holding a horse on the rein.

1. Here Spinoza makes one of his more radical and "heterodox" claims, which, had he made it at the time of his excommunication, would surely have justified his expulsion from the Jewish community. The validity of Jewish law, even in exile, has always been a cardinal point in Judaism. Moreover, Spinoza's reading of Jeremiah

The New Testament, too, plainly supports this view; for, as I have said, it teaches only moral doctrine and the promised reward is the Kingdom of Heaven, while the Apostles made no mention of ceremonial rites once they had extended the preaching of the Gospel to other nations who were bound by the laws of a different commonwealth. The Pharisees did indeed retain these rites, or a great part of them, after the loss of their independent state; but their object in so doing was to oppose the Christians rather than to please God. For when they were led away in captivity to Babylon after the first destruction of the city, they straightway abandoned their observance of ceremonies. Indeed, they turned their backs on the entire Mosaic Law, consigned to oblivion the laws of their native land as being obviously pointless, and began to be assimilated to other nations, as Ezra and Nehemiah make abundantly clear. Therefore there is no doubt that, since the fall of their independent state, Jews are no more bound by the Mosaic Law than they were before their political state came into being. For while they were living among other nations before the exodus from Egypt, they had no special laws to themselves; they were bound by no law other than the natural law, and doubtless the law of the state in which they dwelt, insofar as that was not opposed to the natural Divine Law.

As to the fact that the Patriarchs offered sacrifice to God, I think they did this in order to stimulate a feeling of reverence in their minds, which were accustomed from childhood to seeing sacrifice offered. For all men from the time of Enoch were quite familiar with the offering of sacrifice, and consequently this was the principle means of inducing reverence. Thus the Patriarchs sacrificed to God not through some command imposed on them by God, nor because they were instructed by the universal principles of the Divine Law, but only from contemporary custom. And if they did so by anyone's command, that command was simply the existing law of the commonwealth in which they were dwelling, by which they, too, were bound, as we have remarked both in this chapter and in chapter 3 when speaking of Melchizedek.

With these quotations I think I have confirmed my view by Scriptural authority. It now remains for me to show how and why ceremonial rites served to preserve and strengthen the Hebrew state. This I shall demonstrate as briefly as possible, arguing from universally valid principles.

The formation of a society is advantageous, even absolutely essential, not merely for security against enemies but for the efficient organisation of

---

and other biblical texts can be questioned. Indeed, Jeremiah himself says that God's commandments are as everlasting as the heavenly bodies (Jeremiah 31:35–37). Again, we see Spinoza's selective and sometimes arbitrary reading of Scripture.

an economy. If men did not afford one another mutual aid, they would lack both the skill and the time to support and preserve themselves to the greatest possible extent. All men are not equally suited to all activities, and no single person would be capable of supplying all his own needs. Each would find strength and time fail him if he alone had to plough, sow, reap, grind, cook, weave, stitch and perform all the other numerous tasks to support life, not to mention the arts and sciences which are also indispensable for the perfection of human nature and its blessedness. We see that those who live in a barbarous way with no civilising influences lead a wretched and almost brutish existence, and even so their few poor and crude resources are not acquired without some degree of mutual help.

Now if men were so constituted by nature as to desire nothing but what is prescribed by true reason, society would stand in no need of any laws. Nothing would be required but to teach men true moral doctrine, and they would then act to their true advantage of their own accord, wholeheartedly and freely. But human nature is far differently constituted. All men do, indeed, seek their own advantage, but by no means from the dictates of sound reason. For the most part the objectives they seek and judge to be beneficial are determined only by fleshly desire, and they are carried away by their emotions, which take no account of the future or of other considerations. Hence no society can subsist without government and coercion, and consequently without laws to control and restrain men's lusts and their unbridled urges. Yet human nature will not submit to unlimited repression, and, as Seneca[2] says in his tragedy, rule that depends on violence has never long continued; moderate rule endures. For as long as men act only from fear, they are doing what they are most opposed to doing, taking no account of the usefulness and the necessity of the action to be done, concerned only not to incur capital or other punishment. Indeed, they inevitably rejoice at misfortune or injury to their ruler even when this involves their own considerable misfortune, and they wish every ill on him, and bring this about when they can. Again, men are impatient above all at being subject to their equals and under their rule. Finally, there is nothing more difficult than to take away freedom from men to whom it has once been granted.

From this it follows, first, that either the entire community, if possible, should hold the reins of government as a single body, so that all are thus required to render obedience to themselves and no one to his equal; or, alternatively, if sovereignty is invested in a few men or in one alone, he should be endowed with some extraordinary quality, or must at least make every effort to convince the masses of this. Secondly, in every state laws

2. In the *Troades*. The same quotation occurs in chapter 16.

should be so devised that men may be influenced not so much by fear as by hope of some good that they urgently desire; for in this way each will be eager to do his duty. Finally, since obedience consists in carrying out orders simply by reason of the authority of a ruler, it follows that this has no place in a community where sovereignty is vested in all the citizens, and laws are sanctioned by common consent. In such a community the people would remain equally free whether laws were multiplied or diminished, since it would act not from another's bidding but from its own consent. But the opposite is the case when sovereignty is vested absolutely in one man alone; for all do the state's bidding on the authority of only one man. So unless they have been brought up from the beginning to give unquestioning obedience to a ruler, he will find it difficult to institute new laws when they are needed and to deprive the people of a freedom that has once been granted.

From these general considerations let us pass on to the particular case of the commonwealth of the Hebrews. When they first went out from Egypt, being no longer bound by the laws of any nation, they were at liberty to sanction any new laws they pleased or to establish new ordinances, to maintain a state wherever they wished and to occupy any lands they wished. However, the task of establishing a wise system of laws and of keeping the government in the hands of the whole community was quite beyond them; for they were in general inexperienced in such matters and exhausted by the wretched conditions of slavery. Therefore government had to remain in the hands of one man who would issue commands and enforce them on others; who would, in short, ordain laws and thereafter interpret them. Such sovereignty Moses easily succeeded in keeping in his hands, because he surpassed all others in divine power which he convinced the people that he possessed, providing many proofs thereof (see Exodus chapter 14 last verse and chapter 19 v. 9). He, then, by the divine power with which he was gifted, established a system of law and ordained it for the people. But in so doing he made every effort to see that the people should do their duty willingly rather than through fear. To this he was urged by two considerations, the obstinate nature of a people who cannot be coerced merely by force, and the imminence of war. To achieve military success soldiers have to be encouraged rather than terrorised by threats of punishment, for in this way each will seek to distinguish himself by valorous deeds and courage, and not merely try to avoid punishment. This, then, was the reason why Moses, by his divine power and authority, introduced a state religion: it was to make the people do their duty from devotion rather than fear. Furthermore, he bound them by consideration of benefits received, while promising many more benefits from God in the future. And the laws he established were not unduly harsh, as anyone who studies them will readily grant, especially if he considers the number of circumstantial details required for the conviction of the accused.[3]

Finally, in order that a people incapable of self-rule should be utterly subservient to its ruler, he did not allow these men, habituated as they were to slavery, to perform any action at their own discretion. The people could do nothing without being required at the same time to remember the law and to follow its commands, which were dependent solely on the ruler's will. Ploughing, sowing, reaping were not permitted at their discretion, but had to accord with the fixed and determinate command of the law. They could not even eat, dress, cut their hair, shave, make merry or do anything whatsoever except in accordance with commands and instructions laid down by the law. And this was not all; they had to have certain signs on their doorposts, on their hands and between the eyes, to give them constant reminder of the duty of obedience.

This, then, was the object of ceremonial observance, that men should never act of their own volition but always at another's behest, and that in their actions and inward thoughts they should at all times acknowledge that they were not their own masters but completely subordinate to another. From all these considerations it is quite indisputable that ceremonial observances contribute nothing to blessedness, and that those specified in the Old Testament, and indeed the whole Mosaic Law, were relevant only to the Hebrew state, and consequently to no more than temporal prosperity.

With regard to Christian ceremonies, namely, baptism, the Lord's Supper, festivals, public prayers and all the other ceremonies that are, and always have been, common to all Christendom, if they were ever instituted by Christ or the Apostles (of which I am not yet convinced), they were instituted only as external symbols of a universal Church, not as conducing to blessedness or as containing an intrinsic holiness. Therefore, although it was not to support a sovereign state that these ceremonies were instituted, yet their only purpose was the unification of a particular society, and thus he who lives in solitude is by no means bound by them. Indeed, he who lives under a government where the Christian religion is forbidden is required to abstain from these ceremonies, and can nevertheless live a blessed life. There is an instance of this in Japan, where the Christian religion is forbidden. The Dutch who live there are required by

3. Spinoza is alluding here to the requirements of Jewish criminal law that prescribe in a case involving capital punishment—for example, murder—that the murderer had to be forewarned by two witnesses. These witnesses must have informed the perpetrator of the gravity of the act and the specific punishment for it. If any of these conditions is absent, the killer cannot be punished with death.

the East India Company to refrain from practising any external rites. I do not think it necessary to support this view by other authority; and although it would not be difficult to deduce it also from the fundamental principles of the New Testament and perhaps to demonstrate it by further convincing testimony, I leave this topic the more willingly as I am anxious to move on to other points. I therefore proceed to the second topic I proposed to discuss in this chapter: for whom, and in what way, belief in the narratives of Holy Scripture is requisite. To examine this question by the natural light of reason, I think it proper to proceed as follows.

If anyone, in arguing for or against a proposition which is not self-evident, seeks to persuade others to accept his view, he must prove his point from premises that are granted, and he must convince his audience on empirical grounds or by force of reason; that is, either from what sense-perception tells them occurs in Nature, or through self-evident intellectual axioms. Now unless experience is such as to be clearly and distinctly understood, it cannot have so decisive an effect on a man's understanding and dispel the mists of doubt as when the desired conclusion is deduced solely from intellectual axioms, that is, from the mere force of the intellect and its orderly apprehensions. This is especially so if the point at issue is a spiritual matter and does not come within the scope of the senses.

Now the process of deduction solely from intellectual axioms usually demands the apprehension of a long series of connected propositions, as well as the greatest caution, acuteness of intelligence, and restraint, all of which qualities are rarely to be found among men. So men prefer to be taught by experience rather than engage in the logical process of deduction from a few axioms. Hence it follows that if anyone sets out to teach some doctrine to an entire nation—not to say the whole of mankind—and wants it to be intelligible to all in every detail, he must rely entirely on an appeal to experience, and he must above all adapt his arguments and the definitions relevant to his doctrine to the understanding of the common people, who form the greatest part of mankind. He must not set before them a logical chain of reasoning nor frame the kind of definitions that are best suited to logical thinking. Otherwise he will be writing only for the learned; that is, he will be comprehensible only to a small minority.

Therefore, since the whole of Scripture was revealed in the first place for an entire nation, and eventually for all mankind, its contents had to be adapted particularly to the understanding of the common people, and it had to appeal only to experience. Let us explain more clearly. The teachings of Scripture that are concerned only with philosophic matters can be summed up as follows: that there is a God or Being who made all things and who directs and sustains the world with supreme wisdom; that he takes the utmost care of men, that is, those of them who live moral and righteous lives; and that he severely punishes the others and cuts them off from the good. Now Scripture establishes this simply by appealing to experience, that is, by its historical narratives; it does not provide any definitions of the terms it employs, but its language and reasoning is adapted to the understanding of the common people. And although experience can give no clear knowledge of these matters, and cannot teach what God is and in what way he sustains and directs all things and cares for men, it can still teach and enlighten men as far as suffices to impress on their minds obedience and devotion.

I think we have now shown quite clearly for whom, and in what way, belief in the narratives of Holy Scripture is requisite. From what we have already demonstrated it undoubtedly follows that knowledge of these writings and belief in them is in the highest degree necessary for the common people who lack the ability to perceive things clearly and distinctly. It further follows that he who rejects these writings because he does not believe in God, or does not believe that God cares for the world and mankind, is an impious person. But he who, while unacquainted with these writings, nevertheless knows by the natural light that there is a God having the attributes we have recounted, and who also pursues a true way of life, is altogether blessed—indeed, more blessed than the multitude, because in addition to true beliefs he also has a clear and distinct conception of God. Finally, it follows that he who is neither acquainted with these Biblical narratives nor has any knowledge from the natural light, if he be not impious or obstinate, is yet hardly human and close to being a beast, possessing none of God's gifts.

However, it should here be noted that when we say that it is in the highest degree requisite for the multitude to be acquainted with the Biblical narratives, we do not mean that they need to know absolutely all the narratives of Holy Scripture, but only those narratives that are of the first importance, and which, taken alone, display quite clearly the teachings we have just recounted, and make a striking impression on men's minds. For if all the Scriptural narratives were essential for demonstrating its teachings, and no conclusion could be drawn except by taking complete account of them all without exception, then surely the conclusive demonstration of its doctrine would be beyond the understanding and powers not only of the common people but of any human being. For who could pay attention all at once to such a vast number of narratives, to all the accompanying detail and the partial accounts of a doctrine that would have to be drawn from so many diverse narratives? For my part, I cannot believe that those who bequeathed to us the Scriptures in their present form were men of such outstanding ability as to be capable of following in detail a demonstration of that kind. Still less am I convinced that the doctrine of Scripture cannot be understood without our hearing of the quarrels of Isaac, Achitophel's advice to Absalom, the civil war between the men of Judah and the men of Israel, and other chronicles of this kind. Nor can I believe that historical narratives could not have demonstrated this doctrine to the earlier Jews of the time of Moses quite as well as to the contemporaries of Ezra. The common people, then, need to be acquainted only with those narratives that are most effective in instilling obedience and devotion. But the common people are not themselves qualified to judge of these narratives, being more disposed to take pleasure in the stories and in strange and unexpected happenings than in the doctrine implicit in the narratives; and, therefore, besides reading the narratives they also stand in need of pastors or ministers of the Church to instruct them in a way suited to their limited intelligence.

However, let us not stray from our theme, but proceed to the conclusion which it was our main purpose to prove, namely, that belief in historical narratives of any kind whatsoever has nothing to do with the Divine Law, that it does not in itself make men blessed, that its only value lies in the lesson conveyed, in which respect alone some narratives can be superior to others. So the narratives of the Old and New Testament differ in excellence from non-sacred writings and from one another to the extent that they inspire salutary beliefs. Therefore if a man reads the narratives of Holy Scripture and has complete faith in them, and yet pays no heed to the lesson that Scripture thereby aims to convey, and leads no better life, he might just as well have read the Koran or a poetic drama or at any rate ordinary history, giving the same attention as common people do to such writings. On the other hand, as we have said, he who is totally unacquainted with the Biblical narratives, but nevertheless holds salutary beliefs and pursues the true way of life, is absolutely blessed and has within him the spirit of Christ.

Now the Jews take a completely contrary view. They maintain that true beliefs and a true way of life contribute nothing to blessedness as long as men embrace them only from the natural light of reason, and not as teachings revealed to Moses by prophetic inspiration. This is what Maimonides ventures openly to affirm in chapter 8 of Kings, Law 11, "Every man who takes to heart the seven commandments* and diligently follows them belongs to the pious of nations and is heir to the world to come; that is to say, if he takes them to heart and follows them because God has

---

* N.B. The Jews believe that God gave Noah seven commandments, which alone are binding on all peoples; but to the Jews alone he gave many other commandments, making them more blessed than the rest.

ordained them in his Law, and has revealed to us through Moses that they were formerly ordained for the sons of Noah. But if he follows them through the guidance of reason, he is not a dweller among the pious nor among the wise of nations."[4] Such are the words of Maimonides, to which Rabbi Joseph,[5] son of Shem Tob, in his book called *Kebod Elohim*, or *Glory of God*, adds this, that although Aristotle (whom he considers to have written the finest work on Ethics, esteeming him above all others) may have neglected none of the precepts of true morality—which he also advocated in his own Ethics—and may have diligently followed all these teachings, this could not have furthered his own salvation, because he embraced these doctrines not as divine teachings prophetically revealed, but solely through the dictates of reason.

However, I think that any attentive reader will be convinced that these are mere figments of imagination, unsupported by rational argument or Scriptural authority. To state this view is sufficient to refute it. Nor do I here intend to refute the view of those who maintain that the natural light of reason can give no sound instruction in matters concerning true salvation. Those who deny to themselves a faculty for sound reasoning cannot claim to prove their assertion by reasoning. And if they claim for them-

4. This passage has occasioned a long-standing controversy and has elicited a considerable literature. Spinoza's reference to Maimonides is elliptical; the full citation should be Maimonides' Code of Law (*Mishneh Torah*), *Book of Kings*, chapter 8, law 11. As some modern scholars have noted, Spinoza's text of Maimonides' Code is not accurate. Whereas in the *TTP*, Spinoza reads ". . . nor among the wise of nations," the correct reading is "but only of the wise of nations." That is, according to Maimonides, the non-Jew must accept the moral law as revealed by God in order to merit entry into the World-to-Come, or in Spinoza's language, to be blessed. If not, the non-Jew who observes the moral commandments from rational argument and considerations is just wise, not pious or blessed. Maimonides' position was not universally accepted by Jews. Spinoza, however, uses it as a weapon against Judaism and also by implication any religion that makes dogmatic belief and ritual observances necessary conditions for blessedness (Steven Schwarzschild, "Do Noachites Have to Believe in Revelation? (A Passage in Dispute between Maimonides, Spinoza, Mendelssohn and Hermann Cohen) A Contribution to a Jewish View of Natural Law," *Jewish Quarterly Review,* 52 (1962), 297–308; 53 (1962), 30–65).

5. Joseph ben Shem Tov, a fifteenth-century Spanish Jewish scholar, was a critical Maimonidean, who had reservations concerning the extent to which Aristotelian philosophy could be made consistent with Judaism and conversely. In addition to the treatise cited by Spinoza, he wrote a commentary on Aristotle's *Nicomachean Ethics.*

selves some suprarational faculty, this is the merest fiction, and far inferior to reason. This has been shown clearly enough by the manner of life they usually adopt. But there is no need to speak more openly about such people. This only will I add: we cannot know anyone except by his works. He who abounds in these fruits—charity, joy, peace, patience, kindness, goodness, faithfulness, gentleness and self-control, against which (as Paul says in Galatians chapter 5 v. 22) the law is not laid down, he, whether he be taught by reason alone or by Scripture alone, is in truth taught by God, and is altogether blessed.

Thus I have completed all that I undertook to discuss regarding the Divine Law.

CHAPTER 6

Of Miracles

Just as men are accustomed to call divine the kind of knowledge that surpasses human understanding, so they call divine, or the work of God, any work whose cause is generally unknown. For the common people suppose that God's power and providence are most clearly displayed when some unusual event occurs in Nature contrary to their habitual beliefs concerning Nature, particularly if such an event is to their profit or advantage. They consider that the clearest possible evidence of God's existence is provided when Nature deviates—as they think—from her proper order. Therefore they believe that all those who explain phenomena and miracles through natural causes, or who strive to understand them so, are doing away with God, or at least God's providence. They consider that God is inactive all the while that Nature pursues her normal course, and, conversely, that Nature's power and natural causes are suspended as long as God is acting. Thus they imagine that there are two powers quite distinct from each other, the power of God and the power of Nature, though the latter is determined in a definite way by God, or—as is the prevailing opinion nowadays—created by God. What they mean by the two powers, and what by God and Nature, they have no idea, except that they imagine God's power to be like the rule of some royal potentate, and Nature's power to be a kind of force and energy.

Therefore unusual works of Nature are termed miracles, or works of God, by the common people; and partly from piety, partly for the sake of opposing those who cultivate the natural sciences, they prefer to remain in ignorance of natural causes, and are eager to hear only of what is least comprehensible to them and consequently evokes their greatest wonder. Naturally so, since it is only by abolishing natural causes and imagining supernatural events that they are able to worship God and refer all things to God's governance and God's will; and it is when they imagine Nature's power subdued, as it were, by God that they most admire God's power.

This idea seems to have originated with the early Jews. In order to refute the beliefs of the Gentiles of their time who worshipped visible gods—the Sun, the Moon, the Earth, Water, Sky and so on—and to prove to them that these gods were weak and inconstant, or changeable and under the command of an invisible God, they boasted of their miracles, from which they further sought to prove that the whole of Nature was directed for their sole benefit by command of God whom they worshipped. This idea has found such favour with mankind that they have not ceased to this day to invent miracles with view to convincing people that they are more beloved of God than others, and are the final cause of God's creation and continuous direction of the world.

To what lengths will the folly of the multitude not carry them? They have no sound conception either of God or of Nature, they confuse God's decisions with human decisions, and they imagine Nature to be so limited that they believe man to be its chief part.

I have now devoted enough space to setting forth the beliefs and prejudices of the multitude concerning Nature. However, for the sake of orderly exposition, I shall demonstrate:

1. That no event can occur to contravene Nature, which preserves an eternal fixed and immutable order. At the same time I shall explain what is to be understood by a miracle.

2. That neither God's essence nor God's existence—nor, consequently, God's providence—can be known from miracles. All these can be far better apprehended from Nature's fixed and immutable order.

3. I shall cite a number of passages in Scripture to prove that, by God's decrees and volitions, and consequently God's providence, Scripture itself means nothing other than Nature's order, which necessarily follows from her eternal laws.

4. Finally, I shall discuss the method of interpreting Scriptural miracles, and the chief points to be noted regarding the narratives of miracles.

These are the principal topics which form the subject-matter of this chapter, and which I furthermore consider to be of no small profit in furthering the purpose of this entire work.

As to the first point, this is easily demonstrated from what I have set forth in chapter 4 concerning the Divine Law; namely, that all that God wills or determines involves eternal necessity and truth; for by establishing the identity of God's intellect with God's will we showed that we make the same affirmation in saying that God wills something as in saying that God understands that thing. Therefore the necessity whereby it follows from the divine nature and perfection that God understands some thing as it is, is the same necessity from which it follows that God wills that thing as it is. Now since nothing is necessarily true save by the divine decree, it quite clearly follows that the universal laws of Nature are merely God's decrees, following from the necessity and perfection of the divine nature. So if anything were to happen in Nature contrary to her universal laws, it would also be necessarily contrary to the decree, intellect and nature of God. Or if anyone were to maintain that God performs some act contrary to the laws of Nature, he would at the same time have to maintain that God acts contrary to his own nature—of which nothing could be more absurd. The same could also be easily proved from the fact that the power of Nature is the divine power and virtue, and the divine power is the very essence of God. But I prefer to pass this by for the present.

Nothing, then, can happen in Nature* to contravene her own universal laws, nor yet anything that is not in agreement with these laws or that does not follow from them. For whatever occurs does so through God's will and eternal decree; that is, as we have already shown, all that happens does so in accordance with laws and rules which involve eternal necessity and truth. Nature, then, always observes laws and rules involving eternal necessity and truth although these are not all known to us, and thus it also observes a fixed and immutable order. Nor can any sound reasoning persuade us to attribute to Nature a limited power and virtue, and to regard her laws as having only a restricted application. For since the virtue and power of Nature is the very virtue and power of God, and the laws and rules of Nature are God's very decrees, there can be no doubt that Nature's power is infinite, and her laws sufficiently wide to extend to everything that is conceived even by the divine intellect. Otherwise it would surely have to be maintained that God created Nature so ineffective and prescribed for her laws and rules so barren that he is often constrained to come once more to her rescue if he wants her to be preserved, and the course of events to be as he desires. This I consider to be utterly divorced from reason.

So from these considerations—that nothing happens in Nature that does not follow from her laws, that her laws cover everything that is conceived even by the divine intellect, and that Nature observes a fixed and immutable order—it follows most clearly that the word miracle can be understood only with respect to men's beliefs, and means simply an event whose natural cause we—or at any rate the writer or narrator of the miracle—cannot explain by comparison with any other normal event. I might indeed have said that a miracle is that whose cause cannot be explained on scientific principles known to us by the natural light of reason. However, since miracles were wrought according to the understanding of the common people who were quite ignorant of the principles of science, men of old doubtless regarded as a miracle whatever they could not explain in the way in which the common people are accustomed to explain natural phenomena, that is, by resorting to memory so as to call to mind a similar happening which is ordinarily regarded without wonder. For the common people are not satisfied that they understand a thing until they can regard it without wonder. So men of old, and in general all men

---

* Here, by Nature, I do not mean simply matter and its modifications, but infinite other things besides matter.

up to the present day, had no other criterion of a miracle, and therefore there are undoubtedly many alleged miracles in Scripture whose causes can be easily explained from known scientific principles. This is what we indicated in chapter 2 when we spoke of the sun standing still in the time of Joshua and its retrogression in the time of Ahaz. But we shall presently treat of this matter more fully in discussing the interpretation of miracles, as I have undertaken to do in this chapter.

It is now time to pass on to our second point, namely, to show that miracles cannot provide us with any understanding either of God's essence or his existence or his providence, and that on the contrary these are far better apprehended from the fixed and immutable order of Nature. My proof proceeds as follows. Since God's existence is not self-evident,* it must necessarily be inferred from axiomatic truths which are so firm and incontrovertible that there can neither be, nor be conceived, any power that could call them into question. At any rate, once we have inferred from them God's existence, we are bound to regard them as such if we seek to establish beyond all shadow of doubt our inference from them to God's existence. For if we could conceive that these axiomatic truths themselves can be impugned by any power, of whatever kind it be, then we should doubt their truth and consequently the conclusion following therefrom, namely God's existence; nor could we ever be certain of anything. Further, we know that something agrees with or contravenes Nature only when we can prove that it agrees with or contravenes those basic truths. Therefore if we could conceive that in Nature something could be produced by some power, of whatever kind it be, to contravene Nature, it would contravene those primary axioms. So it must be rejected as absurd, or else (as we have just shown) the primary axioms, and consequently God, and all our apprehensions of every kind must be called into doubt. It is therefore far from being the case that miracles—understanding thereby something that contravenes the order of Nature—prove for us God's existence; on the contrary, they cast doubt on it, since but for them we could be absolutely certain of God's existence, in the assurance that all Nature follows a fixed and immutable order.

But let it be supposed that a miracle is that which cannot be explained through natural causes. This can be understood in two ways: either that it does have natural causes which the human intellect cannot ascertain, or that it owns no cause but God, or the will of God. However, since all things that come to pass through natural causes are also attributable solely to the power and will of God, it really comes down to this, that a miracle, whether or not it has natural causes, is an event that cannot be explained

* See Supplementary Note 6.

through a cause, that is, an event that surpasses human understanding. But from such an event, and from anything at all that surpasses our understanding, we can understand nothing. For whatever we clearly and distinctly understand must become known to us either through itself or through some other thing that is clearly and distinctly understood through itself. Therefore from a miracle, or an event that surpasses our understanding we can understand neither God's essence nor his existence nor anything whatsoever of God or Nature. On the contrary, knowing that all things are determined and ordained by God and that the workings of Nature follow from God's essence, while the laws of Nature are God's eternal decrees and volitions, we must unreservedly conclude that we get to know God and God's will all the better as we gain better knowledge of natural phenomena and understand more clearly how they depend on their first cause, and how they operate in accordance with Nature's eternal laws. Therefore, as far as concerns our understanding, those events which we understand clearly and distinctly have far better right to be termed works of God, and to be referred to God's will, than those of which we are quite ignorant, even though the latter appeal strongly to the imagination and evoke men's wonder. For it is only those works of Nature which we clearly and distinctly understand that afford us a higher knowledge of God, and indicate with the utmost clarity God's will and decrees. So those who have recourse to the will of God when there is something they do not understand are but trifling; this is no more than a ridiculous way of avowing one's ignorance.

Furthermore, granting that any conclusion could be drawn from miracles, God's existence could not possibly be concluded therefrom. For since a miracle is an event of a limited nature, expressing a power that is never other than fixed and limited, from such an effect we could not possibly conclude the existence of a cause whose power is infinite; the most we could conclude is the existence of a cause whose power is greater than that effect. I say 'the most' because an event can also be the result of several simultaneously concurring causes, the force and power of the result being less than all the causes taken together, but far greater than the power of each separate cause. Now since the laws of Nature (as we have shown) are infinite in their scope and are conceived by us as having an eternal quality, and since Nature operates in accordance with them in a fixed and immutable order, the laws themselves give us some indication of the infinity, eternity and immutability of God.

Therefore we conclude that from miracles we cannot gain knowledge of God, his existence and providence, and that these can be far better inferred from Nature's fixed and immutable order. In arriving at this conclusion I am speaking of miracle insofar as it means only an event that surpasses, or is thought to surpass, man's understanding. For insofar as it were supposed to destroy or interrupt the order of Nature or to contravene her laws, in that sense (as I have just shown) not only could it give us no knowledge of God but it would take from us what knowledge we naturally have, and would cast doubt on God and on all things.

And here I do not acknowledge any difference between an event contrary to Nature and a supernatural event; (that is, according to some, an event that does not contravene Nature but nevertheless cannot be produced or brought about by Nature). For since a miracle occurs not externally to Nature but within Nature, even though it be claimed to be supernatural, yet it must necessarily interrupt Nature's order which otherwise we would conceive as fixed and immutable by God's decrees. So if there were to occur in Nature anything that did not follow from her laws, this would necessarily be opposed to the order which God maintains eternally in Nature through her universal laws. So this would be contrary to Nature and Nature's laws, and consequently such a belief would cast doubt on everything, and would lead to atheism.[1]

I think I have now established my second point on a firm footing, from which we may once more reach the conclusion that a miracle, either contrary to Nature or above Nature, is mere absurdity, and therefore a miracle in Scripture can mean nothing else (as we have said) but a natural event which surpasses, or is believed to surpass, human understanding. But before moving on to my third point, I should like to confirm by Scriptural authority our assertion that we cannot gain knowledge of God through miracles. Although Scripture never states this overtly, this conclusion can readily be inferred from it, especially from the passage where Moses (Deut. ch. 13) commands that a false prophet should be con-

---

1. Here Spinoza rejects a common medieval doctrine that distinguishes events that are contrary to the laws of nature from events that are above nature (Aquinas, *Commentary, IV Sentences,* XVII.1.5iii, cited in *St. Thomas Aquinas: Philosophical Texts,* ed. Thomas Gilby (New York: Oxford University Press, 1960), page 125, para. 366; Maimonides, *Treatise on Resurrection of the Dead*). According to this distinction, miracles are indeed contrary to the laws of nature, but they are not logically impossible, such that they do not fall within God's power. Divine omnipotence is on this theory "limited" only by the laws of logic: God can do whatever is logically possible. Miracles are doable insofar as they are logically possible, though contrary to the laws of nature; in this sense they are above or beyond natural—"supranatural."

Spinoza's metaphysics does not allow this distinction, since for him the laws of nature are the laws of God's nature. There is nothing for him that is "above" nature, or God. Or, there is for Spinoza no distinction between the natural and the supranatural (*Ethics,* Part 1).

demned to death even though he should perform miracles. It runs as follows: "(Although) the sign of wonder come to pass, whereof he spoke unto thee . . . thou shalt not hearken to the voice of that prophet . . . for the Lord your God proveth you . . . that prophet shall be put to death. . . ." For this it clearly follows that miracles can be performed by false prophets, too, and that from miracles men may accept false gods quite as readily as the true God, unless they are well fortified by true knowledge and love of God. For he adds, "For the Lord your God proveth you, to know whether ye love him with all your heart and with all your soul."

Again, their many miracles did not enable the Israelites to form any sound conception of God, as the facts bear witness. When they were convinced that Moses had departed from them, they asked Aaron to give them visible deities, and their idea of God, formed after all their many miracles, was—a calf! Asaph, although he had heard of so many miracles, nevertheless doubted God's providence, and might have turned aside from the true path had he not finally achieved an understanding of true blessedness (see Psalm 73). Solomon, too, in whose time the Jews reached the height of their prosperity, suspects that all things happen by chance. See Ecclesiastes chapter 3 v. 19, 20, 21, and chapter 9 v. 2, 3 etc.

Finally, nearly all the prophets found considerable difficulty in reconciling the order of Nature and vicissitudes of men with the conception they had formed of God's providence, whereas this has never afforded difficulty to philosophers, who endeavour to understand things not from miracles but from clear conceptions. For they place true happiness solely in virtue and peace of mind, and they strive to conform with Nature, not to make Nature conform with them; for they are assured that God directs Nature in accordance with the requirements of her universal laws, and not in accordance with the requirements of the particular laws of human nature. Thus God takes account of the whole of Nature, and not of the human race alone.

Therefore even Scripture itself makes it evident that miracles do not afford true knowledge of God, nor do they clearly teach God's providence. As to the many passages in Scripture to the effect that God wrought wonders so as to make himself known to men—as in Exodus chapter 10 v. 2, where God deceived the Egyptians and gave signs of himself so that the Israelites might know that he was God—it does not follow therefrom that miracles really conveyed this; it only follows that the beliefs of the Jews were such that they could be readily convinced by these miracles. For we have already shown clearly in chapter 2 that deliverances of a prophetic nature—i.e. those that are inspired by revelation—are not derived from universal and fundamental axioms, but from the prior assumptions and beliefs, however absurd, of those to whom the revelation is made, or those whom the Holy Spirit seeks to convince. This is a point I have illustrated with many examples, and also with the testimony of Paul, who was a Greek with the Greeks and a Jew with the Jews. But although these miracles succeeded in carrying conviction with the Egyptians and the Jews on the basis of their prior assumptions, they could not impart the true idea and knowledge of God but could only bring about these peoples' admission that there was a Deity more powerful than anything known to them, and that he cared above all men for the Hebrews, whose affairs at that time had prospered beyond expectation. Miracles did not teach them that God cares equally for all; only philosophy can teach that. So the Jews, and all those for whom God's providence was exemplified solely by differences in the condition of human affairs and by inequalities of fortune, were convinced that the Jews were more beloved of God than other peoples, in spite of the fact that, as we showed in chapter 3, the Jews did not excel others in true human perfection.

I now proceed to my third point, demonstrating from Scripture that God's decrees and commandments, and consequently God's providence, are in truth nothing but Nature's order; that is to say, when Scripture tells us that this or that was accomplished by God or by God's will, nothing more is intended than that it came about by accordance with Nature's law and order, and not, as the common people believe, that Nature for that time suspended her action, or that her order was temporarily interrupted. But Scripture does not directly teach what is not relevant to its doctrine; for it is not the part of Scripture (as we showed in connection with the Divine Law) to teach things through their natural causes or to engage in pure philosophy. Therefore the point we here seek to establish must be gathered by implication from certain Scriptural narratives which happen to be related more fully and in more detail. I shall therefore cite a number of these passages.

In 1 Samuel chapter 9 v. 15, 16 it is related that God revealed to Samuel that he would send Saul to him. Yet God did not send Saul to Samuel in the way that men ordinarily send someone to someone else; God's sending was merely the ordinary course of Nature. Saul was in search of his lost asses (as related in the previous chapter) and was thinking of returning home without them when, at his servant's suggestion, he went to the prophet Samuel to learn where he might find them. Nowhere in the entire narrative is it stated that, beyond this natural course of events, Saul received any command of God to visit Samuel.

In Psalm 105 v. 24 we are told that God changed the hearts of the Egyptians so as to hate the Israelites. But this, again, was a quite natural change, as is evident from Exodus chapter 1, where a weighty reason is given as to why the Egyptians were moved to reduce the Israelites to slavery.

In Genesis chapter 9 v. 13 God tells Noah that he will set a rainbow in the cloud. This act of God, again, is assuredly nothing other than the refraction and reflection of the sun's rays which they undergo in droplets of water.

In Psalm 147 v. 18 the natural action and warmth of the wind whereby frost and snow are melted is called the word of God; and in v. 15, wind and cold are called the command and word of God.

In Psalm 104 v. 4 wind and fire are called the messengers and ministers of God, and there are many other such passages in Scripture which clearly indicate that God's decree, command, edict and word are nothing other than the action and order of Nature.

Therefore there can be no doubt that all the events narrated in Scripture occurred naturally; yet they are referred to God because, as we have already shown, it is not the part of Scripture to explain events through their natural causes; it only relates to those events that strike the imagination, employing such method and style as best serves to excite wonder, and consequently to instil piety in the minds of the masses. So if we find in Scripture some things for which we can assign no cause and which seems to have happened beyond—indeed, contrary to—Nature's order, this should not perplex us. We need have no hesitation in believing that what truly happened, happened naturally.

This view receives further confirmation from the fact that many circumstantial details were found to accompany miracles, although these are not always recorded, especially where the style is of a poetic character. The circumstances accompanying miracles, I repeat, clearly show that miracles need natural causes. For instance, so that the Egyptians should be infected with boils, Moses had to scatter ashes in the air (Exodus ch. 9 v. 10). The locusts, too, invaded the land of Egypt by God's command through natural means, namely, through an east wind which blew a whole day and night, and it was through a strong west wind that they quitted the land (Exodus ch. 10 v. 14, 19). By that same command of God, too, the sea opened a path for the Jews (Exodus ch. 14 v. 21), that is, through an east wind which blew strongly all night long. Again, in order that Elisha could revive a child who was thought to be dead, he had to lie over him several times until the child first regained warmth and at last opened his eyes (2 Kings ch. 4 v. 34, 35). So, too, in St. John's Gospel chapter 9 we are told of some accompanying actions which Christ employed to heal the blind man, and there are numerous other instances in Scripture, all going to show that miracles need something other than the absolute command of God, as it is called. Therefore we are justified in believing that, although the circumstances attendant on miracles and the natural causes of miracles are not narrated always and in full, the miracles did not occur without them. This is again clear from Exodus chapter 14 v. 27, where we are merely told that the sea returned to its strength once more solely at the bidding of Moses, no mention being made of any wind; yet in the Song of Moses (ch. 15 v. 10) it is said that this came about because God blew with his wind (that is, a very strong wind). So this attendant circumstance is omitted in the narrative, thereby making the miracle appear all the greater.

But perhaps someone will insist that we find numerous events in Scripture which defy explanation through natural causes, as that the sins of men and their prayers can be the cause of rain and the earth's fertility, or that faith could heal the blind, or other incidents of a similar kind narrated in the Bible. But I consider that I have already replied to such objections. For I have shown that Scripture does not explain things through their proximate causes; in its narratives it merely employs such order and such language as is most effective in moving men—and particularly the common people—to devotion. That is why it speaks of God and events in terms far from correct, its aim being not to convince on rational grounds but to appeal to and engage men's fantasy and imagination. If Scripture were to describe the downfall of an empire in the style adopted by political historians, the common people would not be stirred, whereas they are deeply affected when all is described in poetical language and referred to God, as is customary in Scripture. So when Scripture tells us that the earth is barren because of men's sins, or that the blind were healed by their faith, we should accept this in the same way as when it tells us that God is angry because of men's sins, that he is grieved, that he repents of the good he has promised or done, or that he remembers a promise as a result of seeing a sign, and numerous other assertions that are either of a poetical character or are narrated in accordance with the beliefs and preconceptions of the writer.

Therefore we may now conclude with absolute assurance that everything related in Scripture as having truly happened came to pass necessarily according to the laws of Nature, as everything does. If anything be found in Scripture which can be conclusively proved to contravene the laws of Nature, or which could not possibly follow from them, we have to believe that this was inserted into Holy Scripture by sacrilegious men. For whatever is contrary to Nature is contrary to reason, and whatever is contrary to reason is absurd, and should therefore be rejected.

It now remains for us to remark on just a few more points regarding the interpretation of Scripture, or rather, to recall them—for the main points have already been mentioned—and to illustrate them with a few examples, as I proposed to do here in the fourth section. My purpose is that no one, by misinterpreting some miracle, should heedlessly come to think that he has found something in Scripture contrary to the light of Nature.

It very rarely happens that men relate an event exactly as it took place without introducing into it something of their own judgment. Indeed, when they see or hear something strange, they will generally be so much influenced by their own preconceived beliefs—unless they are strictly on their guard against them—that what they perceive is something quite different from what they really see or hear to have happened. This is especially so if the occurrence surpasses the understanding of the narrator or listener, and in particular if it is to his interest that the event should come about in a certain way. In consequence, chronicles and histories reflect the writer's own beliefs rather than the actual facts, and one and the same occurrence is so differently related by two men holding different beliefs that they seem to be speaking of two different events, and there is often little difficulty in elucidating the beliefs of the chronicler and historian simply from their narratives.

In confirmation I could quote many examples both from writers of natural history and from chroniclers, did I not think it superfluous; but I will cite one example from Holy Scripture, leaving the reader to judge of the rest. In the time of Joshua, the Hebrews (as I have previously indicated) shared the common belief that the sun moves with a diurnal motion (as it is termed) and the earth is at rest, and to this preconceived belief they adapted the miracle that befell them in the battle against the five kings. They did not simply relate that the day in question was longer than usual; they said that the sun and moon stood still, ceasing from their motion. At that time this interpretation may have stood them in good stead in refuting the Gentiles who worshipped the sun, and in proving by actual experience that the sun was under the control of another deity, at whose bidding it must alter its natural course. So partly through piety and partly influenced by preconceived beliefs, they conceived and related this event quite differently from the way it could really have come about.

Therefore, to interpret Scriptural miracles and to understand from their accounts how they really took place, one must know the beliefs of those who originally related them and left us written records of them, and one must distinguish between these beliefs and what could have been presented to their senses. Otherwise we shall confuse their beliefs and judgments with the miracle as it really happened. And awareness of their beliefs is of further importance in avoiding confusion between what really happened and what was imagined and was no more than prophetic symbolism. For many things are related in Scripture as real, and were also believed to be real, but were nevertheless merely symbolical and imaginary; as that God, the supreme Being, came down from heaven (Exodus ch. 19 v. 18 and Deut. ch. 5 v. 19) and that Mount Sinai smoked because God descended upon it surrounded by fire, and that Elijah ascended to heaven in a chariot of fire and with horses of fire. All these were merely symbolical representations, adapted to the belief of those who have transmitted them to us as they were represented to them, that is, as actual happenings. All who have any smattering of education know that God does not have a right hand or a left hand, that he neither moves nor is at rest, nor is he in any particular place, but is absolutely infinite, and contains within himself all perfections. These truths, I say, are known by those whose judgment is formed from the perceptions of pure intellect, and not from the way the imagination is affected by their outward senses. This latter is the case with the masses, who therefore imagine God as corporeal, holding royal sway from his throne in the vault of heaven above the stars— which they believe to be at no great distance from the earth. Numerous occurrences in Scripture are adapted to these and similar beliefs, as we have pointed out, and therefore ought not to be accepted as real by philosophers.[2]

Finally, for the proper understanding of the reality of miracles, it is important to be acquainted with the diction and metaphors affected by the Hebrews. He who does not pay sufficient attention to this will ascribe to Scripture many miracles which Scriptural writers never intended as such, thus completely failing to understand not only events and miracles as they really happened but also the meaning of the writers of the Sacred Books. Thus Zechariah (ch. 14 v. 7), speaking about some future war, says, "It shall be one day known only to the Lord, (for it shall be) neither day nor night, but at evening time it shall be light." By these words he seems to be predicting a great miracle; yet his meaning is quite simply that the battle will be in balance throughout the whole day, its issue being known only to God, and that at evening time they will gain victory. For it was with expressions like these that the prophets used to predict and write of the victories and defeats of nations. Similarly, we see Isaiah (ch. 13) describing the destruction of Babylon in the following way, ". . . since the stars of heaven and the constellations thereof shall not give their light, the sun shall be darkened in his going forth, and the moon shall not cause her light to shine." Surely nobody, I imagine, believes that these things happened at the destruction of that empire, nor, as he goes on to add, ". . . therefore I will make the heavens to tremble, and the earth shall be removed from her place."

---

2. Maimonides, too, insists upon these points (Maimonides, *Guide*, Preface, Part 1, chapter 26).

Similarly Isaiah, in the penultimate verse of chapter 48, intending to convey to the Jews that they would return from Babylon to Jerusalem in safety and would not suffer from thirst on the journey, says, "And they thirsted not when he led them through the wilderness, he caused water to flow out of the rocks for them, he clave the rock and the waters flowed." By these words, I say, he means no more than that the Jews would find springs in the desert—as is not unusual—from which they would quench their thirst; for when the Jews returned to Jerusalem by Cyrus' consent, there is no record of any such miracles befalling them. In Holy Scripture we find many such passages which are simply modes of speech affected by the Jews. There is no need for me to review them all now in detail, but I should like only to make the general point that the Hebrews used to employ this style of speech not merely for rhetorical effect but also—and most of all—from motives of piety. It is for this reason that in Holy Scripture 'Bless God' is substituted for 'Curse God' (see 1 Kings ch. 21 v. 10 and Job ch. 2 v. 9); and for the same reason they referred everything to God, with the result that Scripture appears to be relating nothing but miracles even when it is speaking of the most natural things, as we have already illustrated with many examples. Therefore we should believe that when Scripture says that God hardened Pharaoh's heart, no more is meant than that Pharaoh was obstinate; when it is said that God opened the windows of heaven, this means no more than there was a heavy rainstorm, and so on. If we bear these points well in mind, and also reflect that many of the narratives are very brief, shorn of all detail and defective in many ways, we shall find practically nothing in Scripture that can be shown to contradict the light of Nature, whereas many passages which seemed very obscure we can understand and readily interpret with a little thought.

I think I have now demonstrated quite clearly what I had proposed to demonstrate. Nevertheless, before I bring this chapter to a close, there remains a further point to which I should like to draw attention, namely, that in here discussing miracles I have adopted a method very different from that employed in dealing with prophecy. In the matter of prophecy I made no assertion that I could not infer from grounds revealed in Holy Scripture, whereas in this chapter I have drawn my main conclusions solely from basic principles known by the natural light of reason. This procedure I have adopted deliberately because in dealing with prophecy, since it surpasses human understanding and is a purely theological question, revelation provided the only basis for making any assertion about it, or even for understanding its essential nature. So in the case of prophecy I had no alternative but to compile a historical account, and from that to formulate certain principles which would give me some degree of insight into the nature and properties of prophecy. But in the matter of miracles, since the object of our inquiry—namely, whether we can admit that something can happen in Nature which is contrary to her laws, or which could not follow therefrom—is plainly of a philosophical character, no such procedure was necessary. On the contrary, I deemed it the wiser course to attempt to solve this problem from basic principles known by the natural light, these being of all things best known to us. I say that I deemed it the wiser course, for I might also have solved this problem quite easily from the pronouncements and basic doctrines of Scripture alone. This I shall here briefly demonstrate, so that it may be clear to all.

In certain passages Scripture asserts of Nature in general that she observes a fixed and immutable order, as in Psalm 138 verse 6 and Jeremiah chapter 31 verses 35, 36. Furthermore, in Ecclesiastes chapter 1 verse 10 the Sage tells us quite clearly that nothing new happens in Nature, and in verses 11, 12 to illustrate this same point he says that although occasionally something may happen that seems new, it is not new, but has happened in ages past beyond recall. For, as he says, there is today no remembrance of things past, nor will there be remembrance of things today among those to come. Again, in chapter 3 verse 11 he says that God has ordered all things well for their time, and in verse 14 he says that he knows that whatever God does will endure forever, neither can anything be added to it nor taken away from it. All these passages clearly convey the teaching that Nature observes a fixed and immutable order, that God has been the same throughout all ages that are known or unknown to us, that the laws of Nature are so perfect and fruitful that nothing can be added or taken away from them, and that miracles seem something strange only because of man's ignorance.

These, then, are the express teachings of Scripture: nowhere does it say that something can happen in Nature that contravenes her laws or that cannot follow from her laws; so neither should we impute such a doctrine to Scripture. Then there is the further fact that miracles stand in need of causes and attendant circumstances (as we have already shown); they do not result from some kind of royal government which the masses attribute to God, but from the divine government and decree; that is (as we have also shown from Scripture), from Nature's laws and order. Finally, miracles can be wrought even by false prophets, as is proved from Deuteronomy chapter 13 and Matthew chapter 24 verse 24.

Hence it follows on the plainest evidence that miracles were natural occurrences, and therefore they should be explained in such a way that they seem to be neither 'new' things (to use Solomon's expression) nor things contrary to Nature, but things approximating as closely to natural occurrences as the facts allowed. To render this interpretation easier for everyone, I have set forth certain rules drawn only from Scripture. Nevertheless, although I say that this is Scripture's teaching, I do not mean to suggest that Scripture enjoins this teaching as something requisite for salvation; I mean only that the prophets take the same view as I. Therefore on these matters everyone is entitled to hold whatever view he feels will better bring him with sincere heart to the worship of God and to religion. This was also the opinion of Josephus, for towards the end of Book 2 of his *Antiquities*, he writes as follows: "Let no one baulk at the word miracle, if men of ancient times, unsophisticated as they were, see the road to safety open up through the sea, whether revealed by God's will or of its own accord. Those men, too, who accompanied Alexander, king of Macedon, men of much more recent times,[3] found the Pamphylian sea divide for them, offering a passage when there was no other way, it being God's will to destroy the Persian empire through him. This is admitted to be true by all who have written of Alexander's deeds. Therefore on these matters let everyone think as he will." Such are the words of Josephus, showing his attitude to belief in miracles.

---

3. Here the Latin "*olim et antiquitus a resistentibus*" is transcribed by Spinoza from Rufinus Aquileiensis (1475), whose translation of Josephus was found in Spinoza's library. As it stands, the passage makes no sense. Either the reading was corrupt, or Rufinus failed to understand the Greek idiom χθὲς καὶ πρώην γεγόνασιν. I have therefore translated this phrase from the Greek of Josephus.

CHAPTER 7

Of the Interpretation of Scripture

On every side we hear men saying that the Bible is the Word of God, teaching mankind true blessedness, or the path to salvation. But the facts are quite at variance with their words, for people in general seem to make no attempt whatsoever to live according to the Bible's teachings. We see that nearly all men parade their own ideas as God's Word, their chief aim being to compel others to think as they do, while using religion as a pretext. We see, I say, that the chief concern of theologians on the whole has been to extort from Holy Scripture their own arbitrarily invented ideas, for which they claim divine authority. In no other field do they display less scruple and greater temerity than in the interpretation of Scripture, the mind of the Holy Spirit, and if while so doing they feel any misgivings, their fear is not that they may be mistaken in their understanding of the Holy Spirit and may stray from the path to salvation, but that others may convict them of error, thus annihilating their personal prestige and bringing them into contempt.

Now if men were really sincere in what they profess with regard to Holy Scripture, they would conduct themselves quite differently; they would not be racked by so much quarrelling and such bitter feuding, and they would not be gripped by this blind and passionate desire to interpret Scripture and to introduce innovations in religion. On the contrary, they would never venture to accept as Scriptural doctrine what was not most clearly taught by Scripture itself. And finally, those sacrilegious persons who have had the hardihood to alter Scripture in several places would have been horrified at the enormity of the crime and would have stayed their impious hands. But ambition and iniquity have reached such a pitch that religion takes the form not so much of obedience to the teachings of the Holy Spirit as of defending what men have invented. Indeed, religion is manifested not in charity but in spreading contention among men and in fostering the bitterest hatred, under the false guise of zeal in God's cause and a burning enthusiasm. To these evils is added superstition, which teaches men to despise reason and Nature, and to admire and venerate only that which is opposed to both. It is therefore not surprising that, to make Scripture appear more wonderful and awe-inspiring, they endeavour to explicate it in such a way that is seems diametrically opposed both to reason and to Nature. So they imagine that the most profound mysteries lie hidden in the Bible, and they exhaust themselves in unravelling these absurdities while ignoring other things of value. They ascribe to the Holy Spirit whatever their wild fancies have invented, and devote their utmost strength and enthusiasm to defending it. For human nature is so constituted that what men conceive by pure intellect, they defend only by intellect and reason, whereas the beliefs that spring from the emotions are emotionally defended.

In order to escape from this scene of confusion, to free our minds from the prejudices of theologians and to avoid the hasty acceptance of human fabrications as divine teachings, we must discuss the true method of Scriptural interpretation and examine it in depth; for unless we understand this we cannot know with any certainty what the Bible or the Holy Spirit intends to teach. Now to put it briefly, I hold that the method of interpreting Scripture is no different from the method of interpreting Nature, and is in fact in complete accord with it. For the method of interpreting Nature consists essentially in composing a detailed study of Nature from which, as being the source of our assured data, we can deduce the definitions of the things of Nature. Now in exactly the same way the task of Scriptural interpretation requires us to make a straightforward study of Scripture, and from this, as the source of our fixed data and principles, to deduce by logical inference the meaning of the authors of Scripture. In this way—that is, by allowing no other principles or data for the interpretation of Scripture and study of its contents except those that can be gathered only from Scripture itself and from a historical study of Scripture—steady progress can be made without any danger of error, and one can deal with matters that surpass our understanding with no less confidence than those matters which are known to us by the natural light of reason.

But to establish clearly that this is not merely a sure way, but the only way open to us, and that it accords with the method of interpreting Nature, it should be observed that Scripture frequently treats of matters that cannot be deduced from principles known by the natural light; for it is chiefly made up of historical narratives and revelation. Now an important feature of the historical narratives is the appearance of miracles; that is, as we showed in the previous chapter, stories of unusual occurrences in Nature, adapted to the beliefs and judgment of the historians who recorded them. The revelations, too, were adapted to the beliefs of the prophets, as we showed in chapter 2; and these do, indeed, surpass human understanding. Therefore knowledge of all these things—that is, of almost all the contents of Scripture—must be sought from Scripture alone, just as knowledge of Nature must be sought from Nature itself.

As for the moral doctrines that are also contained in the Bible, although these themselves can be demonstrated from accepted axioms, it cannot be

proved from such axioms that Scripture teaches these doctrines: this can
be established only from Scripture itself. Indeed, if we want to testify,
without any prejudgment, to the divinity of Scripture, it must be made
evident to us from Scripture alone that it teaches true moral doctrine; for
it is on this basis alone that its divinity can be proved. We have shown that
the chief characteristic which established the certainty of the prophets was
that their minds were directed to what was right and good; hence this must
be made evident to us, too, before we can have faith in them. We have
already shown that miracles can never give proof of God's divinity, apart
from the fact that they could be wrought even by a false prophet. Therefore the divinity of Scripture must be established solely from the fact that
it teaches true virtue. Now this can be established only from Scripture. If
this could not be done, our acceptance of Scripture and our witness to its
divinity would argue great prejudice on our part. Therefore all knowledge
of Scripture must be sought from Scripture alone.

Finally, Scripture does not provide us with definitions of the things of
which it speaks, any more than Nature does. Therefore, just as definitions
of the things of Nature must be inferred from the various operations of
Nature, in the same way definitions must be elicited from the various
Biblical narratives as they touch on a particular subject. This, then, is the
universal rule for the interpretation of Scripture, to ascribe no teaching to
Scripture that is not clearly established from studying it closely. What
kind of study this should be, and what are the chief topics it should
include, must now be explained.

1. It should inform us of the nature and properties of the language in
which the Bible was written and which its authors were accustomed to
speak. Thus we should be able to investigate, from established linguistic
usage, all the possible meanings of any passage. And since all the writers of
both the Old and the New Testaments were Hebrews, a study of the
Hebrew language must undoubtedly be a prime requisite not only for an
understanding of the books of the Old Testament, which were written in
that language, but also for the New Testament. For although the latter
books were published in other languages, their idiom is Hebraic.

2. The pronouncements made in each book should be assembled and
listed under headings, so that we can thus have to hand all the texts that
treat of the same subject. Next, we should note all those that are ambiguous or obscure, or that appear to contradict one another. Now here I term
a pronouncement obscure or clear according to the degree of difficulty
with which the meaning can be elicited from the context, and not according to the degree of difficulty with which its truth can be perceived by
reason. For the point at issue is merely the meaning of the texts, not their
truth. I would go further: in seeking the meaning of Scripture we should

take every precaution against the undue influence, not only of our own prejudices, but of our faculty of reason insofar as that is based on the principles of natural cognition. In order to avoid confusion between true meaning and truth of fact, the former must be sought simply from linguistic usage, or from a process of reasoning that looks to no other basis than Scripture.

For further clarification, I shall give an example to illustrate all that I have here said. The sayings of Moses, "God is fire," and "God is jealous," are perfectly clear as long as we attend only to the meanings of the words; and so, in spite of their obscurity from the perspective of truth and reason, I classify these sayings as clear. Indeed, even though their literal meaning is opposed to the natural light of reason, this literal meaning must nevertheless be retained unless it is in clear opposition to the basic principles derived from the study of Scripture. On the other hand, if these statements in their literal interpretation were found to be in contradiction with the basic principles derived from Scripture, they would have to be interpreted differently (that is, metaphorically) even though they were in complete agreement with reason. Therefore the question as to whether Moses did or did not believe that God is fire must in no wise be decided by the rationality or irrationality of the belief, but solely from other pronouncements of Moses. In this particular case, since there are several other instances where Moses clearly tells us that God has no resemblance to visible things in heaven or on the earth or in the water, we must hence conclude that either this statement or all those others must be explained metaphorically. Now since one should depart as little as possible from the literal meaning, we should first enquire whether this single pronouncement, 'God is fire,' admits of any other than a literal meaning; that is, whether the word 'fire' can mean anything other than ordinary natural fire. If the word 'fire' is not found from linguistic usage to have any other meaning, then neither should this statement be interpreted in any other way, however much it is opposed to reason, and all other passages should be made to conform with it, however much they accord with reason. If this, too, should prove impossible on the basis of linguistic usage, then these pronouncements would have to be regarded as irreconcilable, and we should therefore suspend judgment regarding them. However, since the word 'fire' is also used in the sense of anger or jealousy (Job ch. 31 v. 12), Moses' pronouncements are easily reconciled, and we can properly conclude that these two statements, 'God is fire' and 'God is jealous' are one and the same statement.

Again, as Moses clearly teaches that God is jealous and nowhere tells us that God is without passions or emotions, we must evidently conclude that Moses believed this, or at least that he intended to teach this, however strongly we may be convinced that this opinion is contrary to reason. For, as we have shown, it is not permissible for us to manipulate Scripture's meaning to accord with our reason's dictates and our preconceived opinions; all knowledge of the Bible is to be sought from the Bible alone.

3. Finally, our historical study should set forth the circumstances relevant to all the extant books of the prophets, giving the life, character and pursuits of the author of every book, detailing who he was, on what occasion and at what time and for whom and in what language he wrote. Again, it should relate what happened to each book, how it was first received, into whose hands it fell, how many variant versions there were, by whose decision it was received into the canon, and, finally, how all the books, now universally regarded as sacred, were united into a single whole. All these details, I repeat, should be available from a historical study of Scripture; for in order to know which pronouncements were set forth as laws and which as moral teaching, it is important to be acquainted with the life, character and interests of the author. Furthermore, as we have a better understanding of a person's character and temperament, so we can more easily explain his words. Again, to avoid confusing teachings of eternal significance with those which are of only temporary significance or directed only to the benefit of a few, it is also important to know on what occasion, at what period, and for what nation or age all these teachings were written down. Finally, it is important to know the other details we have listed so that, in addition to the authenticity of each book, we may also discover whether or not it may have been contaminated by spurious insertions, whether errors have crept in, and whether these have been corrected by experienced and trustworthy scholars. All this information is needed by us so that we may accept only what is certain and incontrovertible, and not be led by blind impetuosity to take for granted whatever is set before us.

Now when we possess this historical account of Scripture and are firmly resolved not to assert as the indubitable doctrine of the prophets anything that does not follow from this study or cannot be most clearly inferred from it, it will then be time to embark on the task of investigating the meaning of the prophets and the Holy Spirit. But for this task, too, we need a method and order similar to that which we employ in interpreting Nature from the facts presented before us. Now in examining natural phenomena we first of all try to discover those features that are most universal and common to the whole of Nature, to wit, motion-and-rest and the rules and laws governing them which Nature always observes and through which she constantly acts; and then we advance gradually from these to other less universal features. In just the same way we must first seek from our study of Scripture that which is most universal and forms the basis and foundation of all Scripture; in short, that which is commended in Scripture by all the prophets as doctrine eternal and most profitable for all mankind. For example, that God exists, one alone and omnipotent, who alone should be worshipped, who cares for all, who loves above all others those who worship him and love their neighbours as themselves. These and similar doctrines, I repeat, are taught everywhere in Scripture so clearly and explicitly that no one has ever been in any doubt as to its meaning on these points. But what God is, in what way he sees and provides for all things and similar matters, Scripture does not teach formally, and as eternal doctrine. On the contrary, we have clearly shown that the prophets themselves were not in agreement on these matters, and therefore on topics of this kind we should make no assertion that claims to be the doctrine of the Holy Spirit, even though the natural light of reason may be quite decisive on that point.

Having acquired a proper understanding of this universal doctrine of Scripture, we must then proceed to other matters which are of less universal import but affect our ordinary daily life, and which flow from the universal doctrine like rivulets from their source. Such are all the specific external actions of true virtue which need a particular occasion for their exercise. If there be found in Scripture anything ambiguous or obscure regarding such matters, it must be explained and decided on the basis of the universal doctrine of Scripture. If any passages are found to be in contradiction with one another, we should consider on what occasion, at what time, and for whom they were written. For example, when Christ says, "Blessed are they that mourn, for they shall be comforted," we do not know from this text what kind of mourners are meant. But as Christ thereafter teaches that we should take thought for nothing save only the kingdom of God and His righteousness, which he commends as the highest good (Matth. ch. 6 v. 33), it follows that by mourners he means only those who mourn for man's disregard of the kingdom of God and His righteousness; for only this can be the cause of mourning for those who love nothing but the kingdom of God, or justice, and utterly despise whatever else fortune has to offer.

So, too, when Christ says, "But if a man strike you on the right cheek, turn to him the left also" and the words that follow, if he were laying this command on judges in the role of lawgiver, this precept would have violated the law of Moses. But he expressly warns against this (Matth. ch. 5 v. 17). Therefore we should consider who said this, to whom, and at what time. This was said by Christ, who was not ordaining laws as a lawgiver, but was expounding his teachings as a teacher, because (as we have already shown) he was intent on improving men's minds rather than their external actions. Further, he spoke these words to men suffering under oppression, living in a corrupt commonwealth where justice was utterly disregarded, a commonwealth whose ruin he saw to be imminent. Now we see that this very same teaching, which Christ here expounds when the ruin of the city was imminent, was also given by Jeremiah in similar circumstances at the first destruction of the city (Lamentations ch. 3 v. 30). Thus it was only at the time of oppression that the prophets taught this doctrine which was nowhere set forth as law; whereas Moses (who did not write at a time of oppression, but—please note—was concerned to found a good common-wealth), although he likewise condemned revenge and hatred against one's neighbour, yet demanded an eye for an eye. Therefore it clearly follows simply on Scriptural grounds that this teaching of Christ and Jeremiah concerning the toleration of injury and total submission to the wicked applies only in situations where justice is disregarded and at times of oppression, but not in a good commonwealth. Indeed, in a good common-wealth where justice is upheld, everyone who wants to be accounted as just has the duty to go before a judge and demand justice for wrongdoing (Lev. ch. 5 v. 1), not out of revenge (Lev. ch. 19 v. 17, 18), but with the purpose of upholding justice and the laws of his country, and to prevent the wicked from rejoicing in their wickedness. All this is plainly in accord with the natural reason. I could produce many more similar examples, but I think this is sufficient to explain my meaning and the usefulness of this method, which is my only object at present.

Now up to this point we have confined our investigation to those Scriptural pronouncements which are concerned with moral conduct, and which can be the more easily elucidated because on such subjects there has never been any real difference of opinion among the writers of the Bible. But other biblical passages which belong only to the field of philosophical speculation do not yield so easily to investigation. The approach is more difficult, for the prophets differed among themselves in matters of philo-sophical speculation (as we have already shown) and their narratives con-form especially to the prejudices of their particular age. So we are debarred from deducing and explaining the meaning of one prophet from some clearer passages in another, unless it is most plainly established that they were of one and the same mind. I shall therefore briefly explain how in such cases we should elicit the meaning of the prophets from the study of Scripture. Here, again, we must begin from considerations of a most general kind, first of all seeking to establish from the clearest Scriptural pronouncements what is prophecy or revelation and what is its essential nature; then what is a miracle, and so on with other subjects of a most general nature. Thereafter we must move on to the beliefs of individual prophets, and from there finally to the meaning of each particular revela-tion or prophecy, narrative and miracle. We have already pointed out with many apposite examples what great caution we should exercise in these matters to avoid confusing the minds of the prophets and historians with the mind of the Holy Spirit and with factual truth, and so I do not think it necessary to say any more on this subject. But with regard to the meaning of revelation, it should be observed that this method only teaches us how to discover what the prophets really saw or heard, and not what they intended to signify or represent by the symbols in questions. The latter we can only guess at, not infer with certainty from the basis of Scripture.

We have thus set out our plan for interpreting Scripture, at the same time demonstrating that this is the only sure road to the discovery of its true meaning. I do indeed admit that those are better informed (if there are any) who are in possession of a sure tradition or true explanation transmitted from the prophets themselves, as the Pharisees claim, or those who have a pontiff whose interpretation of Scripture is infallible, as the Roman Catholics boast. However, as we cannot be sure either of the tradition in question or of the authority of the pontiff, we cannot base any certain conclusion on them. The latter is denied by the earliest Christians, the former by the most ancient sects of the Jews; and if, furthermore, we examine the succession of years (to mention nothing else) through which this tradition is traced right back to Moses, which the Pharisees have accepted from their Rabbis, we shall find that it is incorrect, as I prove elsewhere. Therefore such a tradition should be regarded with the utmost suspicion; and although our method requires us to accept as uncorrupted a certain tradition of the Jews—namely, the meaning of the words of the Hebrew language, which we have accepted from them—we can be quite sure of the one while doubting the other. For while it may occasionally have been in someone's interest to alter the meaning of some passage, it could never have been to anyone's interest to change the meaning of a word. Indeed, this is very difficult to accomplish, for whoever would try to change the meaning of a word would also have to explain all the writers who wrote in that language and used that word in its accepted meaning, in each case taking account of the character or intention of the writer; or else he would have to falsify the text, a task requiring much circumspection. Then again, a language is preserved by the learned and unlearned alike, whereas books and the meaning of their contents are preserved only by the learned. Therefore we can readily conceive that the learned may have altered or corrupted the meaning of some passage in a rare book which they had in their possession, but not the meaning of words. Besides which, if anyone should wish to change the customary meaning of a word, he would find it difficult to maintain consistency thereafter both in his writing and in his speaking.

For these and other reasons we may readily assume that it could never have entered anyone's mind to corrupt a language, whereas there may frequently have been an intention to corrupt the meaning of a writer by altering what he wrote or by giving it a wrong interpretation. Therefore, since our method (based on the principle that knowledge of Scripture must be sought only from Scripture) is the only true method, if there is anything that it cannot achieve for us in our pursuit of a complete understanding of Scripture, we must regard this as quite unattainable.

At this point I have to discuss any difficulties and shortcomings in our method which may stand in the way of our acquiring a complete and assured knowledge of the Holy Bible. The first important difficulty in our method is this, that it demands a thorough knowledge of the Hebrew language. Where is this now to be obtained? The men of old who used the Hebrew language have left to posterity no information concerning the basic principles and study of this language. At any rate, we possess nothing at all from them, neither dictionary nor grammar nor textbook on rhetoric. The Hebrew nation has lost all its arts and embellishments (little wonder, in view of the disasters and persecutions it has suffered) and has retained only a few remnants of its language and of its books, few in number. Nearly all the words for fruits, birds, fishes have perished with the passage of time, together with numerous other words. Then again, the meanings of many nouns and verbs occurring in the Bible are either completely unknown or subject to dispute. We are deprived not only of these, but more especially of the knowledge of Hebrew phraseology. The idiom and modes of speech peculiar to the Hebrew nation have almost all been consigned to oblivion by the ravages of time. So we cannot always discover to our satisfaction all the possible meanings which a particular passage can yield from linguistic usage; and there are many passages where the sense is very obscure and quite incomprehensible although the component words have a clearly established meaning.

Besides our inability to present a complete account of the Hebrew language, there is the further problem presented by the composition and nature of that language. This gives rise to so many ambiguities as to render it impossible to devise a method* that can teach us with certainty how to discover the true meaning of all Scriptural passages; for apart from the sources of ambiguity that are common to all languages, there are others peculiar to Hebrew which give rise to many ambiguities. These I think it worth listing here.

First, ambiguity and obscurity in the Bible are often caused by the fact that letters involving the same organ of speech are substituted one for

---

* See Supplementary Note 7.

another. The Hebrews divide all letters of the alphabet into five classes in accordance with the five oral instruments employed in their pronunciation, namely, the lips, the tongue, the teeth, the palate and the throat. For example, ה, ע, ח, א *alef, ḥet, 'ayin, hē* are called gutturals, and are used one in place of another without any distinction apparent to us. For instance, אל *el*, which means 'to', is often used for על *'al*, which means 'above', and vice-versa. As a result, any parts of a text may often be rendered ambiguous or appear to be meaningless utterances.

A second ambiguity arises from the multiple meanings of conjunctions and adverbs. For example, ו *vav* serves indiscriminately to join and to separate, and can mean 'and', 'but', 'because', 'however' and 'then'. כי *ki* has seven or eight meanings: 'because', 'although', 'if', 'when', 'just as', 'that', 'a burning' and so on. This is the case with almost all particles.

Thirdly—and the source of many ambiguities—verbs in the Indicative mood lack the Present, the Past Imperfect, the Pluperfect and the Future Perfect, and other tenses in common use in other languages. In the Imperative and Infinitive moods verbs lack all the tenses except the Present, and in the Subjunctive there are no tenses at all. And although all the tenses and moods thus lacking could have been supplied, with ease and even with great elegance, by definite rules deduced from the fundamental principles of language, the writers of old showed complete disregard for such rules, and indiscriminately used Future for Present and Past, and contrariwise Past for Future, and furthermore used Indicative for Imperative and Subjunctive, to the great detriment of clarity.

Besides these three sources of ambiguity in Hebrew there remain two more to be noted, both of which are of far greater importance. First, the Hebrews do not have letters for vowels. Secondly, it was not their custom to punctuate their texts, nor to give them force or emphasis; and although vowels and punctuation thus lacking are usually supplied by points and accents, these cannot satisfy us, having been devised and instituted by men of a later age whose authority should carry no weight with us. The ancient writers did not employ points (that is, vowels and accents), as is abundantly testified; men of later ages added both of these in accordance with their own interpretation of the Bible. Therefore the accents and points that we now have are merely contemporary interpretations, and deserve no more credibility and authority than other commentaries. Those who fail to realise this do not understand the justification of the author of the Epistle to the Hebrews (ch. 11 v. 21) in giving an interpretation of the text of Genesis ch. 47 v. 31 very different from that of the pointed Hebrew text— as if the Apostle ought to have been taught the meaning of Scripture by those who inserted points! In my opinion it is the latter who should be regarded as at fault. To make this clear to all, and to show how different interpretations arise simply from the absence of vowels, I shall here set down both interpretations.

Those who inserted the points interpreted the passage as follows: 'and to Israel bent over (or, changing ע *'ayin* into א *alef*, a letter of the same organ, towards) the head of the bed.' The author of the Epistle reads 'and Israel bent over the head of his staff,' reading 'mate' for '*mita*', the only difference being in the vowels. Now since in this part of the story there is only a question of Jacob's age, and not of his illness which is mentioned in the next chapter, it seems more probable that the historian intended to say that Jacob bent over the head of his staff (which men of advanced age employ to support themselves), not of the bed; and this is especially so because this interpretation does not require the substitution of one letter for another. Now my purpose in giving this example is not only to harmonise the passage in the Epistle to the Hebrews with the text of Genesis, but also to show how little confidence is to be placed in modern points and accents. Thus he who would interpret Scripture without any prejudice is in duty bound to hold these in doubt and to examine them afresh.

To return to our theme, such being the structure and nature of the Hebrew language, it is quite understandable that such a number of ambiguities must arise that no method can be devised for deciding them all. For we have no grounds for expecting that this can be completely achieved from a comparison of different passages, which we have shown to be the only way to elicit the true meaning from the many senses which a particular passage can yield with linguistic justification. It is only by chance that a comparison of passages can throw light on any particular passage, since no prophets wrote with the deliberate purpose of explaining another's words, or his own. And furthermore, we can draw no conclusion as to the meaning of one prophet or apostle from the meaning of another except in matters of moral conduct, as we have already convincingly demonstrated; no such conclusions can be drawn when they are dealing with philosophical questions, or are narrating miracles or history. I could bring further examples to prove this point, that there are many inexplicable passages in Scripture; but I prefer to leave this subject for the present, and I shall proceed to a consideration of the points that still remain: the further difficulties we encounter in this true method of Scriptural interpretation, or in what way it falls short.

One further difficulty consequent upon this method is this, that it requires an account of the history of all the biblical books, and this for the most part we cannot provide. As I shall make clear at some length at a later stage, we either have no knowledge at all or but doubtful knowledge of the authors—or if you prefer the expression, the writers—of many of the books. Again, we do not even know on what occasion or at what time these books of unknown authorship were written. Furthermore, we do not know into whose hands all these books fell, or in whose copies so many different readings were found, nor yet again whether there were not many other versions in other hands. When I touched on this topic I did make a brief reference to the importance of knowing all these details, but there I deliberately passed over certain considerations which must now be taken up.

If we read a book relating events which are incredible or incomprehensible, or which is written in a very obscure style, and if we do not know the author or the time or the occasion of its composition, it well be vain for us to try to achieve a greater understanding of its true meaning. Deprived of all these facts we cannot possibly know what was, or could have been, the author's intention. But if we are fully informed of these facts, we are in a position to form an opinion free from all danger of mistaken assumptions; that is to say, we ascribe to the author, or to him for whom he wrote, no more and no less than his just meaning, concentrating our attention on what the author could have had in mind, or what the time and the occasion demanded. I imagine that everyone is agreed on this; for it often happens that we read in different books stories that are much alike, and form very different judgments of them according to our opinions of the writers. I remember once having read a book about a man named Orlando Furioso who used to ride a winged monster in the sky, fly over any regions he chose and singlehanded slay huge numbers of men and giants, together with other similar fantastic happenings which are quite incomprehensible in respect to our intellect. Now I had read a similar story in Ovid about Perseus, and another story in the books of Judges and Kings about Samson, who singlehanded and unarmed slew thousands of men, and of Elijah, who flew through the air and finally went to heaven in a chariot and horses of fire. These stories, I repeat, are obviously similar, yet we form a very different judgment of each. The first writer was concerned only to amuse, the second had a political motive, the third a religious motive, and it is nothing else but our opinion of the writers that brings us to make these judgments. It is therefore evident that in the case of obscure or incomprehensible writings, it is essential for us to have some knowledge of the authors if we seek to interpret their writings. And for the same reasons, to choose the correct reading out of the various readings of unclear narratives, we have to know in whose manuscript these different readings are found, and whether there were ever some other versions supported by men of greater authority.

In the case of certain books of the Bible, our method of interpretation involves the further difficulty that we do not possess them in the language in which they were first written. The Gospel according to Matthew and undoubtedly the Epistle to the Hebrews were written in Hebrew, it is commonly held, but are not extant in that form. There is some doubt as to the language in which the Book of Job was written. Ibn Ezra, in his commentaries, asserts that it was translated into Hebrew from another language, and that this is the reason for its obscurity. I say nothing of the apocryphal books, since their authority is of a very different kind.

Such then, is a full account of the difficulties involved in this method of interpreting Scripture from its own history, such as we possess. These difficulties, which I undertook to recount, I consider so grave that I have no hesitation in affirming that in many instances we either do not know the true meaning of Scripture or we can do no more than make conjecture. But on the other hand I must again emphasise, with regard to all these difficulties, that they can prevent us from grasping the meaning of the prophets only in matters beyond normal comprehension, which can merely be imagined; it is not true of matters open to intellectual perception, whereof we can readily form a clear conception.* For things which of their own nature are readily apprehended can never be so obscurely worded that they are not easily understood; as the proverb says, 'a word to the wise is enough.' Euclid, whose writings are concerned only with things exceedingly simple and perfectly intelligible, is easily made clear by anyone in any language; for in order to grasp his thought and to be assured of his true meaning there is no need to have a thorough knowledge of the language in which he wrote. A superficial and rudimentary knowledge is enough. Nor need we enquire into the author's life, pursuits and character, the language in which he wrote, and for whom and when, nor what happened to his book, nor its different readings, nor how it came to be accepted and by what council. And what we here say of Euclid can be said of all who have written on matters which of their very nature are capable of intellectual apprehension.

Thus we can conclude that, with the help of such a historical study of Scripture as is available to us, we can readily grasp the meanings of its moral doctrines and be certain of their true sense. For the teachings of true piety are expressed in quite ordinary language, and being directed to the generality of people they are therefore straightforward and easy to understand. And since true salvation and blessedness consist in true contentment of mind and we find our true peace only in what we clearly understand, it most evidently follows that we can understand the meaning of Scripture with confidence in matters relating to salvation and necessary to blessedness. Therefore we have no reason to be unduly anxious con-

* See Supplementary Note 8.

cerning the other contents of Scripture; for since for the most part they are beyond the grasp of reason and intellect, they belong to the sphere of the curious rather than the profitable.

I consider that I have now displayed the true method of Scriptural interpretation and have sufficiently set forth my opinion on this matter. Furthermore, I have no doubt that it is now obvious to all that this method demands no other light than the natural light of reason. For the nature and virtue of that light consists essentially in this, that by a process of logical deduction that which is hidden is inferred and concluded from what is known, or given as known. This is exactly what our method requires. And although we grant that our method does not suffice to explain with certainty everything that is found in the Bible, this is the consequence not of the defectiveness of the method but of the fact that the path which it tells us is the true and correct one has never been pursued nor trodden by men, and so with the passage of time has become exceedingly difficult and almost impassable. This I imagine is quite clear from the very difficulties I have recounted.

It now remains for me to examine the views of those who disagree with me. The first to be considered is held by those who maintain that the natural light of reason does not have the power to interpret Scripture, and that a supernatural light is absolutely essential for this task. What they mean by this light that is beyond the natural light I leave them to explain. For my own part, I can only surmise that they wish to admit, using rather obscure terminology, that they too are for the most part in doubt as to the true meaning of Scripture; for if we consider their explanations, we find that they contain nothing of the supernatural—indeed, nothing but the merest conjectures. Let them be compared if you please, with the explanations of those who frankly admit that they possess no other light but the natural light. They will be found to be remarkably similar; that is to say, their explanations are human, the fruit of long thought, and elaborately devised. As to their assertions that the natural light is insufficient for this task, that is plainly false, for two reasons. In the first place, we have already proved that the difficulty of interpreting Scripture arises not from the lack of power of the natural light, but from the negligence (not to say malice) of those who failed to compile a historical study of Scripture while that was still possible. Secondly, everyone will admit, I imagine, that this supernatural light is a divine gift granted only to the faithful. Now the prophets and the apostles preached not only to the faithful, but especially to unbelievers and the impious. So their audiences must have been capable of understanding the meaning of the prophets and the apostles; otherwise these latter would have appeared to be preaching to children and babies, not to men endowed with reason. Moses, too, would have ordained his laws in vain if they could have been understood only by the faithful, who stand in no need of law. Therefore those who look to a supernatural light to understand the meaning of the prophets and the apostles are sadly in need of the natural light; and so I can hardly think that such men possess a divine supernatural gift.

Maimonides took a quite different view; for he held that every passage of Scripture admits of various—and even contrary—meanings, and that we cannot be certain of the true meaning of any passage unless we know that, as we interpret it, there is nothing in that passage that is not in agreement with reason, or is contrary to reason. If in its literal sense it is found to be contrary to reason, then however clear the passage may appear, he maintains that it must be interpreted in a different way. This view he sets out most clearly in chapter 25 of part 2 of his book '*More Nebuchim*,'[1] where he says: "Know that it is not the Scriptural texts concerning the creation of the world that withholds me from saying that the world has existed from eternity. The texts that teach that the world was created are not more numerous than those that teach that God is corporeal. There are ways, not barred to us, nor even difficult of access, by which we can explain those texts that deal with the question of the world's creation. Our explanation could have followed the same lines as when we denied corporeality of God; and perhaps this might have been much easier to achieve, and we might have explained the texts and established the eternity of the world more plausibly than when we explained Scripture in a way that removed the notion of corporeality from God, blessed be He. Yet there are two reasons that prevent me from so doing and from believing that the world is eternal. First, there is clear proof that God is not corporeal, and it is necessary to explain all those passages whose literal meaning is contrary to that proof; for it is certain that they must then have an explanation other than the literal. But the eternity of the world has not been proved; so it is not necessary to do violence to the Scriptural texts and explain them away merely because of a plausible opinion, when we might incline to a contrary opinion with some degree of reason. Secondly, the belief that God is incorporeal is not contrary to the basic tenets of the Law, whereas the belief that the world is eternal, in the way that Aristotle held, destroys the very foundations of the Law."

Such are the words of Maimonides, and they clearly confirm what we said above. For if he had been convinced on rational grounds that the world is eternal, he would not have hesitated to distort and explain away

1. The title of the book that Spinoza cites is the Hebrew title for Maimonides' *Guide of the Perplexed.*

Scripture until it appeared to teach the same doctrine. Indeed, he would have been quite convinced that Scripture, in spite of its plain denials at every point, intended to teach this same doctrine of the eternity of the world. So he cannot be sure of the true meaning of Scripture, however clearly stated, as long as he can doubt the truth of what it says, or as long as he is not convinced of it. For as long as we are not convinced of the truth of a statement, we cannot know whether it is in conformity with reason or contrary to it, and consequently neither can we know whether the literal meaning is true or false.

If this view were correct, I would unreservedly concede that we need a light other than the natural light to interpret Scripture; for nearly all the contents of Scripture are such as cannot be deduced from principles known by the natural light, as we have already shown. Thus the natural light does not enable us to reach any decisions as to their truth, nor therefore as to the true sense and meaning of Scripture. For this purpose we should necessarily need another kind of light. Then again, if this view were correct, it would follow that the common people, for the most part knowing nothing of logical reasoning or without leisure for it, would have to rely solely on the authority and testimony of philosophers for their understanding of Scripture, and would therefore have to assume that philosophers are infallible in their interpretations of Scripture. This would indeed be a novel form of ecclesiastical authority, with very strange priests or pontiffs, more likely to excite men's ridicule than veneration. And although our own method demands a knowledge of Hebrew, for which study the common people can likewise have no leisure, it is not open to the same sort of objection. The common people of the Jews and Gentiles for whom the prophets and apostles once preached and wrote, understood the language of the prophets and apostles and thereby they also comprehended the meaning of the prophets, but without understanding the rational justification of the prophets' message. Yet, according to Maimonides, this understanding was also necessary if they were to grasp the meaning of the prophets. There is nothing, then, in our method that requires the common people to abide by the testimony of biblical commentators, for I can point to a people who were familiar with the language of the prophets and apostles. But Maimonides cannot point to a people capable of understanding the causes of things, which would be a necessary basis for understanding the meaning of the prophets. And as to the common people of our own time, we have already shown that whatsoever is necessary for salvation, even though its rational justification be not understood, can be readily grasped in any language, because it is couched in ordinary and familiar terms; and it is this understanding, not the testimony of biblical commentators, that gains acceptance with the common people. And as for the rest of Scripture, the common people are on the same footing as the learned.

But let us return to the view put forward by Maimonides, and examine it more closely. In the first place, he assumes that the prophets were in agreement on all matters, and that they were outstanding philosophers and theologians; for he holds that they based their conclusions on scientific truth. But in chapter 2 we have shown that this is not so. Then again, he assumes that the meaning of Scripture cannot be established from Scripture itself. For scientific truth is not established from Scripture itself, which does not engage in demonstrations and does not validate its teaching by appealing to definitions and first causes. And therefore, according to Maimonides, neither can Scripture's true meaning be established from itself, and should not be sought from it. But it is evident from this chapter that this point, too, is false. We have demonstrated both by reasoning and by examples that the meaning of Scripture is established from Scripture alone, and should be sought only from Scripture even when it is speaking of matters known by the natural light of reason. Finally, he assumes that it is legitimate for us to explain away and distort the words of Scripture to accord with our preconceived opinions, to deny its literal meaning and change it into something else even when it is perfectly plain and absolutely clear. Such licence, apart from being diametrically opposed to the proofs advanced in this chapter and elsewhere, must strike everyone as excessive and rash.

However, granting him this considerable degree of liberty, what in the end can it effect? Assuredly, nothing whatsoever. Those things that are not subject to proof and which make up the greater part of Scripture cannot yield to an enquiry of this sort, nor be explained or interpreted according to this rule; whereas by pursuing our method we can explain many things of this kind and investigate them with confidence, as we have already shown both by reason and by concrete example. And in the case of things that are by their nature comprehensible, their meaning can easily be elicited merely from their context, as we have also shown. Thus this method of Maimonides is plainly of no value. Furthermore, he clearly deprives the common people of any confidence they can have in the meaning of Scripture derived from simply perusing it; and yet this confidence is available to all by pursuing a different method. Therefore we can dismiss Maimonides' view as harmful, unprofitable and absurd.

As to the tradition of the Pharisees, we have already declared that it lacks consistency, while the authority of the Popes of Rome stands in need of clearer evidence. This is my only reason for impugning the latter, for if they could prove it from Scripture itself with the same degree of certainty as did the Jewish High Priests of long ago, I should not be influenced by the fact that among the Popes there have been found heretics and impious men. Among the Hebrew High Priests, too, in the past were found heretics and impious men, who gained the priesthood by underhanded means; and yet by Scriptural sanction they possessed the supreme power to interpret the Law. See Deut. ch. 17 v. 11, 12 and ch. 33 v. 10, and Malachi ch. 2 v. 8. But since the Popes can produce no such evidence, their authority remains highly suspect. The example of the Jewish High Priest ought not to deceive one into thinking that the Catholic religion also stands in need of a high priest; for it should be noted that the laws of Moses, being his country's civil laws, necessarily stood in need of some public authority to uphold them. If every man were free to interpret the civil laws as he chose, no state could survive; by that very fact it would be instantly dissolved, and public right would become private right.

Now with religion the case is quite different. Since it consists in honesty and sincerity of heart rather than in outward actions, it does not pertain to the sphere of public law and authority. Honesty and sincerity of heart is not imposed on man by legal command or by the state's authority. It is an absolute fact that nobody can be constrained to a state of blessedness by force or law; to this end one needs godly and brotherly exhortation, a good upbringing, and most of all, a judgment that is independent and free.

Therefore, as the sovereign right to free opinion belongs to every man even in matters of religion, and it is inconceivable that any man can surrender this right, there also belongs to every man the sovereign right and supreme authority to judge freely with regard to religion, and consequently to explain it and interpret it for himself. The supreme authority to interpret laws and the supreme judgment on affairs of state is vested in magistrates for this reason only, that these belong to the sphere of public right. Thus for the same reason the supreme authority to explain religion and to make judgment concerning it is vested in each individual, because it belongs to the sphere of individual right.

It is, then, far from true that the authority of the Hebrew High Priest in interpreting his country's laws enables us to infer the Pope's authority to interpret religion; on the contrary, a more obvious inference is that the interpretation of religion is vested above all in each individual. And this again affords further proof that our method of Scriptural interpretation is the best. For since the supreme authority for the interpretation of Scripture is vested in each individual, the rule that governs interpretation must be nothing other than the natural light that is common to all, and not any supernatural light, nor any eternal authority. Nor must this rule be so difficult as not to be available to any but skilled philosophers; it must be suited to the natural and universal ability and capacity of mankind. We have shown that our rule answers to this description; for we have seen that such difficulties as are now to be found in it have arisen from the negligence of men, and are not inherent in our method.

CHAPTER 8

In which it is shown that the Pentateuch and the Books of Joshua,
Judges, Ruth, Samuel and Kings were not written by themselves.
The question of their authorship is considered. Was there one
author, or several, and who were they?

In the preceding chapter we discussed the foundations and principles of
Scriptural knowledge, and showed that this consists simply in a thorough
historical study of Scripture. In spite of its indispensability, the writers of
ancient times failed to compile such a study, or if in fact they did compile
or transmit one, it has disappeared through the ravages of time, consequently leaving us to a great extent deprived of the foundations and
principles of Scriptural knowledge. This loss would not have been so
serious if later generations had kept within the bounds of truth and had
faithfully transmitted to their successors the few facts they had received or
discovered, without the addition of new ideas of their own devising. As it
is, the historical study of Scripture has remained not merely incomplete
but prone to error; that is, the foundations of Scriptural knowledge are not
only too scanty to form the basis for a complete understanding, but are
also unsound. It belongs to my purpose to correct these faults and to
remove common theological prejudices. But I fear that I approach this task
too late; for matters have almost reached such a pass that men will not
endure correction on this subject, and will obstinately defend what they
have embraced in the name of religion. It is only with very few, com-
paratively speaking, that there seems any place left for reason, so perva-
sively have these prejudices seized upon men's minds. However, I shall
make the attempt and persevere in my efforts, since there is no reason for
utter despair.

To treat the matter in logical order, I shall first deal with misconcep-
tions regarding the true authorship of the Sacred Books, beginning with
the Pentateuch. The author is almost universally believed to be Moses, a
view so obstinately defended by the Pharisees that they have regarded any
other view as heresy. It was for this reason that ibn Ezra, a man of
enlightened mind and considerable learning, who was the first, as far as I
know, to call attention to this misconception, did not venture to explain
his meaning openly, and expressed himself somewhat obscurely in words
which I shall here not hesitate to elucidate, making his meaning quite
plain.

The words of ibn Ezra in his commentary on Deuteronomy are as follows: "'Beyond the Jordan, etc.' If you understand the mystery of the twelve, and also 'Moses wrote the Law,' and, 'the Canaanite was then in the land,' 'it shall be revealed on the Mount of God,' and again 'Behold his bed, a bed of iron,' then shall you know the truth." In these few words he gives a clear indication that it was not Moses who wrote the Pentateuch but someone else who lived long after him, and that it was a different book that Moses wrote. To make this clear, he draws attention to the following points:

1. The preface to Deuteronomy could not have been written by Moses, who did not cross the Jordan.

2. The Book of Moses was inscribed in its entirety on no more than the circumference of a single altar (Deut. ch. 27 and Joshua ch. 8 v. 30 etc.), and this altar, according to the Rabbis, consisted of only twelve stones. From this it follows that the Book of Moses must have required far less space than the Pentateuch. This, I say, was what our author meant by his reference to 'the mystery of the twelve,' unless he was referring to the twelve curses in the aforementioned chapter of Deuteronomy. Perhaps he believed that these could not have been contained in Moses' Book of the Law, because Moses bids the Levites read out these curses in addition to the recital of the Law, so as to bind the people by oath to observe the recited laws. Or again he may have wished to draw attention to the last chapter of Deuteronomy concerning the death of Moses, a chapter consisting of twelve verses. But there is no need here to give closer scrutiny to these and other conjectures.

3. Deuteronomy ch. 31 v. 9 says, "And Moses wrote the Law." These words cannot be ascribed to Moses; they must be those of another writer narrating the deeds and writings of Moses.

4. In Genesis ch. 12 v. 6 when the narrative tells of Abraham journeying through the land of Canaan, the historian adds, "the Canaanite was then in the land," thereby clearly excluding the time at which he was writing. So this passage must have been written after the death of Moses when the Canaanites had been driven out and no longer possessed those lands. In his commentary of this passage ibn Ezra makes the same point in these words: "'And the Canaanite was then in the land.' It appears that Canaan (the grandson of Noah) took the land of Canaan which had been in the possession of another. If this is not the true meaning, some mystery lies here, and let him who understands it keep silent." That is to say, if Canaan invaded that land, then the sense will be that the Canaanite was already in the land, as opposed to some past time when the land was inhabited by another nation. But if Canaan was the first to settle in that region (as

follows from Gen. ch. 10), then the words are intended to exclude the present time, that is, the time of the author. This could not be Moses, in whose time the land was still possessed by the Canaanites; and this is the mystery concerning which ibn Ezra urges silence.

5. In Genesis ch. 22 v. 14 Mount Moriah* is called the Mount of God, a name it did not acquire until after it was assigned to the building of the temple. This choice of mountain was not made in the time of Moses, for Moses does not indicate any position as chosen by God. On the contrary, he foretells that God will at some time choose a place to which his name will be given.

6. Lastly, in Deuteronomy ch. 3 v. 11, in the narrative about Og, king of Bashan, these words are inserted, "Only Og, king of Bashan, remained as the sole survivor of the giants.** Behold, his bedstead was a bedstead of iron, the bedstead that is now in Rabbah of the children of Ammon, nine cubits long. . . ." This parenthesis shows most clearly that the writer of these books lived long after the time of Moses, for this manner of speaking can characterise only one who is narrating ancient history and is pointing to relics to prove his assertion. There is no doubt that this bed was first discovered in the time of David, who conquered this city, as related in 2 Sam. ch. 12 v. 30. A further example of words being inserted in Moses' narrative occurs a little further on, where the same historian says, "Jair, the son of Manasseh, took all the region of Argob as far as the Geshurite and Maacathite border, and called them after his own name Bashan Havvoth Jair unto this day." The historian, I say, added these words so as to explain the words of Moses which he had just related, to wit, "And the rest of Gilead and all Bashan, the kingdom of Og, gave I unto the half-tribe of Manasseh, all the region of Argob with all Bashan, which is called the land of giants." There is no doubt that at the time of this writer the Hebrews knew what was Havvoth Jair of the tribe of Judah, but not under the name of the region of Argob, nor the land of giants. So he was forced to explain what these places were that were so called in antiquity, and at the same time give reason why in his time they took the name of Jair, who was of the tribe of Judah, not Manasseh (see 1 Chron. ch. 2 v. 21, 22).

We have now set forth the view of ibn Ezra, and the passages of the Pentateuch which he cites in support. Yet he did not call attention to all such passages, nor even the principal ones; for there are many other

---

* See Supplementary Note 9.

** The Hebrew '*rephaim*' means 'the condemned,' and from 1 Chron. ch. 20 it also appears to be a proper name. For this reason I think it is here a family name.

passages in these books, and of greater significance, which have yet to be cited.

1. The writer of these books not only speaks of Moses in the third person, but also bears witness to many details concerning him: for instance, 'God talked with Moses' 'God spake with Moses face to face' 'Moses was the meekest of men' (Num. ch. 12 v. 3), 'Moses was wrath with the captains of the host' (Num. ch. 31 v. 14), 'Moses, the man of God' (Deut. ch. 33 v. 1), 'Moses, the servant of God, died,' 'There has never arisen in Israel a prophet like Moses,' and so on. On the other hand, in Deuteronomy, where the Law, which Moses had expounded to the people and put in written form, is set forth, Moses speaks and narrates his deeds in the first person; for instance, 'God spoke to me' (Deut. ch. 2 v. 1, 17 etc.), 'I prayed to God,' and so on. However, later on towards the end of the book, after the historian has reported the words of Moses, he again continues the narrative in the third person, telling how Moses handed over to the people in written form the Law he had expounded, with his last admonition, and how he came to the end of his life. All these considerations—the manner of speaking, the giving of testimony, the very structure of the entire history—lead us to the plain conclusion that these books were written not by Moses, but by another.

2. It should further be added that this history not only narrates the death of Moses, his burial, and the thirty days mourning of the Hebrews, but also draws a comparison between Moses and all the other prophets who came after him, declaring that he excelled them all. "There has never arisen in Israel a prophet like Moses," he says, "whom God knew face to face." Such testimony could never have been given by Moses of himself, nor by any immediate successor, but by someone who lived many generations later, and particularly so since the historian seems to be speaking of some remote time, as in "there has never arisen a prophet," etc. And he says of his place of burial, "Nobody knows it unto this day."

3. Some places are indicated not by the names they bore in Moses' time, but by other names which they only later acquired. For instance, Abraham "pursued the enemy even unto Dan" (Gen. ch. 14 v. 14), a name not given to that city until long after the death of Joshua (Judges ch. 18 v. 29).

4. The narrative sometimes continues beyond the death of Moses, for in Exodus ch. 16 v. 35 we are told that 'the children of Israel did eat manna forty years until they came to a land inhabited, until they came unto the borders of the land of Canaan;' that is to say, until the time referred to in Joshua ch. 5 v. 12. Again, in Genesis ch. 36 v. 31 we read, 'These are the kings that reigned in Edom before there reigned any king over the children of Israel.' Undoubtedly the historian here lists the kings of Idumaea

before David conquered that people* and set up governors in the land (2 Sam. ch. 8 v. 14).

Thus from the foregoing it is clear beyond a shadow of doubt that the Pentateuch was not written by Moses, but by someone who lived many generations after Moses. But let us now turn our attention, if you please, to the books which Moses did write and which are cited in the Pentateuch; for we shall see from them that they were different from the Pentateuch. In the first place, then, Exodus ch. 17 v. 14 tells us that Moses, by God's command, wrote an account of the war against Amalek. In that chapter we are not told what book this was, but in Numbers ch. 21 v. 12 reference is made to a certain book called the 'Book of the Wars of God,' which undoubtedly included the history of this war against Amalek together with all the stages of their journeyings (which in Numbers ch. 33 v. 2 the author of the Penteteuch testifies were also written by Moses). Again, Exodus ch. 24 v. 4, 7 gives evidence of another book called the 'Book of the Covenant,'** which Moses read before the Israelites when they first entered into a covenant with God. Now this book or document contained very little, namely, the laws or commandments of God which are set out in Exodus from chapter 20 v. 22 to chapter 24, and this no one will deny who reads the aforesaid chapter impartially and with sound judgment. There we read that as soon as Moses realised the feelings of the people with regard to a covenant with God, he immediately wrote down God's utterances and laws, and in the morning, when certain ceremonies had been performed, he read out the terms of the covenant to the whole congregation. When the terms had been read out and no doubt understood by the entire assembly, the people bound themselves with full consent. It therefore follows both from the brief time taken in writing down the book and from the manner of the ratifying of the covenant, that this book contained nothing more than the few items I have mentioned.

Lastly, it is clear that in the fortieth year from the departure out of Egypt Moses explained all the laws that he made (see Deut. ch. 1 v. 5) and bound the people anew to observe them (Deut. ch. 29 v. 14), and finally wrote a book containing these laws as explained and this new covenant (see Deut. ch. 31 v. 9). This book was called the Book of the Law of God, to which Joshua later added an account of the covenant by which the people of his time bound themselves once more, making a covenant with God for the third time (see Josh. ch. 24 v. 25, 26). Now since there is no extant book containing this covenant of Moses together with the covenant of Joshua, we have to grant that this book has perished—or else we must share in the

---

* See Supplementary Note 10.
** The Hebrew word '*sepher*' often means letter or writing.

madness of the Chaldaean Paraphrast Jonathan,[1] distorting the words of Scripture just as we please. Confronted by this problem, this commentator preferred to corrupt Scripture rather than admit his ignorance. The passage in the book of Joshua (ch. 24 v. 26) which runs, "And Joshua wrote these words in the book of the Law of God," he translates in Chaldaic, "And Joshua wrote these words and kept them together with the book of the Law of God." What can you do with those who see nothing but what they please? What else is this, I ask, but to reject Scripture itself and fashion a new Scripture of one's own devising?

We may therefore conclude that the book of the Law of God which Moses wrote was not the Pentateuch, but a quite different book which the author of the Pentateuch inserted in proper order in his own work; and this conclusion follows on the clearest evidence not only from what has just been said but also from what I am about to state. In the passage of Deuteronomy just quoted which tells us that Moses wrote the book of the Law, the historian adds that Moses gave it into the hands of the priests, and that he further ordered them to read it out to the entire people at an appointed time. This indicates that the book in question was much shorter than the Pentateuch, seeing that it could be read through at a single assembly so as to be understood by all. Nor must we here omit to mention that, of all the books that Moses wrote, it was only this one of the second covenant and the Canticle[2] (which he later added so that all the people might learn it) that he commanded to be religiously guarded and preserved. For by the first covenant he had bound only those who were present, whereas by the second covenant he also bound those who should come after them (Deut. ch. 29 v. 14, 15). He therefore commanded that this book of the second covenant be religiously preserved for future generations, and with it, as we have said, the Canticle, which particularly concerns future generations. Since, then, there is no evidence that Moses wrote any other books but these, and he gave no instructions for any other book but this book of the Law together with the Canticle to be preserved religiously for posterity, and finally, since there are many passages in the Pentateuch that could not have been written by Moses, it follows that there are no grounds for holding Moses to be the author of the Pentateuch, and that such an opinion is quite contrary to reason.

Now at this point someone will perhaps ask whether, in addition to the above, Moses did not write down laws when they were first revealed to

---

1. The Chaldaean Paraphrast Jonathan was Jonathan ben Uzziel, first century A.D., who produced an Aramaic (Chaldaean) translation or paraphrase of the Bible, called a Targum. Maimonides held him in high regard.

2. Spinoza is referring to Moses' song in Deuteronomy 33.

him; that is, whether over the space of forty years he did not write down any of the laws which he made except those few which I have stated were contained in the book of the first covenant. To this I reply that, although I would grant it to be a reasonable assumption that Moses wrote down the laws at the time and place where he happened to promulgate them, I deny that it is therefore legitimate for us to affirm this. We have previously shown that in matters like this we must assert nothing but what is established from Scripture itself, or what logically proceeds solely from the fundamental principles of Scripture. It is not enough that such an assertion should appear reasonable. Moreover, neither does reason itself compel us to this conclusion. It is possible that the elders communicated Moses' decrees to the people in writing, and that later the historian gathered these together and inserted them in due order in the life of Moses.

So much for the five books of Moses; it is now time for us to examine the other books. The book of Joshua can likewise be shown, by similar arguments, not to be by the hand of Joshua; for it is someone else who testifies of Joshua that his fame was spread throughout the world (ch. 6 v. 27), that he omitted nothing of what Moses had commanded him (ch. 8 last verse and ch. 11 v. 15), that he grew old and summoned the entire people to an assembly, and that finally he breathed his last. Then again, some events are narrated that happened after Joshua's death, as that after his death the Israelites continued to worship God as long as men who had known him were still alive. And in chapter 16 v. 10 we read that Ephraim and Manasseh 'did not drive out the Canaanites that dwelt in Gezer, but (he adds) the Canaanites have dwelt among the Ephraimites unto this day, and served as tributaries.' This is the same as the narrative in Judges, chapter 1, and the turn of phrase 'even unto this day' indicates that the writer is speaking of ancient times. Similar to this is the text of chapter 15, last verse, concerning the sons of Judah, and the history of Caleb from verse 13 of the same chapter. Again, the events narrated in chapter 22 from verse 10 on, when the two tribes and a half built an altar beyond Jordan, seem to have taken place after the death of Joshua; for throughout the story there is no mention of Joshua, and it is the people alone who hold council as to waging war, send delegates and await the reply they bring, which they finally approve. Lastly, the passage in chapter 10 v. 14 clearly proves that this book was written many generations after Joshua, for it testifies, "There was no day like that, either before it or after it, that the Lord hearkened unto the voice of a man," etc. Therefore if Joshua wrote any book at all, it must be that which is quoted in ch. 10 v. 13 of this same history.

As for the book of Judges, I imagine that nobody of sound judgment can believe that it was written by the judges themselves, for the summary of the whole book in chapter 2 clearly shows that the entire book is the work of a single historian. Then again, since the writer often remarks that in those times there was no king in Israel, there can be no doubt that it was written after the institution of monarchy.

We need spend little time in considering the books of Samuel, inasmuch as the history is continued long after his lifetime. However, I should like it to be noted that this book, too, was written many generations after Samuel. In book 1, chapter 9 v. 9 the historian remarks in parenthesis, "Beforetimes in Israel, when a man went to inquire of God, thus he spoke, 'Come, let us go to a seer'; for he that is now called a prophet was beforetime called a seer."

Lastly, the books of Kings, as is made clear by their contents, are taken from the books of the Acts of Solomon (see 1 Kings ch. 11 v. 41), from the chronicles of the kings of Judah (1 Kings ch. 14 v. 19, 29), and from the chronicles of the kings of Israel.

We may therefore conclude that all the books we have so far considered are the works of other hands, and that their contents are narrated as ancient history.

If we now turn our attention to the interconnection and the main theme of all these books, we shall easily see that they are all the work of a single historian who set out to write the antiquities of the Jews from their first beginnings until the first destruction of the city.[3] These books are so connected with one another that this alone is sufficient to enable us to decide that they form the narrative of a single historian. As soon as he reaches the end of the narrative of the life of Moses, the historian passes on to the life of Joshua with these words: "Now after the death of Moses, the servant of the Lord, it came to pass that the Lord spake unto Joshua . . . ," and when this narrative ends with the death of Joshua, he begins the history of the Judges with exactly the same transitional words, "Now after the death of Joshua it came to pass that the children of Israel asked the Lord. . . ." To this book he joins the story of Ruth as an appendix, with these words: "Now it came to pass in the days when the Judges ruled that there was a famine in the land." Then there is the same sort of transition between Ruth and the first Book of Samuel, at the end of which he proceeds with his customary transitional phrase to the second book. Then, without completing the history of David, he moves on to the first Book of Kings, and, continuing the history of David, he goes on with the same transition to the second Book of Kings.

Again, the construction and order of the narratives also shows that there was only one historian, with a fixed aim in view. He begins by narrating

3. This is Jerusalem.

the first origins of the Hebrew nation, and then continues in an orderly way to relate on what occasions and at what times Moses made his laws and his numerous prophecies. He then goes on to tell how the Israelites invaded the promised land in accordance with Moses' prophecies (see Deut. ch. 7), and how, after possessing the land, they forsook their laws (Deut. ch. 31 v. 16) and thereafter met with many misfortunes (same ch. v. 17). Then he relates how the people decided to choose kings (Deut. ch. 17 v. 14), who likewise prospered or failed according to the reverence they paid to the laws, and, finally, how their kingdom was destroyed as Moses had foretold. With regard to other matters that are not relevant to the observance of the Law, our historian either keeps silent or refers the reader to other historians. Thus all these books have but a single theme, to set forth the words and commandments of Moses and to demonstrate their truth by the course of history.

When we consider in unison these three points, namely, the unity of theme of all these books, their interconnections, and the fact that they were written by a later hand many generations after the events, we may conclude, as I have just stated, that they were all the work of a single historian. The identity of this historian is not susceptible to certain proof, but I believe it was Ezra, a conjecture supported by a number of weighty reasons.

The historian (whom we already know to be a single individual) continues his history up to the liberation of Jehoiachin, adding that he sat at the king's table all the days of his life (that is, either Jehoiachin's life or the life of the son of Nebuchadnezzar, for the meaning is by no means clear). Hence it follows that the historian could not have been anyone before Ezra. Now Scripture testifies of Ezra alone of all men of his time (Ezra ch. 7 v. 10) that he devoted himself to seek the Law of God and to set it forth, and that he was a scribe learned in the Law of Moses (Ezra ch. 7 v. 6). Therefore I cannot imagine anyone but Ezra as the writer of these books.

Again, on examining this testimony concerning Ezra, we note that he devoted himself not only to seek the Law of God but also to set it forth, and in Nehemiah ch. 8 v. 8 we are also told that "they read the book of the Law distinctly, and caused them to understand, and they understood the Scripture." Now since Deuteronomy contains not only the book of the Law of Moses, or most of it, but also many passages inserted for its fuller explanation, I conjecture that Deuteronomy is that book of the Law of God, written, set forth and explained by Ezra, which they read at that time. As to the numerous parenthetic insertions in Deuteronomy which serve for fuller explanation, I gave two examples of this in discussing the views of ibn Ezra, and there are many more such passages to be found; for example, chapter 2 v. 12, "The Horites also dwelt in Seir beforetime, but the children of Esau drove them out and destroyed them from before them, and dwelt in their stead, as Israel did unto the land of his possession, which the Lord gave unto him." Here he is explaining verses 3 and 4 of the same chapter, saying that Mount Seir, which had come to the children of Esau for their possession, was not seized by them uninhabited, but that they invaded it and expelled and destroyed the Horites who formerly dwelt there, just as after Moses' death the Israelites expelled the Canaanites.

Other parenthetic insertions in the words of Moses are verses 6, 7, 8, 9 of chapter 10; for it is obvious that verse 8, which begins, "At that time the Lord separated the tribe of Levi" must refer back to verse 5, and not to the death of Aaron, which Ezra seems to have inserted at this point only because Moses, when he recounted the story of the worship of the calf, had said (ch. 9 v. 20), that he had prayed to God on Aaron's behalf. Ezra then goes on to explain that, at the time of which Moses is here speaking, God had chosen for himself the tribe of Levi, thus giving reason for the election and the exclusion of the Levites from a share in the inheritance; and thereafter he continues the thread of the history in the words of Moses. Then there is also the preface to the book, and all those passages where Moses is spoken of in the third person. And there were doubtless many other passages, which we cannot now identify, which were added or given a different expression by the historian, so that they might be more easily comprehended by his contemporaries.

If, I say, we possessed Moses' original book of the Law, I doubt not that we should find considerable differences both in the wording of his commandments and in the order of the text and in the explanations given. If only the Decalogue of Deuteronomy be compared with the Decalogue of Exodus (where its history is explicitly given) the former is found to differ from the latter on all these points. In the former the fourth commandment not only takes a different form but is set out at much greater length, and the reasoning on which it is based is quite different from that given in the Exodus Decalogue. And finally, the order in which the tenth commandment is here set forth is also quite different from that of Exodus.

It is my opinion, as I have already said, that the discrepancies here and elsewhere are due to Ezra because he was explaining the Law of God to the people of his own time, and therefore this is the book of the Law of God as presented and set forth by Ezra. And this book, I believe, was the first of all the books which I have attributed to him. This conjecture is supported by the fact that it contains the laws of his country—which are the most urgent need of a people—and also that this book, unlike all the others, is not joined to the preceding book by a transitional phrase, but begins independently with 'These are the words of Moses. . . .' Now when he had completed this task and had instructed the people in the laws, I believe he applied himself to composing a complete history of the Hebrew nation from the creation of the world to the final destruction of the city, and into this work he inserted the book of Deuteronomy in its appropriate place. Perhaps he called the first five books by the name of Moses because their principal subject is the life of Moses, the name deriving from the main theme. For the same reason he called the sixth book the book of Joshua, the seventh the book of Judges, the eighth Ruth, the ninth and perhaps the tenth the books of Samuel, and the eleventh and twelfth the books of Kings. On the question as to whether Ezra put the final touches to this work and completed it as he intended, see the next chapter.

CHAPTER 9

An enquiry into further matters relating to these same books, namely, whether Ezra gave them a final revision, and whether the marginal notes found in the Hebrew codices were variant readings

In the preceding chapter we discussed the question of the true authorship of the books therein considered. In support of our theory we considered some obscure passages which can be clarified only by this theory, a fact which in itself emphasises how much our theory contributes to a complete understanding of these books. But apart from the question of authorship, we have yet to draw attention to some other points of interest in the books themselves, the comprehension of which is denied to people in general by the prevalence of superstition. Of these the most important is this, that Ezra (whom I shall regard as the author of the aforementioned books until a more likely candidate appears) did not make a final revision of the narratives contained in these books and confined himself to making a collection of the histories from various writers, sometimes simply copying them down as they were and leaving them to posterity without proper scrutiny and arrangement.

The reasons (if it was not his untimely death) which prevented him from completing this work in final detail are beyond my conjecture. But although the ancient Hebrew historians are lost to us, the few remnants that we do possess make the fact indisputable. The history of Hezekiah (2 Kings ch. 18 from v. 17 on) was copied from Isaiah's account just as it appeared in the chronicles of the kings of Judah, for we have it in its entirety in the book of Isaiah—which was included in the chronicles of the kings of Judah (see 2 Chron. ch. 32 v. 32)—in exactly the same words as in the other narrative, with a few exceptions.* Hence we are bound to conclude that there existed various versions of this narrative of Isaiah— unless one should prefer to imagine that here, again, there lurk some mysteries. Moreover, the ending of 2 Kings is repeated in the last chapter of Jeremiah v. 31–34. In addition, we find that 2 Sam. ch. 7 is repeated in 1 Chron. ch. 17; but in a number of places the words are seen to have undergone such a remarkable change** that it is obvious that the two chapters are taken from two different copies of the story of Nathan.

* See Supplementary Note 11.
** See Supplementary Note 12.

Finally, the genealogy of the kings of Idumaea, in Gen. ch. 36 v. 31 on, is also repeated in the same words in 1 Chron. ch. 1, although it is clear that the author of the latter book took his materials from other historians, and not from the twelve books we have ascribed to Ezra. Therefore there can be no doubt that if the historians themselves were available to us, we should have direct proof of our contention. But since they are lost to us, our only resource is to examine the histories that we do possess, considering their order and interconnections, the various repetitions and the discrepancies in the reckoning of years, from which we may judge of the rest.

Let us then consider these histories, or at least the most noteworthy; and in the first place the story of Judah and Tamar (Gen. 38), where the historian begins his narration thus: "And it came to pass at that time that Judah departed from his brethren. . . ." The time here mentioned must refer not to the passage that immediately precedes it in Genesis but to a quite different time* of which it is the immediate continuation. For from the former time—that is, the time when Joseph was taken away to Egypt—until the time when the patriarch Jacob also set out thither with all his household, we can reckon no more than twenty-two years. Joseph was seventeen years old when he was sold by his brothers, and he was thirty years old when he was summoned by Pharaoh from prison. If we add to this the seven years of plenty and the two years of famine, we arrive at a total of twenty-two years. Now nobody can conceive that in this space of time so many events could have taken place: that Judah begat three children, one after another, from the one wife whom he married at that time, that the eldest of these married Tamar when he was of age, that when he died the second son married her in turn, and also died, that some time after these events Judah unwittingly had intercourse with his own daughter-in-law Tamar, that she bore him twins, of whom one also became a father within the aforesaid period. Thus, since all these events cannot be accommodated within the time specified in Genesis, the reference must be to some immediately preceding time in the narrative of a different book. Therefore Ezra must have simply copied out this story, too, inserting it into the rest of his work without critical examination.

Now it has to be admitted that not only this chapter but the entire story of Joseph and Jacob was gathered and copied down from different sources, such are the number of inconsistencies to be found in it. Genesis chapter 47 tells us that Jacob was 130 years old when first Joseph brought him to salute Pharaoh. If we subtract the twenty-two years he passed in sorrow-

* See Supplementary Note 13.

ing for Joseph's absence, and the seventeen years which was Joseph's age when he was sold, and finally the seven years he served for Rachel, we find that he was old indeed, eighty-four in fact, when he married Leah, while Dinah was scarcely seven years old* when she was violated by Shechem, and Simeon and Levi had scarcely reached the ages of twelve and eleven when they spoiled that entire city and slew all its people with the sword.

There is no need for me here to review the whole of the Pentateuch. If one merely observes that all the contents of these five books, histories and precepts, are set forth with no distinction or order and with no regard to chronology, and that frequently the same story is repeated, with variations, it will readily be recognised that all these materials were collected indiscriminately and stored together with view to examining them and arranging them more conveniently at some later time. And not only the contents of these five books but the other histories in the remaining seven books right down to the destruction of the city were compiled in the same way. Nobody can fail to see that in chapter 2 of Judges at verse 6 there appears on the scene a new historian who had also written of Joshua's deeds, and that his words are simply set down unchanged. For after our historian has related in the last chapter of Joshua how Joshua died and was buried, and in the first chapter of Judges has promised to continue the history after Joshua's death, what logical connection—if he really intended to pursue the thread of his story—could he have claimed between the preceding verses and what he here begins to relate of Joshua?**

In the same way, too, chapters 17, 18 etc. of 1 Samuel are taken from another historian, who held that the reason why David began to frequent Saul's court was very different from that given in chapter 16 of this same book. He did not think that it was by his servants' advice that Saul summoned David to his presence (as is related in chapter 16), but that, happening to be sent by his father to his brothers in camp, David first came to Saul's attention through his victory over the Philistine Goliath, and was detained at his court. I suspect that the same applies to chapter 26 of this same book, where the historian appears to repeat the narrative of chapter 24, but gives a different version. But I pass over this point, and proceed to examine the question of chronology.

In 1 Kings chapter 6 we are told that Solomon built his temple 480 years after the exodus from Egypt, but the narratives themselves require a much greater number of years.

---

* See Supplementary Note 14.
** See Supplementary Note 15.

	Years
Moses governed the people in the desert	40
According to Josephus and other writers, Joshua, who lived to the age of 110, led the people for no more than	26
Cushan Rishathaim held the people in subjection	8
Othniel, son of Kenaz, was judge*	40
Eglon, king of Moab, held rule over the people	18
Ehud and Shamgar were judges	80
Jabin, king of Canaan, again held the people in subjection	20
Thereafter the people were at peace	40
Then they were in subjection to Midian	7
In the time of Gideon they were free	40
They were under the rule of Abimelech	3
Tola, son of Pua, was judge	23
Jair was judge	22
The people were again in subjection to the Philistines and the Ammonites	18
Jephtha was judge	6
Ibzan the Bethlehemite was judge	7
Elon the Zebulunite was judge	10
Abdon the Pirathonite was judge	8
The people were again in subjection to the Philistines	40
Samson was judge**	20
Eli was judge	40
The people were again in subjection to the Philistines until they were freed by Samuel	20
David reigned	40
Solomon reigned before building the temple	4
Total	**580**

To this total must be added the period after the death of Joshua when the Hebrew state flourished before it was subjugated by Cushan Rishathaim, a period which I believe covered a considerable number of years. For I cannot be persuaded that immediately after the death of Joshua all those who witnessed his marvelous doings perished all at once, and that their successors rejected their laws at a single stroke and plunged from the heights of virtue into the depths of wickedness and indolence, or that Cushan Rishathaim subjugated them at one blow. Since each of these

---

* See Supplementary Note 16.
** See Supplementary Note 17.

circumstances requires about a generation, there can be no doubt that the book of Judges, chapter 2 v. 7, 9, 10 covers the history of many years which it passes over in silence.

Furthermore, we must add the years when Samuel was judge, the number of which is again not given in Scripture; and then there are the years of Saul's reign, which I have omitted in the above calculation because the history of Saul does not make clear the length of his reign. There is indeed the statement in 1 Samuel chapter 13 v. 1 that he reigned two years, but the text there is mutilated, and the narrative itself also postulates a longer period. That the text is mutilated cannot be doubted by anyone who has the slightest acquaintance with the Hebrew language, for it begins thus, "Saul was in his __ year when he began to reign, and he reigned for two years over Israel." Who can fail to see, I repeat, that the number of years of Saul's age when he began to reign has been omitted? And I do not think that anyone can doubt too that the narrative itself requires a greater number for the years of his reign. For chapter 27 v. 7 of the same book tells us that David sojourned among the Philistines, to whom he had fled for refuge from Saul, a year and four months. By this calculation the other events of his reign must have occupied eight months, a conclusion which I imagine no one will accept. Josephus, at least, at the end of his sixth book of *Antiquities*, emends the text thus: "Saul reigned eighteen years during Samuel's lifetime, and two years after his death."

Indeed, this entire narrative in chapter 13 is in complete disagreement with what has gone before. At the end of chapter 7 we are told that the Philistines were so crushed by the Hebrews that they dared not invade their borders during Samuel's lifetime. Yet in chapter 13 we are told that, in Samuel's lifetime, the Hebrews were invaded by the Philistines and reduced to such a state of wretchedness and poverty that they were deprived of weapons wherewith to defend themselves, and even of the means of making them. I should certainly be hard put to it if I were to attempt to reconcile all the narratives of the first book of Samuel so that they might present the appearance of having been written and arranged by a single historian. But I return to my theme. The years of Saul's reign, then, should be added to our previous calculation. And finally, I have not taken into account the years of anarchy of the Hebrews, since their number is not clear from Scripture. I cannot be sure, I say, of the time taken up by those events which are recorded from chapter 17 to the end of the book of Judges.

Thus it clearly follows that neither can a true system of chronology be established from the narratives nor are the narratives consistent with one another in this matter, but differ widely. Therefore it must be admitted that these narratives were compiled from different sources, without any proper arrangement or scrutiny. And there seems to have been just as great a chronological discrepancy between the books of the chronicles of the kings of Judah and those of the kings of Israel. The chronicles of the kings of Israel recorded that Jehoram, the son of Ahab, began his reign in the second year of the reign of Jehoram, the son of Jehoshaphat (2 Kings ch. 1 v. 17); but in the chronicles of the kings of Judah we are told that Jehoram, the son of Jehoshaphat, began his reign in the fifth year of the reign of Jehoram, the son of Ahab (2 Kings ch. 8 v. 16).

Furthermore, anyone who cares to compare the narratives of the book of Chronicles with the narratives of the books of Kings will find many similar discrepancies, which I need not recount here, and far less need I consider the commentaries wherein writers seek to reconcile these narratives. The Rabbis run quite wild, and such commentators as I have read indulge in dreams, fantasies, and in the end corrupt the language altogether. For example, in the second book of Chronicles where we read that "Forty and two years old was Ahaziah when he began to reign," some of them pretend that these years are reckoned from the reign of Omri, not from the birth of Ahaziah. If they could prove this to be the real meaning of the author of the book of Chronicles, I should not hesitate to declare that he did not know how to speak. They indulge in many other fancies of this sort; and if these were true, I should declare outright that the ancient Hebrews knew neither their own language nor how a narrative should be arranged, I should acknowledge no method or rule for the interpretation of Scripture, and there would be no restriction whatsoever on the imagination.

If anyone thinks that my criticism here is of too sweeping a nature and lacking sufficient foundation, I would ask him to undertake to show us in these narratives a definite plan such as might legitimately be imitated by historians in their chronicles. In his attempts to interpret the narratives and to harmonise them, let him adhere with absolute strictness* to the actual diction and to the manner of exposition, arrangement and organisation of the texts, and then provide such an explanation as may furnish us with a model to imitate in our own writing. If he succeeds, I shall at once admit defeat, and he will be my mighty Apollo. For I confess that all my efforts over a long period have resulted in no such discovery. Indeed, I may add that I write nothing here that is not the fruit of lengthy reflection; and although I have been educated from boyhood in the accepted beliefs concerning Scripture, I have felt bound in the end to embrace the views I here express. But there is no point in taking up the reader's time on this subject, presenting him with a hopeless task: it has been necessary to

* See Supplementary Note 18.

confront this issue in order to make my position clearer, and so I now pass
on to the remaining topics which I undertook to discuss, concerning the
fate that befell these books.

In addition to our previous remarks, we have to observe that these books
were not so preserved by posterity as not to suffer the intrusion of some
errors. The scribes of old have noted several doubtful readings and also a
number of mutilated passages, but not all that there are. I shall not at this
point discuss the question as to whether the errors are of such a kind as to
cause serious difficulty to the reader. In my opinion, however, they are of
minor importance, at any rate to those who have an enlightened approach
to Scripture. This much I can say with certainty, that in the matter of
moral doctrine I have never observed a fault of variant reading that could
give rise to obscurity or doubt in such teaching. But there are many who
deny the possibility of any fault having occurred even in the other texts;
they maintain that God by some singular act of providence has preserved
all the Sacred Books uncorrupted. They say that the variant readings
signal mysteries most profound; they contend that the same is true of the
twenty-eight cases of asterisks in mid-paragraph, and that great secrets
lurk even in the markings above the letters. I do not know whether these
views proceed from folly and a feeble-minded devoutness or from ar-
rogance and malice, to the end that they alone may be credited with
possessing the secrets of God. This much I do know, that I have found in
their writings nothing that smacks of divine secrets, but mere childishness.
I have also read, and am acquainted with, a number of Cabbalistic[1] triflers
whose madness passes the bounds of my understanding.

That some errors have crept in, as we have said, will not be denied, I
believe, by anyone of sound judgment who reads the passages concerning
Saul (which I have already quoted from 1 Sam. ch. 13 v. 1) and also 2 Sam.
ch. 6 v. 2, "And David arose and went with all the people that were with
him from Judah to bring up from there the ark of God." Nobody can fail
to see that the place to which they went to bring up from there the ark of
God, namely, Kirjath Jeharim,* has been omitted. Nor again can we deny
that 2 Sam. ch. 13 v. 37 has been corrupted and mutilated: "And Absalom
fled and went to Talmai, the son of Ammihud, king of Geshur, and he
mourned for his son every day, and Absalom fled and went to Geshur, and

1. Spinoza alludes here to the Jewish mystical tradition, commonly known as
Qabbalah. One of Spinoza's own teachers, Menasseh ben Israel, was a keen Qab-
balist. Indeed, Qabbalah was widely disseminated among Spanish Jewish scholars
after the Expulsion.

* See Supplementary Note 19.

was there three years.'"* There are other instances of this kind which I
know I have previously noted, but cannot at present recall.

That the marginal notes which are found in many places in the Hebrew
Codices were doubtful readings, nobody again can doubt who notices that
most of these have originated from the remarkable similarity between
Hebrew letters; the similarity between כ *kaf,* and ב *bet,* י *yad* and ו *vav,* ד
dalet and ר *resh* and so on. For example, in 2 Sam. ch. 5 v. 24, we have
בשמעך 'in the (time) in which thou hearest,' and in the margin כשמעך
'when thou hearest.' And in Judges ch. 21 v. 22 'when their fathers or
brothers come to us לרוב in multitude' (that is, 'often'), in the margin is
written לריב 'to complain.'

In the same way, many other variant readings have also arisen from the
use of letters called mutes, which for the most part are not pronounced,
and are used indiscriminately one in place of another. For example, in
Leviticus chapter 25 verse 30 we have 'and the house will be established
which is in the city without a wall'—אשר לא חומה, but in the margin is
written אשר לו חומה, 'which is in the walled city.'

Although this is self-evident, I should like to reply to the arguments of
certain Pharisees whereby they try to convince us that the marginal notes
were inserted by the writers of the Sacred Books themselves with the
purpose of signifying some mystery. The first of these arguments, to
which I attach little weight, derives from the practice of reading the
Scriptures aloud. If, they say, these notes are added because of a difference
of reading on which later generations could not decide, why has the
custom prevailed that the marginal readings should everywhere be given
preference? Why, they ask, has the preferred reading been written in the
margin? They could on the contrary have written the text itself as they
wished it to be read, and they should not have relegated to the margin the
meaning and reading of which they most approved.

The second argument, which has some plausibility, derives from the
nature of the case, namely, that errors find their way into a text by chance,
not by design; and that which is the effect of chance occurs at random.
Now in the Pentateuch the word נערה 'girl', is always, with one exception,
incorrectly written without the ה *hē,* contrary to grammatical rule, whereas
in the margin it is correctly written according to the universal grammatical
rule. Could this, too, have come about through a scribe's copying error?
How could it have happened that the pen always slipped up when this
word occurred? Then again, they could easily have supplied what was
missing and made the correction with good conscience, according to the

---

* See Supplementary Note 20.

rules of grammar. Therefore, since these readings are not due to chance and such obvious faults have remained uncorrected, the argument runs that they were the deliberate work of the original writers, so as to signify something.

However, these arguments are easily answered. The argument from the development of their usage in reading aloud the Scriptures carries no weight with me. Superstition may have played some part, and perhaps the custom developed because they considered both versions equally good or feasible, and so decided that the one should be written and the other read so that neither should be rejected. That is to say, in so important a matter they feared to make a final decision lest they should mistakenly prefer the false to the true. So they resolved to show no preference for the one above the other, as must certainly have been the case if they had ordered only the one to be written and read, especially so when the marginal notes are not written in the Sacred Books. Or perhaps this came about through their deciding that certain things, although correctly written down, should nevertheless be read in the way indicated by a marginal note. Thus came the general rule that the Bible should be read according to the marginal notes.

I shall now discuss the motive that induced the scribes to mark certain words to be read expressly from the margin. For not all marginal notes are doubtful readings; they also occur in the case of expressions that had passed out of common usage, namely, obsolete words, and terms that the approved manners of the time did not permit to be read aloud in a public assembly. Writers of old, in their simple way, called things plainly by their names with no courtly circumlocution. Later on, when vice and intemperance were rife, words which in the mouths of the ancients were free from obscenity began to be regarded as obscene. There was no need to alter Scripture on this account, but in concession to the weak-mindedness of the common people they introduced the custom in public readings of substituting more acceptable words for sexual intercourse and excrement, as are marked in the marginal notes.

Finally, whatever the reason for the development of the practice of reading and interpreting Scripture according to the marginal version, it was certainly not that a true interpretation must thus result. For apart from the fact that the Rabbis themselves in the Talmud are often at variance with the Massoretes,[2] and possessed other readings which they regarded as correct—as I shall show in due course—there are also some

2. Massoretes. A name given to the succession of scholars who labored from about the sixth century to the tenth century to produce an authoritative version of the Hebrew Bible. They introduced vowel signs.

marginal notes which seem less in accord with Hebrew linguistic usage. For example, in 2 Samuel ch. 14 v. 22 we read "in that the king hath fulfilled the request of his servant," a quite regular construction, and in agreement with that of verse 15 of the same chapter. But the margin has עבדך 'of thy servant,' which does not agree with the person of the verb. So, too, in the last verse of chapter 16 of the same book, we read 'as when one enquires (ישאל) of the word of God,' while in the margin the word איש (someone) is added as the subject of the verb. This appears to have been done in error, for it is the common practice of the Hebrew language to express the impersonal of a verb by the third person singular active, as grammarians well know. And there are several marginal notes of this kind which cannot be given preference over the written version.

As for the second argument of the Pharisees, this is also easily met by my earlier statement, namely, that besides doubtful readings the scribes also marked obsolete words. For there is no doubt that in the Hebrew language, as in other languages, many words were rendered obsolete and antiquated by later usage; and these were found in the Bible by the latest generation of scribes, who, as we have said, marked them all as having to be read in public according to contemporary usage. It is for this reason that the word נער *na'ar* is always found marked, because in antiquity it was of common gender, and meant the same as the Latin word '*juvenis*' (a young person). So, too, the capital city of the Hebrews used to be called in ancient times Jerusalem, not Jerusalaim. I take a similar view regarding the pronoun הוא meaning 'he' or 'she', that is, that the later scribes changed the ו *vav* into י *yad* (a frequent change in Hebrew) when they intended to signify the feminine gender, whereas the ancients used to distinguish the feminine from the masculine only by a change of vowel. So, too, the irregular forms of certain verbs in earlier times differed from those of later times. Finally, the ancient writers made use of the paragogic[3] letters האמנתיו with an elegance peculiar to their time. All this I could illustrate with many more examples, were I not afraid of wearying the reader.

If I am asked what are my grounds for classifying words as obsolete, I reply that I do so because I often find them in the most ancient writers— that is, the Bible—and yet later writers ceased to use them; and in the case of other languages this is the only justification for classifying words as obsolete, even though they are also dead languages. But perhaps I shall be further pressed with the question why, since I have maintained that most of these marginal notes are doubtful readings, there are never more than

---

3. This is a technical grammatical term deriving from Greek grammar. It is the addition of a letter or syllable to the end of a word, especially to give emphasis or to modify the meaning.

two readings of a single passage. Why are there not sometimes three or more? Then again, some passages in Scripture, corrected in a marginal note, are so obviously contrary to grammar that we cannot believe that the scribes could have had any hesitation in deciding which was correct.

But here again there is no difficulty in answering. In reply to the first point, I say that there were in fact more readings than we now find marked in the codices. The Talmud notes several that were passed over by the Massoretes, differing so markedly from their version in many passages that the superstitious editor of the Bomberg Bible[4] was finally forced to admit in his preface that he could not reconcile them. "Here we can make no reply," he said, "except what we have stated above, namely, that the Talmudic practice is in contradiction with the Massoretes." So we do not have sufficient grounds for maintaining that there never were more than two readings of a single passage. Nevertheless, I do readily grant—indeed, I positively believe—that no more than two readings of a single passage have ever been found, and this for two reasons. First, what we have shown to be the cause of the difference in these readings can admit of no more than two readings. We have shown that the chief source of ambiguity was the similarity of certain letters, and therefore this ambiguity nearly always resolved itself into the question as to which of two letters should be accepted, ב *bet* or כ *kaf*, י *yad* or ו *vav*, ד *dalet* or ר *resh* and so on. These letters are of frequent occurrence, and thus it could often come about that either letter yielded a reasonable meaning. Again, it might be a question of whether a syllable was long or short, its quantity depending on the letters called mutes. There is the further point that not all marginal notes are doubtful readings: we have mentioned that many were inserted for the sake of decency, and others to explain obsolete and antiquated words. The second reason that convinces me that not more than two readings of a single passage are found is this, that I believe that the scribes found very few original manuscripts, perhaps not more than two or three. In the Treatise of the Scribes,[5] סופרים chapter 6, there is mention of only three, which they allege were made by Ezra himself. Be that as it may, if they possessed three manuscripts we can naturally suppose that two would always be in agreement in any one passage. Indeed, it would have been quite extraordinary if in the case of three manuscripts each gave a different reading of one and the same text.

How it came about that after the time of Ezra there existed so few manuscripts will surprise no one who has read either the first book of the

---

4. The Bomberg Bible was printed by D. Bomberg (a Christian) at Venice, 1524–1525, edited by Jacob ben Hayyim.

5. This is a treatise in the Babylonian Talmud.

Maccabees, chapter 1, or Josephus' *Antiquities*, Book 12, chapter 5. Indeed, it seems miraculous that they could have saved these few after such a fierce and lengthy persecution. Nobody, I imagine, can doubt this if he has read the history of these times with any attention. Thus we can see why nowhere do we find more than two doubtful readings. Therefore this cannot possibly lead to the conclusion that the marked passages in the Bible were deliberately written incorrectly so as to signify some mysteries.

As to the second argument, that certain passages are so incorrectly written that there could be no shadow of doubt that they violated the grammatical rules of all times, and that therefore they should have been unhesitatingly corrected and not merely accompanied by a marginal note, I attach little weight to this. I am not bound to know what religious scruple induced the scribes to refrain from so doing. Perhaps they were prompted by a sincere wish to transmit the Bible to posterity in the exact condition in which they had found it in the few original manuscripts, while noting in the margin the discrepancies in the manuscripts, not as doubtful readings, but as variant readings. The only reason for my calling them doubtful readings is that in fact I find them nearly all to be of such a kind that I cannot determine which should be preferred to the other.

Finally, apart from these doubtful readings, the scribes have noted a number of cases of mutilated texts by leaving a space in mid-paragraph. The Massoretes have counted them, enumerating twenty-eight cases where a space is left in mid-paragraph. Whether they believe that some mystery also lurks in this number I do not know, but the Pharisees religiously preserve a fixed area of empty space. To take one example, in Genesis chapter 4 v. 8 we read, "And Cain said to his brother . . . and it came to pass while they were in the field that Cain. . . ." A space is left where we might have expected to learn what Cain said to his brother. There are twenty-eight such spaces left by the scribes, apart from passages we have already noted. Yet many of these passages would not be recognised as mutilated, were it not for the space. But I have said enough on this subject.

CHAPTER 10

An examination of the remaining books of the Old Testament
by the same method as was used with the previous books

I now pass on to the remaining books of the Old Testament. Of the two books of Chronicles I have nothing particular or important to remark, except that they were written some considerable time after Ezra, and perhaps after the restoration of the temple by Judas Maccabee.* For in chapter 9 of the first book the historian tells us 'what families first of all (that is, in the time of Ezra) dwelt in Jerusalem,' and then in verse 17 he gives the names of the porters, two of whom are also mentioned in Nehemiah ch. 11 v. 19. This shows that these books were written some considerable time after the rebuilding of the city. As to the authorship of these books, their authority, usefulness and doctrine, I can say nothing. Indeed, I find it quite astonishing that they were accepted among the Sacred Books by those who excluded from the canon the book of Wisdom, the book of Tobit, and other books that are called apocryphal. But it is not my purpose to disparage the authority of the Chronicles; since they have been given universal acceptance, I also leave them, for what they are.

The Psalms were also gathered together and divided into five books in the time of the second temple; for on the evidence of Philo Judaeus[1] Psalm 88 was published while king Jehoiachin was still a prisoner in Babylon, and Psalm 89 when Jehoiachin obtained his freedom. I do not believe that Philo would ever have made this statement unless either it was the accepted belief of his time or he had learned it from trustworthy sources.

The Proverbs of Solomon, I believe, were also collected at that time, or at least in the time of king Josiah, for in chapter 25 v. 1 we read, "These are

---

* See Supplementary Note 21.

1. The Philo Judaeus mentioned here by Spinoza is *not* the famous Jewish philosopher and biblical exegete of Alexandria, Egypt (first century A.D.). Later in this chapter (page 133) Spinoza refers to a Philo Judaeus again and mentions his work, *The Book of Times*. The philosopher Philo of Alexandria wrote no such book. According to the modern Hebrew translator of the *TTP*, Chayyim Wirszubski, Spinoza is actually referring to a book attributed to "Philo Judaeus" by the Italian scholar Johannes Annius of Viterbo. Most probably, suggests Wirszubski, Spinoza found this reference in the Renaissance Italian Jewish historian Azariah de Rossi's *Me'or 'Einaiyyim*, Book 3, chapter 32.

also the Proverbs of Solomon, which the men of Hezekiah, king of Judah, copied out." At this point I cannot refrain from remarking on the audacity of the Rabbis who wanted this book, and also Ecclesiastes, to be excluded from the canon and to be kept with the others that are now missing. This they would actually have done had they not found some passages where the Law of Moses is commended. It is indeed a matter of deep regret that decisions of high and sacred import rested with these men. However, I am obliged to them for allowing these books, too, to come down to us, though I cannot help doubting their good faith in transmitting them, a matter which I shall not here subject to keen scrutiny.

I pass on, then, to the books of the Prophets. On turning my attention to these, I find that the prophecies they contain were gathered from other books, and were not always set down in these books in the same order in which they were spoken or written by the prophets themselves; nor again are they all contained there, but only those that the compilers could find in various sources. Hence these books are only fragmentary writings of the prophets. For Isaiah began to prophesy in the reign of Uzziah, as the writer himself testifies in the first verse. Now Isaiah not only prophesied at that time but also wrote a full account of Uzziah's acts (see 2 Chron. ch. 26 v. 22), a book that is now lost. We have shown that what we do possess is taken from the chronicles of the kings of Judah and Israel. Furthermore, the Rabbis maintain that Isaiah also prophesied in the reign of Manasseh, by whom he was finally put to death; and although this may be a myth, it does appear that they believed that not all of Isaiah's prophecies are extant.

The prophecies of Jeremiah, which are narrated in the manner of history, were selected and compiled from various chronicles. For not only are they gathered together in a confused mass with no regard to chronological order but, furthermore, there are different versions of the same story. In chapter 21 the writer gives as the reason for Jeremiah's arrest that, on being consulted by Zedekiah, he prophesied the destruction of the city; then, interrupting his narrative, in chapter 22 he passes on to Jeremiah's outcry against Jehoiachin, who reigned before Zedekiah, predicting the king's captivity. Then in chapter 25 the writer describes the prophet's revelations prior to these events, in the fourth year of Jehoiachin's reign. Then he moves on to the events of the first year of this king's reign, continuing to pile up prophecies with no regard of chronological order, until in chapter 38 he resumes what he began to relate in chapter 21, as if the intervening fifteen chapters were a parenthesis. For the connecting words at the beginning of chapter 38 relate to verses 8, 9 and 10 of chapter 21. He then describes Jeremiah's final arrest in very different terms, and assigns a reason for his long stay in prison which is very different from that related in chapter 37. Thus one may clearly see that all these narratives were taken from different historians, and the incoherence can have no other explanation.

The prophecies contained in the remaining chapters of the book, where Jeremiah speaks in the first person, seem to have been copied from a volume that Baruch wrote at Jeremiah's dictation; for, as chapter 36 v. 2 makes clear, this contained only what was revealed to the prophet from the time of Josiah to the fourth year of Jehoiachin, the point at which this book begins. The narrative from chapter 45 v. 2 to chapter 51 v. 59 also seems to have been copied from the same volume.

The book of Ezekiel, too, is only a fragment, as is clearly indicated by the early verses. Who can fail to see that the transitional words with which the book begins relate to things previously said, making a connection between those things and things yet to come? But it is not only the transition, it is the entire structure of the work that presupposes other writings. That the book begins with the thirtieth year shows that the prophet is continuing a narrative, not beginning one; and this is noted by the writer himself in a parenthesis in verse 3, "And the word of the Lord came often unto Ezekiel, the son of Buzi, a priest in the land of the Chaldeans . . .," as if to say that the words of Ezekiel which he had thus far written related to other revelations that had come to him before his thirtieth year. Then again, Josephus in his *Antiquities*, Book 10, chapter 7 tells us that Ezekiel foretold that Zedekiah would not see Babylon; but this is not told us in the book of Ezekiel now extant, which on the contrary tells us in chapter 17 that he would be taken to Babylon as captive.*

With regard to Hosea, we cannot say with certainty that he wrote more than is contained in the book of his name. Yet I am surprised that we do not possess more writings of one who, on the testimony of the author, prophesied for eighty-four years. This much we know as a general fact, that the writers of these books did not collect the prophecies of all who prophesied, nor all the prophecies of those prophets whom we do possess. Of the prophets who prophesied in the reign of Manasseh, of whom general mention is made in 2 Chron. ch. 33 v. 10, 18, 19, we possess no prophecies whatsoever, nor do we possess all the prophecies of our twelve prophets. In the case of Jonah, only the prophecies concerning the Ninevites are available, although he also prophesied to the Israelites, for which see 2 Kings ch. 14 v. 25.

With regard to the book of Job, and Job himself, there has been considerable controversy among writers.[2] Some think that Moses wrote the

---

* See Supplementary Note 22.

2. The authorship of the Book of Job was debated by the Rabbis in the Talmud

book, and that the whole story is nothing but a parable. This is the view of certain Rabbis in the Talmud, and is also favoured by Maimonides in his '*More Nebuchim*.' Others have believed that the story is true, of whom some have thought that Job lived in the time of Jacob and married his daughter Dinah. But ibn Ezra, as I have previously said, asserts in his commentary on this book that it was translated into Hebrew from another language. I wish he could have demonstrated this more convincingly, for we might therefrom conclude that the Gentiles, too, possessed sacred books. I therefore leave the question unresolved, but I would surmise that Job was a Gentile, a man of great steadfastness who experienced first of all prosperity, then calamity, and finally the utmost good fortune; for he is so named among others by Ezekiel chapter 14 v. 14. I believe that the vicissitudes of Job and his steadfastness gave occasion for much discussion concerning God's providence, or at least induced the author of this book to compose his dialogue. The contents of the book, and likewise its style, seem not to be the work of a man wretchedly ill, lying amid ashes, but of one meditating at ease in a library. I am also inclined to agree with ibn Ezra that this book is a translation from another language, for its poetic style seems to be characteristic of the Gentiles. The Father of the gods twice summons a council; Momus,[3] who is here called Satan, criticises God's words with the utmost freedom and so on. But these are mere conjectures, and not firmly founded.

I pass on to the book of Daniel. From chapter 8 on it undoubtedly contains the writings of Daniel himself, but I do not know whence the first seven chapters were derived. Since they were written in Chaldaic except for the first chapter, we may surmise that they were taken from the chronicles of the Chaldeans. If this could be clearly established, it would afford striking evidence to prove that Scripture is sacred only insofar as we understand through it the matters therein signified, and not insofar as we understand merely the words or the language and sentences whereby these matters are conveyed. It would further prove that books that teach and tell of the highest things are equally sacred, in whatever language and by whatever nation they were written. This much, at least, we can remark,

---

(Babylonian Talmud, Treatise Bava Batrah, 15a). They also discussed the question of whether Job was a historical figure or only an allegorical type. Maimonides favored the latter view (*Guide of the Perplexed*, 3.22).

3. In ancient Greek literature and mythology Momus was a fault-finding personification (Hesiod, *Theogony*, 214). Spinoza's identification of Momus with the biblical Satan suggests that the Bible, too, is a literary document analogous to Greek myths and that we should regard and study the former as we do the latter.

that these chapters were written in Chaldaic, and are nevertheless as sacred as the rest of the Bible.

To this book of Daniel the first book of Ezra is so linked that it is easily recognised to be the work of the same author, who continues the history of the Jews from their first captivity on. And I have no doubt that the book of Esther is linked with this book, for the connective words with which it begins can refer to no other book. It cannot be believed that this is the same book as that which Mordecai wrote, for in chapter 9 v. 20, 21, 22 somebody else tells of Mordecai that he wrote letters, giving their contents; and again in verse 31 of the same chapter he says that Queen Esther established by edict the arrangements pertaining to the feast of Lots (Purim), and that this was written in the book—that is, as the Hebrew idiom indicates, in a book well known at the time of writing. This book has perished along with the others, as ibn Ezra admits and must be universally admitted. Finally, for the rest of the acts of Mordecai the historian refers us to the chronicles of the kings of Persia. Therefore there can be no doubt that this book was also written by the same historian who related the history of Daniel and Ezra; and so, too, was the book of Nehemiah,* for it is called the second book of Ezra. We can affirm, then, that these four books—the books of Daniel, Ezra, Esther and Nehemiah—were written by one and the same historian. As to the identity of the writer, I cannot even hazard a guess. But to help us to understand from what sources the historian, whoever he was, may have acquired his knowledge of these histories, perhaps simply transcribing the greatest part of them, it should be observed that the governors or rulers of the Jews in the time of the second temple, like the kings in the time of the first temple, kept a succession of scribes or chroniclers who wrote their annals or chronicles. For the chronicles or annals of the kings are quoted in numerous places in the books of Kings, while those of the rulers and priests of the second temple are first quoted in Nehemiah chapter 12 v. 23, and then again in 1 Maccabees chapter 16 v. 24. This is undoubtedly the book (see Esther ch. 9 v. 31) of which we have just spoken, containing the decree of Esther and the acts of Mordecai, a book which we said, with ibn Ezra, is no longer extant. From this book, then, were derived or copied all the contents of the four books in question, for no other book is quoted by their author, nor do we know of any other book of acknowledged authority.

That these books were not written by Ezra or Nehemiah is obvious from Nehemiah chapter 12 v. 10, 11, where the genealogy of the high priests is traced from Jeshua to Jaddua, the sixth high priest, a man who met Alexander the Great at a time when the Persian Empire was almost

---

* See Supplementary Note 23.

completely subjugated (see Josephus' *Antiquities*, Book 11, chapter 8), or who, according to Philo Judaeus in his book of *Times*, was the sixth and last high priest under the Persians. Indeed, in verse 22 of this same chapter of Nehemiah, this is made quite clear. "The Levites," says the historian, "in the days of Eliashab, Joiada, Johanan and Jaddua were recorded above* the reign of Darius the Persian," that is, in the chronicles. Now I cannot imagine that anyone would believe that Ezra** or Nehemiah lived long enough to survive fourteen Persian kings. For Cyrus was the first to grant the Jews permission to rebuild their temple, and from this time to Darius, the fourteenth and last Persian king, is a period of more than 200 years. Therefore I have no doubt that these books were written some time after Judas Maccabee restored the worship in the temple; and this is supported by the fact that at that time the spurious books of Daniel, Ezra and Esther were published by certain ill-disposed persons who were no doubt of the sect of the Sadducees,⁴ for the Pharisees never accepted these books, to the best of my knowledge. And although we find in the so-called fourth book of Ezra certain stories that also appear in the Talmud, these books should not on that account be attributed to the Pharisees; for, except for the most ignorant, they are all of them convinced that these stories were added by some trifler. In fact, I believe that this was the work of some people whose object was to bring universal ridicule on the traditions of the Pharisees.

Perhaps the reason why these four books were written and published at that particular time was to demonstrate to the people that Daniel's prophecies were fulfilled, thereby strengthening their devotion to religion and giving them, in the midst of such grievous misfortunes, some hope of better things and salvation to come. However, although these books belong to a period so much later and more recent, many errors have crept in as a result, I imagine, of the hastiness of the writers. Marginal notes, which I discussed in the preceding chapter, are to be found in these books as in the others, but in greater number, and there are in addition some passages which can have no other explanation, as I shall proceed to show. But let me first observe with regard to the marginal readings in these books, that if we take the Pharisees' view that these notes go back as far as the writers of these books, then we shall have to say that the writers—if there were more

---

* Unless this means 'beyond' it was an error of the scribe who wrote עַל 'above' instead of עַד—'up to'.

** See Supplementary Note 24.

4. A conservative sect, belonging mainly to the upper class and associated with the priestly families. On certain matters of doctrine they differed from the Pharisees, who, according to Josephus, "profess to be more religious than the rest and to explain the laws more precisely."

than one—must have marked these marginal notes because they found that the chronicles which were their sources had been incorrectly written, and although there were some glaring faults, they did not venture to correct the writings of their predecessors of long ago. There is no need for me to enlarge once again on this subject; and I shall therefore move on to point out such errors as are not indicated in the margin.

In the first place, there is no way of knowing how many faults have found their way into chapter 2 of Ezra. Verse 64 gives the sum total of all the items separately enumerated in the chapter as 42,360, yet the addition of the items there enumerated gives the figure of 29,818. Thus there must be a mistake either in the sum total or in the separate items. Now the total is probably to be regarded as correct, because everyone would doubtless have remembered it as a noteworthy thing, whereas this does not apply to the separate items. If an error had occurred in the sum total, everyone would have noticed it, and it would easily have been corrected. This view is plainly confirmed by chapter 7 of Nehemiah, where this chapter of Ezra (called the register of genealogy) was copied, as is expressly stated in verse 5 of the same chapter of Nehemiah. The sum total here given agrees exactly with that given in the book of Ezra, whereas the items are very different, some being greater and some less than in Ezra, and totalling 31,089. Therefore there can be no doubt that, both in Ezra and Nehemiah, it is only in the separate items that errors have occurred.

The commentators who attempt to reconcile these obvious discrepancies exercise each one his imagination according to his ingenuity, and while paying homage to every letter and word of Scripture, they merely succeed, as I have previously indicated, in exposing to contempt the writers of the Bible, as if these did not know how to speak or to arrange what they had to say. Indeed, they do no more than obscure the plain meaning of Scripture. If it were legitimate to extend their mode of interpretation to the whole of Scripture, there would not be a sentence whose true meaning could not be called into doubt. But I shall waste no more time on this subject, for I am convinced that if an historian were to allow himself the same liberties that the commentators in their religious fervour grant to the writers of the Bible, he would be laughed to scorn by those very commentators. And if they regard as blasphemous anyone who asserts that Scripture is in some places faulty, by what name, pray, shall I call those who read into Scripture whatever takes their fancy, who expose the sacred historians as stammering in utter confusion, who reject the plainest and most evident meaning of Scripture? What can be clearer in Scripture than that Ezra with his companions, in the register of genealogy written in chapter 2 of the book called by his name, has given the itemised total of all those who set out for Jerusalem? For he included in that total not only those who could give account of their lineage but also those who could not do so. What can be clearer than that Nehemiah (ch. 7 v. 5) simply copied down this register? Those who offer another explanation are just denying the true meaning of Scripture, and consequently Scripture itself. They think it a mark of piety to alter some passages of Scripture to harmonise with others—an absurd piety, in that they adapt clear passages to suit the obscure, the correct to suit the faulty, and they contaminate what is sound with what is corrupt. Yet far be it from me to accuse of blasphemy those who have no malicious intent, for to err is human.

But I return to my theme. Besides the undoubted arithmetical errors in the register of genealogy both in Ezra and in Nehemiah, several others are to be remarked in family names, and many more in the genealogies, in the histories, and even in the prophecies, I fear. The prophecy of Jeremiah, chapter 22, concerning Jeconiah seems in no way to agree with his history (see the end of 2 Kings, and Jeremiah, and 1 Chron. ch. 3 v. 17, 18, 19), and especially the words of the last verse of that chapter. Nor again do I see how he could have said, "Thou shalt die in peace" of Zedekiah, whose eyes were put out after his sons were slain before him (Jer. ch. 34 v. 5). If prophecies are to be interpreted by the event, these names should be interchanged, Jeconiah for Zedekiah and Zedekiah for Jeconiah. But this would be too paradoxical a proceeding, and so I prefer to leave this as an insoluble problem, especially since any mistake here must be attributed to the historian, and not to a fault in the original manuscripts.

As for the other difficulties I have mentioned, I do not intend to deal with them here as I would only weary the reader, and in any case they have already been noticed by others. Faced with the glaring contradictions which he saw in the genealogies I have spoken of, R. Shlomo[5] was driven to give vent to these words (see his commentaries on 1 Chron. ch. 8): "The fact that Ezra (whom he takes to be the author of Chronicles) differs from Genesis in the names he gives to the sons of Benjamin and in the genealogy he establishes, and that again he differs from Joshua in his references to most of the cities of the Levites, is due to differences that he found in the original manuscripts." A little further on he says: "The genealogy of Gibeon and others is set down twice in different ways because in the case of each genealogy Ezra found several registers giving different versions. In copying these he followed the version of the majority of manuscripts; but when there were an equal number of differing genealogies, he gave both versions." Thus he unquestionably admits that these books were compiled

5. R. Shlomo—this is R. Shlomo Yitzhaki 1040–1105, better known by the abbreviation Rashi. A French rabbinical scholar, whose commentary on the Bible won great fame.

from original manuscripts of doubtful accuracy and certainty. Indeed, the commentators themselves, in their attempts to reconcile various passages, frequently do nothing more than indicate the causes of errors. Finally, no one of sound judgment, I imagine, can believe that the sacred historians deliberately wrote in such a way as to present the appearance of contradicting one another over and over again.

Perhaps someone will object that in this way I am plainly subverting Scripture, for according to this argument all may suspect it of being faulty at all points. But on the contrary, I have shown that by my approach to the problem I am doing a service to Scripture by preventing its clear and uncontaminated passages from being made to fit with faulty passages, and thus being corrupted. Nor does the corrupt state of certain passages give grounds for bringing them all under suspicion. No book is ever free from faults; has anyone ever suspected books of being faulty through and through on that account? Surely no one would think so, especially if a book is clearly expressed and the author's meaning unmistakable.

Having now completed my task of enquiring into the books of the Old Testament, I find no difficulty in concluding that no canon of the Sacred Books existed before the Maccabees,* that those books which we now possess were chosen from many others by the Pharisees of the second temple—who were also responsible for the set form of prayers—and that these books were accepted solely on their authority. Therefore those who propose to prove the authority of Holy Scripture are required to prove the authority of each separate book. Proving the divine origin of one book does not sufficiently prove the divine origin of all; otherwise one would have to maintain that the council of Pharisees was infallible in making its selection, which is impossible to demonstrate. Now the evidence that compels me to maintain that the Pharisees alone were responsible for selecting the books of the Old Testament and introducing them into the canon is this, that in the last chapter of Daniel, verse 2, the resurrection of the dead is foretold, a doctrine denied by the Sadducees. Secondly, in the Talmud the Pharisees themselves clearly confirm my view: in the Treatise of Sabbatus, chapter 2, folio 30, page 2, we read, "R. Jehuda, entitled Rabi, has said, 'The learned sought to suppress the book of Ecclesiastes because its words are at variance with the words of the Law (i.e. the book of the Law of Moses). Why did they not suppress it? Because its beginning is in accordance with the Law and its ending is in accordance with the Law.'" And a little further on, "They also sought to suppress the book of Proverbs." And finally, in the same treatise, chapter 1, folio 13, page 2, "Verily, name that man for good, he who was called Nehunya, son of Hezekiah.

* See Supplementary Note 25.

Had it not been for him, the book of Ezekiel would have been suppressed because its words were at variance with the words of the Law. . . ." Here is clear evidence that men learned in the Law summoned a council to decide what books should be received as sacred and what books should be excluded. Therefore whoever seeks assurance as to the authority of all the books, let him again call a council and require each book to be justified.

At this point we should proceed to a similar examination of the books of the New Testament. But I gather that this has been done by men highly skilled in the sciences and particularly in languages, and furthermore my knowledge of Greek is insufficient for venturing upon such an undertaking. And finally, we are without the originals of the books, which were written in Hebrew. For these reasons I prefer to leave this task. However, there are certain points particularly relevant to my general theme, and to these I shall draw attention in the following chapter.

CHAPTER 11

An enquiry as to whether the Apostles wrote their
Epistles as Apostles and prophets, or as teachers.
The function of the Apostles is explained

Nobody who reads the New Testament can doubt that the Apostles were prophets.[1] However, prophets did not speak at all times from revelation, but only on rare occasions, as we showed towards the end of chapter 1; and so the question may be raised as to whether the Apostles wrote their Epistles as prophets, from revelation and express mandate like Moses, Jeremiah and others, or as private individuals or teachers. This is particularly a matter of some doubt because in 1 Cor. ch. 14 v. 6 Paul speaks of two kinds of preaching, one from revelation and the other from knowledge, so that the question may properly be raised as to whether the Apostles in their Epistles were prophesying or teaching.

Now if we examine the style of the Epistles, we shall find it to be entirely different from that of prophecy. It was the constant practice of the prophets to declare at all points that they were speaking at God's command, as in the phrases, 'Thus saith the Lord,' 'The Lord of hosts saith,' 'The commandment of the Lord' and so on. This seems to have been the case not only when they addressed public assemblies but also in their epistles containing revelations, as is clear from that of Elijah written to Jehoram (2 Chron. ch. 21 v. 12), which likewise begins 'Thus saith the Lord.' But in the Epistles of the Apostles we find nothing like this; on the contrary, in 1 Cor. ch. 7 v. 40 Paul speaks according to his own opinion. Indeed, there are numerous instances of expressions indicating lack of positive certainty, such as 'We therefore think"* (Rom. ch. 3 v. 28) and 'For I think' (Rom. ch. 8 v. 18) and many others of this kind. There are, furthermore, many expressions far removed from the authoritativeness of prophecy, such as 'But I speak this by way of concession to weakness, not of command' (1 Cor. ch. 7 v. 6), and 'I give my judgment as one that hath

---

1. As Spinoza's subsequent discussion will show, this sentence should be taken with the proverbial grain of salt. At any rate, since the earlier chapters of the *TTP* have demonstrated that prophets do not really reveal to us anything but some basic moral principles, Spinoza's concession to the Apostles in this sentence doesn't cost him much.

* See Supplementary Note 26.

obtained the mercy of the Lord to be faithful' (1 Cor. ch. 7 v. 25), and many other instances. We must also remember that when in the aforementioned chapter the Apostle says that he has or has not the instruction or commandment of God, he does not mean an instruction or commandment revealed to him by God, but only the teachings of Christ in the Sermon on the Mount.

Furthermore, if we examine the manner in which the Apostles expound the Gospel in their Epistles, we see that this, too, is markedly different from that of the prophets. For the Apostles everywhere employ argument, so that they seem to be conducting a discussion rather than prophesying. The prophetic writings, on the other hand, contain only dogma and decrees, for they represent God as speaking not like one who reasons, but one who makes decrees issuing from the absolute power of his nature. Then again, the authority of a prophet does not permit of argumentation, for whoever seeks to base his dogmatic assertions on reason thereby submits them to the arbitrary judgment of the individual. This is just what Paul, because he reasons, seems to have done, declaring in 1 Cor. ch. 10 v. 15, "I speak as to wise men; judge ye what I say."

Finally, as we demonstrated in chapter 1, it was not by virtue of the natural light—that is, by the exercise of reason—that the prophets perceived what was revealed to them. Although the Pentateuch contains some instances where conclusions seem to follow from a process of inference, a closer examination will show that these can in no way be regarded as instances of conclusive argumentation. For example, when Moses said to the Israelites in Deut. ch. 31 v. 27, "If, while I am yet alive with you, ye have been rebellious against the Lord, how much more so after my death," this must not be taken as meaning that Moses intends to prove by rational argument that the Israelites will necessarily turn away from the true worship of God after his death. The argument would have been false, as can be shown from Scripture itself; for the Israelites continued faithful during the lifetime of Joshua and the elders, and again later on during the lifetime of Samuel, David, Solomon and others. Therefore these words of Moses are merely a moral exhortation where, in a rhetorical expression, he predicts the future backsliding of the people as his lively imagination enabled him to picture it. The view that Moses, in seeking to make his prediction credible to the people, spoke not as a prophet from revelation but on his own initiative, I reject for the following reason: in verse 21 of the same chapter we are told that God revealed this very thing to Moses in different words. Now surely Moses stood in no need of plausible reasoning in order to give him greater assurance of God's prediction and decree, but it was necessary that it should be vividly impressed on his imagination, as we showed in chapter 1. This could be most effectively achieved by his imagining the people's present obstinacy, which he had often experienced, as extending into the future.

All the arguments employed by Moses in the Pentateuch are to be understood in this same way. They are not derived from textbooks of logic, but are merely figures of speech whereby he expressed God's decrees more effectively and imagined them in lively fashion. I do not absolutely deny that the prophets may have argued from the basis of revelation, but this much I will assert, that the more use the prophets make of logical reasoning, the more closely does their revelatory knowledge approach to natural knowledge, and the surest mark of supernatural knowledge in the prophets is their proclamation of pure dogma, or decrees, or judgment. And thus Moses, the greatest of the prophets, never engaged in logical argument, whereas in the case of Paul the lengthy chains of logical argumentation such as we find in the Epistle to the Romans were most certainly not written from supernatural revelation.

Therefore the modes of expression and discussion employed by the Apostles in the Epistles clearly show that these originated not from revelation and God's command but from their own natural faculty of judgment, and contain nothing but brotherly admonitions mingled with courteous expressions (very different, indeed, from prophetic authoritativeness), such as Paul's apology in Rom. ch. 15 v. 15, "I have written to you more boldly in some sort, my brethren." We can also reach the same conclusion from the fact that nowhere do we read that the Apostles were commanded to write, but only to preach whithersoever they went, and to confirm their words by signs. Their personal presence and their signs were essential for the conversion of the Gentiles to religion, and their strengthening therein, as Paul himself expressly indicates in Rom. ch. 1 v. 11, "But I long to see you," he said, "so that I may impart to you the gift of the Spirit, to the end that you may be strengthened."

Here it may be objected that the same line of argument could prove that neither was it as prophets that the Apostles did their preaching; for in journeying to various places to preach they were not acting by the express mandate of God, as were the prophets in time gone by. We read in the Old Testament that Jonah went to Nineveh to preach, and at the same time that he was expressly sent there, and that it was revealed to him what he should there preach. So also it is related of Moses in considerable detail that he set out to Egypt as God's emissary, and at the same time he was told what he must say to the people of Israel and to Pharaoh, and what wonders he must perform to gain their credence. Isaiah, Jeremiah and Ezekiel are expressly ordered to preach to the Israelites. Lastly, the prophets preached only what Scripture tells us they had received from God, whereas the New Testament very rarely tells us anything like this of the Apostles when they travelled about preaching. On the contrary, there are some passages which expressly indicate that the Apostles used their own initiative in deciding where to preach, as illustrated by the argument, amounting to a quarrel, between Paul and Barnabas (Acts ch. 15 v. 37, 38 etc.). And they were often frustrated, too, in their proposed journey, as Paul again testifies in Rom. ch. 1 v. 13, "Oftentimes I proposed to come to ye, and was prevented," and in ch. 15 v. 22, "For which cause I have been oftentimes hindered from coming to you," and in the last chapter of 1 Cor. v. 12, "And touching my brother Apollos, I greatly desired him to come unto you with the brethren, but his will was not at all to come; but when he shall have convenient time. . . ." Therefore, taking into account expressions like these and the disagreements among the Apostles, and also that Scripture does not testify, as in the case of the prophets of old, that it was by God's command that they went about to preach, the conclusion should have been that in their preaching, too, the Apostles acted as teachers, not as prophets.

But this difficulty is easily resolved if we consider the difference between the Apostles and the prophets of the Old Testament, in respect of their calling. The latter were called to preach and prophesy only to certain nations, not to all nations, and they therefore needed a clear specific mandate for each nation. But the Apostles were called to preach to all men without restriction, and to convert all men to religion. So wherever they went they were fulfilling Christ's command. Nor did they need, before their mission, a revelation of what they were to preach; for they were disciples of Christ, who had told them: "But when they deliver you up, take no thought of how or what ye shall speak, for it shall be given you in that same hour what ye shall speak" (see Matth. ch. 10 v. 19, 20). We may conclude, then, that the Apostles were inspired by special revelation only in what they orally preached when confirmed by signs, while that which they taught in writing or orally without the attestation of signs was spoken or written from knowledge, that is, natural knowledge (see 1 Cor. ch. 14 v. 6).

There is no problem for us in the fact that all the Epistles begin by setting forth the credentials of apostleship, because the Apostles, as I shall go on to show, were granted not only the gift of prophecy but also authority to teach. That is why we grant that they wrote the Epistles as Apostles, and it was for this reason that each began by affirming the credentials of his apostleship. Or perhaps it was with view to winning the good will of the reader, and gaining his attention, that they first of all testified that they were those who were well known to all the faithful from their preaching, and had already shown on clear evidence that they were teaching true religion and the way of salvation. For I observe that all the statements made in these Epistles regarding the calling of the Apostles and their possessing the Holy and Divine Spirit refer to their past preaching, except only for those passages where 'the Spirit of God' and 'the Holy Spirit' are used in the sense of a mind, pure, blessed, devoted to God and so on (a point we discussed in our first chapter). For instance, in 1 Cor. ch. 7 v. 40, Paul says, "But she is happy if she so abide after my judgment, and I think that I also have the Spirit of God," where by the Spirit of God he means his very mind, as the context shows. For his meaning is, 'I count as blessed a widow who does not remarry, I, who have resolved to live unmarried, and think myself blessed.' There are other similar passages, which I need not quote here.

Since, then, we must maintain that the Epistles of the Apostles were dictated solely by the natural light, we have now to consider how the Apostles were able, from natural knowledge alone, to teach matters that do not fall within its scope. But if we attend to what we said in chapter 7 of this treatise regarding Scriptural interpretation, the difficulty will disappear. For although the contents of the Bible for the most part surpass our understanding, they may safely be the subject of discourse provided that we admit no principles of interpretation other than those that Scripture presents. In the same way the Apostles, on the basis of what they had seen and heard and had acquired by revelation, were able to reach many conclusions and make many inferences, and to teach these to men at their own discretion. Furthermore, although religion as preached by the Apostles— who simply related the story of Christ—does not come within the scope of reason, yet its substance, which consists essentially in moral teachings as does the whole of Christ's doctrine,* can be readily grasped by everyone by the natural light of reason.

Finally, the Apostles needed no supernatural light to adapt a religion, which they had previously confirmed with signs, to the common understanding of mankind so as to be readily and sincerely accepted by everyone; nor yet did they need a supernatural light in their task of exhortation. This is the object of the Epistles, to teach and exhort men in whatever way each Apostle judged would best strengthen them in religious faith. And here we should recall a point recently mentioned, namely, that the Apostles had received not only the power to preach the story of Christ as prophets—that is, confirming it with signs—but also the authority to teach and exhort in whatever way each should think best. Both these gifts are clearly indicated by Paul in 2 Timoth. ch. 1 v. 11, "Whereunto I am appointed a preacher, and an Apostle, and a teacher of the Gentiles," and again in 1 Timoth. ch. 2 v. 7, "Whereunto I am ordained a preacher and an

---

* See Supplementary Note 27.

Apostle (I speak the truth in Christ, and lie not), a teacher of the Gentiles in faith (note this) and verity." In these passages, I say, he clearly indicates his credentials both as an Apostle and as a teacher, while his authority to exhort whomsoever he would, on all occasions, is indicated in Philem. v. 8, thus, "Although I might be much bold in Christ to enjoin thee that which is fitting, yet. . . ." Here we should observe that if Paul had received from God, in his capacity of prophet, that which it behoved him to enjoin on Philemon, and which it was his duty as a prophet to enjoin on him, surely it would have been wrong for him to change God's command into an entreaty. Therefore he must be understood as referring to his freedom to exhort, which belonged to him as a teacher, not a prophet.

However, it does not as yet clearly follow that the Apostles were empowered to choose the method of teaching which each one judged the best; we have merely shown that by virtue of their apostleship they were not only prophets but teachers. To justify the former assertion we might call on the assistance of reason, which clearly tells us that he who has the authority to teach has also the authority to choose his own way of teaching. But it would be more satisfactory to demonstrate this entirely from Scripture, which makes it perfectly clear that each of the Apostles chose his own particular way, as shown by these words of Paul, Rom. ch. 15 v. 20, "striving to preach the Gospel not where Christ was named, lest I should build upon another man's foundation." Now if all the Apostles employed the same method of teaching and had built the Christian religion on the same foundation, Paul could have had no justification in referring to another Apostle's work as 'another man's foundation,' inasmuch as it was the same as his own. But since he does so refer to it, we have to conclude that each Apostle built religion on a different foundation, and that in their capacity as teachers the Apostles were in just the same position as other teachers; they each have their own method, so that they always prefer to instruct those who are beginners and have never studied under any other master, whether in the case of languages, the sciences, and even mathematics, of whose truth no one can doubt.

Again, if we study the Epistles themselves with some care, we shall see that, while the Apostles were in agreement about religion itself, they differed widely as to its foundations. In order to strengthen men in their religious faith and to show that salvation depends solely on the grace of God, Paul taught that no one can boast by reason of works, but only his faith, and no one can be justified by works (see Rom. ch. 3 v. 27, 28), and he goes on to teach the complete doctrine of predestination. James, on the other hand, in his Epistle teaches that man is justified by works, and not by faith alone (ch. 2 v. 24), and his doctrine of religion is confined within a small compass, leaving out all those discussions we find in Paul.

Finally, there can be no doubt that these differences between the Apostles in the grounding of their religion gave rise to many disputes and schisms to vex the Church continually right from the time of the Apostles, and they will assuredly continue to vex the Church until the day comes when religion shall be separated from philosophic speculation and reduced to the few simple doctrines that Christ taught his people. This was impossible for the Apostles, because the Gospel was then unknown to mankind; so to avoid offending men's ears by the novelty of its doctrine, they adapted it, as far as possible, to the character of their contemporaries (see 1 Cor. ch. 9 v. 19, 20 etc.), building on foundations that were most familiar and accepted at that time. Thus none of the Apostles did more philosophising than Paul, who was called to preach to the Gentiles. The other Apostles, preaching to the Jews[2] who despised philosophy, likewise adapted themselves to the character of their listeners (see Galat. ch. 2 v. 11 etc.), and taught a religious doctrine free from all philosophic speculation. Happy indeed would be our age, if we were to see religion freed again from all superstition.

2. Spinoza seems to contradict himself here. On page 141 he says that the Apostles were ordained by Jesus to preach to all peoples. Here he says that the Apostles, except Paul, preached to the Jews.

CHAPTER 12

Of the true original of the Divine Law. In what respect Scripture
is called holy and the Word of God. It is shown
that Scripture, insofar as it contains the Word of God,
has come down to us uncorrupted

Those who look upon the Bible, in its present form, as a message for
mankind sent down by God from heaven, will doubtless cry out that I have
committed the sin against the Holy Spirit in maintaining that the Word of
God is faulty, mutilated, adulterated and inconsistent, that we possess it
only in fragmentary form, and that the original of God's covenant with the
Jews has perished. However, I am confident that reflection will at once put
an end to their outcry; for not only reason itself, but the assertions of the
prophets and the Apostles clearly proclaim that God's eternal Word and
covenant and true religion are divinely inscribed in men's hearts—that is,
in men's minds—and that this is the true handwriting of God which he
has sealed with his own seal, this seal being the idea of himself, the image
of his own divinity, as it were.

To the early Jews religion was transmitted in the form of written law
because at that time they were just like children; but later on Moses (Deut.
ch. 30 v. 6) and Jeremiah (ch. 31 v. 33) told them of a time to come when
God would inscribe his law in their hearts. So while it was proper only for
the Jews of long ago, and especially the Sadducees, to strive in defence of a
law written on tablets, this does not apply to those who have the law
inscribed in their minds. Whoever reflects on this will find nothing in
what I have said that is at variance with God's word or true religion and
faith, or can weaken it; on the contrary, he will realise that I am strengthening it, as I have also shown towards the end of chapter 10. If this were
not so, I should have resolved to remain completely silent; indeed, to avoid
creating any difficulties, I should gladly have conceded that in Scripture
there lie hidden mysteries of the deepest kind. But since this approach has
led to gross superstition and other pernicious ills, of which I have spoken
in the preface to chapter 7, I feel I must not abandon my task, and all the
more so because religion stands in no need of the trappings of superstition. On the contrary, its glory is diminished when it is embellished with
such fancies.

But it will be said that, although God's law is inscribed in our hearts,
Scripture is nevertheless the Word of God, and it is no more permissible
to say of Scripture that it is mutilated and contaminated than to say this of

God's Word. In reply, I have to say that such objectors are carrying their piety too far, and are turning religion into superstition; indeed, instead of God's Word they are beginning to worship likenesses and images, that is, paper and ink. This much I do know, I have said nothing unworthy of God's Word, for I have affirmed nothing that I have not proved to be true by the plainest of arguments, and therefore I also declare with certainty that I have said nothing that is impious or that smacks of impiety. I do admit that some ungodly men who find religion a burden can assume from my views a licence to sin and, without any justification and merely to gratify their desires, can conclude therefrom that Scripture is at all points faulty and contaminated, and therefore has no authority. But such people are beyond help; as the old saying goes, nothing can be so accurately stated as to be incapable of distortion by misrepresentation. Those who wish to give rein to their desires can easily find any reason for so doing. Men were no better in time gone by when they had the original writings, the Ark of the Covenant, and indeed the prophets and the Apostles in person, nor were they any more obedient. All men, Jews and Gentiles alike, have always been the same, and in every age virtue has been exceedingly rare.

However, to remove any remaining doubt, we must now demonstrate in what sense the terms 'sacred' and 'divine' should be applied to Scripture and to any inanimate thing, and then we must show what the Word of God really is, that it is not confined within the compass of a set number of books, and, further, that Scripture could not have been corrupted insofar as it teaches what is necessary for obedience and salvation. From such a demonstration everyone will readily be able to see that we have said nothing against the Word of God or given any occasion for impiety.

A thing is called sacred and divine when its purpose is to foster piety and religion, and it is sacred only for as long as men use it in a religious way. If men cease to be pious, the thing will likewise cease to be sacred; if it is devoted to impious uses, then that which before was sacred will become unclean and profane. For example, Jacob called a certain place Beth El (House of God) because there he worshipped God who was revealed to him. But the prophets called that same place 'house of iniquity' (see Amos ch. 5 v. 5 and Hosea ch. 10 v. 5) because the Israelites, at the instigation of Jeroboam, were there wont to sacrifice to idols. Another example will make the point quite clear. Words acquire a fixed meaning solely from their use; if in accordance with this usage they are so arranged that readers are moved to devotion, then these words will be sacred, and likewise the book containing this arrangement of words. But if these words at a later time fall into disuse so as to become meaningless, or if the book falls into utter neglect, whether from malice or because men no longer feel the need of it, then both words and book will be without value and without sanctity.

Lastly, if these words are arranged differently, or if by custom they acquire a meaning contrary to their original meaning, then both words and book will become impure and profane instead of sacred. Thus it follows that nothing is sacred or profane or impure in an absolute sense apart from the mind, but only in relation to the mind. This again is made abundantly clear in many passages of Scripture. To take one case at random, Jeremiah says in ch. 7 v. 4 that the Jews of his time were wrong to call Solomon's temple the temple of God; for, as he goes on to say in the same chapter, the temple was entitled to God's name only as long as it was a place of resort for men who worshipped God and upheld righteousness. If it became a place of resort for murderers, thieves, idolaters and other scoundrels, then it was better termed a den of sinners.

I find it strange that Scripture tells us nothing of what became of the Ark of the Covenant; but there can be no doubt that it perished or was burnt along with the temple, in spite of the fact that the Hebrews regarded nothing as more sacred or more worthy of reverence. So Scripture likewise is sacred, and its words divine, only as long as it moves men to devotion towards God; but if it is utterly disregarded by them, as it was once by the Jews, it is nothing more than paper and ink, and their neglect renders it completely profane, leaving it exposed to corruption. So if it then suffers corruption or perishes, it is wrong to say that the Word of God suffers corruption or perishes, just as in the time of Jeremiah it would have been wrong to say that the temple, which at that time was the temple of God, had perished in flames. Jeremiah makes the same point with regard to the Law, for he rebukes the ungodly of his time with these words: "Wherefore say you that we are the learned, and that the Law of God is with us? Surely, it has been composed in vain, in vain has the pen of the scribes (been made)." That is to say, although Scripture is in your keeping, you are wrong in saying that you have the Law of God, since you have rendered it vain.

So, too, when Moses broke the first tablets, he certainly did not in his anger cast from his hands and shatter the Word of God—this would be inconceivable of Moses and of the Word of God—but merely stones which, although previously sacred because on them was inscribed the Covenant under which the Jews had bound themselves to obey God, were now without any sanctity whatever, the Jews having nullified that Covenant by worshipping the calf. And for the same reason the second tablets could not avoid destruction along with the Ark. It is therefore not surprising that the original of Moses' writing, too, is no longer extant, and that the events we previously described have befallen the books which we do possess, seeing that even the true original of God's Covenant, the most sacred of all things, could have completely perished.

Let them cease, therefore, to bring the charge of impiety against us, who have said nothing contrary to the Word of God, nor corrupted it; let them turn their anger, if they have any just cause for anger, against those men of ages past whose wickedness desecrated the Ark, the temple, the Law and all things sacred, exposing them to corruption. Furthermore, if in accordance with the saying of the Apostle in 2 Cor. ch. 3 v. 3 they have within themselves the Epistle of God, written not with ink but with the Spirit of God, not on tablets of stone but on the fleshly tablets of the heart, let them cease to worship the letter and to show so much concern for it.

I think I have now satisfactorily explained in what sense Scripture should be regarded as sacred and divine. We have next to consider what is to be rightly understood by the phrase '*dabar Jehovah*' (the Word of the Lord). '*Dabar*' means word, speech, command and thing. In chapter 1 we have already explained the reasons why a thing is said in Hebrew to be of God, and is referred to God, and from this we can readily understand what Scripture means by the word, speech, command, thing of God. We therefore need not go over all that ground again, nor repeat what we said in chapter 6 in the third section of our exposition concerning miracles. A reference to the points there made will itself be sufficient to afford a better understanding of what I now intend to say: the phrase 'Word of God,' when used in connection with anything other than God himself, properly means the Divine Law which we discussed in chapter 4; that is, religion universal to the entire human race, or catholic religion. For this, see Isaiah ch. 1 v. 10 etc., where he teaches the true way of life as consisting not in ceremonial observance but in charity and sincerity of heart, calling it God's Law and God's Word without distinction.

The expression is also used metaphorically for Nature's order and destiny (because in reality this is dependent on and follows from the eternal decree of the divine nature), and especially for that part of Nature's order that the prophets had foreseen; for the prophets did not envisage future events as the result of natural causes, but as God's will and decrees. Again, this expression is also used for any edict of any prophet insofar his perception resulted not from the natural light which is common to all, but from his special power or prophetic gift. This use of the expression was natural to the prophets, because in actual fact they were wont to perceive God as a lawgiver, as we showed in chapter 4. There are, then, three reasons why Scripture is called the Word of God: because it teaches true religion, of which God is the eternal Author; because it relates predictions of the future as God's decrees; and lastly, because the real authors of Scripture taught for the most part not from the natural light common to all but from a light peculiar to themselves, and they represented God as making these utterances. And although, besides these features, Scripture contains a great deal of merely historical narrative such as can be apprehended by the natural light, it takes the name 'Word of God' from its most important aspect.

It can thus be readily seen in what sense God is to be understood as the author of the Bible: it is not because God willed to confer on men a set number of books, but because of the true religion that is taught therein. And this also explains for us why the Bible is divided into the Old and New Testaments. Before the coming of Christ the prophets used to proclaim religion as the law of their own country by virtue of the covenant made in the time of Moses, whereas after the coming of Christ the Apostles preached religion to all men as a universal law solely by virtue of Christ's Passion. The books of the New Testament contained no different doctrine, nor were they written as documents of a covenant, nor was the universal religion—which is entirely in accord with Nature—anything new, except in relation to men who knew it not. "He was in the world," says John the Evangelist, ch. 1 v. 10, "and the world knew Him not."

Therefore, even if we possessed fewer books of the Old Testament, we should not be deprived of the Word of God, whose proper meaning, as we have said, is true religion. After all, we do not regard ourselves at present as deprived of the Word of God in spite of being without many very important writings, such as the book of the Law, which was zealously guarded in the temple as the original of the Covenant, and the books of the Wars, the books of the Chronicles, and numerous others from which our Old Testament books were gathered and compiled. And there are many other arguments to confirm this view.

1. In the case of both Testaments, the books were not written by express command at one and the same time for all ages. They were the fortuitous work of certain men who wrote according to the requirements of their age and of their own particular character, as is clearly shown by the calling of the prophets (who were called to admonish the ungodly of their time) and also by the Epistles of the Apostles.

2. To understand Scripture and the mind of the prophets is by no means the same thing as to understand the mind of God, that is, to understand truth itself. This follows from our discussion of the prophets in chapter 2, and we showed in chapter 6 that this also applies to the narratives and the miracles. But this cannot be said of those passages that are concerned with true religion and true virtue.

3. The books of the Old Testament were selected out of many books, and were finally assembled and approved by a council of Pharisees, as we showed in chapter 10. The books of the New Testament were also admitted to the canon by the decrees of certain Councils, who rejected as spurious several other books held by many as sacred. But the membership

of these councils (both of Pharisees and of Christians) did not consist of prophets, but only of teachers and scholars. Still, it must be granted that they took the Word of God as their standard in making their selection, and so they must have been acquainted with the Word of God before they approved all the books.

4. The Apostles wrote not as prophets but as teachers (as we said in the preceding chapter), and they chose such methods of teaching as they thought best adapted to those whom they wished to instruct at the time. Hence it follows (as we showed at the end of that same chapter) that their writings contain many things that are no longer relevant to religion.

5. Finally, there are four Evangelists in the New Testament; and who can believe that God willed to tell the story of Christ and impart it in writing to mankind four times over?[1] And although one version may contain some details that are omitted in another, and one version is often helpful to the understanding of another, we should not thus conclude that all that was related in the four Gospels was essential for us to know, and that God chose the Evangelists to write so that the life of Christ might be better understood. Each Evangelist preached his message in a different place, and each wrote down in simple style what he had preached with view to telling clearly the story of Christ, and not with view to explaining the other Evangelists. If a comparison of their different versions sometimes produces a readier and clearer understanding, this is a matter of chance, and it occurs only in a few passages whose obscurity would not have rendered the story less clear or mankind less blessed.

We have thus shown that it is only in respect of religion—i.e. in respect of the universal divine law—that Scripture can properly be called the Word of God. It remains for us now to show that Scripture, insofar as it is properly thus called, is neither faulty, nor corrupted, nor mutilated. Now I here apply the terms 'faulty', 'corrupted' and 'mutilated' to that which is so incorrectly written and composed that its meaning cannot be arrived at from linguistic usage, or be derived from Scripture alone. I am not going to say that Scripture, insofar as it contains the Divine Law, has always preserved the same markings, the same letters and the same words (I leave this to be proved by the Massoretes, who zealously worship the letter), but I will say this, that its meaning—and only in respect of meaning can any utterance be called divine—has reached us uncorrupted, even if it be supposed that the words by which it was originally expressed have under-

---

1. Spinoza suggests here that just as the Old Testament exhibits repetition, inconsistencies, and omissions, so does the New Testament. Hence, just as these faults indicate the human composition of the former work, so do the analogous faults in the latter books manifest their human origin.

gone many changes. Such alterations, as we have seen, take nothing away from the divinity of Scripture; for Scripture would be just as divine even if it had been written in different words or in a different language. Therefore there can be no doubt that the Divine Law has come down to us in this respect uncorrupted. For from Scripture itself we learn that its message, unclouded by any doubt or any ambiguity, is in essence this, to love God above all, and one's neighbour as oneself. There can be no adulteration here, nor can it have been written by a hasty and errant pen; for if doctrine differing from this is to be found anywhere in Scripture, all the rest of its teaching must also have been different. For this is the basis of the whole structure of religion; if it is removed, the entire fabric crashes to the ground, and then such a Scripture would not be the sort of thing we are now discussing, but a quite different book. It is, then, incontestable that this has always been the teaching of Scripture, and therefore no error capable of corrupting this meaning can have entered without its being immediately observed by all, nor could anyone have deliberately corrupted it without his evil intent being at once detected.

Since, then, it must be maintained that this fundamental principle is uncorrupted, the same must be granted of all that indisputably follows therefrom and is likewise fundamental, such as that God exists, that He provides for all things, that He is omnipotent, that by His decrees the good prosper and the wicked are cast down, and that our salvation depends solely on His grace. For all these are doctrines which are plainly taught throughout Scripture, and which it was at all times bound to teach if all the rest of its teachings were not to be vain and without foundation. And we must accept as equally uncorrupted, inasmuch as they quite clearly follow from this universal basis, all its other moral teachings, such as to uphold justice, to help the helpless, to do no murder, to covet no man's goods and so on. None of these, I say, could have been corrupted by human malice or destroyed by time's decay; for if any part of them had disappeared, the underlying universal principle would at once have restored it, especially the doctrine of charity, which is everywhere commended in the highest degree in both Testaments. Furthermore, although there is no crime so abominable as not to have been committed by someone, there is no one who, to excuse his crimes, would attempt to destroy the law or to introduce some impiety as eternal doctrine and the road to salvation. For we see that human nature is so constituted that any man (be he king or subject) who has committed a base action seeks to cloak his deed with such outward show as to give the impression of having done nothing contrary to justice and decency. We may therefore accept without reservation that the universal Divine Law, as taught by Scripture, has reached us uncorrupted.

Besides the above, there are other things which we cannot doubt have been transmitted to us in good faith, such as the chief historical narratives of Scripture, these being well known to all. It was the custom of the Jewish people in ancient times to chant their nation's history in psalms. The chief facts of the life of Christ, too, and his Passion were immediately spread abroad throughout the whole Roman Empire. It is therefore impossible to believe that, without the connivance of a large part of mankind—which is quite inconceivable[2]—later generations handed down a version of the main outlines of these events different from what they had received. So any alterations or faults can have occurred only with respect to minor matters, such as a few details in history or prophecy designed to foster people's devotion, or in a few miracles so as to perplex philosophers, or in speculative matters after schismatics had begun the practice of introducing these into religion in order that each of them might buttress his own fictions by misusing divine authority. But for salvation it matters little whether these are instances of corruption or not, as I shall explain in full in the next chapter; though I believe this is already proved by what I have previously said, especially in chapter 2.

2. This argument was frequently employed in medieval Jewish thought to vindicate the authenticity of Jewish revelation and tradition. (See Saadia Gaon (882–942), *The Book of Beliefs and Opinions*, Treatise 3, chapter 6.)

CHAPTER 13

It is shown that Scripture teaches only very simple doctrines
and inculcates nothing but obedience, and that concerning
the nature of God it teaches only what men can imitate
by a definite code of conduct

In chapter 2 of this treatise we showed that the prophets possessed only an extraordinary power of imagination, not of intellect; and that God did not reveal to them any philosophic mysteries, but only things of a very simple nature, adapted to their preconceived beliefs. Then in chapter 5 we showed that Scripture conveys and teaches its message in a way best suited to the comprehension of all men, not resorting to a chain of deductive reasoning from axioms and definitions, but speaking quite simply. And to induce belief, it relies only on past events, such as miracles and histories, to confirm its message, employing such style and mode of expression as is most likely to make a strong impression on men's minds. (On this subject see the third section of chapter 6.) Finally, in chapter 7 we showed that the difficulty in understanding Scripture lies only in its language, and not in the high level of its argumentation. We may add furthermore that the prophets preached not to scholars but to all Jews without exception, and the Apostles were wont to teach their Gospel in churches which were places of public assembly. From all these considerations it follows that Scriptural doctrine contains not abstruse speculation or philosophic reasoning, but very simple matters able to be understood by the most sluggish mind.

I am therefore astonished at the ingenuity displayed by those, of whom I have already spoken, who find in Scripture mysteries so profound as not to be open to explanation in any human language, and who have then imported into religion so many matters of a philosophic nature that the Church seems like an academy, and religion like a science, or rather, a subject for debate. Yet why should I be surprised that men who vaunt themselves on possessing a supernatural light refuse to yield precedence in knowledge to men who possess nothing more than the natural light? I should indeed be surprised if they taught any purely philosophic doctrine which was new and not already a commonplace in ages past among Gentile philosophers (whom they nevertheless accuse of blindness); for if you enquire as to the nature of the mysteries which they see lurking in Scripture, you will certainly find nothing but the notions of an Aristotle or a Plato or the like, which often seem to suggest the fantasies of any uneducated person rather than the findings of an accomplished biblical scholar.

However, I do not go so far as to maintain that nothing whatsoever of a purely philosophic nature is to be found in Scripture's teaching, for in the last chapter we set forth certain affirmations of this kind as Scripture's basic principles. But this much I will say, that such affirmations are very few, and of a very simple nature. What they are, and on what grounds they are determined, I now intend to explain; and this we can easily do now that we know that Scripture's aim was not to impart scientific knowledge; for this leads obviously to the conclusion that Scripture demands nothing from men but obedience, and condemns not ignorance, but only obstinacy. Furthermore, since obedience to God consists solely in loving one's neighbour (for he who loves his neighbour in obedience to God's command has fulfilled the Law, as Paul says in Romans chapter 13 v. 8), it follows that Scripture commands no other kind of knowledge than that which is necessary for all men before they can obey God according to this commandment, and without which men are bound to be self-willed, or at least unschooled to obedience. Other philosophic questions which do not directly tend to this end, whether they be concerned with knowledge of God or with knowledge of Nature, have nothing to do with Scripture, and should therefore be dissociated from revealed religion.

Now although, as we have said, this is now quite obvious to all, nevertheless, since this matter is of cardinal importance to the concept of religion, I shall go into the whole question more carefully and explain it more clearly. To this end I must in the first place demonstrate that the intellectual or exact knowledge of God is not a gift shared by all the faithful, as is obedience; secondly, that the knowledge which God through the medium of his prophets has required of all men universally, and which every man is in duty bound to possess, is no other than the knowledge of his divine justice and charity. Both of these points can be readily demonstrated from Scripture.

The first clearly follows from Exodus ch. 6 v. 3, where in order to emphasise the singular grace bestowed on Moses, God says to him, "And I appeared unto Abraham, unto Isaac, and unto Jacob as *El Shaddai*, but by my name Jehovah was I not known to them." For a clearer explanation of this passage it should be observed that *El Shaddai* means in Hebrew 'the God who suffices,' because to each man he gives that which suffices for him; and although '*Shaddai*' is often used by itself to mean God, there can be no doubt that in all cases the word '*El*', God, is to be understood. Again, it should be observed that in Scripture no word but 'Jehovah' is to be found to indicate the absolute essence of God, as unrelated to created things. That is why the Hebrews contend that this is, strictly speaking, God's only name, the other names being forms of address; and it is a fact that the other names of God, whether substantive or adjectival, are attributes belonging to God insofar as he is considered as related to created things, or manifested through them. For example, take אל *El* (or, with the paragogic ה *hē*, אלה *Eloha*), which signifies nothing other than 'powerful', as all agree, and belongs to God only through his pre-eminence, in the way that the term 'Apostle' belongs to Paul. The qualities of his potency are explicated by additional adjectives, such as the great, the awful, the just, the merciful *El* (mighty one); or else, to embrace them all in one, this word is used in the plural with a singular meaning, a common practice in Scripture.

Now since God tells Moses that he was not known to the patriarchs by the name 'Jehovah', it follows that they were not acquainted with any attribute of God that expresses his absolute essence, but only with his deeds and promises, that is, his power as manifested through visible things. Yet in saying this to Moses God is not accusing the patriarchs of want of faith; on the contrary, he is extolling their trust and faith which, although they could not attain to Moses' special knowledge of God, led them to believe in the sureness and certainty of God's promises. In this they were unlike Moses who, despite his more exalted conception of God, yet doubted God's promises, and reproached God for bringing the Jews to a worse plight instead of the promised salvation.

The patriarchs, then, did not know God's distinctive name, and God tells Moses this in praise of their singlemindedness and faith, and also to signify the special grace granted to Moses. Hence it clearly follows, as we asserted in the first place, that men are not bound as a command to know God's attributes; this is a special gift granted only to certain of the faithful. It is not worth the effort to demonstrate this by further Scriptural testimony, for who can fail to see that the faithful have not all possessed an equal knowledge of God, and that nobody can be wise by command any more than he can live and exist by command? Men, women, children, all are equally capable of obedience by command, but not of wisdom by command. Now if anyone says that, while there is no need to understand God's attributes, there is a duty to believe them straightforwardly without proof, he is plainly talking nonsense. In the case of things invisible which are objects only of the mind, proofs are the only eyes by which they can be seen; therefore those who do not have such proofs can see nothing at all of these things. So when they merely repeat what they have heard of such matters, this is no more relevant to or indicative of their mind than the words of a parrot or a puppet speaking without meaning or sense.

However, before going any further, I should explain why Genesis often says that the patriarchs invoked God as Jehovah, which seems flatly to contradict what has been said above. Now if we have regard to the demonstration of chapter 8, we shall find that there is no real contradic-

tion. In that chapter we showed that the writer of the Pentateuch did not
apply to things and places the exact names that were in use at the time to
which he was referring, but names more familiar to the time of the writer.
So in Genesis God as invoked by the patriarchs is signified by the name
'Jehovah', not because he was known to them by this name but because this
was the name most revered by the Jews. This, I say, is the view we must
take, seeing that our Exodus text expressly states that God was not known
to the patriarchs by that name. There is a further reason in Exodus ch. 3 v.
13, where Moses desires to know the name of God: if this name had
previously been known, it must surely have been known to Moses. We
must therefore hold to the view we put forward, that the faithful patriarchs
did not know this name of God, and that knowledge of God is God's gift,
not a command.

It is now time to pass on to our second point, which is to show that God
through his prophets asks no other knowledge of himself than the knowledge of his divine justice and charity, that is, such attributes of God as men
find it possible to imitate by a definite rule of conduct. This is the express
teaching of Jeremiah, who in chapter 22 v. 15, 16 says, speaking of king
Josiah, "Thy father did eat and drink and do judgment and justice; then it
was well with him. He judged the cause of the poor and the needy; then it
was well with him. For (note well) this is what it is to know me, said the
Lord." The passage in chapter 9 v. 23 is no less clear. "But let him that
glorieth glory in this, that he understandeth and knoweth me, that I am the
Lord who exerciseth lovingkindness, judgment and righteousness in the
earth, for in these things I delight, saith the Lord." The same point is also
made in Exodus ch. 34 v. 6, 7, where God reveals to Moses, who desires to
see and know him, no other attributes than those which make manifest the
divine justice and charity. Finally, we should here call particular attention
to that passage in John—of which more hereafter—where he singles out
charity as the only means of making God manifest (since nobody has seen
God), and concludes that he who has charity truly has God, and knows
God.

We see, then, that Jeremiah, Moses and John sum up very briefly the
knowledge of God which it is the duty of every man to have, and they hold
it to consist simply in what we asserted, that God is supremely just and
supremely merciful, that is, the one perfect pattern of the true life. Furthermore, Scripture never expressly gives a definition of God, nor does it
enjoin on us the acceptance of any other attributes than those I have just
described, nor does it formally commend other attributes as it does these.
All this leads us to the conclusion that the intellectual knowledge of God
which contemplates his nature as it really is in itself—a nature which men
cannot imitate by a set rule of conduct nor take as their example—has no

bearing on the practice of a true way of life, on faith, and on revealed religion, and that consequently men can go far astray in this matter without sinning. It is therefore by no means surprising that God adapted himself to the imagination and the preconceived beliefs of the prophets, and that the faithful have entertained very diverse ideas about God, as we demonstrated with many examples in chapter 2. And it is again not at all surprising that the Sacred Books frequently speak so inexactly about God, attributing to him hands, feet, eyes, ears, mind, movement and even emotions such as jealousy, pity and so forth, and depicting him as a judge sitting on a royal throne in heaven, with Christ on his right hand. For they are speaking in accordance with the understanding of the common people, in whom Scripture seeks to inculcate obedience, not learning.

Yet the common run of theologians have argued that those passages which their natural light has convinced them are not in agreement with the divine nature should be interpreted in a metaphorical way, while whatever is beyond their understanding must be taken literally. But if every passage of the former kind in Scripture was meant to be understood and interpreted metaphorically, Scripture must have been written not for the common people and the uneducated masses, but for the learned alone, and for philosophers in particular. Indeed, if it were a sin to believe with simple piety and faith those ideas about God which we have just recounted, then surely the prophets should have exercised the greatest care to avoid such expressions, having regard to the limited intelligence of the common people; and they should have made it their primary aim to teach the attributes of God explicitly and clearly in the manner that every man is required to accept them. Nowhere has this been done.

Thus we should reject the view that anything of piety or impiety attaches to beliefs taken simply in themselves without respect to works. A man's beliefs should be regarded as pious or impious only insofar as he is thereby induced to obey the moral law, or else assumes from them the licence to sin or rebel. Therefore if anyone by believing what is true becomes self-willed, he has a faith which in reality is impious; and if by believing what is false he becomes obedient to the moral law, he has a faith which is pious. For we have shown that true knowledge of God is not commanded, but is a divine gift, and that God has asked no other knowledge from men but knowledge of his divine justice and charity, this knowledge being necessary not for philosophical understanding, but for obedience to the moral law.

CHAPTER 14

An analysis of faith, the faithful and the fundamental
principles of faith. Faith is finally set apart from philosophy

Anyone who gives any thought to this question cannot fail to realise that, for a true comprehension of faith, it is essential to understand that Scripture is adapted to the intellectual level not only of the prophets but of the unstable and fickle Jewish multitude. He who indiscriminately accepts everything in Scripture as being the universal and absolute teaching about God, and does not distinguish precisely what is adapted to the understanding of the masses, is bound to confuse the beliefs of the masses with divine doctrine, to proclaim as God's teaching the figments and arbitrary opinions of men, and to abuse Scriptural authority. Who, I ask, does not see this as the main reason why so many quite contradictory beliefs are taught by different sects as articles of faith, which they confirm with many citations from Scripture, so that in the Netherlands the saying '*Geen ketter sonder letter*'[1] has long become a proverb? The Sacred Books were not the work of a single writer, nor were they written for a people of a single age; they were written by a number of men of different character and different generations over a period of time which, taking them all into account, will be found to extend to about two thousand years, and perhaps much longer.

However, I will not level the charge of impiety against those sectaries simply because they adapt the words of Scripture to their own beliefs. Just as Scripture was once adapted to the understanding of the people of that time, in the same way anyone may now adapt it to his own beliefs if he feels that this will enable him to obey God with heartier will in those matters that pertain to justice and charity. My accusation against them is this, that they refuse to grant this same freedom to others. All those who do not share their opinions, however righteous and truly virtuous the dissenters may be, they persecute as God's enemies, while those who follow their lead, however dissolute they may be, they cherish as God's elect. Surely nothing more damnable than this, and more fraught with danger to the state, can be devised.

So in order to establish what are the limits of individual freedom of opinion in regard to faith, and who should be seen as belonging to the faithful in spite of their diverse opinions, we must define faith and its basic principles. This I propose to do in this present chapter, at the same time

1. No heretic without a text.

distinguishing between faith and philosophy, this being the main object of this entire treatise.

To demonstrate these matters in good order, let us look again at the chief aim of Scripture in its entirety, for this will furnish us with a true norm for defining faith. In the last chapter we said that the aim of Scripture is simply to teach obedience, a statement which surely no one can deny. For who can fail to see that both the Testaments are simply a training for obedience, that each has as its purpose this alone, that men should sincerely hearken to God? Leaving out of account the demonstrations of the last chapter, I shall say that Moses' aim was not to convince the Israelites by reasoned argument, but to bind them by a covenant, by oaths and by benefits received; he induced the people to obey the Law under threat of punishment, while exhorting them thereto by promise of rewards. These are all means to promote obedience, not to impart knowledge. The message of the Gospel is one of simple faith; that is, belief in God and reverence for God, or—which is the same thing—obedience to God. So in order to prove what is already quite plain, there is no need for me to compile a list of the Scriptural texts that commend obedience, which are to be found in abundance in both Testaments. Then again, Scripture itself tells us quite clearly over and over again what every man should do in order to serve God, declaring that the entire Law consists in this alone, to love one's neighbour. Therefore it is also undeniable that he who by God's commandments loves his neighbour as himself is truly obedient and blessed according to the Law, while he who hates or takes no thought for his neighbour is rebellious and disobedient. Finally, there is universal agreement that Scripture was written and disseminated not just for the learned but for all men of every time and race, and this by itself justifies us in concluding that Scripture does not require us to believe anything beyond what is necessary for the fulfilling of the said commandment.

Therefore this commandment is the one and only guiding principle for the entire common faith of mankind, and through this commandment alone should be determined all the tenets of faith that every man is in duty bound to accept. Since it is abundantly clear that this is so, and that from this fundamental principle alone all else can legitimately be inferred simply by the process of reason, let everyone consider for himself how it can have come about that so many disputes have arisen in the Church. Can this be due to any other causes than those I have recounted at the beginning of chapter 7? These, then, are the considerations which now induce me to explain in what manner and by what means necessary the tenets of faith are to be derived from the fundamental principle we have discovered. Unless I can achieve this, operating within definite rules, it will rightly be held that I have so far accomplished nothing. For anyone will still be able to foist on religion whatever doctrine he pleases under this same pretext, that it is a means for inculcating obedience. This is especially so when it is the divine attributes that are at issue.

For a complete and methodical demonstration, I shall begin with the definition of faith. According to our fundamental principle, faith must be defined as the holding of certain beliefs about God such that, without these beliefs, there cannot be obedience to God, and if this obedience is posited, these beliefs are necessarily posited. This definition is so clear, and follows so obviously from what has already been proved, that it needs no explanation. I shall now briefly show what consequences it entails. First, faith does not bring salvation through itself, but only by reason of obedience; or, as James says (ch. 2 v. 17), faith in itself without works is dead. For this point, see the whole of chapter 2 of the Epistle of James. Secondly, it follows that he who is truly obedient necessarily possesses a true and saving faith; for, as we have said, obedience being posited, faith is necessarily posited. This is again expressly stated by the same Apostle in chapter 2 v. 18, "Show me thy faith without thy works, and I will show thee my faith by my works." Likewise John, in 1 Ep. ch. 4 v. 7, 8, "Everyone that loveth (his neighbour) is born of God and knoweth God. He that loveth not, knoweth not God; for God is love." From these considerations it again follows that only by works can we judge anyone to be a believer or an unbeliever. If his works are good, he is a believer, however much he may differ in religious dogma from other believers; whereas if his works are evil, he is an unbeliever, however much he may agree with them verbally. For obedience being posited, faith is necessarily posited, and faith without works is dead. The Apostle John again expressly teaches this same doctrine in verse 13 of the same chapter. "Hereby," he says, "we know that we dwell in him and he in us, because he hath given us his Spirit." By 'spirit' he means love, whence he concludes (that is, from premises he has already accepted) that he who has love truly has the spirit of God. Indeed, since nobody has seen God he concludes therefrom that it is only through love of one's neighbour that one can perceive or be conscious of God, and thus no one can discover any other attribute of God except this love, insofar as we participate therein. Even if this argument is not conclusive, it nevertheless shows John's meaning quite clearly; but a far clearer statement is made in chapter 2 v. 3, 4 of the same Epistle, where he most explicitly teaches what I am here maintaining. "And hereby do we know that we know him, if we keep his commandments. He that saith, I know him, and keepeth not his commandments, is a liar, and the truth is not in him." From this we can again conclude that the true enemies of Christ are those who persecute the righteous and the lovers of justice because these disagree with them and do not uphold the same religious dogmas. Those who love justice and charity we know by that very fact to be the faithful, and he who persecutes the faithful is an enemy of Christ.

Finally, it follows that faith requires not so much true dogmas as pious dogmas, that is, such as move the heart to obedience; and this is so even if many of those beliefs contain not a shadow of truth, provided that he who adheres to them knows not that they are false. If he knew that they were false, he would necessarily be a rebel, for how could it be that one who seeks to love justice and obey God should worship as divine what he knows to be alien to the divine nature? Yet men may err from simplicity of mind, and, as we have seen, Scripture condemns only obstinacy, not ignorance. Indeed, this conclusion necessarily follows simply from the definition of faith, whose every part must be derived from that universal basic principle already demonstrated, and from the single purpose underlying the whole of Scripture, unless we allow ourselves to put our own arbitrary constructions on it. Now this definition does not expressly demand true dogmatic belief, but only such beliefs as are necessary for obedience, that is, those that strengthen the will to love one's neighbour. It is only through this love, as John says, that every man is in God, and God in every man.

Each man's faith, then, is to be regarded as pious or impious not in respect of its truth or falsity, but as it is conducive to obedience or obstinacy. Now nobody questions that there is to be found among men a wide variety of temperament, that all men are not equally in agreement in all matters and are influenced by their beliefs in different ways, so that what moves one man to devotion will move another to ridicule and contempt. Hence it follows that a catholic[2] or universal faith must not contain any dogmas that good men may regard as controversial; for such dogmas may be to one man pious, to another impious, since their value lies only in the works they inspire. A catholic faith should therefore contain only those dogmas which obedience to God absolutely demands, and without which such obedience is absolutely impossible. As for other dogmas, every man should embrace those that he, being the best judge of himself, feels will do most to strengthen him in love of justice. Acceptance of this principle would, I suggest, leave no occasion for controversy in the Church.

I can now venture to enumerate the dogmas of the universal faith, the basic teachings which Scripture as a whole intends to convey. These must all be directed (as evidently follows from what we have demonstrated in these two chapters) to this one end: that there is a Supreme Being who

---

2. In this chapter Spinoza's use of the term 'catholic' must be understood always in its original meaning as "universal." Spinoza in no way has in mind here the Roman Catholic Church.

loves justice and charity, whom all must obey in order to be saved, and must worship by practising justice and charity to their neighbour. From this, all the tenets of faith can readily be determined, and they are simply as follows:

1. God, that is, a Supreme Being, exists, supremely just and merciful, the exemplar of true life. He who knows not, or does not believe, that God exists, cannot obey him or know him as judge.

2. God is one alone. No one can doubt that this belief is essential for complete devotion, reverence, that is, love towards God; for devotion, reverence and love spring only from the pre-eminence of one above all others.

3. God is omnipresent, and all things are open to him. If it were believed that things could be concealed from God, or if it were not realised that he sees everything, one might doubt, or be unaware of the uniformity of the justice wherewith he directs everything.

4. God has supreme right and dominion over all things. He is under no jurisdiction, but acts by his absolute decree and singular grace. All are required to obey him absolutely, while he obeys none.

5. Worship of God and obedience to him consists solely in justice and charity, or love towards one's neighbour.

6. All who obey God by following this way of life, and only those, are saved; others, who live at pleasure's behest, are lost. If men did not firmly believe this, there is no reason why they should obey God rather than their desires.

7. God forgives repentant sinners. There is no one who does not sin, so that without this belief all would despair of salvation, and there would be no reason to believe that God is merciful. He who firmly believes that God forgives men's sins from the mercy and grace whereby he directs all things, and whose heart is thereby the more inspired by love of God, that man verily knows Christ according to the spirit, and Christ is in him.

No one can fail to realise that all these beliefs are essential if all men, without exception, are to be capable of obeying God as prescribed by the law explained above; for if any one of these beliefs is nullified, obedience is also nullified. But as to the question of what God, the exemplar of true life, really is, whether he is fire, or spirit, or light, or thought, or something else, this is irrelevant to faith.[3] And so likewise is the question as to why he

---

3. Spinoza makes clear that these seven principles of the universal religion, which define faith, need not be literally true. In fact, given his 'true philosophy' of the *Ethics*, the first and seventh principles are strictly speaking false. Spinoza denies that God has any moral attributes, such as justice or mercy, and claims that

is the exemplar of true life, whether this is because he has a just and merciful disposition, or because all things exist and act through him and consequently we, too, understand through him, and through him we see what is true, just, and good. On these questions it matters not what beliefs a man holds. Nor, again, does it matter for faith whether one believes that God is omnipresent in essence or in potency, whether he directs everything from free will or from the necessity of his nature, whether he lays down laws as a ruler or teaches them as being eternal truths, whether man obeys God from free will or from the necessity of the divine decree, whether the rewarding of the good and the punishing of the wicked is natural or supernatural. The view one takes on these and similar questions has no bearing on faith, provided that such a belief does not lead to the assumption of greater licence to sin, or hinders submission to God. Indeed, as we have already said, every man is in duty bound to adapt these religious dogmas to his own understanding and to interpret them for himself in whatever way makes him feel that he can the more readily accept them with full confidence and conviction. For, as we have already pointed out, just as in olden days faith was revealed and written down in a form which accorded with the understanding and beliefs of the prophets and people of that time, so, too, every man has now the duty to adapt it to his own beliefs, so as thus to accept it without any misgivings or doubts. For we have shown that faith demands piety rather than truth; faith is pious and saving only by reason of the obedience it inspires, and consequently nobody is faithful except by reason of his obedience. Therefore the best faith is not necessarily manifested by him who displays the best arguments, but by him who displays the best works of justice and charity. How salutary this doctrine is, and how necessary in the state if men are to live in peace and harmony, and how many important causes of disturbance and crime are thereby aborted at source, I leave everyone to judge for himself.

Before proceeding further, it should here be observed that, from what has just been demonstrated, we are now in a position to provide a convincing answer to the difficulties we raised in chapter 1 when we were discussing God's speaking to the Israelites from Mount Sinai. Although the voice which the Israelites heard could not have given those men a philosophical or mathematical certainty of God's existence, it sufficed to strike them with awe of God as they had previously known him, and to induce them to obedience, this being the purpose of that manifestation. For God was not

---

repentance is either idle or absurd (*Ethics*, 1.8, Scholium 2, Appendix; 3. Definitions of the Emotions, 27; 4.54).

seeking to teach the Israelites the absolute attributes of his essence (he revealed none of these things at the time), but to break down their obstinacy and bring them to obedience. Therefore he assailed them, not with arguments, but with the blare of trumpets, with thunder and with lightnings (see Exodus ch. 20 v. 20).

It now remains for me finally to show that between faith and theology on the one side and philosophy on the other there is no relation and no affinity, a point which must now be apparent to everyone who knows the aims and bases of these two faculties, which are as far apart as can be.[4] The aim of philosophy is, quite simply, truth, while the aim of faith, as we have abundantly shown, is nothing other than obedience and piety. Again, philosophy rests on the basis of universally valid axioms, and must be constructed by studying Nature alone, whereas faith is based on history and language, and must be derived only from Scripture and revelation, as we showed in chapter 7. So faith allows to every man the utmost freedom to philosophise, and he may hold whatever opinions he pleases on any subjects whatsoever without imputation of evil. It condemns as heretics and schismatics only those who teach such beliefs as promote obstinacy, hatred, strife and anger, while it regards as the faithful only those who promote justice and charity to the best of their intellectual powers and capacity.

Finally, since what I have here demonstrated forms the most important part of the subject of this treatise, before proceeding further I do most earnestly beg the reader to be good enough to read these two chapters with careful attention and to reflect on them repeatedly. Let him accept my assurance that my purpose in writing these chapters has not been to introduce innovations but to correct abuses, such as I hope one day to see corrected.

4. Spinoza's sharp distinction between faith and philosophy should not be construed as a defense of "fideism," the thesis that human reason is inherently incapable of reaching the truth, especially on the important issues, and hence we must take refuge in religious faith. Fideism is based upon skepticism, and Spinoza is as far removed from skepticism as he is from revealed religion. The "divorce" that Spinoza wants to decree is more akin to a "separation of powers," or domains.

CHAPTER 15

*It is demonstrated that neither is theology ancillary to
reason nor reason to theology. The reason why we
are convinced of the authority of Holy Scripture*

Those who do not understand the distinction between philosophy and theology argue as to whether Scripture should be ancillary[1] to reason, or reason to Scripture; that is, whether the meaning of Scripture should be made to conform with reason, or reason with Scripture. The latter view is upheld by the sceptics who deny the certainty of reason, the former by the dogmatists. But it is clear from our earlier findings that both parties are utterly mistaken, for whichever view we embrace we are forced to do violence either to reason or to Scripture. We have demonstrated that Scripture teaches only piety, not philosophy, and that all its contents were adapted to the understanding and preconceived beliefs of the common people. Therefore he who seeks to make Scripture conform with philosophy is sure to ascribe to the prophets many ideas which they never dreamed of, and will quite distort their meaning. On the other hand, he who makes reason and philosophy ancillary to theology has to accept as divinely inspired utterances the prejudices of a common people of long ago, which will gain a hold on his understanding and darken it. Thus they will both go wildly astray, the one spurning reason, the other siding with reason.

The first among the Pharisees who openly maintained that Scripture must be made to conform with reason was Maimonides, whose opinion we reviewed in chapter 7 and refuted on many grounds. Although this writer was held in great esteem by the Pharisees, most of them desert him on this issue, favouring the view of a certain R. Jehuda Alpakhar,[2] who, while

---

1. Throughout medieval thought it was maintained by many that philosophy is the ancillary, or "handmaiden," to theology, the "queen of the sciences." (Thomas Aquinas, *Summa Theologica*, Part I–I, question 1, article 5)

2. Jehuda Alpakhar (or 'Alfakar') was an important thirteenth-century Spanish Jewish physician residing in Toledo. In the anti-Maimonidean debates in Spain he supported the opponents of Maimonides. Spinoza refers to him also in Letter 43 (Spinoza, *The Letters*, translated by Samuel Shirley, Indianapolis: Hackett Publishing Company, 1995, 240n.228). Alpakhar's letter, to which Spinoza refers in this chapter, has been translated and commented upon by Jacob Adler in *Studia Spinozana* 12 (1996), 141–168.

seeking to avoid the error of Maimonides, fell into the opposite error. He maintained* that reason should be ancillary to Scripture, and completely subservient to it. He held that nothing in Scripture requires a metaphorical explanation merely on the grounds that its literal meaning is contrary to reason, but only if it is contrary to Scripture itself, that is, to the clear pronouncements of Scripture. Hence he formulated the universal rule that whatever Scripture teaches in dogmatic form and quite expressly affirms must be accepted as absolutely true simply on its own authority. No other dogma in the Bible will be found to be in contradiction with this directly, but only by implication, and this comes about because the Scriptural style of expression often appears to assume what is contrary to its express doctrine. Therefore it is only such passages that should be explained metaphorically. For example, Scripture clearly tells us that God is one alone (Deut. ch. 6 v. 4), and nowhere will any passage be found directly asserting that there is more than one God. But there are many passages where God speaks of himself, and the prophets speak of him, in the plural. This is merely a figure of speech, and does not really intend to indicate that there are in fact a number of Gods. Therefore all such expressions are to be explained metaphorically, not on the grounds that it is contrary to reason that there should be more than one God, but because Scripture itself directly asserts that God is one alone. Similarly, since Scripture directly asserts (according to Alpakhar) in Deuteronomy ch. 4 v. 15 that God is incorporeal, it is on the authority of this passage alone, not of reason, that we must believe that God has no body, and consequently it is on the authority of Scripture alone that we have to give a metaphorical explanation to all those passages that attribute to God hands, feet and so on. It is only through their figurative mode of expression that they appear to assume that God is corporeal.

Such is the view of Alpakhar. Insofar as he aims to explain Scripture through Scripture, I give him credit, but I am surprised that a man endowed with reason should seek to abolish reason. It is indeed true that, as long as we are simply concerned with the meaning of the text and the prophets' intention, Scripture should be explained through Scripture; but having extracted the true meaning, we must necessarily resort to judgment and reason before we can assent thereto. Now if reason, in spite of her protests, is nevertheless to be made completely subservient to Scripture, must this submission be effected with reason's concurrence, or without it, blindly? If the latter, then surely we are behaving like fools, without judgment. If the former, then it is only at reason's behest that we accept

---

* I remember once reading this in a letter against Maimonides, contained in a collection of letters said to belong to Maimonides.

Scripture, which we would therefore not accept if it were repugnant to reason. And again, I ask, who can give mental acceptance to something against which his reason rebels? For what else is mental denial but reason's rebellion? I am utterly astonished that men can bring themselves to make reason, the greatest of all gifts and a light divine, subservient to letters that are dead, and may have been corrupted by human malice; that it should be considered no crime to denigrate the mind, the true handwriting of God's word, declaring it to be corrupt, blind and lost, whereas it is considered to be a heinous crime to entertain such thoughts of the letter, a mere shadow of God's word. They think it pious to put no trust in reason and their own judgment, impious to doubt the trustworthiness of those who have transmitted to us the Sacred Books. This is not piety, but mere folly. But what, I ask, is troubling them? What are they afraid of? Is it that religion and faith cannot be upheld unless men deliberately cultivate ignorance and completely turn their backs on reason? Such an attitude is surely the mark of fear on Scripture's behalf rather than confidence. But let it never be said that religion and piety seek to enslave reason, or reason religion, or that either of them is incapable of maintaining its own sovereignty in complete harmony with the other. This is a theme to which I shall soon return, for in the meantime I should like first of all to consider R. Alpakhar's rule.

As we have said, he holds that we must accept as true or reject as false everything that Scripture affirms or denies, and secondly, that Scripture never expressly affirms or denies anything that contradicts what it elsewhere affirms or denies. The rashness of both these assertions will be apparent to all. I pass by his failure to perceive that Scripture consists of different books written at different times for different men by different authors. And there is the further point that these assertions are made on his own authority without any evidence from either reason or Scripture; for he ought to have shown that those passages that contradict other passages only by implication can have a plausible metaphorical explanation based on the nature of language and a consideration of their context; and furthermore that Scripture has come down to us uncorrupted.

But let us examine the question methodically. With regard to his first assertion, I ask whether, if reason protests, we are nevertheless obliged to accept as true or reject as false whatever Scripture affirms or denies. Perhaps he will reply that there is nothing in Scripture which contradicts reason. But I insist that Scripture expressly affirms and teaches that God is jealous (in the Decalogue itself and in Exod. ch. 34 v. 14, in Deut. ch. 4 v. 24 and in many other places); this is contrary to reason, but must still, by his account, be posited as true. Indeed, if there should be any other passages in Scripture implying that God is not jealous, they would have to be explained metaphorically so that they seem to have no such implication.

So, too, Scripture expressly says that God came down to Mount Sinai (Exod. ch. 19 v. 20) and ascribes to him other movements from place to place, nor does it anywhere expressly say that God does not move. So this must be accepted by all as true, and as to Solomon's assertion that God is not contained in any one place (1 Kings ch. 8 v. 27), since it does not maintain but merely implies that God does not move, it must be so explained as not to deprive God of movement. Similarly, the heavens would have to be taken as the dwelling-place and throne of God, because Scripture expressly says so. And there are numerous statements of this kind, made in accordance with the beliefs of the prophets and the multitude, which only reason and philosophy, not Scripture, tells us are false, and which nevertheless are all to be taken as true in our author's view, there being no appeal to reason.

Next, he is wrong in affirming that one passage does not directly contradict another, but only by implication. Moses directly affirms that God is fire (Deut. ch. 4 v. 24) and directly denies that God has any likeness to visible things (Deut. ch. 4 v. 12). If our author replies that the latter statement's denial that God is fire is not direct, but only by implication, and must therefore be made to conform with the former statement so as to avoid the appearance of contradiction, come then, let us grant that God is fire. Or better, lest we seem as crazy as he, let us put this question aside and take another example. Samuel directly denies that God ever repents (1 Sam. ch. 15 v. 29); on the other hand, Jeremiah asserts that God repents of the good and evil that he may have decreed (Jer. ch. 18, v. 8, 10). Well, then, are not these teachings directly opposed to each other? So which of the two is he going to explain metaphorically? Each of these assertions is made as universally valid, and each contradicts the other; what the one directly affirms, the other directly denies. Thus, by his own rule, he is required to accept something as true and at the same time reject it as false.

Then again, what difference does it make if one passage should contradict another not directly but only by implication, if the implication is clear, and if the context and nature of the passage do not permit of a metaphorical interpretation? There are many such instances in the Bible, as we mentioned in chapter 2 where we showed that the prophets held diverse and contrary opinions, and there are the particularly glaring contradictions in the historical narratives to which we drew attention in chapters 9 and 10. There is no need for me here to review them all again, for in my earlier remarks I have said enough to expose the absurdities consequent on the acceptance of this rule, its falsity, and the author's rashness in proposing it.

We may therefore dismiss the views of both Alpakhar and Maimonides, and we may maintain as incontrovertible that neither is theology required to be subordinated to reason nor reason to theology, and that each has its own domain. The domain of reason, as we have said, is truth and wisdom, the domain of theology is piety and obedience. For the power of reason, as we have already demonstrated, does not extend so far as to enable us to conclude that men can achieve blessedness simply through obedience without understanding, whereas this alone is the message of theology, which commands only obedience and neither seeks nor is able to oppose reason. As we showed in the last chapter, theology defines its religious dogmas only so far as suffices to secure obedience, and it leaves it to reason to decide exactly how these dogmas are to be understood in respect of truth; for reason is in reality the light of the mind, without which the mind sees nothing but dreams and fantasies.

By theology I here mean, in precise terms, revelation insofar as it manifests Scripture's objective as we have stated it, that is, the way of achieving obedience, or the dogmas of true piety and faith. In other words, by theology I mean the Word of God properly so called, which does not consist in a set number of books (see chapter 12). Theology thus understood, if you consider its precepts and moral teaching, will be found to agree with reason; and if you look to its purpose and end, it will be found to be in no respect opposed to reason, and is therefore valid for all men.

With regard to Scripture taken in its entirety, we have already shown in chapter 7 that its meaning is not to be derived from investigation of Nature in general—which is the basis of philosophy only—but simply from studying it in itself; and we should not be deterred if, after thus discovering the true meaning of Scripture, we find that it is at some points opposed to reason. Whatever instances of this kind are to be found in the Bible, or whatever things men may fail to understand without detriment to their love of their fellow men, we can be sure that these have no bearing on theology or the Word of God, and consequently anyone may hold whatever opinions he pleases on such matters without censure. We may therefore conclude without reservation that neither must Scripture be made to conform with reason, nor reason with Scripture.

However, since reason cannot demonstrate the truth or falsity of this fundamental principle of theology, that men may be saved simply by obedience, we may also be asked why it is that we believe it. If we accept this principle without reason, blindly, then we too are acting foolishly without judgment; if on the other hand we assert that this fundamental principle can be proved by reason, then theology becomes a part of philosophy, and inseparable from it. To this I reply that I maintain absolutely that this fundamental dogma of theology cannot be investigated by the natural light of reason, or at least that nobody has been successful in proving it, and that therefore it was essential that there should be revelation. Nevertheless, we can use judgment before we accept with at least moral certainty that which has been revealed. I say 'with moral certainty,' for we have no grounds for expecting to reach greater certainty in this matter than did the prophets to whom it was originally revealed; and yet their certainty was only of a moral kind, as we have shown in chapter 2 of this treatise.

So those who attempt to prove Scripture's authority by demonstrations of a mathematical order go far astray, for the authority of the Bible is dependent on the authority of the prophets, and can thus have no stronger arguments to support it than those by which the prophets of old were wont to convince the people of their authority. Indeed, our own certainty as to this authority can have no other foundation than that on which the prophets based their certainty and authority. Now we have shown that the certainty of the prophets rested entirely on these three factors—first, a distinct and vivid imagination, second, a sign, third and most important, a heart turned to what is right and good. They based their claims on no other considerations, and so there are no other considerations by which their authority could be proved either to the people to whom they once spoke face to face, or to us to whom they speak in writing.

The first of these factors, their vivid imagination, was a personal quality confined to the prophets, and therefore our certainty regarding revelation can rest, and ought to rest, entirely on the other two, the sign and the doctrine they taught. And this is what Moses too expressly asserts, for in Deuteronomy ch. 18 he bids the people obey the prophet who should give a true sign in the name of the Lord, but to condemn to death that same man if he should prophesy falsely even in the name of the Lord, and likewise him who should seek to turn the people away from the true religion, even if he were to confirm his authority by signs and wonders (see Deut. ch. 13). Hence it follows that a true prophet can be distinguished from a false prophet by his doctrine and his miracles taken together. For it is such a one that Moses declares to be a true prophet, and bids us trust without fear of deceit; while he condemns as false prophets deserving of death those who make false prophecies even in the name of the Lord, or those who preach false gods, even if they have wrought true miracles.

Therefore we too must accept only this one reason for believing in Scripture—that is, in the prophets—namely, their teaching as confirmed by signs. For since we see that the prophets commend above all else justice and charity and have no other objective, we may hence conclude that it was no evil intent but sincere conviction that prompted them to teach that men may achieve blessedness by obedience and faith. And because they furthermore confirmed this teaching with signs, we are convinced that they were not speaking at random nor were they out of their senses while prophesying. This conclusion is further corroborated when we realise that all their moral teaching is in full agreement with reason, for it is no accident that the Word of God proclaimed by the prophets agrees in all respects with the Word of God that speaks in our hearts. The Bible, I say, conveys to us this certainty just as well as did the living voice of the prophets to the Jews of old. For we showed towards the end of chapter 12 that Scripture has come down to us uncorrupted in respect of its doctrine and its chief historical narratives.

Therefore, although this fundamental principle underlying all theology and Scripture cannot be demonstrated with mathematical exactitude, we may yet accept it without our judgment being called into question. It would be folly to refuse to accept, merely on the grounds that it cannot be proved with mathematical certainty, that which is abundantly confirmed by the testimony of so many prophets, that which is the source of so much comfort to those less gifted with intelligence, and of considerable advantage to the state, and which we can believe without incurring any peril or hurt. Could we live our lives wisely if we were to accept as true nothing that could conceivably be called into doubt on any principle of scepticism? Are not most of our actions in any case fraught with uncertainty and hazard?

I do indeed admit that those who think that philosophy and theology are mutually contradictory and that therefore one or the other must be deprived of its sovereignty and set aside, have good reason for seeking to put theology on a solid foundation and for attempting to prove it with mathematical accuracy. Who but a desperate madman would be so rash as to turn his back on reason, or to hold the arts and sciences in contempt, while denying the certainty of reason? Even so, we cannot entirely absolve them from censure, in that they seek the help of reason in the task of repelling reason, and they try to employ the certainty of reason to disparage reason's certainty. While they are aiming to prove the truth and authority of theology by mathematical demonstrations and to deprive reason and the natural light of its authority, they are simply drawing theology into the domain of reason, and are quite clearly implying that her authority has no brilliance unless it is illuminated by the natural light of reason.

If on the other hand they boast that their own assurance rests entirely on the inward testimony of the Holy Spirit and that they invoke the aid of reason solely for the purpose of convincing unbelievers, we should still give no credit to their words, for we can now readily prove that they are prompted to say this either from emotional bias or from vainglory. From the preceding chapter it quite clearly follows that the testimony of the

Holy Spirit is concerned only with good works—which therefore Paul, too, in his Epistle to the Galatians ch. 5 v. 22 calls 'the fruits of the Holy Spirit'—and that the Holy Spirit itself is nothing other than the peace of mind that results from good actions. As for the truth and certainty of those questions which are the subject only of speculative philosophy, no spirit bears testimony other than reason, which alone, as we have shown, has asserted its claim to the realm of truth. So if they contend that they possess some other spirit that gives them certainty of truth, this is an idle boast; they speak from emotional bias; or else, through dread of being worsted by philosophers and exposed to public ridicule, they seek refuge in the sacred. But all in vain; for what altar can he find to shelter him, who is guilty of betraying reason?

But I will say no more of these men, since I think I have satisfactorily made my case by demonstrating on what grounds philosophy must be distinguished from theology, what is the essential nature of each, and that neither of them is subordinate to the other, each of them holding its own domain without contradicting the other. Finally, as opportunity arose, I have also shown the absurdities, the damage and the harm that have resulted from the fact that men have thoroughly confused these two faculties, failing to make an accurate distinction between them and to separate the one from the other.

Before I continue, I wish to emphasise in express terms—though I have said it before—the importance and necessity of the role that I assign to Scripture, or revelation. For since we cannot perceive by the natural light that simple obedience is a way to salvation,* and since only revelation teaches us that this comes about by God's singular grace which we cannot attain by reason, it follows that Scripture has brought very great comfort to mankind. For all men without exception are capable of obedience, while there are only a few—in proportion to the whole of humanity—who acquire a virtuous disposition under the guidance of reason alone. Thus, did we not have this testimony of Scripture, the salvation of nearly all men would be in doubt.

---

* See Supplementary Note 31.

CHAPTER 16

*The basis of the state; the natural and civil right
of the individual, and the right of sovereign powers*

Up to this point our object has been to separate philosophy from theology
and to show that the latter allows freedom to philosophise for every
individual. It is therefore time to enquire what are the limits of this
freedom of thought, and of saying what one thinks, in a well-conducted
state. To approach this question in an orderly way, we must discuss the
basis of the state, and prior to that, before giving any consideration to the
state and to religion, we must discuss the natural right of the individual.[1]

By the right and established order of Nature I mean simply the rules
governing the nature of every individual thing, according to which we
conceive it as naturally determined to exist and to act in a definite way. For
example, fish are determined by nature to swim, and the big ones to eat the
smaller ones. Thus it is by sovereign natural right that fish inhabit water,
and the big ones eat the smaller ones. For it is certain that Nature, taken in
the absolute sense, has the sovereign right to do all that she can do; that is,
Nature's right is co-extensive with her power. For Nature's power is the
very power of God, who has sovereign right over all things.[2] But since the
universal power of Nature as a whole is nothing but the power of all
individual things taken together,[3] it follows that each individual thing has
the sovereign right to do all that it can do; i.e. the right of the individual is
co-extensive with its determinate power.

Now since it is the supreme law of Nature that each thing endeavours to
persist in its present being, as far as in it lies, taking account of no other
thing but itself,[4] it follows that each individual has the sovereign right to

---

1. Throughout this chapter there are echoes of the political philosophy of Thomas
Hobbes, whose treatise *De Cive* (On the Citizen) Spinoza had read. The relationship of Spinoza's political theory to that of Hobbes is complicated and controversial, and scholars have expressed divergent conclusions and evaluations. A good
essay on this topic is "Liberalism and Hobbes and Spinoza," by D. J. Den Uyl and
S. Warner in *Studia Spinozana* 3 (1987), 261–318; this volume is devoted entirely
to the theme of Spinoza's relationship to Hobbes. In volume 1 of this journal,
focusing on Spinoza's social philosophy, there are several other relevant essays.

2. *Ethics*, 1.17, Scholium 34–35.

3. *Ethics*, 2.13, Lemma 7, Scholium, Letter 32.

4. *Ethics*, 3.6–7.

do this, that is (as I have said), to exist and to act as it is naturally determined. And here I do not acknowledge any distinction between men and other individuals of Nature, nor between men endowed with reason and others to whom true reason is unknown, nor between fools, mad-men and the sane. Whatever an individual thing does by the laws of its own nature, it does with sovereign right, inasmuch as it acts as determined by Nature, and can do no other. Therefore among men, as long as they are considered as living under the rule of Nature alone, he who is not yet acquainted with reason or has not yet acquired a virtuous disposition lives under the sole control of appetite with as much sovereign right as he who conducts his life under the rule of reason. That is to say, just as the wise man has the sovereign right to do all that reason dictates, i.e. to live according to the laws of reason, so, too, a man who is ignorant and weak-willed has the sovereign right to do all that is urged on him by appetite, i.e. to live according to the laws of appetite. This is the same doctrine as that of Paul, who declares that prior to the law—that is, as long as men are considered as living under Nature's rule—there can be no sin.

Thus the natural right of every man is determined not by sound reason, but by his desire and his power. For not all men are naturally determined to act in accordance with the rules and laws of reason. On the contrary, all men are born in a state of complete ignorance, and before they can learn the true way of life and acquire a virtuous disposition, even if they have been well brought up, a great part of their life has gone by. Yet in the meantime they have to live and preserve themselves as far as in them lies, namely, by the urging of appetite alone, for Nature has given them nothing else and has denied them the actualised power to live according to sound reason. Therefore they are no more in duty bound to live according to the laws of a sound mind than a cat to live according to the laws of a lion's nature. Thus whatever every man, when he is considered as solely under the dominion of Nature, believes to be to his advantage, whether under the guidance of sound reason or under passion's sway, he may by sovereign natural right seek and get for himself by any means, by force, deceit, entreaty or in any other way he best can, and he may consequently regard as his enemy anyone who tries to hinder him from getting what he wants.

From this it follows that Nature's right and her established order, under which all men are born and for the most part live, forbids only those things that no one desires and no one can do; it does not frown on strife, or hatred, or anger, or deceit, or on anything at all urged by appetite. This is not surprising, for Nature's bounds are not set by the laws of human reason which aim only at man's true interest and his preservation, but by infinite other laws which have regard to the eternal order of the whole of Nature, of which man is but a particle. It is from the necessity of this order alone that all individual things are determined to exist and to act in a definite way. So when something in Nature appears to us as ridiculous, absurd or evil, this is due to the fact that our knowledge is only partial, that we are largely ignorant of the order and coherence of the whole of Nature and want all things to be arranged to suit our reason. Yet that which our reason declares to be evil is not evil in respect of the order and laws of universal Nature, but only in respect of the laws of our own nature.

However, there cannot be any doubt as to how much more it is to men's advantage to live in accordance with the laws and sure dictates of our reason, which, as we have said, aim only at the true good of men.[5] Furthermore, there is nobody who does not desire to live in safety free from fear, as far as is possible. But this cannot come about as long as every individual is permitted to do just as he pleases, and reason can claim no more right than hatred and anger. For there is no one whose life is free from anxiety in the midst of feuds, hatred, anger and deceit, and who will not therefore try to avoid these as far as in him lies. And if we also reflect that the life of men without mutual assistance must necessarily be most wretched and must lack the cultivation of reason, as we showed in chapter 5, it will become quite clear to us that, in order to achieve a secure and good life, men had necessarily to unite in one body. They therefore arranged that the unrestricted right naturally possessed by each individual should be put into common ownership, and that this right should no longer be determined by the strength and appetite of the individual, but by the power and will of all together. Yet in this they would have failed, had appetite been their only guide (for by the laws of appetite all men are drawn in different directions), and so they had to bind themselves by the most stringent pledges to be guided in all matters only by the dictates of reason (which nobody ventures openly to oppose, lest he should appear to be without capacity to reason) and to keep appetite in check insofar as it tends to another's hurt, to do to no one what they would not want done to themselves, and to uphold another's right as they would their own.

At this point we must consider how this covenant is to be made so as to ensure its stability and validity. Now it is a universal law of human nature that nobody rejects what he judges to be good except through hope of a greater good or fear of greater loss, and that no one endures any evil except to avoid a greater evil or to gain a greater good. That is to say, everyone will choose of two goods that which he judges the greater, and of two evils that which seems to him the lesser. I say expressly 'that which in his belief is the greater or lesser'; I do not say that the facts necessarily correspond with his judgment. This law is so deeply inscribed in human nature that it should

5. *Ethics*, 4.18, Scholium 35, 37, Scholium 2.

be counted among the eternal truths universally known. Now from this law it necessarily follows that nobody is going to promise in all good faith* to give up his unrestricted right, and in general nobody is going to keep any promises whatsoever, except through fear of a greater evil or hope of a greater good. To make the point more clearly understood, suppose that a robber forces me to promise to give him my goods at his pleasure. Now since, as I have already shown, my natural right is determined by power alone, it is quite clear that if I can free myself from this robber by deceit, promising him whatever he wants, I have the natural right to do so, that is, to pretend to agree to whatever he wants. Or suppose that in all good faith I have promised somebody that I will not taste food or any other nourishment for twenty days, and that I later realised that I had made a foolish promise which could be kept only with considerable hurt to myself. Since by natural right I am bound to choose the lesser of two evils, I have the sovereign right to break faith and go back on my pledged word. Now this, I say, is justified by natural right, whether it was true and infallible reasoning or whether it was fallible belief that made me realise I was wrong to have made the promise. For whether my conviction is true or false, I shall be in fear of a terrible evil, one which therefore, by Nature's law, I shall do everything to avoid.

We may thus conclude that the validity of an agreement rests on its utility, without which the agreement automatically becomes null and void. It is therefore folly to demand from another that he should keep his word for ever, if at the same time one does not try to ensure that, if he breaks his word, he will meet with more harm than good. This point is particularly relevant in considering the constitution of a state. Now if all men could be readily induced to be guided by reason alone and to recognise the supreme advantage and the necessity of the state's existence, everyone would entirely forswear deceit. In their desire for this highest good, the preservation of the state, all men would in absolute good faith abide entirely by their agreement, and would regard it as the most important thing in the world to keep their word, this being the strongest shield of the state. But it is by no means the case that all men can always be readily induced to be guided by reason; for each is drawn by his own pleasure,[6] and the mind is frequently so beset by greed, ambition, envy, anger and the like that no room is left for reason. Therefore although men may make promises with every mark of sincerity, and pledge themselves to keep their word, nobody can rely on another's good faith unless the promise is backed by something else; for everyone has the natural right to act deceitfully and is not bound

---

* See Supplementary Note 32.

6. A quotation adapted from Vergil, *Eclogues*, II, 65, "*trahit sua quemque voluptas.*"

to keep his engagements except through hope of greater good or fear of greater evil. However, since we have already demonstrated that everyone's natural right is determined by his power alone, it follows that to the extent that each transfers his power to another, whether by force or voluntarily, to that extent he also necessarily surrenders his right to him, and the sovereign right over all men is held by him who holds the supreme power whereby he can compel all by force and coerce them by threat of the supreme penalty, universally feared by all. This right he will retain only as long as he has this power of carrying into execution whatever he wills; otherwise his rule will be precarious, and nobody who is stronger than he will need to obey him unless he so wishes.

Therefore, without any infringement of natural right, a community can be formed and a contract be always preserved in its entirety in absolute good faith on these terms, that everyone transfers all the power that he possesses to the community, which will therefore alone retain the sovereign natural right over everything, that is, the supreme rule which everyone will have to obey either of free choice or through fear of the ultimate penalty. Such a community's right is called a democracy, which can therefore be defined as a united body of men which corporately possesses sovereign right over everything within its power. Hence it follows that the sovereign power is bound by no law, and all must obey it in all matters; for this is what all must have covenanted tacitly or expressly when they transferred to it all their power of self-defence, that is, all their right. If they intended that there should be anything reserved to themselves, they should have taken the precaution at the same time to make secure provision to uphold it. Since they did not do so, and could not have done so without the division and consequent destruction of the state, they thereby submitted themselves absolutely to the will of the sovereign power. Since they did this without reservation and (as we have shown) by force of necessity and by the persuasion of reason itself, it follows that, unless we wish to be enemies of the state and to act against reason which urges us to uphold the state with all our might, it is our duty to carry out all the orders of the sovereign power without exception, even if those orders are quite irrational. For reason bids us carry out even such orders, so as to choose the lesser of two evils.

Furthermore, the danger involved in submitting oneself absolutely to the command and will of another was not such as to cause grave misgivings. As we have shown, sovereign powers possess the right of commanding whatever they will only for as long as they do in fact hold supreme power. If they lose this power, with it they also lose the right of complete command, which passes to one man or a number of men who have acquired it and are able to retain it. Therefore it is exceedingly rare for governments to issue quite unreasonable commands; in their own interest and to retain their rule, it especially behoves them to look to the public good and to conduct all affairs under the guidance of reason. For, as Seneca says, '*violenta imperia nemo continuit diu*'—tyrannical governments never last long. There is the further fact that in a democracy there is less danger of a government behaving unreasonably, for it is practically impossible for the majority of a single assembly, if it is of some size, to agree on the same piece of folly. Then again, as we have also shown, it is the fundamental purpose of democracy to avoid the follies of appetite and to keep men within the bounds of reason, as far as possible, so that they may live in peace and harmony. If this basic principle is removed, the whole fabric soon collapses. It is for the sovereign power alone, then, to have regard to these considerations, while it is for the subjects, as I have said, to carry out its orders and to acknowledge no other right but that which the sovereign power declares to be a right.

Now perhaps it will be thought that in this way we are turning subjects into slaves, the slave being one who acts under orders and the free man one who does as he pleases. But this is not completely true, for the real slave is one who lives under pleasure's sway and can neither see nor do what is for his own good, and only he is free who lives whole-heartedly under the sole guidance of reason.[7] Action under orders—that is, obedience—is indeed to some extent an infringement of freedom, but it does not automatically make a man a slave; the reason for the action must enter into account. If the purpose of the action is not to the advantage of the doer but of him who commands, then the doer is a slave, and does not serve his own interest. But in a sovereign state where the welfare of the whole people, not the ruler, is the supreme law, he who obeys the sovereign power in all things should be called a subject, not a slave who does not serve his own interest. And so that commonwealth whose laws are based on sound reason is the most free, for there everybody can be free as he wills,* that is, he can live whole-heartedly under the guidance of reason. Similarly, although children are in duty bound to obey all the commands of their parents, they are not slaves; for the parents' commands have as their chief aim the good of the children. We therefore recognise a great difference between a slave, a son, and a subject, who accordingly may be defined as follows. A slave is one who has to obey his master's commands which look only to the interests of him who commands; a son is one who by his

7. Parts 4 and 5 of the *Ethics* are concerned with the main topics of Spinoza's philosophy: human bondage and human freedom.
* See Supplementary Note 33.

father's command does what is to his own good; a subject is one who, by command of the sovereign power, acts for the common good, and therefore for his own good also.

I think I have thus demonstrated quite clearly the basis of the democratic state, which I have elected to discuss before all others because it seemed the most natural form of state, approaching most closely to that freedom which nature grants to every man. For in a democratic state nobody transfers his natural right to another so completely that thereafter he is not to be consulted; he transfers it to the majority of the entire community of which he is part. In this way all men remain equal, as they were before in a state of nature. And there is this further reason why I have chosen to discuss at some length only this form of state: thereby my main purpose is best served, which is to discuss the benefits of freedom in a commonwealth. I therefore omit the discussion of the basic principles of other forms of government. To understand their right we do not now need to know how they have arisen, and frequently continue to arise, for this has been made abundantly clear from what we have already proved. Whoever holds sovereign power, be it vested in one person or a few persons or in all the people, it is quite clear that to him belongs the sovereign right of commanding what he will. Furthermore, whoever transfers to another his power of self-defence, whether voluntarily or under compulsion, has fully ceded his natural right and has consequently resolved to obey the other absolutely in all matters; and this he is obliged to do without reservation, as long as the king, or the nobles, or the people retain the sovereign power they have received, which was the basis for the transference of right. I need say no more.

Now that we have demonstrated the basis and right of the state, we can easily determine what is a citizen's civil right, what is a wrong, and what is justice and injustice in a state; and then what is an ally, what is an enemy, and what is treason. By a citizen's civil right we can only mean the freedom of every man to preserve himself in his present condition, a freedom determined by the edicts of the sovereign power and upheld by its authority alone. For when the individual has transferred to another the right to live as he pleases, a right which is limited only by his power—in other words, when he has transferred to another his freedom and power of self-defence—he is then bound to live entirely as the other directs and to trust in him entirely for his defence.

A wrong occurs when a citizen or subject is forced to suffer some injury at the hands of another, contrary to his civil right, i.e. contrary to the edict of the sovereign power. For a wrong cannot be conceived except in a civil condition, nor yet can a wrong be done to subjects by sovereign powers, whose right is not limited. Therefore it can occur only as between private citizens, who are bound by law not to injure one another.

Justice is a set disposition to render to every man what is his by civil right. Injustice is to deprive a man, under the guise of legality, of what belongs to him by true interpretation of the law. These are also called equity and inequity, because those appointed to judge lawsuits are required to hold all men as equal without respect to persons, and to uphold equally everyone's right, neither envying the rich nor despising the poor.

Allies are the men of two states who, to avoid being exposed to the hazards of war or to gain some other advantage, pledge themselves to abstain from mutual aggression and to afford each other aid when occasion demands, each state still retaining its independence. This contract will remain in force for as long as its basis—namely, the consideration of danger or advantage—persists; for nobody makes a contract, or is bound to abide by an agreement, except through hope of some good or apprehension of some evil. If the basis is removed, the agreement becomes void of itself, a fact abundantly illustrated by experience. For although two different states may make a treaty of mutual non-aggression, they nevertheless try as far as they can to prevent the other from becoming too powerful, and they place their trust in words only if they are well assured of the purpose and interest of each party in making the treaty. Without this assurance they fear a breach of faith, and rightly so. For who but a fool who knows nothing of the right of sovereign powers will rest content with the words and promises of someone who maintains the sovereign power and right to do whatever he pleases, one for whom the welfare and advantage of his own state must be his supreme law? And even if piety and religion are taken into account, we shall still see that no one who holds the reins of government can, without doing wrong, abide by his promises to the harm of his country. For he cannot keep whatever promise he sees likely to be detrimental to his country without violating his pledge to his subjects, a pledge by which he is most firmly bound, and whose fulfilment usually involves the most solemn promises.

An enemy is one who lives outside the state on such terms that neither as an ally nor as a subject does he recognise its sovereignty. For it is not hatred but the state's right that makes a man an enemy; and the state's right against one who does not recognise its sovereignty by any kind of treaty is the same as its right against one who has done it an injury, for it can rightly compel him either to submit or to enter into alliance, by any means.

Treason applies only in the case of subjects or citizens who by agreement, whether implicit or explicit, have transferred all their right to the state. A subject is said to have committed this crime if he has attempted for any reason to seize for himself the sovereign power's right or to transfer it to another. I say 'if he has attempted,' for if men were to be condemned only after the deed was done, in most cases it would be too late for the state to try to do this after the seizure of its right or its transference to another. Again, I say without qualification 'he who for any reason attempts to seize for himself the sovereign power's right,' thus making no distinction between cases where either injury or gain to the entire state would have unquestionably resulted. Whatever be the reason for the attempt, he is guilty of treason and is rightly condemned. In war, indeed, there is complete agreement that this is fully justified. If a man leaves his post and approaches the enemy without his commander's knowledge, even though he has ventured on this action with good intention—but nevertheless his own—and has overcome the enemy, he is rightly condemned to death because he has violated his oath and the commander's right. Now it is not universally realised quite so clearly that all citizens without exception are always bound by this right, yet the point at issue is exactly the same. For since the state must be preserved and governed solely by the policy of the sovereign power and it is covenanted that this right belongs absolutely to it alone, if anyone embarks on some undertaking of public concern on his own initiative and without the knowledge of the supreme council, he has violated the right of the sovereign power and is guilty of treason and is rightly and properly condemned, even if, as we have said, the state was sure to gain some advantage from his action.

To remove the last shadow of doubt, it remains for us now to deal with the following objection. Is not our earlier assertion, that everyone who is without the use of reason has the sovereign natural right in a state of nature to live by the laws of appetite, in clear contradiction with the divine law as revealed? For since all men without exception, whether or not they have the use of reason, are equally required by God's command to love their neighbour as themselves, we cannot, without doing wrong, inflict injury on another and live solely by the laws of appetite.

However, we can easily answer this objection if we confine our attention to the state of nature only, for this is prior to religion in nature and in time. For nobody knows by nature* that he has any duty to obey God. Indeed, this knowledge cannot be attained by any process of reasoning; one can gain it only by revelation confirmed by signs. Therefore prior to revelation nobody can be bound by a divine law of which he cannot be aware. So a state of nature must not be confused with a state of religion; we must conceive it as being without religion and without law, and consequently without sin and without wrong, as we have in fact done, quoting Paul in

* See Supplementary Note 34.

confirmation. And it is not only in respect of men's ignorance that we conceive the state of nature as prior to, and lacking, the revelation of God's law, but also in respect of that freedom with which all men are born. For if men were by nature bound by the divine law, or if the divine law were a law by nature, there would have been no need for God to enter into a contract with men and to bind them by covenant and by oath. Therefore we must concede without qualification that the divine law began from the time when men by express covenant promised to obey God in all things, thereby surrendering, as it were, their natural freedom and transferring their right to God in the manner we described in speaking of the civil state. But I shall later treat of these matters at greater length.

But we still have to meet the objection that sovereign powers are no less bound by this divine law than are their subjects, whereas we have said that they retain their natural right and are not restricted in their right. In order to dispose completely of this difficulty, which originates from consideration of natural right rather than the state of nature, I assert that in a state of nature everyone is bound to live by the revealed law from the same motive as he is bound to live according to the dictates of sound reason, namely, that to do so is to his greater advantage and necessary for his salvation. He may refuse to do so, but at his own peril. He is thus bound to live according as he himself wills, and no other, and to acknowledge no man as judge or as rightful arbitrator over religion. This is the right, I say, that has been retained by the sovereign, who can indeed consult others but is not bound to acknowledge anyone as judge or any person but himself as claiming any right, except a prophet expressly sent by God and proving his mission by indisputable signs. Yet not even then is he forced to acknowledge a human judge, but only God himself. And if the sovereign power refuses to obey God as revealed in his Law, he may do so to his own peril and hurt without any violation of right, civil or natural. For civil right depends only on his decree, while natural right depends on the laws of Nature, which are adapted not to religion (whose sole aim is the good of man) but to the order of Nature as a whole, that is, to God's eternal decree, which is beyond our knowledge. This truth seems to have been glimpsed by those who maintain that man can sin against the revealed will of God, but not against the eternal decree by which he has pre-ordained all things.

We may now be asked, "What if the sovereign's command contravenes religion and the obedience we have promised to God by express covenant? Should we obey the divine command or human command?" As I shall later be dealing with this question in more detail, I shall here make only this brief reply: we must obey God before all things when we have a sure and indubitable revelation. But in matters of religion men are especially prone to go astray and contentiously advance many ideas of their own devising, as is abundantly testified by experience. It is therefore quite clear that, if nobody were bound by right to obey the sovereign power in those matters which he thinks to pertain to religion, the state's right would then inevitably depend on judgments and feelings that vary with each individual. For nobody would be bound by it if he considered it to be contrary to his own faith and superstitious belief, and so on this pretext everyone could assume unrestricted freedom to do as he pleases. Now since the right of the state is in this way utterly destroyed, it follows that it belongs completely to the sovereign power, on whom alone both divine and natural right impose the duty of preserving and safeguarding the laws of the state, to make what decisions it thinks fit concerning religion, and all are bound by their pledged word, which God bids them keep inviolate, to obey the sovereign power's decrees and commands in this matter.[8]

But if those at the head of government are heathens, we must either make no contract with them, resolving to suffer anything rather than to transfer our right to them; or, if we have made a contract transferring our right to them and thereby deprived ourselves of the right to defend ourselves and our religion, we are bound, or may be compelled, to obey them and keep our pledge. An exception is made in the case of one to whom God, by sure revelation, has promised his special help against the tyrant, or has given specific exemption. Thus we see that three young men alone out of all the Jews in Babylon refused to obey Nebuchadnezzar, being assured of God's help. All the rest—with the exception of Daniel also, whom the king had worshipped—no doubt obeyed, being compelled by right, perhaps with the thought that they were given into the king's hands by God's decree, and that it was by God's design that the king held and preserved his supreme dominion. On the other hand Eleazar[9] while his country still stood, resolved to give his people an example of steadfastness, so that by following him they would be encouraged to endure anything rather than allow their right and power to be transferred to the Greeks, and would go to any lengths to avoid having to swear allegiance to heathens.

What I have said is confirmed by common experience. In the interests

---

8. Spinoza will qualify somewhat this thesis in chapter 20.

9. Spinoza is referring here to Eleazar, a brother of Judah Maccabee, whose family, the Hasmoneans, revolted against the Greek king of Syria and Mesopotamia, Antiochus ("Epiphanes") IV in 166 B.C. Although the Israelites were victorious, Eleazar was killed in battle. According to Josephus, he attacked an elephant on which he believed Antiochus was seated, and died when it fell upon him (Josephus, *The Wars*, 1.1.5; *Jewish Antiquities*, 12.6.1, 12.9.5).

of greater security the rulers of Christian countries do not hesitate to make treaties with Turks and heathens, and to order those of their subjects who go to dwell with them not to assume more freedom in secular and religious matters than is specified in the treaty or is granted by the government concerned. This is clear from the treaty made by the Dutch with the Japanese, of which I have already made mention.

CHAPTER 17

It is demonstrated that nobody can, or need, transfer all his rights to the sovereign power. An account of the Hebrew state as it was in the time of Moses, and after his death before the institution of monarchy, and its success. Finally, the reasons why it came about that the theocratic state fell, and could scarcely have continued without civil strife

The picture presented in the last chapter of the overriding right of sovereign powers and the transference to them of the individual's natural right, though it comes quite close to actual practice and can increasingly be realised in reality, must nevertheless remain in many respects no more than theory. Nobody can so completely transfer to another all his right, and consequently his power, as to cease to be a human being, nor will there ever be a sovereign power that can do all it pleases. It would be vain to command a subject to hate one to whom he is indebted for some service, to love one who has done him harm, to refrain from taking offence at insults, from wanting to be free of fear, or from numerous similar things that necessarily follow from the laws of human nature. This is shown I think, quite clearly by actual experience; for men have never transferred their right and surrendered their power to another so completely that they were not feared by those very persons who received their right and power, and that the government has not been in greater danger from its citizens, though deprived of their right, than from its external enemies. If men could in fact be so completely deprived of their natural right as thereafter to be powerless* to do anything except by the will of those who hold the supreme right, then indeed the subjects of the most violent tyranny would be without resource, a condition which I imagine no one can possibly envisage. It must therefore be granted that the individual reserves to himself a considerable part of his right, which therefore depends on nobody's decision but his own.

However, for a proper understanding of the extent of the government's right and power, it should be observed that the government's power is not strictly confined to its power of coercion by fear, but rests on all the possible means by which it can induce men to obey its commands. It is not the motive for obedience, but the fact of obedience, that constitutes a subject. Whatever be the motives that prompt a man to carry out the

---

* See Supplementary Note 35.

commands of the sovereign power, whether it be fear of punishment, hope of reward, love of country or any other emotion, while it is he who makes the decision, he is nevertheless acting under the control of the sovereign power. From the fact, then, that a man acts from his own decision, we should not forthwith conclude that his action proceeds from his own right, and not from the right of the government. For whether a man is urged by love or driven by fear of a threatened evil, since in both cases his action always proceeds from his own intention and decision, either there can be no such thing as sovereignty and right over subjects or else it must include all the means that contribute to men's willingness to obey. Consequently, whenever a subject acts in accordance with the commands of the sovereign power, whether he is motivated by love, or fear, or (and this is more frequently the case) a mixture of hope and fear, or by reverence—which is an emotion compounded of fear and awe—or whatever be his motive, he acts from the ruler's right, not from his own.

This point is again clearly established from the fact that obedience is not so much a matter of outward act as internal act of mind. Therefore he who whole-heartedly resolves to obey another in all his commands is fully under another's dominion, and consequently he who reigns over his subjects' minds holds the most powerful dominion. If the strongest dominion were held by those who are most feared, then it would assuredly be held by tyrants' subjects, for they are most feared by their tyrants. Then again, although command cannot be exercised over minds in the same way as over tongues, yet minds are to some degree under the control of the sovereign power, who has many means of inducing the great majority to believe, love, hate etc. whatever he wills. Thus, although it is not by direct command of the sovereign power that these results are produced, yet experience abundantly testifies they often proceed from the authoritative nature of his power and from his guidance, that is, from his right. Therefore there is no absurdity in conceiving men whose beliefs, love, hatred, contempt and every single emotion is under the sole control of the governing power.

But although the right and power of government, when conceived in this way, are quite extensive, there can never be any government so mighty that those in command would have unlimited power to do anything they wish. This, I think, I have already clearly shown. As to the question of how, in spite of this, a state can be formed so as to achieve constant stability, I have already said that it is not my intention to discuss this. Still, in pursuing my theme, I shall draw attention to the means of achieving this end which Moses of old learned from divine revelation; then we shall consider the course taken by the history of the Jews, from which we shall eventually see what exactly are the most important concessions that sovereign powers should make to their subjects to ensure the greater security and prosperity of the state.

Reason and experience tell us quite clearly that the preservation of the state depends mainly on the subjects' loyalty and virtue and their steadfastness in carrying out orders, but the means whereby they should be induced to persevere in their loyalty and virtue are not so readily apparent. For all, both rulers and ruled, are but men, and as such prone to forsake duty for pleasure.[1] Indeed, those who have experienced the fickleness of the masses are almost reduced to despair; for the masses are governed solely by their emotions, not by reason; they rush wildly into everything, and are readily corrupted either by avarice or by luxurious living. Every single man thinks he knows everything, and wants to fashion the world to his liking; he considers things to be fair or unfair, right or wrong, according as he judges them to be to his profit or loss. Vanity makes him despise his equals, nor will he be guided by them. Through envy of superior fame or fortune—which is never equal for all men—he desires another's misfortune and takes pleasure therein. There is no need for me to go through the whole catalogue, for everyone knows to what wickedness men are frequently persuaded by dissatisfaction with their lot and desire for change, by hasty anger, by disdain of poverty, and how their minds are engrossed and agitated by these emotions.

To guard against all these dangers, to organise a state in such a way as leaves no place for wrongdoing, or better still, to frame such a constitution that every man, whatever be his character, will set public right before private advantage, this is the task, this the toil.[2] The need to find a solution has driven men to devise many expedients, yet the position has never been attained where the state was not in greater danger from its citizens than from the external enemy, and where its rulers were not in greater fear of the former than the latter. Let Rome be witness, unconquerable by her enemies, yet so often conquered and wretchedly oppressed by her own citizens, and particularly in the civil war between Vespasian and Vitellius. (See Tacitus' *Histories*, at the beginning of Book 4, where he describes the sad plight of the city.) Alexander, as Curtius says towards the end of Book 8, thought it a less exacting task to maintain prestige abroad than at home, believing that his greatness might be destroyed by his own people. Fearing such a fate for himself, he besought his friends with these words: "Do you but keep me safe from internal treachery and domestic plots; I will fearlessly face the hazards of war and fighting. Philip was safer in battle than in the theatre. He often emerged unscathed from the enemy's violence: he

1. A quotation from Terence, *Andria*, 77–78, "*a labore proclives ad libidenem.*"
2. Vergil, *Aeneid*, VI, 129, "*hoc opus, hic labor est.*"

could not escape from that of his own people. And if you reflect on the deaths of other kings, you will find more who died at the hands of their own people than at the hands of the enemy." See Q. Curtius, Book 9, chapter 6.

It was for this reason, then, to render themselves secure, that kings who in ancient times seized power, tried to persuade men that they were descended from the immortal gods, thinking that if only their subjects and all men should regard them not as their equals but should believe them to be gods, they would willingly suffer their rule and would readily submit. Thus Augustus persuaded the Romans that he traced his origin to Aeneas, who was thought to be the son of Venus and ranked among the gods. He wanted to be worshipped with temples and godlike statues, with attendant flamens and priests (Tac. *Ann.* 1). Alexander wished to be saluted as the son of Jupiter, a wish that seems to have been motivated by policy rather than pride, as shown by his reply when attacked by Hermolaus. "It was," he said, "quite absurd for Hermolaus to demand of me that I should take no account of Jupiter, by whose oracle I am recognised. Am I responsible even for the answers of the gods? He offered me the name of son; to accept this"—note well!—"was by no means incongruous with the designs we are pursuing. Would that the Indians, too, might believe me to be a god! In war, prestige is an important factor, and a false belief has often done duty for truth" (Curtius, Book 8, chapter 8). In these few remarks he cleverly contrives to foist a deception on the ignorant, while at the same time hinting at the reason for the pretence. The same is true of Cleon's speech, attempting to persuade the Macedonians to bow to the king's demand. After giving pretence the gloss of truth by extolling Alexander's deeds and reviewing his achievements, he passes on to the question of expedience, as follows: "The Persians show wisdom as well as piety in worshipping their kings as gods, for majesty is the bulwark of the state's security." And he concludes by saying, "For my part, I will prostrate myself to the ground when the king enters the banquet. Others should do likewise, especially those endowed with wisdom" (Curtius, Book 8, chapter 5).

But the Macedonians were too sensible, and only utter barbarians allow themselves to be so blatantly deceived and to become slaves instead of subjects, with no interests of their own. Others, however, have succeeded more easily in convincing men that royalty is sacred and is God's regent on earth, that it is established by God, not by the votes and consent of men, and is preserved and sustained by God's special providence and help. Other ideas of this kind have been devised by monarchs for the security of their rule, but all these I pass over, and in order to reach my intended goal I shall confine myself, as I have said, to noting and examining only the things that Moses of old learned to this end by divine revelation.

We have already said in chapter 5 that, after their departure from Egypt, the Hebrews were no longer bound by the laws of any other nation, but were free to establish new laws as they pleased, and to occupy whatever lands they wished. For after their liberation from the intolerable oppression of the Egyptians, being bound by no covenant to any mortal man they regained their natural right over everything that lay within their power, and every man could decide afresh whether to retain it or to surrender it and transfer it to another. Finding themselves thus placed in this state of nature, they hearkened to Moses, in whom they all placed the greatest confidence, and resolved to transfer their right not to any mortal man, but to God alone. Without much hesitation they all promised, equally and with one voice, to obey God absolutely in all his commands and to acknowledge no other law but that which he should proclaim as such by prophetic revelation. Now this promise, or transference of right to God, was made in the same way as we have previously conceived it to be made in the case of an ordinary community when men decide to surrender their natural right. For it was by express covenant and oath (Exod. ch. 24 v. 7) that they surrendered their natural right and transferred it to God, which they did freely, not by forcible coercion or fear of threats. Furthermore, to ensure that the covenant should be fixed and binding with no suspicion of deceit, God made no covenant with them until they had experienced his wonderful power which alone had saved them, and which alone might save them in time to come (Exod. ch. 19 v. 4, 5). For it was through this very belief, that God's power alone could save them, that they transferred to God all their natural power of self-preservation—which they probably thought they themselves had hitherto possessed—and consequently all their right.

It was God alone, then, who held sovereignty over the Hebrews, and so this state alone, by virtue of the covenant, was rightly called the kingdom of God, and God was also called the king of the Hebrews. Consequently, the enemies of this state were the enemies of God; citizens who aimed to seize the sovereignty were guilty of treason against God, and the laws of the state were the laws and commands of God. So in this state civil law and religion—which we have shown to consist only in obedience to God— were one and the same thing; the tenets of religion were not just teachings but laws and commands; piety was looked upon as justice, impiety as crime and injustice. He who forsook his religion ceased to be a citizen and by that alone became an enemy, and he who died for his religion was regarded as having died for his country. In short, there was considered to be no difference whatsoever between civil law and religion. Hence this form of government could be called a theocracy, its citizens being bound only by such law as was revealed by God. However, all this was a matter of theory rather than fact, for in reality the Hebrews retained their sovereign right completely, as will become clear when I describe the manner and method of the government of this state, which I now intend to set forth.

Since the Hebrews did not transfer their right to any other man, but, as in a democracy, they all surrendered their right on equal terms, crying with one voice, "Whatever God shall speak, we shall do" (no one being named as mediator), it follows that this covenant left them all completely equal, and they all had an equal right to consult God, to receive and interpret his laws; in short, they all shared equally in the government of the state. It was for this reason, then, that on the first occasion they all approached God on equal terms to hear what he wished to command. But on this first appearance before God they were so terrified and so thunderstruck at hearing God speak that they thought their last hour had come. So, overwhelmed with fear they went to Moses again, saying, "Behold, we have heard God speaking in the midst of the fire; now therefore why should we die? For this great fire will surely consume us; if again we are to hear the voice of God, we shall surely die. Go thou near therefore, and hear all that our God shall say. And speak thou (not God) to us. All that God shall speak unto thee, we shall hear and do (Exod. ch. 20 v. 18)."

By this they clearly abrogated the first covenant, making an absolute transfer to Moses of their right to consult God and to interpret his decrees. For at this point what they promised was not, as before, to obey all that God should speak to them, but what God should speak to Moses. (See Deut. ch. 5 after the Decalogue, and ch. 18 v. 15, 16.) Therefore Moses was left as the sole lawgiver and interpreter of God's laws, and thus also the supreme judge, whom no one could judge, and who alone acted on God's behalf among the Hebrews, that is, held the supreme kingship, since he alone had the right to consult God, to give God's answers to the people, and to compel them to obey. He alone, I say, for if anyone during Moses' lifetime sought to make any proclamation in God's name, even if he were a true prophet he was nevertheless guilty of claiming the supreme sovereignty (Num. ch. 11 v. 28).*

Here we should observe that although the people chose Moses, they had no right to choose his successor. For as soon as they transferred to Moses their right to consult God and promised without reservation to regard him as the divine oracle, they completely lost all their right and were bound to accept as chosen by God whichever successor Moses should choose. Now if Moses had chosen a successor to have, like himself, complete control over the state, that is, the right to consult God alone in his tent, and consequently the authority to make and repeal laws, to make decisions on

* See Supplementary Note 36.

war and peace, to send envoys, to appoint judges, to choose a successor, in short, to exercise all the functions of a sovereign, the state would have become simply a monarchy. There would have been no difference but this, that ordinarily a monarchy is ruled in accordance with a decree of God which is hidden even from the monarch, whereas the Hebrew state would be, or should have been, ruled in a definite way by God's decree revealed to the monarch alone. This difference does not diminish the monarch's dominion and right over all his subjects; on the contrary, it increases it. As for the people, in both cases they are equally subject and equally ignorant of God's decree, for in both cases they are dependent on what the monarch says, understanding from him alone what is right and what is wrong. And by believing that the monarch issues commands only in accordance with God's decree as revealed to him, the people would in fact be more, not less, under the monarch's dominion. However, Moses appointed no such successor, but left the state to be so governed by those who came after him that it could be called neither a democracy nor an aristocracy nor a monarchy, but a theocracy. While the right to interpret the laws and to promulgate God's answers was vested in one man, the right and power to govern the state in accordance with laws thus expounded and answers thus made known was vested in another. See Num. ch. 27 v. 21.* For a clearer understanding of this situation, I shall explain in an orderly way how the whole state was governed.

First, the people were commanded to build a dwelling to serve as the palace of God, the state's supreme sovereign. This palace was to be built at the expense not of one man but of the entire people, so that the dwelling where God was to be consulted should belong to the nation as a whole. The Levites were chosen to be the courtiers and administrators of this palace of God, while Aaron, the brother of Moses, was chosen to be at their head, in second place, as it were, to God their king, to be succeeded by his sons by hereditary right. Therefore Aaron, as next to God, was the supreme interpreter of God's laws, giving the people the answers of the divine oracle and entreating God on the people's behalf. Now if, along with these functions, he had held the right of issuing commands, his position would have been that of an absolute monarch. But this right was denied him, and in general the whole tribe of Levi was so completely divested of civil rights that they did not have even a legal share of territory, like the other tribes, to provide them at least with a livelihood. Moses ordained that they should be maintained by the rest of the people, yet always be held in the highest honour by the common people as the only tribe dedicated to God.

* See Supplementary Note 37.

Next, a military force was formed from the remaining twelve tribes, and they were ordered to invade the land of Canaan and to divide it into twelve parts which would be allocated to the tribes by lot. For this task twelve captains were chosen, one from each tribe, who, together with Joshua and the high priest Eleazar, were given the right to divide the territory into twelve equal parts to be allocated by lot. Joshua was chosen as commander-in-chief of the armed forces, and he alone had the right in emergencies to consult God, not, however, like Moses, alone in his tent or in the tabernacle, but through the mediation of the high priest, to whom alone God's answers were given. Furthermore, Joshua alone had the authority to promulgate God's commands as told him by the high priest and to compel the people's obedience, to devise and apply the means of executing these commands, to choose from the armed forces whom he wished and as many as he wished, to send envoys in his own name; in short, the complete control of war was in his hands alone. There was no successor to his position by hereditary right; only at a time of national emergency was one chosen, and then only by God's direct intervention. At all other times all matters concerning war and peace were in the hands of the captains of the tribes, as I shall presently show. Finally, all men between the ages of twenty and sixty were ordered to bear arms and to form armies recruited only from the people, which swore allegiance not to the commander-in-chief nor to the high priest, but to their religion and to God. They were thus called the armies and hosts of God, and correspondingly God was called by the Hebrews the Lord of Hosts. It was for this reason that in great battles on whose issue depended victory or defeat for the whole people the ark of the covenant was borne in the midst of the army, so that on seeing their king in their midst, as it were, the people would fight with all their might.[3]

From these commands left by Moses to his successors we can plainly see that it was ministers, not masters of the state, that Moses appointed. To no one did he give the right to consult God in solitude and wherever he wished, and therefore to no one did he give the authority, which he himself possessed, to make and repeal laws, to decide on war and peace, and to choose men for religious and secular office, all these being the prerogative of a sovereign. The high priest did indeed have the right to interpret the laws and to deliver God's answers, but only when requested by the

3. Like Machiavelli, for whom Spinoza had considerable respect, Spinoza advocates a citizen military, not mercenaries. This was one of the good features of the ancient Israelite state (Machiavelli, *The Prince*, chapters 12–14. Spinoza, *Political Treatise*, 5.7).

commander-in-chief or the supreme council or similar authorities, and not whenever he wished, like Moses. On the other hand the commander-in-chief and the councils could consult God whenever they wished but could receive God's answers only from the high priest. Therefore God's words as given by the priest were not decrees, as when given by Moses, but only answers; only when accepted by Joshua and the councils did they have the force of commands and decrees. Moreover, the high priest who received God's answers from God possessed no armed force and held no rightful command, while those who had the right to the possession of land did not have the right to make laws.

Then again, the high priest, in the case both of Aaron and his son Eleazar, was indeed chosen by Moses; but after the death of Moses nobody had the right to choose the high priest; son succeeded father by hereditary right. The commander-in-chief was also appointed by Moses, and assumed his office not by virtue of the high priest's right, but by the right of Moses granted to him. So on the death of Joshua the high priest did not choose anyone in his place, nor did the captains consult God on the question of a new commander. Each captain retained Joshua's command over the military force of his own tribe, and they all collectively took over Joshua's command over the entire military force. There seems to have been no need for a commander-in-chief except when they had to join forces against a common enemy, a circumstance which occurred mainly in Joshua's time when not all the tribes had as yet a fixed territory and everything was held in common. But when all the tribes had divided among themselves those territories which they held by right of conquest and those which it was their mission yet to conquer, and all things were no longer held in common, thereby there ceased to be any reason for a common commander; for as a result of the allocation the different tribes must have been regarded as confederated states rather than as fellow citizens. With respect to God and religion they must indeed have been regarded as fellow citizens, but in respect of the right of one tribe as against another they were only members of a confederation, in much the same position (disregarding the common temple) as the High Confederated Estates of the Netherlands. For the division into shares of property held in common simply implies that each member now owns his share alone, the others having surrendered their right to that particular share. This, then, was Moses' purpose in appointing captains of the tribes, that after the division of the state each captain should assume control over his own part, including the right to consult God through the high priest about the affairs of his own tribe, to command his own military forces, to found and fortify cities, to appoint judges in each city, to attack the enemies of his own particular state, in short, to carry out all the duties of war and peace. He was not required to recognise any other judge than God* or a prophet expressly sent by God. If he rebelled against God, it was the duty of the other tribes to attack him as an enemy who had violated the terms of his agreement, not to pass judgment on him as a subject.

That this was the situation is exemplified in Scripture. After Joshua's death it was the children of Israel who consulted God, not a new commander-in-chief. Now when it was learnt that it fell to the tribe of Judah to be the first to attack its enemy, this tribe alone made an agreement with the tribe of Simeon to join forces in attacking their common enemies. The other tribes were not included in this agreement (Judges ch. 1 v. 1, 2, 3); each tribe waged war separately (as we are told in the same chapter) against its own enemy, imposing terms of submission and alliance on whom it would, although they had been commanded to spare no one on any terms and to destroy them utterly. For this sin they were no doubt reproved, but nobody was in a position to call them to account. It was not for such reasons that the tribes began to take up arms against one another and to interfere in another's affairs. But the tribe of Benjamin, which had wronged other tribes and had so violated the bond of peace that none of the confederates could lodge safely among them, was attacked as an enemy, and after three battles the victors slaughtered them all indiscriminately, guilty and innocent alike, by right of war, a deed which they later bewailed with a repentance that came too late.

These examples plainly confirm what we have just said regarding the right of each tribe. But perhaps the question will be raised—who appointed the successor to the captains of each tribe? Now on this point I cannot find anything definite in Scripture itself, but I conjecture that, since each tribe was divided into families whose heads were chosen from their more senior members, the senior of these succeeded by right to the office of captain. For it was from the seniors that Moses chose his seventy colleagues to sit with him on the supreme council. Those who had charge of the government after Joshua's death are called 'elders' in Scripture; and, finally, the use of the word 'elders' to mean judges was a common practice among the Hebrews, as I think everyone knows. But for our purpose it matters little if this point remains undecided; it is enough to have shown that after Moses' death no one exercised all the functions of a sovereign. The management of affairs was not entirely in the hands of one man, or one council, or the people; some affairs were managed by one tribe and others by the rest, with equal right in each case. Thus it clearly follows that after Moses' death the state was left neither as a monarchy nor

* See Supplementary Note 38.

an aristocracy nor a democracy, but, as we have said, a theocracy, and for the following reasons. First, the royal seat of government was the temple, and it was only in respect of the temple that all the tribes were fellow citizens, as we have shown. Secondly, all their citizens had to swear allegiance to God, their supreme judge, to whom alone they had promised absolute obedience in all things. Finally, when a commander-in-chief was needed, he was chosen only by God. This is what Moses explicitly foretold to the people in God's name in Deut. ch. 18 v. 15, and was confirmed in actual fact by the choosing of Gideon, Samson and Samuel. Hence we cannot have any doubt that the other faithful leaders were also chosen in like manner, even though this is not expressly stated in the narrative.

Our survey being now complete, it is time for us to see how far a constitution framed on these lines was able to exercise control over men's minds and to so restrain both rulers and ruled that neither would the latter rebel nor the former become tyrants.

Those who govern the state or hold the reins of power always strive to cloak with a show of legality whatever wrong they commit, persuading the people that this action was right and proper; and this they can easily achieve when the interpretation of the law is entirely in their hands. For this in itself undoubtedly affords them the greatest latitude in doing whatever they want and whatever their appetite suggests, whereas they are largely deprived of this freedom if the right to interpret the laws is vested in somebody else, and likewise if the true interpretation of the laws is so obvious that it is not open to doubt. This makes it clear that the captains of the Hebrews found their scope for transgression severely curtailed by the fact that the entire right to interpret the laws was assigned to the Levites (Deut. ch. 21 v. 5) who had no share either in the administration of the state or in its territory, and who saw their entire welfare and prestige dependent on a true interpretation of the law. Furthermore, the entire populace was required to assemble at an appointed place every seventh year to learn the laws from the priest, and in addition everyone was expected to read and re-read the book of the Law on his own, constantly and with the utmost concentration. See Deut. ch. 31 v. 9 etc. and ch. 6 v. 7. Thus, if only in their own interests, the captains had to take great care to govern entirely in accordance with laws laid down and familiar to all, if they wished to enjoy the highest esteem of a people who would then revere them as ministers of God's kingdom and as God's vice-regents. If they acted otherwise they must have inevitably encountered the bitterest hatred—such as religious hatred is wont to be—on the part of their subjects.

Among other considerations that restrained the unbridled licence of the captains was one of considerable importance, in that the armed forces were recruited from the whole citizen body with no exceptions between the ages of twenty and sixty, and that the captains were not allowed to hire foreign mercenaries. This, I repeat, was of considerable importance, for it is a fact that rulers can subjugate a people simply by means of hired mercenaries, while there is nothing they fear more than the independence of a citizen soldiery who have won freedom and glory for their country by their valour, their toil, and the heavy price of blood. It was for this reason that when Alexander was about to fight his second battle against Darius, he refrained from rebuking Parmenio on hearing his advice, but instead rebuked Polypercon, who was merely supporting Parmenio. For, as Curtius says in Book 4, chapter 13, having recently rebuked Parmenio more severely than he might have wished, he did not venture to castigate him again. Nor was he able to suppress the Macedonians' freedom—of which, as I have already said, he was in great fear—until he had increased the number of troops recruited from prisoners of war far above the level of the Macedonians. Only then could he give rein to the vicious propensities that had long been held in check by the independence of his best countrymen. Now if this independence of a citizen soldiery can restrain the rulers of a secular state who usually claim for themselves all the credit for victories, it must have exercised far greater restraint on the Hebrew captains whose soldiers fought not for their captain's glory, but for the glory of God, and who did not join battle until they had received God's assent.

Another check on the Hebrew captains was the fact that religion was the only tie that bound them all together. Therefore if one of them transgressed against religion and began to violate individual rights given by God, the others could treat him as an enemy and lawfully subdue him.

A third check was afforded by the fear of the appearance of a new prophet. If a man of proven virtue could show by certain acknowledged signs that he was a prophet, he thereby, like Moses, assumed the supreme right to command in the name of God to him alone revealed, not consulted only through the mediation of a priest, as was the case with the captains. And there is no doubt that if the people were oppressed, such prophets could easily gain support, and by signs of no great significance they could convince the people of whatever they wished. On the other hand, if the government were properly conducted, the captain could ensure in good time that the prophet should first stand before him to be examined as to whether he was of proven virtue, whether he possessed sure and indubitable signs of his mission, and whether his message in God's name was consistent with the accepted teachings and common laws of his country. If his signs were less than satisfactory, or his teaching innovatory, he could rightly be condemned to death. In the other event, he was accepted only on the captain's authority and testimony.

Fourthly, there was the fact that the captain had no superiority over others by nobility of descent or right of birth; the government of the state was in his hands only by reason of his age and qualities.

Finally, the captains and the entire armed force did not have any reason to prefer war to peace. The army, as we have said, was entirely a citizen force, and therefore matters of both war and peace were in the same hands. Thus the soldier in the camp was a citizen in the forum, the officer in the camp was a judge in the law-court, and the commander-in-chief in the camp was a ruler in civil life. Therefore nobody could want war for war's sake, but only for the sake of peace and the defence of freedom; and possibly the captain refrained from new ventures as far as he could so as to avoid having to approach the high priest and stand before him to the detriment of his dignity. So much, then, for the reasons that kept the captains within due bounds.

We must now consider what were the restraints on the people, though these are also plainly indicated by the basic principles of the state. Even a cursory examination will at once reveal that these must have kindled such an ardent patriotism in the hearts of the citizens that it could never enter anyone's mind to betray or desert his country; on the contrary, they must all have been of such a mind as to suffer death rather than a foreign yoke. For having transferred their right to God, believing that their kingdom was God's kingdom and that they alone were God's children, while the other nations were God's enemies for whom they therefore felt an implacable hatred (for this, too, they believed to be a mark of piety; see Psalm 139 v. 21, 22), they could think of nothing more abhorrent than to swear allegiance and promise obedience to a foreigner, and they could conceive of nothing more wicked and abominable than to betray their country, that is, the very kingdom of the God whom they worshipped. Indeed, it was regarded as utterly disgraceful even to emigrate, for the religious rites which it was their constant duty to practise could be performed only on their native soil; it alone was held to be holy ground, the rest of the world being unclean and profane. It was for this reason that David, when driven into exile, complained to Saul in these words: "If those who stir thee up against me be men, they are accursed, for they shut me out from walking in the inheritance of the Lord, saying, 'Go and worship other gods.'" For the same reason—and this is here specially noteworthy—no citizen was condemned to exile; for the wrongdoer does indeed deserve to be punished, but not to be outraged.

Therefore the patriotism of the Hebrews was not simply patriotism but piety, and this, together with hatred for other nations, was so fostered and nourished by their daily ritual that it inevitably became part of their nature. For their daily worship was not merely quite different, making them altogether unique and completely distinct from other peoples, but also utterly opposed to others. Hence this daily invective, as it were, was bound to engender a lasting hatred of a most deep-rooted kind, since it was a hatred that had its source in strong devotion or piety and was believed to be a religious duty—for that is the bitterest and most persistent of all kinds of hatred. And this was reinforced by the universal cause of the continuous growth of hatred, to wit, the reciprocation of hatred; for the other nations inevitably held them in bitter hatred in return.[4]

How all these factors—their freedom from human rule, their devotion to their country, their absolute right against all others and a hatred that was not only permissible but a religious duty, the hostility of all around them, their distinctive customs and rites—how all these factors, I say, combined to fortify the hearts of the Hebrews to endure all things for their country with unexampled steadfastness and valour, is confirmed by reason and attested by experience. Never while their city stood could they long endure foreign dominion, and that was why Jerusalem was wont to be called the rebellious city (Ezra ch. 4 v. 12, 15). It was with the greatest difficulty that the Romans succeeded in destroying their second state (a mere shadow of the first, the priests having usurped the right to govern), as Tacitus bears witness in these words in *Histories*, Book 2: "Vespasian had brought to an end the Jewish War except for the siege of Jerusalem, a task rendered more severe and difficult by the character of the people and the obstinacy of their superstitious beliefs rather than by the sufficiency of their resources to endure the hardships of a siege."

But beside these factors, whose influence is a matter of subjective assessment, there was another feature of this state, peculiar to it and of indisputable weight, which must have been most effective in deterring citizens from contemplating defection and from ever wanting to desert their country, to wit, the motive of self-interest, the strength and life of all human action. This, I say, was a feature peculiar to this state. Nowhere else did citizens have stronger right to their possessions than did the subjects of this state, who had an equal share with the captain in lands and fields,

---

4. This is not Spinoza at his best; here he expresses his "revenge" against his former coreligionists. Throughout the Hebrew Bible the commandment to love the stranger is repeated (Deuteronomy 10:19). The Israelites are forbidden to hate the Edomites, despite the latter's ill treatment of them nor are they to abhor the Egyptians, their former slave-masters (Deuteronomy 23:8). In later times a special sacrifice on behalf of the nations was offered in the Temple in Jerusalem. Spinoza knew all of this well, but his political agenda led him to make these false allegations.

and were each the owners of their share in perpetuity. For if any man was compelled by poverty to sell his farm or field, it had to be restored to him when the jubilee came round, and there were other similar enactments to prevent the alienation of real estate. Then again, nowhere could poverty have been lighter to endure than there, where charity to one's neighbour, that is, to one's fellow citizen, was a duty to be practised with the utmost piety so as to gain the favour of God, their king. Thus the Hebrew citizens could enjoy a good life only in their own country; abroad they could expect only hurt and humiliation.

Moreover, the following considerations were particularly effective not only in keeping them in their native land but also in avoiding civil war and in removing the causes of strife, namely, that no man served his equal, but only God, that charity and love towards one's fellow citizen was regarded as a supreme religious duty and was fostered to no small degree by the common hatred they had for other nations, and other nations for them. A further important factor was their training in strict obedience, imposing the duty of following a definite prescribed law in all that they did. A man might not plough when he pleased, but only at fixed times and seasons, and then with only one kind of animal at a time; likewise, he might sow and reap only in a certain way and at a certain time. To sum up, their life was one long schooling in obedience (see chapter 5 regarding ceremonial practices). Therefore to men so habituated to it obedience must have appeared no longer as bondage, but freedom. From this it must also have followed that nobody desired what was forbidden and all desired what was commanded, an attitude considerably encouraged by the requirement to give themselves up to rest and rejoicing at certain seasons of the year, not for self-indulgence, but to serve God with a cheerful heart. Three times a year they feasted before the Lord (Deut. ch. 16). On the seventh day of every week they had to cease from all work and give themselves over to rest; and in addition to these, other times were appointed when innocent rejoicing and feasting were not merely permitted but enjoined. In my opinion no more effective means can be devised to influence men's minds, for nothing can so captivate the mind as joy springing from devotion, that is, love mingled with awe. Nor was there much likelihood that repetition would bring about boredom; the ceremonial appointed for feast days recurred only at lengthy intervals and was varied in character. Further-more, there was their deep reverence for their temple because of its special rites and the ceremonies required before one was allowed to enter, a reverence which they most religiously preserved at all times, so that even today Jews cannot read without the deepest horror of Manasseh's crime in daring to introduce an idol into the very temple. No less was the people's reverence for the Law, which was most zealously guarded in the inmost shrine. Hence in this state there was little danger of murmurings and unorthodoxy on the part of the people. No one ventured to pass judgment in matters of religion; they had to obey all that was commanded them on the authority of God's answer received in the temple, or of the Law established by God, without any resort to reason.

I have thus, I think, set forth quite clearly, though briefly, the main features of the Hebrew state. It now remains for me to enquire into the reasons why the Hebrews so frequently forsook the Law, and why they were so many times conquered, and why it came about in the end that their state was utterly destroyed. Perhaps at this point it will be suggested that this resulted from the stubbornness of the race. However, this is a foolish suggestion, for why was this nation more stubborn than others? Was it by nature? But surely nature creates individuals, not nations, and it is only difference of language, of laws, and of established customs that divides individuals into nations. And only the last two, laws and customs, can be the source of the particular character, the particular mode of life, the particular set of attitudes that signalise each nation. So if it had to be allowed that the Hebrews were stubborn beyond other mortals, this would have to be attributed to the defectiveness of their laws or of their established customs. It is, of course, true that if God had willed their state to be of longer duration, he would also have given them laws and ordinances of a different kind and would have established a different mode of government. So we can only say that their God was angry with them, not only, as Jeremiah says in chapter 32 verse 21, from the foundation of their city, but right from the time when their laws were ordained. Ezekiel, too, makes the same point in chapter 20 verse 25, where he says: "I gave them also statutes that were not good and judgments whereby they should not live, in that I polluted them in their gifts by rejecting all that opened the womb (that is, the firstborn) so that I might make them desolate, to the end that they might know that I am the Lord."

In order that we may rightly understand these words and the cause of the destruction of the state, we should observe that it had first been intended to entrust the entire ministry of religion to the firstborn, not to the Levites (Num. ch. 8 v. 17); but when all except the Levites had worshipped the calf, the firstborn were rejected as defiled and the Levites were chosen in their place (Deut. ch. 10 v. 8). The more I consider the change, the more I am forced to exclaim in the words of Tacitus, "At that time, God's concern was not for their security, but for vengeance."[5] I

---

5. Tacitus, *Histories*, I, 3. An adaptation of "*non esse curae deis securitatem nostram, esse ultionem.*"

cannot sufficiently marvel that such was the wrath of heaven[6] that God framed their very laws, whose sole end should always be the honour, welfare and security of the people, with the intention of avenging himself and punishing the people, with the result that their laws appeared to them to be not so much laws—that is, the safeguard of the people—as penalties and punishments. All the gifts that they were required to make to the Levites and priests, as likewise the compulsory redemption of their first-born by a payment to the Levites for each one, and the fact that the Levites alone were privileged to perform the sacred rites—all this was a constant reminder of their defilement and rejection. Then again, the Levites were continually finding occasion to rebuke them, for among so many thousands of people one may well imagine there were many would-be theologians making themselves a nuisance. As a result, the people were keen to keep watch over the Levites—who were no doubt just human—and, as often happens, to accuse them all for the misdeeds of one. Hence there were continual murmurings, culminating in a sense of resentment at having to maintain in idleness men who were unpopular and unrelated to them by blood, especially when food was dear. Little wonder, then, that in times of peace when there were no more striking miracles and no men of unquestionable authority appeared on the scene, the people's morale began to fail through discontent and greed, and eventually they looked for change, forsaking a worship which, although worship of God, nevertheless involved their humiliation and was also the object of suspicion. Little wonder that their rulers—and rulers are always seeking ways to keep for themselves supreme sovereignty over the state—made every concession to the people and introduced new forms of worship, with the view to securing the people's favour and alienating them from the high priest.

Now if the constitution of the state had been as first intended, all the tribes would have enjoyed equal right and honour, and the whole structure of the state would have been quite sound. For who would have wished to violate the sacred right of their own kinsfolk? What more could they have wanted than to maintain their own kinsfolk, their brothers and fathers, as a religious duty, to be taught by them the interpretation of the laws, and to await God's answers from them. Moreover, if all the tribes had preserved equal right to the sacred offices, they would thus have remained far more closely united. Even so, there would still have been no dangerous consequences if the election of the Levites had been inspired by anything other than anger and revenge. However, as I have said, their God was angry with

---

6. An adaptation of Vergil, *Aeneid*, I, 11, *"tantaene animis caelestibus irae?"*

them, and, to repeat the words of Ezekiel, he polluted them in their gifts by rejecting all that opened the womb, so as to make them desolate.

The historical narratives themselves provide further confirmation of this view. As soon as the people found themselves with abundant leisure in the wilderness, many of them, of no mean standing, began to resent this election, and found in this a reason for believing that Moses was acting not by divine decree, but at his own pleasure, in that he had chosen his own tribe before all others and had bestowed on his own brother the office of high priest in perpetuity. They therefore went to him, raising a tumult and crying that all were equally holy and that it was wrong for him to be exalted above all others.[7] In no way could Moses pacify them, but a miracle intervened as a sign of his faithfulness, and they were all wiped out. Then came a new and widespread revolt of the entire people, who believed that the men had perished not by God's judgment but by the devising of Moses. When a great disaster or plague had at last reduced them to exhaustion, he succeeded in pacifying them, but their condition was such that they all preferred death to life. It would therefore be truer to say of that time that there was a cessation of rebellion rather than a restoration of harmony. This is confirmed by the words of Scripture in Deuteronomy chapter 31 verse 21, where, after foretelling that the people would fall away from the practice of their religion after his death, God says to Moses, "For I know their desire, and what they are about this day, even before I have brought them to the land which I swore." And a little later Moses speaks thus to the people, "For I know thy rebellion and thy stiff neck. If while I have lived among you ye have been rebellious against the Lord, how much more after my death."

And this is what in fact occurred, as we know. There ensued great changes, unbounded licence, self-indulgence and sloth, leading to a general decline until, after being frequently subjugated, they came to open rupture with divine rule and sought a mortal king, making the seat of government a court rather than a temple, with all the tribes no longer retaining a common citizenship on the basis of the divine rule and the priesthood, but by allegiance to a king. But here was ample material for fresh sedition, which led ultimately to the downfall of the entire state. For what can be more intolerable to kings than to rule by sufferance, and to allow a dominion within their dominion? The first kings to be chosen from private station were content with the rank to which they had been elevated, but when their sons succeeded by hereditary right they gradually began to bring about extensive changes so as to hold the absolute sovereignty in their own hands alone. This they lacked to a considerable

---

7. Here Spinoza is alluding to the rebellion of Korah, related in Numbers 16.

extent as long as control over the laws was exercised not by them but by the high priest, who guarded the laws in the sanctuary and interpreted them to the people. Thus the kings were bound by the laws no less than their subjects, and had no right to repeal them or to enact new laws of equal authority. A further contributory factor was that the right of the Levites debarred kings just as much as their subjects from administering the sacred rites: they were equally unholy. Lastly, there was the fact that the security of their rule depended solely on the will of one man, who was seen as a prophet. Of this last they had seen examples, such as the emphatic independence shown by Samuel in giving orders to Saul, and the facility with which he was able to transfer the sovereignty to David because of a single fault. Therefore they saw an empire within their empire, and they ruled on sufferance.

To overcome these restrictions they permitted other temples to be dedicated to the gods to avoid further occasion to consult the Levites, and then they sought out other men to prophesy in God's name, so as to have prophets to counter the true prophets. But their various attempts never succeeded in achieving their aims. For the prophets, always resourceful, awaited their opportunity in the rule of a successor, which is always precarious as long as the memory of his predecessor remains fresh. Then, by their divine authority, they could readily induce someone hostile to the king and of high repute to champion the divine right and claim the sovereignty, or some portion of it, by right. Yet the prophets in their turn met with no great success by these methods; for even though they removed a tyrant, the causes of tyranny remained. Thus they merely succeeded in installing a new tyrant at the cost of much citizen blood. There was no end, then, to discord and civil wars, but the causes which led to the violation of the divine law were always the same, and could be removed only along with the whole constitution.

We have now seen in what manner religion was introduced into the Hebrew commonwealth, and how the state might have lasted indefinitely if the just anger of the lawgiver had allowed it to continue in its original form. But since this was impossible, it was bound eventually to come to an end. I have here been discussing only the first state; the second[8] was a mere shadow of the first, in that people were bound by the right of the Persians to whom they were subject, and after the restoration of independence the priests usurped the right of government, thereby holding abso-

---

8. The destruction of the Temple in 586 B.C. by the Babylonians is commonly taken to be the end of the First Commonwealth; the Second Commonwealth is usually understood to have commenced with the restoration of the High Priesthood in Jerusalem in 538 B.C. under the sponsorship of the Persian King Cyrus.

lute power. Hence the priests became inflamed with the desire to combine secular and religious rule. For this reason I have thought it unnecessary to say more about the second state. As to whether the first state, regarding only its lasting qualities, is a model to be imitated, or whether it is a pious duty to imitate it as far as possible, this will become clear in the following chapters. Here, in conclusion, I would like merely to emphasise a point already indicated. From the findings of this present chapter it clearly emerges that the divine right, or the right of religion, originates in a contract, without which there is no right but natural right, and so the Hebrews were not required as a religious duty to practise piety towards peoples who were not party to the contract, but only towards their fellow citizens.

CHAPTER 18

From the commonwealth of the Hebrews and their history
some political principles are deduced

Although the Hebrew state, as in the previous chapter we have conceived it to be, might have lasted indefinitely, it is not possible to imitate it now, nor would it be advisable. If any people should resolve to transfer their right to God, they would have to make a covenant expressly with God, as did the Hebrews, and so it would be necessary to have not only the consent of those transferring their right but also the consent of God to whom the right was to be transferred. God, however, has revealed through his Apostles that his covenant is no longer written in ink or engraved on tablets of stone, but is inscribed by God's spirit in men's hearts. Then again, this form of state might possibly meet the needs of those who intend to live for themselves alone with no external ties, shutting themselves away within their own boundaries and cutting themselves off from the rest of the world; but it would not suit those who have to have dealings with the outside world. It follows that this form of state would be practicable for only a very few. However, although it cannot be imitated in all respects, it possessed many features which are at least worthy of note, and which it may perhaps be quite profitable to imitate. But since, as I have mentioned, it is not my purpose to compose a full-length treatise on the state, I shall omit most of these features and shall draw attention only to those that are relevant to my goal.

First, it is not inconsistent with God's kingship to elect a supreme ruler who would have complete command over the state. For after the Hebrews had transferred their right to God, they gave the supreme sovereignty to Moses, who thus had sole authority to enact and repeal laws in God's name, to choose ministers of the sacred rites, to judge, to instruct, to punish—in short, to be an absolute ruler in all matters. Secondly, although the ministers of the sacred rites were the interpreters of the laws, it was not for them to judge citizens or to excommunicate anyone: this right belonged only to judges and captains chosen from the people. (See Joshua chapter 6 verse 26; Judges chapter 21 verse 18; and 1 Samuel chapter 14 verse 24.) And if, furthermore, we turn our attention to the course of events in the history of the Hebrews, we shall find other points equally worthy of note.

1. There were no religious divisions among the people until the high priests in the second state acquired the authority to issue decrees and to

transact government business—an authority which they sought to render permanent by usurping the government and finally demanding the title of kings. The reason for these sectarian divisions is readily seen. In the first state no decrees could bear the name of a high priest: they had no right to issue decrees, only the right to give God's answers when requested by the captains or the councils. Therefore during that period they could have had no desire to make innovations: they wanted only to administer and uphold what was approved by custom and tradition. For the only way in which they could safely preserve their own independence in the face of the captains was to keep the laws intact. But after they had acquired the power to transact government affairs and had added to the priesthood the right of secular rule, they each began to seek self-glorification both in religious and secular matters. They extended pontifical authority to all areas, and in the field of religious rites, dogma and all else they continually issued new decrees for which they claimed no less sanctity and authority than for the laws of Moses. As a result, religion degenerated into pernicious superstition, and the true meaning and interpretation of the laws was corrupted.

Furthermore, while the priests at the beginning of the restoration were pursuing the path to secular rule, in order to gain the support of the masses they indulged them in every way, approving their deeds, however impious, and adapting Scripture to suit their immorality. Malachi bears witness to their conduct in the most impressive terms. Rebuking the priests of his day, he calls them despisers of God's name, and then goes on to chide them thus: "The priest's lips are the guardians of knowledge and the law is sought from his mouth, because he is the emissary of God. But ye have departed out of the way, ye have made the Law a stumbling-block to many, ye have corrupted the covenant of Levi, saith the Lord of hosts" (Malachi ch. 2 v. 1–9). He then proceeds to accuse them of interpreting the laws at their pleasure, and of having no regard for God, but only for persons. But the priests, however careful they were, must certainly have failed to conceal these actions from the more intelligent citizens, who therefore maintained with increasing boldness that the only laws to be kept were the written laws, while the decrees which the Pharisees (who, as Josephus tells us in his *Antiquities*, were drawn mainly from the common people) mistakenly called 'the traditions of the fathers' should be discarded. Be that as it may, there is no possible doubt that the servile attitude of the high priests, the corruption of religion and the laws, the enormous proliferation of the latter, all gave serious and frequent occasion for arguments and quarrels that could never be appeased. For when men begin to dispute with superstitious fervour, and the civil authority favours one side or the other, they cannot be reconciled and inevitably split into sects.

2. It is worthy of remark that the prophets, men of private station, in exercising their freedom to warn, to rebuke and to censure, succeeded in annoying men rather than reforming them, whereas men who were admonished or castigated by kings were more apt to turn from their ways. Indeed, even devout kings often found prophets intolerable because of their assumption of authority to decide what action was pious or impious, and even to berate the kings themselves if the latter had the hardihood to transact any business, public or private, against their judgment. King Asa, who according to Scripture was a pious ruler, consigned the prophet Hanani to prison (2 Chron. ch. 16) for venturing to reproach him too freely in the matter of the treaty made with the king of Aramaea. There are other examples to show that such freedom brought religion more harm than good, not to mention that great civil wars also originated from the prophets' retention of so important a right.

3. It is also noteworthy that as long as the people was sovereign there was only one civil war, and even that ended with peace completely restored, the victors showing such compassion to the conquered that they sought every means to restore them to their former dignity and power. But after the people, who were little accustomed to kings, changed the original form of their state to monarchy, there was practically no end to civil wars, and the fighting reached such ferocity as to surpass all previous record. In a single battle—and this is almost incredible—500,000 Israelites were slain by the men of Judah, while in turn in another battle the Israelites slew a great number of the men of Judah (the figure is not given in Scripture), captured their king, almost demolished the walls of Jerusalem and, as proof of an anger that knew no bounds, completely sacked the temple. Laden with the enormous booty of their brethren and glutted with blood, they took hostages and, leaving the king in his almost devastated kingdom, they laid down their arms, relying for their security on the weakness rather than the good faith of the men of Judah. For the men of Judah, recovering their strength a few years later, once more went forth to battle, where the Israelites were again victorious, slaying 120,000 of the men of Judah, taking captive their women and children to the number of 200,000, and again seizing considerable booty. Exhausted by these battles and by others that are narrated in the course of their history, they eventually fell prey to their enemies.

Furthermore, if we reckon up the periods of unbroken peace enjoyed under the two forms of government, we shall again find a considerable difference. Before the monarchy there were several periods of forty years, and one incredible period of eighty years, when peace prevailed both at home and abroad. But after the establishment of monarchy wars were no longer to be fought for peace and freedom, but for glory, and we find that all the kings waged war with the exception of Solomon, whose outstanding quality, wisdom, could find better scope in peace than in war. Add to this the fatal ambition for royal power, which in most cases made the path to the throne a very bloody one.

Finally, as long as the people held the reins of government, the laws remained uncorrupted and were observed with greater constancy. For before the monarchy very few prophets arose to admonish the people, whereas after the election of kings we find an abundance of them at the same time. Obadiah rescued a hundred from death, hiding them so as to save them from execution along with the rest. Nor do we see the people being deceived by false prophets until the rule of kings, whose favour is eagerly sought by most men. Then there is the further fact that the people—in whom there is generally a proud or humble spirit according to changing circumstance—was ready to mend its ways in time of disaster, turning to God, restoring the laws, and thus extricating itself from all peril; whereas kings, who are unvaryingly proud-spirited and who cannot change course without humiliation, adhered obstinately to their faults right up to the final destruction of the city.

From these considerations we can clearly see:

1. How disastrous it is for both religion and state to grant to religious functionaries any right to issue decrees or to concern themselves with state business. Stability is far better assured if these officials are restricted to giving answers only when requested, and at other times to teaching and practising only what is acknowledged as customary and traditional.

2. How dangerous it is to refer to religious jurisdiction matters that are purely philosophical, and to legislate concerning beliefs that are frequently subject to dispute, or can so be. Tyranny is most violent where individual beliefs, which are an inalienable right, are regarded as criminal. Indeed, in such circumstances the anger of the mob is usually the greatest tyrant of all. It was in giving way to the anger of the Pharisees that Pilate ordered the crucifixion of Christ, whom he knew to be innocent. Then again, it was with the purpose of casting down the rich from their privileged position that the Pharisees began to instigate religious inquisitions and to accuse the Sadducees of impiety. Following this example of the Pharisees, the vilest hypocrites, urged on by that same fury which they call zeal for God's law, have everywhere persecuted men whose blameless character and distinguished qualities have excited the hostility of the masses, publicly denouncing their beliefs and inflaming the savage crowd's anger against them. And this shameless licence, sheltering under the cloak of religion, is not easy to suppress. This is especially so where sovereign powers have introduced a religious sect of which they are not themselves

the founders; for they are then regarded not as interpreters of religious law but as mere members of the sect, that is, as acknowledging the sectarian teachers to be the interpreters of religious law. So in these matters the common people have little regard for the authority of magistrates, holding in high esteem the authority of sectarian leaders, and they believe that even kings should bow down to interpretations made by the latter. To avoid these evils, then, the safest course for the commonwealth is to define piety and religious observance as consisting only in works, that is, simply in the exercise of charity and just dealing, and to allow individual free judgment in all other matters. But more of this later.

3. How essential it is for both commonwealth and religion that the sovereign power should be given the right to decide what is right and what is wrong. For if the right to pass judgment on actions could not be given even to the prophets of God without great harm to the commonwealth and religion, far less should it be given to those who can neither foretell the future nor work miracles. However, I shall be dealing with this at full-length in the next chapter.

4. Finally, we see how fatal it is for a people unaccustomed to the rule of kings, and already possessing established laws, to set up a monarchy. For neither will the people be able to endure such autocratic rule nor the monarch to tolerate laws and rights of the people which have been instituted by someone of inferior authority. Still less could the sovereign persuade himself to uphold these laws, since they could not have been designed to take any account of a king, but were instituted for a people, or a council, which regarded itself as sovereign. So in upholding the ancient rights of the people the king would appear to be its servant rather than its master. Therefore a newly established monarch will make every effort to introduce new laws and to reconstitute the state's legal code to his own advantage, reducing the people to a point where it will find it not so easy to abolish monarchy as to set it up.

Here, however, I must not fail to point out that there is also no less danger involved in removing a monarch, even if his tyranny is apparent to all. The people, accustomed to royal rule and constrained by that alone, will despise and mock a lesser authority; and therefore, on removing one king, it will find it necessary to appoint another in his place, as did the prophets of old. And the successor will be a tyrant not by choice, but by necessity; for how will he be able to endure the sight of the citizens' hands reeking with royal blood, of the people rejoicing in regicide as in a glorious deed, a deed perpetrated as a warning for him alone? Surely, if he wants to be a king, if he does not wish to acknowledge the people as judge of kings and master over him, if he does not wish to reign on sufferance, he must avenge the death of his predecessor, and for his own sake make an example that will warn the people against daring to repeat such a crime. But he cannot easily avenge the tyrant's death by the execution of citizens without defending the cause of the tyrant who preceded him, approving his actions, and consequently following in his footsteps.

This, then, is the reason why a people has often succeeded in changing tyrants, but never in abolishing tyranny or substituting another form of government for monarchy. A sad example of this truth is provided by the English people, who under the form of law sought grounds for removing their monarch,[1] but with his disappearance found it quite impossible to change their form of government. After much bloodshed they resorted to hailing a new monarch by a different name[2] (as if the whole question at issue was a name), and he succeeded in maintaining his place only by utterly destroying the royal line, killing the king's friends, or those thought to be so. He went to war, disrupting the peace whose leisure might breed murmurings, so that the populace would turn its thoughts away from the execution of the king to fresh matters that would engage its full attention. Too late, then, did the people come to realise that to save their country they had done nothing other than violate the right of their lawful king and change everything for the worse. Therefore, when the opportunity came, it decided to retrace its steps, and was not satisfied until it saw a complete restoration of the former state of affairs.[3]

Now perhaps the Romans will be produced as an example to prove that a people can easily remove a tyrant; but I hold that this example entirely confirms my view. It is true that the Romans found it far easier to remove a tyrant and change the form of their state because the right to appoint the king and his successor was vested in the people itself; and furthermore the people, composed as it was of rebels and criminals, had not yet acquired the habit of obedience to kings, having killed three of the previous six. Yet all that they succeeded in doing was to appoint several tyrants in place of one,[4] and these kept them wretchedly embroiled in wars, foreign and civil, until at last the government became once more a monarchy with merely a change of name, as in England.[5]

As for the Estates of Holland, as far as we know they never had kings, but counts, to whom the right of sovereignty was never transferred. As the High Estates of Holland make plain in the document published by them at

1. Charles I, executed in 1649.
2. Cromwell assumed the title of Protector.
3. The Restoration of 1660.
4. This seems a very odd account of the period of the Roman Republic.
5. Presumably a reference to Augustus, who was styled '*princeps*'.

the time of Count Leicester,[6] they have always reserved to themselves the authority to remind the said counts of their duty, and have retained the power to uphold this authority of theirs and the freedom of the citizens, to assert their rights against the counts if the latter proved tyrannical, and to keep them on such a tight rein that they could do nothing without the permission and approval of the Estates. From this it follows that sovereign right was always vested in the Estates, and it was this sovereignty that the last count[7] attempted to usurp. Therefore it is by no means true that the Estates revolted against him, when in fact they recovered their original sovereignty which had almost been lost.

These examples, then, fully confirm our assertion that every state must necessarily preserve its own form, and cannot be changed without incurring the danger of utter ruin. These are the points which I have here thought worthy of remark.

6. The Earl of Leicester, sent by Elizabeth with some forces to help the Dutch in 1585, was offered and accepted the title of supreme governor of the United Provinces. Spinoza here refers to the document setting forth the rights of the Provinces, which Leicester swore to uphold. He resigned in 1588.

7. Philip II of Spain.

CHAPTER 19

It is shown that the right over matters of religion is vested
entirely in the sovereign, and that the external forms of
worship should be such as accord with the peace of
the commonwealth, if we would serve God aright

When I said above that only those who hold the sovereign power have an overall right and that all law is dependent on their decision alone, I intended not only civil but religious law; for in the case of the latter, too, they must be both interpreters and guardians. I now wish to draw particular attention to this point and to discuss it at full length in this chapter; for there are many who emphatically deny that this right over religion belongs to sovereign powers, and they refuse to acknowledge them as interpreters of the divine law. Hence they presume to accuse and traduce sovereigns, and even to excommunicate them from the Church, as Ambrose once did to the Emperor Theodosius.[1] But in so doing they are making a division of the sovereignty and actually paving the way to their own supremacy, as I shall demonstrate in the course of this chapter. But first I intend to show that religion acquires the force of law only by decree of those who hold the sovereignty, and that God has no special kingdom over men except through the medium of temporal rulers. Furthermore, the practice of religion and the exercises of piety must accord with the peace and welfare of the commonwealth, and consequently must be determined only by sovereigns, who therefore must also be its interpreters. I speak expressly of acts of piety and the outward forms of religion, not of piety itself and the inward worship of God, or of the means whereby the mind is inwardly led to worship God in sincerity of heart; for inward worship of God and piety itself belong to the sphere of individual right (as we showed at the end of chapter 7) which cannot be transferred to another. Furthermore, the meaning I here attach to the kingdom of God is, I think, quite clear from chapter 14. There we showed that he who practises justice and charity in accordance with God's command is fulfilling God's law, from which it follows that the kingdom of God is where justice and charity have the force of law and command. And here I acknowledge no distinction whether it is by the natural light of reason or by revelation that God teaches and commands the true practice of justice and charity, for it matters not how the practice of these virtues is revealed to us as long as it holds the place of

1. In A.D. 390.

supreme authority and is the supreme law for men. So if I now show that justice and charity can acquire the force of law and command only through the right of the state, I can readily draw the conclusion—since the state's right is vested in the sovereign alone—that religion can acquire the force of law only from the decree of those who have the right to command, and that God has no special kingdom over men save through the medium of those who hold the sovereignty.

Now this truth, that the practice of justice and charity does not acquire the force of law save from the right of the state, is clear from our previous discussion. For we showed in chapter 16 that in a state of nature reason possesses no more right than does appetite, and those who live in accordance with the laws of appetite have just as much right to everything within their power as those who live in accordance with the laws of reason. It was in consequence of this that we could not conceive sin to exist in a state of nature, nor God as a judge who punishes men for their sins: all things came to pass in accordance with laws common to universal Nature, and the same fate—to quote Solomon—befell the righteous and the wicked, the pure and the impure, and there was no place for justice and charity. In order that the precepts of true reason—that is, as we showed in our discussion of the divine law in chapter 14, the very precepts of God— might have the absolute force of law, we saw that every man must surrender his natural right and that they must all transfer that right to the whole community, or to a number of men, or to one man. And not until then did we obtain a clear idea of what is justice and injustice, right and wrong. Therefore justice and, in sum, all the precepts of true reason, including charity towards one's neighbour, acquire the force of law and command only from the right of the state, that is (as we demonstrated in the same chapter), only from the decree of those who possess the right to command. And since (as I have already shown) God's kingdom consists simply in the rule of justice and charity, or true religion, it follows (as we asserted) that God has no kingdom over men save through the medium of those who hold the sovereignty. And this is equally so, I repeat, whether we consider religion to be revealed by the natural light or by prophecy; the proof applies in all cases, since religion is the same and equally revealed by God in whatever way we suppose men have come to know it.

Thus it was that, even in the case of religion revealed through prophecy, before it could have the force of law with the Hebrews it was necessary that every one of them should first surrender his natural right, and that all should by common consent resolve to obey only what was revealed to them by God through prophecy. This is an exact parallel to what we have shown to be the development of a democracy, where all by common consent resolve to live only by the dictates of reason. Now although the

Hebrews went further by transferring their right to God, this transference was notional rather than practical; for in reality (as we have seen above) they retained their sovereignty absolutely until they transferred it to Moses, who from then on remained an absolute ruler, and through him alone did God reign over the Hebrews. Moreover, this fact—that religion acquires the force of law solely from the right of the state—also explains why Moses could not punish those who violated the Sabbath before the covenant, and were thus still in possession of their own right (Exod. ch. 16 v. 27); but this he could do after the covenant (Num. ch. 15 v. 36), that is, after every man had surrendered his right and the Sabbath had acquired the force of law from the right of the state.

Finally, this also explains why, with the destruction of the Hebrew state, their revealed religion ceased to have the force of law. We cannot doubt that, as soon as the Hebrews transferred their right to the king of Babylon, the kingdom of God and the divine law came to an abrupt end; for in so doing they completely annulled the covenant whereby they had promised to obey all that God should speak, which had been the basis of God's kingdom. They were no longer able to abide by it, because from that time on they were no longer possessed of their own right (as they had been in the wilderness or in their own country), but were subject to the king of Babylon whom, as we have shown in chapter 16, they were bound to obey in all things. Jeremiah expressly reminds them of this in chapter 29 verse 7, "Seek the peace of that city whither I have brought you captive; for in the peace thereof shall ye have peace." Now they could not seek the peace of that city as officers of state—for they were captives—but only as slaves, that is, by rendering the absolute obedience that shuns insurrection, by keeping the laws and ordinances of the state, however different they might be from the laws to which they were accustomed in their own land, and so forth.

From all these considerations it follows quite clearly that among the Hebrews religion acquired the force of law solely from the right of the state, and, with the destruction of the state, religion could no longer be regarded as the command of a particular state, but as the universal doctrine of reason. I say 'of reason,' for the universal religion had not yet become known through revelation. We may therefore conclude with finality that religion, whether revealed by the natural light or by prophecy, acquires the force of command solely from the decree of those who have the right to command, and that God has no special kingdom over men save through those who hold the sovereignty. This also follows, and can be more clearly understood, from what we said in chapter 4; for there we showed that God's decrees all involve eternal truth and necessity, and that God cannot be conceived as a ruler or lawgiver enacting laws for mankind.

Therefore the divine teachings revealed by the natural light or by prophecy do not acquire the force of command from God directly; they must acquire it from those, or through the medium of those, who have the right to command and to issue decrees, and consequently it is only by their mediation that we can conceive of God as reigning over men and directing human affairs according to justice and equity. This conclusion is supported by experience; for indications of divine justice are to be found only where just men reign; elsewhere—to quote Solomon once more—we see the same fate befalling the just and the unjust, the pure and the impure. And this it is that has caused many men, who thought that God rules directly over men and orders the whole of Nature to their advantage, to doubt the divine providence. Therefore, since it is established both by reason and experience that the divine law is entirely dependent on the decrees of rulers, it follows that these are also the interpreters of the divine law. How this is so we shall see presently, for it is now time to demonstrate that the external forms of religion and the entire practice of piety must accord with the peace and preservation of the commonwealth, if we would serve God aright. When this has been proved, we shall readily understand in what way sovereigns are the interpreters of religion and piety.

There can be no doubt that devotion to one's country is the highest form of devotion that can be shown; for if the state is destroyed nothing good can survive, everything is endangered, and anger and wickedness reign supreme amidst universal fear. Hence it follows that any act of piety towards one's neighbour must be impious if it results in harm to the commonwealth as a whole, and any impious act committed against him must be accounted pious if it is done for the sake of the preservation of the commonwealth. For example, if someone who is quarrelling with me wants to take my coat, it is an act of piety to give him my cloak as well; but when it is judged that this is detrimental to the preservation of the state, it is then a pious act to bring him to justice, even though he must be condemned to death. That is why Manlius Torquatus[2] gained renown: the people's welfare had more weight with him than devotion to his son.

This being so, it follows that the welfare of the people is the highest law, to which all other laws, both human and divine, must be made to conform. But since it is the duty of the sovereign alone to decide what is necessary for the welfare of the entire people and the security of the state, and to command what it judges to be thus necessary, it follows that it is also the duty of the sovereign alone to decide what form piety towards one's neighbour should take, that is, in what way every man is required to obey

---

2. He executed his son for disobeying orders in a battle against the Latins, 340 B.C. (Livy, VIII).

God. From this we clearly understand in what way the sovereign is the interpreter of religion; and, furthermore, we see that no one can rightly obey God unless his practice of piety—which is the duty of every man—conforms with the public good, and consequently, unless he obeys all the decrees of the sovereign. For since we are bound by God's command to practise piety towards all men without exception and to harm no man, it follows that no one is permitted to assist anyone to another's hurt, far less to the detriment of the commonwealth as a whole. So no one can exercise piety towards his neighbour in accordance with God's command unless his piety and religion conform to the public good. But no private citizen can know what is good for the state except from the decrees of the sovereign, to whom alone it belongs to transact public business. Therefore no one can practise piety aright nor obey God unless he obeys the decrees of the sovereign in all things. This is confirmed by actual practice. For whether a man be a citizen or an alien, a person in private station or one holding command over others, if the sovereign condemns him to death or declares him an enemy, no subject is permitted to come to his assistance. Similarly, although the Hebrews were told that everyone should love his neighbour as himself (Lev. ch. 19 v. 17, 18), they were nevertheless required to inform the judge of anyone who had committed an act that contravened the edicts of the law (Lev. ch. 5 v. 1 and Deut. ch. 13 v. 8, 9) and to kill him if he was condemned to death (Deut. ch. 17 v. 7).

Then again, in order to preserve the freedom they had won and keep complete control over the territories they had seized, the Hebrews, as we explained in chapter 17, found it necessary to adapt religion to the needs of their own state alone and to separate themselves from other nations. It was for this reason that they were told: "Love thy neighbour and hate thine enemy"[3] (Matth. ch. 5 v. 43). But when they had lost their independence and were led captive to Babylon, Jeremiah counselled them to take thought for the safety of that city (as well), to which they had been led captive. And after Christ saw that they would be dispersed throughout the whole world, he taught that they should practise piety to all without exception. All these considerations clearly show that religion has always been adapted to the good of the commonwealth.

If I am now asked by what right were Christ's disciples, men of private station, enabled to preach religion, I reply that they did so by right of the power they had received from Christ against unclean spirits (Matth. ch. 10 v. 1). For I expressly stated above at the end of chapter 16 that all men are

---

3. As the editors of the New Oxford Edition of the Bible comment, there is no such commandment in the Hebrew Bible (see on Matthew 5:43). Nevertheless, Spinoza lets it pass, even though he knows better.

bound to keep faith even with a tyrant except for him to whom God, by sure revelation, has promised his special aid against the tyrant. Therefore no one may take precedent from this unless he also has the power to perform miracles. This point is likewise made manifest by the fact that Christ also bade his disciples not to fear those who kill the body (Matth. ch. 10 v. 28). If this command had been laid on every man, no state could continue in existence, and that saying of Solomon (Prov. ch. 24 v. 21), "My son, fear God and the king," would have been impiety, which is far from true. Thus it must be granted that the authority which Christ gave the disciples was a unique occurrence, and cannot be regarded as an example for others.

As for the arguments by which my opponents seek to separate religious right from civil right, maintaining that only the latter is vested in the sovereign while the former is vested in the universal church, these are of no account, being so trivial as not even to merit refutation. But one thing I cannot pass over in silence, how lamentably deceived they are when, to support this seditious opinion (pardon the bluntness of this expression) they cite the example of the Hebrew high priest who once had control over matters of religion—as if the priests did not receive this right from Moses (who, as I have shown above, alone possessed the sovereignty) and could not also have been deprived of it by his decree. For it was Moses who appointed not only Aaron but his son Eleazar and his grandson Phineas, and gave them the authority to carry out their priestly duties. This authority was held by successive high priests only insofar as they were regarded as representatives of Moses, that is, of the sovereign power. For, as I have already shown, Moses did not choose anyone to succeed to his rule: he divided all its functions in such a way that those who followed him were regarded as his deputies, carrying on the government as if the king were absent, not dead. It is true that in the second Hebrew state the high priests held this right absolutely, but that was after they combined the right of secular rule with the priesthood. Therefore the right of the priesthood has always depended on the edict of the sovereign, and the high priests have never held it except when it was combined with secular power. Indeed, the right over religion was always vested absolutely in the kings (as will become clear from what I have still to say at the end of this chapter) with this one exception: they were not permitted to set their hands to the ministry of sacred rites in the temple, because all who were not descended from Aaron were regarded as unholy. Such a situation, of course, does not obtain in a Christian state.

Thus we cannot doubt that in modern times religion—whose ministry demands outstanding moral qualities, not lineage, and therefore does not exclude as unholy those who hold the sovereignty—belongs solely to the right of the sovereign. No one has the right and power to exercise control over it, to choose its ministers, to determine and establish the foundations of the church and its doctrine, to pass judgment on morality and acts of piety, to excommunicate or to accept into the church, and to provide for the poor, except by the authority and permission of the sovereign. These doctrines are not only shown to be true (which we have just done) but also to be essential both to religion and to the preservation of the state. For everyone knows how much importance the people attach to the right and authority over religion, and how they all revere every single word of him who possesses that authority, so that one might even go so far as to say that he to whom this authority belongs has the most effective control over minds. Therefore anyone who seeks to deprive the sovereign of this authority is attempting to divide the sovereignty; and as a result, as happened long ago in the case of the kings and priests of the Hebrews, there will inevitably arise strife and dissensions that can never be allayed. Indeed, he who seeks to deprive the sovereign of this authority is paving the way to his own ascendancy, as we have already said. For what decisions can be taken by sovereigns if this right is denied them? They can decide nothing whatsoever, whether concerning war or peace or any other matter, if they are to wait on the utterance of another who will tell them whether that which they judge to be beneficial is pious or impious. On the contrary, everything will be done according to the decree of him who has the right to judge and decide what is pious or impious, right or wrong.

Every age has seen such instances, of which I will quote only one, as typical of them all. The Pope of Rome, being granted this right absolutely, began gradually to establish his ascendancy over all the kings until he actually attained the pinnacle of dominion. Whenever attempts were later made by monarchs, in particular by the Emperors of Germany, to diminish his authority in the slightest degree, they met with no success; these very efforts merely increased that authority to a considerable degree. Yet what no monarch could achieve by fire and sword, churchmen succeeded in doing by pen alone;[4] and this in itself provides a clear indication of the strength and power of religious authority, and gives further warning of the necessity for the sovereign to keep it in his own hands. Now if we also reflect on the points made in the previous chapter, we shall see that his retention of this authority is also a strong influence in promoting religion and piety. For there we saw that, although the prophets were endowed with a divine virtue, yet, being men of private station, in exercising their freedom to admonish, to rebuke and to denounce, they had the effect of provoking men rather than reforming them, whereas those who were

4. A reference to Luther and Calvin.

admonished or castigated by kings were more likely to turn from their ways. Then again, the kings themselves, simply because this right did not fully belong to them, frequently forsook their religion, taking with them nearly all the people. It is a well-established fact that this has frequently occurred even in Christian states for the same reason.

Now perhaps at this point I shall be asked: "Then if those who hold the sovereignty choose to be impious, who will be the rightful champion of piety? Are the rulers still to be regarded as the interpreters of religion?" To this I ask in return: "What if churchmen (who are also but human, and, as private citizens, are entitled to have regard for their own affairs) or any others to whom it is proposed to entrust control over religion, should choose to be impious? Are they even then to be regarded as the interpreters of religion?" It is indeed true that if those who hold the sovereignty choose to go what way they will, then, whether or not they have control over religion, all things, both religious and secular, will go to ruin: but this will come about far more quickly if private citizens seditiously seek to be the champions of religious law. Therefore nothing whatsoever is gained by denying this right to sovereigns; on the contrary, evil is aggravated. For, as was the case with the Hebrew kings to whom this right was not unconditionally granted, this very fact is likely to drive them to impiety, and in consequence injury and damage to the entire commonwealth become certain and inevitable instead of uncertain and possible. So whether we have regard to the truth of the matter, or the security of the state, or the advancement of piety, we are forced to maintain that divine law, or religious law, also depends absolutely on the decree of sovereigns, who are its interpreters and champions. It follows that the ministers of God's word are those who are authorised by their sovereign to teach piety in the form that, by decree of the sovereign, is adapted to the public good.

It now remains for me, in addition, to indicate the reason why this right has always been the subject of disputes in Christian states, whereas the Hebrews, to the best of my knowledge, never entertained any doubt about it. It would certainly seem extraordinary that a matter so plain and so vitally important should always have been called into question, and that sovereigns have never held this right without controversy—nay, without grave danger of sedition and harm to religion. Indeed, if we could not assign any assured cause for this phenomenon, I might easily be convinced that all the findings of this chapter are merely theoretical, the kind of speculative thinking that can never be of practical importance. But in fact, when we review the origins of the Christian religion, the cause of this phenomenon is completely revealed. It was not kings who were the first teachers of the Christian religion, but men of private station who, despite the will of those who held the sovereignty and were their rulers, were long

accustomed to address private religious assemblies, to institute and perform sacred rites, to make all arrangements and decisions on their own
responsibility without any regard to the state. Many years later, when their
religion began to be adopted by the state, the churchmen were obliged to
teach it to the emperors themselves in the form they had given it, from
which it was an easy step for them to gain recognition as its teachers and
interpreters, and furthermore as the pastors of the church and virtually
God's representatives. And to prevent Christian kings from later seizing
this authority for themselves, the churchmen devised the very effective
precaution of forbidding marriage to the chief ministers of the church and
to the supreme interpreter of religion. In addition, they multiplied religious dogmas to such an extent and confused them with so much philosophy that the supreme interpreter of religion had to be a consummate
philosopher and theologian and to have time for a host of idle speculations.
This effectively ruled out all but men of private station with abundant
leisure.

Now with the Hebrews the position was quite different. Their church
originated together with their state, and Moses, the absolute ruler of that
state, taught the people their religion, arranged the sacred offices and
appointed those who were to administer them. Thus a quite different
situation developed, where the royal authority carried the greatest weight
with the people, and kings most decidedly held the right over religion. For
although no one held absolute sovereignty after Moses' death, the right to
make decisions both in matters religious and in other matters was vested in
the captains, as I have already shown. Then again, for instruction in
religion and piety the people were required to attend on the supreme
judge no less than the high priest (Deut. ch. 17 v. 9, 11). Finally, although
the kings did not possess a right equal to that of Moses, almost all the
organisation of religious ministry and appointment thereto depended on
their decision. David, for instance, arranged the entire construction of the
temple (1 Chron. ch. 28 v. 11, 12 etc.); then out of all the Levites he chose
24,000 for the psalm-singing, 6,000 to supply candidates for appointment
as judges and officers, 4,000 doorkeepers and 4,000 to play musical instruments (1 Chron. ch. 23 v. 4, 5). He further divided these into companies
(of which he also chose the leaders), so that each company should do duty
as its turn came round (same chapter, verse 6). The priests he likewise
divided into as many companies. But to avoid having to go into every
detail, I refer the reader to 2 Chron. ch. 8 v. 13, where we read that the
worship of God, as established by Moses, was conducted in the temple by
Solomon's command; and in verse 14 that he (Solomon) appointed companies of priests in their ministries and companies of Levites, etc. in
accordance with the command of David, the man of God. And finally, in

verse 15, the historian testifies that "they departed not from the commandment of the king unto the priests and Levites in any matter, nor in the administration of the treasuries."

From all these considerations, together with other narratives concerning the kings, it follows quite clearly that the entire practice of religion and its ministry depended solely on the command of the kings. When I stated above that they did not have the same right as Moses to appoint the high priest, to consult God directly and to condemn prophets who should prophesy during their lifetime, this was only because the prophets, from the nature of the authority they possessed, could appoint a new king and pardon regicide. I did not mean that they were permitted to summon to judgment and lawfully impeach* a king if he dared to contravene the laws. Therefore if there had been no prophets who by special revelation could assuredly grant pardon for regicide, the kings would have had absolute right over all matters, both sacred and secular. Hence sovereigns of our times, who neither have prophets nor are bound by right to acknowledge any (not being subject to the laws of the Hebrews), even if they be not celibate, possess this right absolutely; and provided they do not allow religious dogmas to be multiplied or to be confused with philosophy, they will always retain this right.

* See Supplementary Note 39.

CHAPTER 20

*It is shown that in a free commonwealth every man may
think as he pleases, and say what he thinks* [1]

If minds could be as easily controlled as tongues, every government would
be secure in its rule, and need not resort to force; for every man would
conduct himself as his rulers wished, and his views as to what is true or
false, good or bad, fair or unfair, would be governed by their decision
alone. But we have already explained at the beginning of chapter 17 that it
is impossible for the mind to be completely under another's control; for no
one is able to transfer to another his natural right or faculty to reason
freely and to form his own judgment on any matters whatsoever, nor can
he be compelled to do so. Consequently, a government that attempts to
control men's minds is regarded as tyrannical, and a sovereign is thought
to wrong his subjects and infringe their right when he seeks to prescribe
for every man what he should accept as true and reject as false, and what
are the beliefs that will inspire him with devotion to God. All these are
matters belonging to individual right, which no man can surrender even if
he should so wish.

I admit that judgment can be influenced in numerous ways—some of
them almost past belief—and to such an extent that, although it is not
directly subject to another's command, it may be so dependent on another's words that it can properly be said in that respect to belong to his
right. But in spite of all that ingenuity has been able to devise in this field,
it has never attained such success that men did not ever find that the
individual citizen has his own ideas in plenty, and that opinions vary as
much as tastes. Moses had gained the strongest of holds on the minds of
his people not by deception but by his divine virtue, for he was thought to
be a man of God whose every word and action was divinely inspired; yet
even he was not exempt from their murmurings and criticisms, and far less
so were other monarchs. Now if such exemption from criticism were
conceivable, it would surely be in the case of a monarchy, not a democracy,
where the sovereignty is corporately held by all the people, or a great part
of them. The reason for this, I imagine, is obvious to all.

So however much sovereigns are believed to possess unlimited right and
to be the interpreters of law and piety, they will never succeed in preventing men from exercising their own particular judgment on any matters

1. Tacitus, *Histories*, I, 1, 4, "*ubi sentire quae velis et quae sentias dicere licet.*"

whatsoever and from being influenced accordingly by a variety of emotions. It is true that sovereigns can by their right treat as enemies all who do not absolutely agree with them on all matters, but the point at issue is not what is their right, but what is to their interest. I grant that by this right they can govern in the most oppressive way and execute citizens on the most trivial pretexts, but no one can imagine that by so doing they are acting in accordance with the judgment of sound reason. Indeed, since they cannot so act without endangering the whole fabric of the state, we can even argue that they do not have the absolute power to do these and other such things, and consequently that they do not have the absolute right to do so. For we have demonstrated that the right of sovereigns is determined by their power.

If no man, then, can give up his freedom to judge and think as he pleases, and everyone is by absolute natural right the master of his own thoughts, it follows that utter failure will attend any attempt in a commonwealth to force men to speak only as prescribed by the sovereign despite their different and opposing opinions. Not even men well versed in affairs can keep silent, not to say the lower classes. It is the common failing of men to confide what they think to others, even when secrecy is needed. Therefore the most tyrannical government will be one where the individual is denied the freedom to express and to communicate to others what he thinks, and a moderate government is one where this freedom is granted to every man. However, it is also undeniable that words can be treasonable as well as deeds; and so, while it is impossible to deprive subjects completely of this freedom, to grant it unreservedly could have the most disastrous consequences. Therefore it is our present task to enquire to what extent this freedom can and should be granted to all without endangering the peace of the commonwealth and the right of the sovereign. This, as I indicated at the beginning of chapter 16, was the main purpose of this part of my treatise.

It follows quite clearly from my earlier explanation of the basis of the state that its ultimate purpose is not to exercise dominion nor to restrain men by fear and deprive them of independence, but on the contrary to free every man from fear so that he may live in security as far as is possible, that is, so that he may best preserve his own natural right to exist and to act, without harm to himself and to others. It is not, I repeat, the purpose of the state to transform men from rational beings into beasts or puppets, but rather to enable them to develop their mental and physical faculties in safety, to use their reason without restraint and to refrain from the strife and the vicious mutual abuse that are prompted by hatred, anger or deceit. Thus the purpose of the state is, in reality, freedom.

Furthermore, we have seen that the one essential feature in the formation of a state was that all power to make laws should be vested in the entire citizen body, or in a number of citizens, or in one man. For since there is a considerable diversity in the free judgment of men, each believing that he alone knows best, and since it is impossible that all should think alike and speak with one voice, peaceful existence could not be achieved unless every man surrendered his right to act just as he thought fit. Thus it was only the right to act as he thought fit that each man surrendered, and not his right to reason and judge. So while to act against the sovereign's decree is definitely an infringement of his right, this is not the case with thinking, judging, and consequently with speaking, too, provided one does no more than express or communicate one's opinion, defending it through rational conviction alone, not through deceit, anger, hatred, or the will to effect such changes in the state as he himself decides. For example, suppose a man maintains that a certain law is against sound reason, and he therefore advocates its repeal. If he at the same time submits his opinion to the judgment of the sovereign power (which alone is competent to enact and repeal laws), and meanwhile does nothing contrary to what is commanded by that law, he deserves well of the state, acting as a good citizen should do. But if on the contrary the purpose of his action is to accuse the magistrate of injustice and to stir up popular hatred against him, or if he seditiously seeks to repeal that law in spite of the magistrate, he is nothing more than an agitator and a rebel.

Thus we see how the individual citizen can say and communicate to others what he thinks without infringing the right and authority of the sovereign, that is, without violating the peace of the commonwealth. He must leave it to the sovereign to decide what action is to be taken in all circumstances, and must not act contrary to its decision, even if frequently his action has to be in conflict with what he judges and openly proclaims to be good. This entails no violation of justice and piety; indeed, he is bound to act thus if he wants to be a just and pious man. For, as we have shown, justice depends solely on the decree of the sovereign, and nobody save one who lives in accordance with the sovereign's established decrees can be a just man. As for piety, this (by our findings in the previous chapter) is demonstrated in its highest form in the service of the peace and tranquillity of the commonwealth, which, however, cannot be preserved if every man is to live simply as he thinks fit. So it is impious, as well, for the subject to contravene his sovereign's decree just as he pleases; for if this were permitted to everyone, the ruin of the state would inevitably ensue. Indeed, as long as a man is acting in accordance with the sovereign's decrees, he cannot be acting against the decree and dictates of his own reason; for it was with the full approval of reason that he resolved to transfer to the sovereign his right to live by his own judgment. But my argument is further confirmed by actual practice: in the councils of authorities, both sovereign and subordinate, it rarely happens that there is a unanimous vote in favour of some measure; yet everything is done by the common decision of all, whether they have voted for or against. But I must return to my theme.

Our discussion of the basis of the state has revealed how the individual citizen can exercise freedom of judgment without infringing the right of the sovereign. The same considerations enable us just as well to determine what political beliefs are seditious: they are those which, when posited, immediately have the effect of annulling the covenant whereby everyone has surrendered his right to act just as he thinks fit. For example, if anyone holds the opinion that the sovereign is not possessed of full power, or that promises need not be kept, or that it behoves everyone to live as he pleases, or if he holds other such views as are directly opposed to the said covenant, he is guilty of sedition, not so much because of his judgment and belief as because of the action that is implicit therein. For merely to hold such an opinion is to violate the pledge tacitly or expressly given to the sovereign. And therefore other beliefs, those in which there is no implication of action such as the breaking of the covenant, the exaction of revenge, the indulgence of anger and so forth, are not seditious, except perchance in a state which is in some way corrupted, a state where superstitious and ambitious men who cannot tolerate men of integrity have gained such a great reputation that the common people pay more heed to them than to the sovereign. We do not deny, however, that there are in addition certain views, which have the appearance of being concerned merely with questions of truth and falsity, but are nevertheless put forward and popularised with malicious purpose. But these, too, we have already dealt with in chapter 15, and reached a conclusion that left reason nonetheless free.

Finally, if we also reflect on the fact that every man's loyalty to the state can be known only from his works—just as his devotion to God can be known only from his works, that is, his charity to his neighbour—we are left in no doubt that a good commonwealth grants to every man the same freedom to philosophise as we have seen is granted by religious faith. I do indeed admit that there may sometimes be some disadvantages in allowing such freedom, but what institution was ever so wisely planned that no disadvantage could arise therefrom? He who seeks to regulate everything by law will aggravate vices rather than correct them. What cannot be prohibited must necessarily be allowed, even if harm often ensues. How many are the evils that arise from dissipation, envy, avarice, drunkenness and the like? Yet we tolerate these, because although they are in reality vices they cannot be prohibited by legal enactment. Much more, then, should we allow freedom of judgment, which is assuredly a virtue, and cannot be suppressed. Furthermore, it can produce no untoward results that cannot be contained, as I shall presently show, by the magistrates' authority; not to mention that this freedom is of the first importance in fostering the sciences and the arts, for it is only those whose judgment is free and unbiased who can attain success in these fields.[2]

But let it be supposed that this freedom can be suppressed and that men can be kept under such control that they dare not whisper anything that is not commanded by the sovereign. Still, it will certainly never come to pass that men will think only what they are bidden to think. It would thus inevitably follow that in their daily lives men would be thinking one thing and saying another, with the result that good faith, of first importance in the state, would be undermined and the disgusting arts of sycophancy and treachery would be encouraged. This is the source of false dealing and the corruption of all honest accomplishments. But it is far beyond the bounds of possibility that all men can be made to speak to order. On the contrary, the greater the effort to deprive them of freedom of speech, the more obstinately do they resist: not indeed the greedy, the flatterers and other poor-spirited souls who find their greatest happiness in gloating over their money-bags and cramming their bellies, but those to whom a good up-bringing, integrity and a virtuous disposition have given a more liberal outlook. Men in general are so constituted that their resentment is most aroused when beliefs which they think to be true are treated as criminal, and when that which motivates their pious conduct to God and man is accounted as wickedness. In consequence, they are emboldened to de-nounce the laws and go to all lengths to oppose the magistrate, considering it not a disgrace but honourable to stir up sedition and to resort to any outrageous action in this cause.

Granted, then, that human nature is thus constituted, it follows that laws enacted against men's beliefs are directed not against villains but against men of good character, and their purpose is to provoke honourable men rather than to restrain the wicked. Nor can they be enforced without great danger to the state. Furthermore, such laws are quite ineffective; for those who are convinced of the validity of beliefs that are condemned by law will not be able to obey the law, while those who reject these beliefs as false will regard the law in question as enacted for their special benefit, and their exultation over such laws will make it difficult for the magistrate to repeal them thereafter, even if he should so wish. In addition to these

---

2. Spinoza's defense of free speech here is similar to that of J. S. Mill's argument on its behalf in his essay *On Liberty*.

considerations, there are the lessons learnt from the history of the Hebrews, chapter 18, under the second heading.

Finally, how many divisions in the church have arisen mainly from attempts made by magistrates to settle the disputes of scholars by legislation! If men were not possessed by the hope of enlisting the law and the magistrate on their side, of triumphing over their opponents amid the universal applause of the mob and of gaining office, they would never engage in such malicious strife against one another nor would they be agitated by such frenzy. This is demonstrated not only by reason but by experience with its daily examples. Laws of this kind, prescribing what everyone must believe and prohibiting the saying or writing of anything that opposes this or that opinion, have often been enacted to pander to, or rather to surrender to, the anger of those who cannot endure enlightened minds, men who, by the exercise of a stern authority can easily turn the devotion of the unruly masses into a rage, inciting them against whomsoever they will. Yet how much better it would be to curb the frenzied anger of the mob instead of passing useless laws which can be broken only by those who love the virtues and the arts, and reducing the state to such straits that it cannot endure men of noble character! What greater misfortune can be imagined for a state than that honourable men should be exiled as miscreants because their opinions are at variance with authority and they cannot disguise the fact? What can be more calamitous than that men should be regarded as enemies and put to death, not for any crime or misdeed, but for being of independent mind? That the scaffold, the terror of evildoers, should become the glorious stage where is presented a supreme example of virtuous endurance, to the utter disgrace of the ruling power? Those who are conscious of their own probity do not fear death as criminals do, nor do they beg for mercy, for they are not tormented with remorse for shameful deeds. On the contrary, they think it an honour, not a punishment, to die in a good cause, and a glorious thing to die for freedom. What sort of lesson, then, is learnt from the death of such men, whose cause is beyond the understanding of those of sluggish and feeble spirit, is hated by troublemakers, but is dear to the hearts of all good men? The only lesson to be drawn from their death is to emulate them, or at least to revere them.

Therefore, if honesty is to be prized rather than obsequiousness, and if sovereigns are to retain full control and not be forced to surrender to agitators, it is imperative to grant freedom of judgment and to govern men in such a way that the different and conflicting views they openly proclaim do not debar them from living together in peace. This system of government is undoubtedly the best and its disadvantages are fewer because it is in closest accord with human nature. For we have shown that in a democracy (which comes closest to the natural state) all the citizens undertake to act, but not to reason and to judge, by decision made in common. That is to say, since all men cannot think alike, they agree that a proposal supported by a majority of votes shall have the force of a decree, meanwhile retaining the authority to repeal the same when they see a better alternative. Thus the less freedom of judgment is conceded to men, the further their distance from the most natural state, and consequently the more oppressive the regime.

Moreover, to confirm that any disadvantages consequent on this freedom can be avoided simply by the sovereign's authority, and by this authority alone men can be restrained from harming one another even when their opinions are in open conflict, examples are ready to hand, and I need go no distance to find them. Take the city of Amsterdam, which enjoys the fruits of this freedom, to its own considerable prosperity and the admiration of the world. In this flourishing state, a city of the highest renown, men of every race and sect live in complete harmony; and before entrusting their property to some person they will want to know no more than this, whether he is rich or poor and whether he has been honest or dishonest in his dealings. As for religion or sect, that is of no account, because such considerations are regarded as irrelevant in a court of law; and no sect whatsoever is so hated that its adherents—provided that they injure no one, render to each what is his own, and live upright lives—are denied the protection of the civil authorities. On the other hand, in time past when politicians and the Estates of the Provinces began to intervene in the religious controversy between the Remonstrants and the Counter-Remonstrants,[3] it resulted in a division in the church. Many other instances in that period provide clear evidence that laws enacted to settle religious controversies have the effect of angering men rather than reforming them, that they give some men the opportunity to assume unbounded licence, and that, furthermore, divisions in the church do not arise from zeal for truth (which breeds only courtesy and tolerance) but from lust for supremacy. From this it is clearer than the sun at noon that the real schismatics are those who condemn the writings of others and seditiously incite the quarrelsome mob against the writers, rather than the writers themselves, who usually write only for scholars and appeal to

---

3. During the seventeenth century the new Dutch Republic was theologically and politically divided between two Protestant groups, the Remonstrants and the Counter-Remonstrants. The former supported the republic and favored a more liberal theology, rejecting for example the Calvinist doctrine of predestination. The Counter-Remonstrants sided with the monarchist faction and adhered to orthodox Calvinist theology.

reason alone; and that, finally, the real disturbers of peace are those who, in a free commonwealth, vainly seek to abolish freedom of judgment, which cannot be suppressed.

I have thus shown:

1. That it is impossible to deprive men of the freedom to say what they think.

2. That this freedom can be granted to everyone without infringing the right and authority of the sovereign, and that the individual citizen can preserve this freedom without infringing that right, provided that he does not presume therefrom to make any innovation in the constitution or to do anything that contravenes the established laws.

3. That every man can possess this freedom without endangering public peace, and any troubles that may arise from this freedom can easily be held in check.

4. That every man can also possess that freedom without endangering piety.

5. That laws enacted concerning speculative matters are quite useless.

6. Finally, we have shown not only that this freedom can be granted without detriment to public peace, to piety, and to the right of the sovereign, but also that it must be granted if these are to be preserved. For when a contrary course is taken and attempts are made to deprive men of this freedom, and the beliefs of dissenters (but not their minds, which alone are capable of wrongdoing) are brought to trial, the exemplary punishment inflicted on honourable men seems more like martyrdom, and serves not so much to terrorise others as to anger them and move them to compassion, if not to revenge. Upright dealing and good faith are undermined, sycophants and traitors are encouraged, and opponents of freedom exult because their anger has won the day and they have converted the government to their creed, of which they are regarded as the interpreters. As a result, they even venture to usurp the government's authority and right, and they unashamedly boast that they have been chosen directly by God and that their decrees are divinely inspired, whereas those of the sovereign are merely human and should therefore give way before divine decrees—that is, their own. Nobody can fail to see that all this is directly opposed to the welfare of the state. Therefore we have to conclude, as we did in chapter 18, that the state can pursue no safer course than to regard piety and religion as consisting solely in the exercise of charity and just dealing, and that the right of the sovereign, both in religious and secular spheres, should be restricted to men's actions, with everyone being allowed to think what he will and to say what he thinks.

I have now completed the task I set myself in this treatise. It only remains for me to state expressly that it contains nothing that I would not willingly submit to the scrutiny and judgment of my country's government. If they consider any part of my writing to be contrary to the laws of my country or to be prejudicial to the general good, I retract it. I know that I am human, and may have erred. Yet I have taken great pains not to err, and I have made it my prime object that whatever I have written should be in complete accord with my country's laws, with piety and with morality.

SPINOZA'S SUPPLEMENTARY NOTES TO THE
TRACTATUS THEOLOGICO-POLITICUS

[Notes numbered 28, 29, 30 in Gebhardt's edition have been omitted. Those notes merely refer the reader to *Philosophia S. Scripturae Interpres*, a tract written by Spinoza's friend Lodewijk Meyer, and bound together with Spinoza's *Tractatus* in one of its editions.]

Chapter 1

Note 1: '*nabi*'. If the third radical is one of those termed 'mutes', it is customarily omitted and instead the second letter is doubled. Thus קָלַל by the omission of the mute ה becomes קוֹלֵל and then קוֹל and נָבָא becomes נוֹבֵב whence נִיב שְׂפָתִים—utterance or speech. Similarly בוֹא becomes בַז or בוֹ. (משגה שגג שהג, המה המם : בלה בלל בלעל : שגה). Therefore R. Shlomo was quite correct in interpreting this word as נָבָא, and was wrongly criticised by ibn Ezra, whose knowledge of Hebrew was not profound. It should further be noted that the word נבואה—prophecy is of general application, and embraces every kind of prophesying, whereas other nouns are more specific and refer to a particular kind of prophesying. This point, I believe, is familiar to all scholars.[1]

Note 2: 'its professors cannot be called prophets'. That is, interpreters of God. For an interpreter of God is one who has a revelation of God's decrees which he interprets to others who have not had this revelation, and who accept it solely in reliance on the prophet's authority and the confidence he enjoys. Now if those who listen to prophets were themselves to become prophets just as those who listen to philosophers become philosophers, the prophet would not be an interpreter of divine decrees; for his hearers would rely not on the testimony and authority of the prophet but on the divine revelation itself and on their own inward testimony, just as the prophet does. Similarly, sovereign powers are the interpreters of their own sovereign right, since the laws that they enact are upheld only by their own sovereign authority, and are supported only by their own testimony.

Note 3: 'that the prophets were endowed with an extraordinary virtue exceeding the normal'. Although some men possess gifts that nature does not bestow on others, they are not said to surpass human nature unless the gifts that are peculiar to them are such as cannot be understood from the definition of human nature. For example, a giant is of unusual size, but his size is still human. It is granted to few to

---

1. Here Spinoza takes back his earlier compliments to ibn Ezra and transfers them to Rabbi Shlomo, or Rashi (see chapter 10, footnote 5). This is a curious reversal, since no one familiar with both medieval Jewish exegetes would say that Rashi's command of Hebrew philology was greater than that of ibn Ezra. Rashi's commentaries favored the midrashic, or free, method, whereas ibn Ezra argued for the strict, literal reading of the text.

be able to compose poetry extempore, but this is still a human gift, as also is the gift whereby someone, while wide awake, imagines certain things as vividly as if they were actually present before him. But if someone were to possess a quite different means of perception and quite different grounds of knowledge, he would assuredly surpass the bounds of human nature.

Chapter 3

Note 4: 'Patriarchs'. In chapter 15 of Genesis we are told that God said to Abraham that he would be his protector and would give him an exceedingly great reward; to which Abraham replied that he had nothing very much to look forward to, since he was childless and stricken with years.

Note 5: 'their security'. It is clear from Mark ch. 10 v. 21 that to achieve eternal life it is not enough to keep the commandments of the Old Testament.

Chapter 6

Note 6: 'Since God's existence is not self-evident'. We doubt the existence of God, and consequently everything else, as long as we do not have a clear and distinct idea of God, but only a confused idea. Just as he who does not rightly know the nature of a triangle does not know that its three angles are equal to two right angles, so he who conceives the divine nature in a confused way does not see that existence pertains to the nature of God. Now in order that we may conceive God's nature clearly and distinctly, we have to fix our attention on certain very simple axioms called universal axioms, and connect to them those attributes that belong to the divine nature. Only then does it become clear to us that God necessarily exists and is omnipresent, and only then do we see that all our conceptions involve God's nature and are conceived through God's nature. and, finally, that everything that we adequately conceive is true. But for this see the Preface to my book entitled '*The Principles of Philosophy Demonstrated in a Geometrical Manner.*'

Chapter 7

Note 7: 'impossible to devise a method'. That is, impossible for us who are not used to this language and lack a systematic account of its phraseology.

Note 8: 'conception'. By things comprehensible I mean not only those which can be logically proved but also those which we are wont to accept with moral certainty and to hear without surprise, although they can by no means be proved. Anyone can comprehend Euclid's propositions before they are proved. Similarly, I call comprehensible those narratives, whether of future or past events, that do not exceed human belief, and likewise laws, institutions and customs, although they cannot be proved with mathematical certainty. But mysterious symbols, and narratives that exceed all human belief, I call incomprehensible. Yet even among these there are many that yield to examination by our method, so that we can perceive the author's meaning.

Chapter 8

Note 9: 'Mount Moriah'. Thus named not by Abraham, but by the historian, who says that the place which in his day was called 'in the mount of the Lord it shall be revealed' was called by Abraham 'the Lord will provide.'

Note 10: 'before David conquered that people'. From this time until the reign of Jehoram, when they gained independence (2 Kings ch. 8 v. 20), the Idumaeans had no king. Governors, appointed by the Jews, took the place of kings (1 Kings ch. 22 v. 47), and therefore the governor of Edom is called 'king' (2 Kings ch. 3 v. 9). There is some doubt as to whether the last of the Idumaean kings had begun his reign before Saul became king, or whether in this chapter of Genesis, Scripture intended to list only the kings who were unconquered until their death. However, it is plain folly to attempt to include Moses, who by the divine will established a Hebrew state very different from monarchy, in the list of Hebrew kings.

Chapter 9

Note 11: 'exceptions'. For example, in 2 Kings ch. 18 v. 20 the text has the second person, 'Thou hast said—but they are no more than words—etc.', whereas in Isaiah ch. 36 v. 5 we have 'I have said—but they are no more than words—that war needs counsel and courage.' Again, in verse 22 the text of Kings reads 'But ye may say unto me', the verb being in the plural, whereas Isaiah has the verb in the singular. Furthermore, the words in Kings, same chapter, verse 32, 'a land of oil olive and of honey, that ye may live and not die: and hearken not to Hezekiah' are missing in Isaiah. There are many other differences of reading of this kind, and no one can determine which is to be preferred.

Note 12: 'remarkable change'. For example, in 2 Sam. ch. 7 v. 6 we have (וָאֶהְיֶה מִתְהַלֵּךְ בְּאֹהֶל וּבְמִשְׁכָּן)—'and I have continually wandered with tent and tabernacle'; but in 1 Chron. ch. 17 v. 5 we have (וָאֶהְיֶה מֵאֹהֶל אֶל-אֹהֶל וּמִמִּשְׁכָּן)—'and I have been from tent to tent and from tabernacle', with a change of מִתְהַלֵּךְ to מֵאֹהֶל, מִמִּשְׁכָּן to בְמִשְׁכָּן and אֶל-אֹהֶל to בְּאֹהֶל. Again in verse 10 of the same chapter of Samuel we have לְעַנּוֹתוֹ—'to afflict him', while in verse 9 of the quoted chapter of Chronicles we have לְבַלֹּתוֹ—'to wear him down'. For anyone who is not quite blind or completely mad a single reading of these chapters will reveal many discrepancies of this kind, some of considerable importance.

Note 13: 'the time here mentioned must refer . . . to a quite different time'. That this passage refers to the time when Joseph was sold is not only evident from the context itself but can also be inferred from the age of Judah, who was then in his twenty-second year at the most, if one may base one's calculation on his preceding history. From the last verse of Genesis ch. 29 it is clear that Judah was born ten years after the patriarch Jacob began to serve Laban, and Joseph fourteen years. Now since Joseph was seventeen years old at the time he was sold, Judah could not have been more than twenty-one. So those who believe that Judah's long absence from home took place before Joseph was sold are seeking to delude themselves, and are more concerned for the sanctity of Scripture than for accuracy.

Note 14: 'while Dinah was scarcely seven years old'. The opinion advanced by some that Jacob wandered about between Mesopotamia and Bethel for eight or ten years savours of the ridiculous, if I may say so without disrespect to ibn Ezra. Jacob had good reason for haste, not only because he no doubt longed to see his aged parents, but also for a most important purpose, to fulfill the vow he had made when he fled from his brother (Gen. ch. 28 v. 20, ch. 31 v. 13 and ch. 35 v. 1), a vow which God also bade him fulfill, promising to help him to return to his country. However, if these considerations seem mere conjectures rather than cogent reasoning, let us grant that Jacob, driven by a more malignant fate than Ulysses, spent eight or ten or even more years on this short journey. Even so our objectors cannot deny that Benjamin was born in the last year of this wandering, that is, according to their view and their theory, when Joseph was fifteen or sixteen or thereabouts; for Jacob parted from Laban seven years after Joseph was born. Now the period of time from Joseph's seventeenth year until the patriarch travelled to Egypt does not exceed twenty-two years, as I have shown in this chapter. Thus at that point of time—that is, when he set out to Egypt—Benjamin was twenty-three or twenty-four years old at the most, at which time, in the early flowering of his life, he must have been a grandfather (see Gen. ch. 46 v. 21, and compare with Num. ch. 26 v. 38, 39, 40 and with 1 Chron. ch. 8 v. 1 and the verses that follow); for Belah, his firstborn, had already begotten two sons, Ard and Naaman. This is surely no less absurd than to maintain that Dinah was seven years old when she was violated, not to mention the other absurdities that are entailed by this manner of arranging history. Thus it is clear that unscholarly attempts to solve difficulties produce further difficulties, confusing and clouding the question even more.

Note 15:   'he here begins to relate of Joshua'. That is to say, the terms used and the order of narration differ from those employed in the book of Joshua.

Note 16:   'Othniel, son of Kenaz, was judge 40 years'. Rabbi Levi ben Gerson[2] and some others believe that these 40 years, which Scripture declares to have been passed in freedom, should be calculated from the death of Joshua and thus include the preceding 8 years when the people were subject to Cushan Rishathaim, while the following 18 years should be included in the total of the 80 years when Ehud and Shamgar were judges. In the same way, they think that the other years of subjection are always included in the years which Scripture declares to have been passed in freedom. But Scripture expressly computes how many years the Hebrews passed in subjection and how many years in freedom, and in chapter 2 v. 18 it expressly tells us that the Hebrews always enjoyed prosperity in the time of the Judges. So it is perfectly clear that our Rabbi (in other respects a man of great learning) and the others who follow him, when trying to solve such difficulties, are not so much explaining Scripture as emending it.

This is also true of those who maintain that, in the summation of years which Scripture here makes, only the years of a properly administered Jewish state were taken into account, while the periods of anarchy and subjection, being unhappy interludes in the history of the Jewish state, must have been ignored. Now Scripture does indeed pass over in silence the periods of anarchy, but the years of subjection are narrated quite as fully as the years of independence, and are not

2. Gersonides, of Provence, 1288–1344, the most outstanding scholar of his age. Biblical exegete and philosopher.

erased from Jewish history, as is wildly suggested. Ezra—whom we have shown to be the author of these books—in 1 Kings ch. 6 intended to include in that complete total all the years from the exodus from Egypt to the fourth year of Solomon's reign, a fact so clear that no biblical scholar has ever doubted it. For, leaving aside for the present the precise wording of the text, the genealogy of David given at the end of the book of Ruth and in 1 Chron. ch. 2 fails to account in full for such a large figure as 480 years. Nahshon was chief of the tribe of Judah in the second year after the exodus (Num. ch. 7 v. 11, 12), and thus died in the wilderness along with all those who at the age of 20 were capable of military service; and his son Salmon crossed the Jordan with Joshua. Now this Salmon, according to the said genealogy, was David's great-great-grandfather. If we subtract from this grand total of 480 years the 4 years of Solomon's reign, the 70 years of David's life and the 40 years spent in the wilderness, we find that David was born 366 years after the passage of the Jordan, and that his father, grandfather, great-grandfather and great-great-grandfather must each have begotten children when they were 90 years old.

Note 17: 'Samson was judge'. Samson was born after the Philistines had subjugated the Hebrews. There is some doubt as to whether the 20 years here mentioned should be reckoned among the years of independence, or whether they are included in the immediately preceding 40 years when the people were under the yoke of the Philistines. For my part, I am of the opinion that it is more probable and more credible that the Hebrews recovered their freedom at the time when the most eminent of the Philistines perished along with Samson. My only reason for refusing to include Samson's 20 years in the period of subjugation to the Philistines is this, that Samson was born after the Philistines had subjugated the Hebrews. There is a further reason, the mention made in the Tractate Shabbat of a certain book of Jerusalem where it is stated that Samson judged the people for 40 years. However, it is not a question of these years alone.

Note 18: 'with absolute strictness'. Otherwise, they are not explaining the words of Scripture, but emending them.

Note 19: 'Kirjath Jeharim'. Kirjath Jeharim is also called Baal Judah. Hence Kimhi[3] and some others think that the words 'Baale Judah', which I have here translated as 'from the people of Judah', signify the name of a town. But they are wrong, because בַּעֲלֵי is plural. Moreover, comparing the text of Samuel with the text of 1 Chronicles, we see that David did not arise and go forth from Baal, but that he went thither. If the author of 2 Samuel had intended to indicate the place whence David removed the ark, then the Hebrew would have run as follows: "Then David arose and set forth . . . etc. from Baal Judah, and took from there the ark of God."

Note 20: 'and was there three years'. Some commentators have emended the text as follows: "And Absalom fled and went to Talmai, the son of Ammihud, king of Geshur, where he remained for three years, and David wept for his son all the time that he was at Geshur." Now if this is to be called interpretation, and if one

---

3. David Kimhi was a thirteenth-century French Jewish biblical exegete and defender of Maimonides.

can assume such licence in expounding Scripture, transposing entire phrases, adding to them and subtracting from them, then I declare that it is permissible to corrupt Scripture and to treat it as a piece of wax on which one can impose whatever forms one chooses.

Chapter 10

Note 21: 'and perhaps after the restoration of the temple by Judas Maccabee'. This possibility—though it is more akin to certainty—is based on the genealogy from king Jeconiah, given in 1 Chron. ch. 3 and continuing as far as the sons of Elioneai, who were thirteenth in direct line from Jeconiah. It should be observed that Jeconiah had no children when he was imprisoned, but he had two children while in prison, as far as can be conjectured by the names he gave them. Now he seems to have had grandchildren—again making conjecture from their names— after his release from prison; and therefore Pedaiah (which means 'God hath delivered'), who according to this chapter is said to be the father of Zerubbabel, was born in the thirty-seventh or thirty-eighth year of Jeconiah's captivity, that is, thirty-three years before Cyrus gave the Jews permission to return. Therefore Zerubbabel, whom Cyrus put in charge of the Jews, seems to have been thirteen or fourteen years old at the most. But I have preferred to keep silent on these matters for reasons which our difficult times do not allow me to explain. A word to the wise is enough. If they will peruse with some care the list of the descendants of Jeconiah given in 1 Chron. ch. 3 from verse 17 to the end of the chapter, and compare the Hebrew text with the Septuagint version, they will have no difficulty in seeing that these books were published after the second restoration of the city by Judas Maccabee when the descendants of Jeconiah had lost the throne, and not before then.

Note 22: 'he would be taken to Babylon as captive'. Thus no one could have suspected that Ezekiel's prophecy contradicted Jeremiah's prediction, as everyone suspected according to Josephus' narrative. But the event proved them both right.

Note 23: 'Nehemiah'. The historian himself testifies in chapter 1 verse 1 that the greater part of this book is taken from the book that Nehemiah wrote. But there can be no doubt that the passage from chapter 8 to chapter 12 verse 26, and also the last two verses of chapter 12 inserted as a parenthesis into the words of Nehemiah, were added by the historian who lived after Nehemiah.

Note 24: 'Ezra'. Ezra was the uncle of the first high priest, Joshua (see Ezra ch. 7 v. 1 and 1 Chron. ch. 6 v. 13, 14, 15), and accompanied Zerubbabel from Babylon to Jerusalem (see Nehem. ch. 12 v. 1). But it appears that when he saw the state of confusion among the Jews, he returned to Babylon, as also did some others (Nehem. ch. 1 v. 2), and remained there until the reign of Artaxerxes when, being granted his request, he went for a second time to Jerusalem. Nehemiah, too, went with Zerubbabel to Jerusalem in the time of Cyrus. See Ezra, ch. 2 v. 2 and 63, and compare with ch. 10 v. 2 and ch. 12 v. 1 of Nehemiah. As to the translation of the word '*Atirshata*' by 'ambassador', there is no authority for this, whereas it is quite certain that those Jews whose duty it was to attend the court were given new names. Thus Daniel was Balteshazzar, and Zerubbabel Sheshbazzar (see Dan. ch. 1 v. 7, Ezra ch. 1 v. 8 and ch. 5 v. 14). Nehemiah was called Atirshata, but by virtue of his office he was termed פֶּחָה—procurator or president. See Nehem. ch. 5 v. 14 and ch. 12 v. 26.

Note 25: 'that no canon of the Sacred Books existed before the Maccabees'. The Synagogue termed 'the Great' did not originate until after Asia had been subjugated by the Macedonians. As to the assertion made by Maimonides, R. Abraham ben David[4] and others, that the presidents of the Council were Ezra, Daniel, Nehemiah, Haggai, Zechariah etc., this is an absurd fiction, based only on a rabbinical tradition that the Persian empire lasted no more than 34 years. This is their only way of proving that the decrees of the Great Synagogue or Synod—which was composed of Pharisees only, and whose decrees were rejected by the Sadducees—were transmitted by prophets who had received them from other prophets all the way back to Moses, who had received them from God himself and had transmitted them orally, not in writing. But let the Pharisees cling to their belief with their wonted obstinacy. The wise, being well acquainted with the reasons for councils and Synods and knowing of the quarrels between Pharisees and Sadducees, can easily imagine the reasons for the summoning of that Great Synagogue or Council. This much is certain, that no prophets took part in that council, and that the decrees of the Pharisees, which they call 'traditions', derived their authority from that Council.

Chapter 11

Note 26: 'we therefore think'. Translators here render λογίζομαι as *'concludo'*—I infer, and they maintain that in Paul's writing the word λογίζομαι is synonymous with συλλογίζομαι, whereas in fact the Greek λογίζομαι has the same force as the Hebrew חשב—to reckon, think, consider. This meaning is in full agreement with the Syriac text. The Syriac translation (if indeed it is a translation, which is a matter of doubt since we know neither the translator nor the time of publication, and the vernacular language of the Apostles was none other than Syriac) renders this text of Paul as 'מתרעינן הכיל', which Tremellius correctly translates as *'arbitramur igitur'*—'we therefore think'. For the word 'רעינא' which derives from this verb means 'arbitratus'—thinking. In Hebrew 'רעינא' is רְעוּתָא *reutha*—'will'. Therefore the Syriac word means 'we will' or 'we think'.

Note 27: 'the whole of Christ's doctrine'. In effect, the teachings of Jesus in the Sermon on the Mount, related in Matthew, chapter 5.

4. Abraham ben David was a twelfth-century Spanish Jewish historian and philosopher. Spinoza seems to be referring to the latter's historical treatise *Sefer Ha-Qabbalah* (*The Book of Tradition*), which is available in an English translation by Gerson Cohen (Philadelphia: Jewish Publication Society, 1967).

Chapter 15

Note 31: 'that simple obedience is a way to salvation'. That is, it is not reason but revelation that can teach us that it is enough for blessedness or salvation for us to accept the divine decrees as laws or commandments, and that there is no need to conceive them as eternal truths. This is made clear by what we have demonstrated in chapter 4.

Chapter 16

Note 32: 'promise in all good faith'. In a civil state, where what is good and what is evil is decided by the right of the whole community, it is correct to make a distinction between deception with good intent (*dolus bonus*) and deception with malicious intent (*dolus malus*). But in a state of nature, where everyone is his own judge and possesses the perfect right to prescribe and interpret laws for himself and even to repeal them if he thinks this is to his advantage, it is impossible to conceive that anyone can act with malicious intent to deceive.

Note 33: 'everybody can be free as he wills'. A man can be free in any kind of state, for a man is free, of course, to the extent that he is guided by reason. Now (although Hobbes[5] thinks otherwise) reason is entirely in favour of peace; but peace cannot be secured unless the general laws of the state are kept inviolate. Therefore the more a man is guided by reason, that is, the more free he is, the more steadfastly he will observe the laws of the state and obey the commands of the sovereign whose subject he is.

Note 34: 'For nobody knows by nature'. When Paul says that men are without means of escape, he is speaking in merely human terms. For in chapter 9 v. 18 of the same Epistle he expressly teaches that God has mercy on whom he will and makes stubborn whom he will, and that men are without excuse not because they have been forewarned but because they are in God's power like clay in the hands of the potter, who from the same lump makes one vessel to honour and another vessel to dishonour. As for the divine natural law whose chief commandment, as we have said, is to love God, I have called it a law in the same sense as philosophers apply the term 'law' to the universal rules of Nature according to which all things come to pass. For love of God is not obedience but a virtue necessarily present in a man who knows God aright, whereas obedience has regard to the will of him who commands, and not to necessity and truth. Now since we do not know the nature of God's will, while we are quite certain that everything that happens comes to pass from God's power alone, it is only from revelation that we can know whether God wishes to receive honour from men like some temporal ruler. Furthermore, we have shown that the divine commandments appear to us as commandments or ordinances only as long as we do not know their cause. Once this is known, they cease to be commandments, and we embrace them as eternal truths, not as commandments; that is, obedience forthwith passes into love, which arises from true

5. The only occasion in this work where Hobbes (1588–1679) is mentioned by name, although his influence is clear. Spinoza must have carefully studied his *De Cive.*

knowledge by the same necessity as light arises from the sun. Therefore by the guidance of reason we can love God, but not obey him; for by virtue of reason we can neither accept divine commandments as divine while not knowing their cause, nor can we conceive God as a ruler enacting laws.

Chapter 17

Note 35: 'as thereafter to be powerless'. Two common soldiers undertook to make one man Emperor of Rome in place of another, and they succeeded. Tacitus, *Histories,* Book 1.[6]

Note 36: '(Num. ch. 11 v. 28)'. In this passage two men are accused of prophesying in the camp, and Joshua urges their arrest. This he would not have done if it had been lawful for anyone to deliver God's oracles to the people without Moses' permission. But Moses thought fit to acquit the accused, and he rebuked Joshua for urging him to assert this royal right at a time when he was so weary of ruling that he preferred to die rather than continue to rule alone, as is clear from verses 14 and 15 of the same chapter. For he replied to Joshua thus: "Enviest thou for my sake? Would God that all the Lord's people were prophets!" That is to say, would that the right to consult God were vested in the entire people, who would thus be sovereign. Therefore Joshua's error lay not in the question of right but in the occasion of its exercise, and he was rebuked by Moses in the same way as Abishai was rebuked by David when he urged David to condemn to death Shimei, who was undoubtedly guilty of treason. See 2 Sam. ch. 19 v. 22, 23.

Note 37: 'See Num. ch. 27 v. 21'. Verses 19 and 23 of this chapter are mistranslated in such versions as I have seen. These verses do not mean that Moses gave Joshua commands or instructions, but that he properly constituted or established him as captain. This turn of phrase is quite common in Scripture, as in Exod. ch. 18 v. 23, 1 Sam. ch. 13 v. 14, Josh. ch. 1 v. 9, 1 Sam. ch. 25 v. 30 and elsewhere.

Note 38: 'to recognise any other judge than God'. The Rabbis imagine that what is known as the Great Sanhedrin was instituted by Moses, and many Christians share in this delusion. Moses did indeed choose seventy colleagues to assist him in the task of government, being unable to bear alone the burden of the whole people. But at no time did he enact a law establishing a college of seventy members. On the contrary, he commanded that each tribe should appoint judges in the cities that God had given them, to decide lawsuits in accordance with the laws that he had laid down. If it should happen that the judges themselves were in doubt as to the law, they were to approach the high priest, as being the supreme interpreter of the laws, or the judge who was at that time their superior (for he had the right to consult the high priest) so as to settle the question according to the high priest's interpretation. If a lower judge should maintain that he was not bound to pass judgment in accordance with the opinion of the high priest as received from the high priest himself or from his own superior, he was to be condemned to death by whatever supreme judge had appointed him a subordinate judge. See Deut. ch.

6. A reference to the murder of Caligula and the accession of Claudius.

17 v. 9. This person might be the commander-in-chief of all Israel, like Joshua, or he might be the captain of a single tribe (in whom, after the partition of the land was vested the right of consulting the high priest concerning the affairs of his tribe, of deciding on war or peace, of fortifying cities, of appointing judges and so on), or he might be the king, to whom all or some of the tribes had transferred their right.

In confirmation I could cite many instances from history, but I will confine myself to one of outstanding importance. When the Shilonite prophet appointed Jeroboam king, he thereby gave him the right of consulting the high priest and of appointing judges; in short, Jeroboam held over the ten tribes all the right that Rehoboam held over two tribes. Therefore Jeroboam could set up a supreme council of state at his court by the same right by which Jehoshaphat set up his council at Jerusalem (see 2 Chron. ch. 19 v. 8 on). For it is clear that Jeroboam, insofar as he was king by God's command, and consequently Jeroboam's subjects, were not required by the law of Moses to submit to the jurisdiction of Rehoboam, since they were not his subjects, and far less to the jurisdiction of the court established by Rehoboam at Jerusalem and subordinate to him. Thus a supreme court was established in each of the separate and independent divisions of the Hebrew state. Those who disregard the varied political arrangements of the Hebrews and fail to distinguish between them find themselves involved in many difficulties.

Chapter 19

Note 39: 'and lawfully impeach'. Here particular attention should be paid to my discussion of right in chapter 16.

BIBLICAL REFERENCES

Old Testament

Genesis	*page*
1.2	17, 29
4.7	32
4.8	127
6.3	17
9.13	79
Ch. 10	107
12.3	41
12.6	106
14.14	108
14.18ff.	39
Ch. 15	232
15.8	22
18.19	28
18.24	28
20.6	11
22.14	107
26.5	39
28.20	234
29.35	233
31.13	234
31.29	28
35.1	234
35.2	30
36.31	108, 117
Ch. 38	117
46.21	234
Ch. 47	117
Ch. 49	95
49.29, 33	61

Exodus	
Ch. 1	78
3.13	156
3.18	28
4.1	28
4.8	28
4.24	42
6.3	154
7.1	9
9.10	79

10.2	77
10.14, 19	79
11.8	24
14.21	79
14.27	80
14.31	64
15.10	80
15.11	29
16.27	214
16.35	108
17.14	109
18.11	29
18.23	239
19.4	189
19.9	64
19.18	82
19.20	168
20.18	190
20.20	164
20.22	109
Ch. 24	12, 109
24.4	109
24.7	109, 189
25.22	11
31.3	17
Ch. 33	13
33.2	30
33.11	13
33.16	31, 42
33.18	30
34.6	30, 40, 156
34.7	30, 32, 156
34.9	43
34.10	43
34.14	167

Leviticus	
5.1	92, 216
18.27	45
19.17	18, 92, 216
25.30	123

New Testament

INDEX

Abraham: 28, 232n.4
Abravanel, Isaac: x
Adam: ix, 28, 53, 55–56
Alexander the Great: 2, 85, 132, 187–188, 196
allies: 180
Alpakhar, Jehuda: 165–168, 165n.2
ambition: 4, 228
Ambrose: 212
Amsterdam: 228
angels: 54
anthropocentrism: xxvi
anti-Semitism: xxiii
Apostles, the: xxxi, 138–144, 150
Aquinas: 76n.1, 165n.1
aristocracy: 191, 195
Aristotle: xxxvii–xxxviii, xlii, 69, 100, 153
Ark of the Covenant: 147–148
Arminians: see Remonstrants and Counter-Remonstrants
army: see military
assimilation, of the Jews: xxiii, 45–46
atheism: xii, xiii
Augustus: 188
author of Scripture: see Bible, authorship and composition of
authority: religious, xiii, 218; political, 64, 185–186, 218
axioms: see method, philosophical or axiomatic-deductive

Bacon, Francis: xii
belief: 160–163
ben Shem Tov, Joseph: 69n.5
ben Uzziel, Jonathan: 110n.1
Bible: authorship and composition of, xix, xxvi, xxx, xxxi–xxxii, 96–97, 105–115, 128–133, 136, 149,

158; chronology of, 117–122, 128–130, 132–133, 136, 233n.13–14, 234n.15–16, 235n.17, 236n.21, 237n.25; errors and marginal notations within, 122–127, 133–136, 145–146, 150–152; interpretation of, ix, x, xviii–xix, xxi, xxii, xxvi, xxvii, xxviii–xxxiii, 5–6, 10, 21, 26–27, 33–34, 66–68, 72, 78–83, 86–104, 121, 122, 124, 131, 134–135, 136, 142, 157, 165–169, 235n.18 and n.20; purpose of Biblical narratives, 51, 67–70; in relation to the Word of God, 145–147, 149–151; teaching and purpose of, 6, 33, 66–68, 78, 151, 153–154, 156–157, 158, 159, 161–163, 172
blessedness: 50, 52, 56, 59, 60–61, 63, 65, 68, 98, 169, 238n.31; see also happiness
Blyenburgh: xv
Bomberg Bible: 126
Boyle, Robert: xiv
Burgh, Albert: xv

Cabbalists: 122
Calvinism: xxx, 218n.4
Cartesianism: see Descartes
Catholicism: 93, 102–103
causality: see causes
causes: 10, 37, 48–49, 50, 71, 74–75, 78–80; see also determinism, natural
ceremonial rites and observance: xxv, 45–46, 51–52, 59–62, 65, 197–198, 199
certainty: 21–23, 50, 163, 170–171, 232n.8
Charles I: 210n.1